The
Civil War

THE
7
SEVEN-DAY
SCHOLAR

The
Civil War

EXPLORING HISTORY
ONE WEEK AT A TIME

DENNIS GAFFNEY AND
PETER GAFFNEY

HYPERION
NEW YORK

Unless indicated below, images in this book were reproduced from the Prints & Photographs Division of the Library of Congress.

1865 Map of U.S.: General Collections, Library of Congress [LOC]

p. 63 (slave map): Geography & Map Division, Library of Congress [LOC]

p. 36 (Ruffin), p. 219 (Jackson), p. 429 (recruit poster): National Archives & Records Administration [NARA]

p. 132 (Hunley): Naval Historical Foundation

Library of Congress Cataloging-in-Publication Data has been applied for.

ISBN: 978-1-4013-2374-5

Hyperion books are available for special promotions and premiums. For details contact the HarperCollins Special Markets Department in the New York office at 212-207-7528, fax 212-207-7222, or email spsales@harpercollins.com.

BOOK DESIGN BY DEBORAH KERNER

FIRST EDITION

10 9 8 7 6 5 4 3 2 1

THIS LABEL APPLIES TO TEXT STOCK

We try to produce the most beautiful books possible, and we are also extremely concerned about the impact of our manufacturing process on the forests of the world and the environment as a whole. Accordingly, we made sure that all of the paper we used has been certified as coming from forests that are managed to insure the protection of the people and wildlife dependent upon them.

To our parents,

Anne and Walter Gaffney,

who taught us that curiosity

and perseverance

get you most of the way there

CONTENTS

AN ALL-CONSUMING BATTLE
(1863)   207

THE PEOPLE, WEARY OF WAR
(1864)   311

THE "MIGHTY SCOURGE" ENDS, THE NATION IS TRANSFORMED
(1865)   371

ACKNOWLEDGMENTS

We came to this book as history buffs; we complete it humbled not only by the ordeal Americans passed through, but by all those who have since written so intelligently about the war. For general guidance, we relied on a few mainstays in the field, well-read for good reason, including James McPherson's *Battle Cry of Freedom*, Shelby Foote's *The Civil War: A Narrative*, and all of Bruce Catton's books. As ours isn't an academic book, footnotes were omitted. That said, we are indebted to hundreds of scholarly books and articles, and whenever we relied heavily on any one source, we cited them in our endnotes.

Our other crucial guides were the historians and rangers at the national parks and historic sites related to the Civil War. These experts pointed us in the right direction and, by the time they were done, reviewed nearly the entire manuscript, helping refine interpretations and correct mistakes. At the risk of leaving out some, we would like to thank Robert E. L. Krick, Historian, Richmond National Battlefield Park; Callie Hawkins, Curator of Education at President Lincoln's Cottage at the Soldier's Home; Cathy Ingram and Padraic Benson, the Frederick Douglass National Historic Site; David Fox, Park Ranger, Harpers Ferry National Historical Park; Charlie Spearman, Park Ranger, Shiloh National Military Park; Donald Pfanz, Historian, Fredericksburg & Spotsylvania National Military Park; Gary Scott, Regional Chief Historian, National Capital Region, National Park Service; Jim Burgess, Museum Specialist, Manassas National Battlefield Park; John Heiser, Historian, Gettysburg National Military Park; John R. George, Museum Technician, Stones River National Battlefield; Joseph M. Judge, Curator, Hampton Roads Naval Museum; Maria Jacobsen, Senior Archaeologist on the Hunley Project and Kellen Correia, Executive Director, Friends of the Hunley; Kimberly Robinson, Acting Museum Curator, Clara Barton National Historic Site & Glen Echo Park; Pam Sanfilippo, Site Historian, Ulysses S. Grant National Historic Site; Patrick A. Schroeder, Historian, Appomattox Court House National Historical Park; Richard W. Hatcher III, Historian, Fort Sumter National Monument; Ryan McNabb, Park Ranger, Boston African American National Historic Site; Terrence Winschel, Historian, Vicksburg National Military Park; Timothy P. Townsend, Historian, Lincoln Home National Historic Site; Dr. Frank Smith, Founding Director of the African American Civil War Memorial Freedom Foundation.

Also, thanks to those at the Capital District Civil War Roundtable; Allen Ballard, Professor of History and Africana Studies at the University at Albany, for pointing us to sources for African-American issues; Valarie Ziegler, Department of Religious Studies, at DePauw University, for her expertise on Julia Ward Howe; Iver Bernstein, Professor of History at Washington University, for his expertise on the draft riots in New York City.

A special thanks to Alain Jehlen for researching and writing several chapters of the book and for thinking about the big picture; to Kate Cohen for her extraordinary editing skills; to Charles Bryan, our consultant and a true devotee of the Civil War, who suggested course corrections large and small with patience and grace. He also introduced us to Cornelia Peake McDonald, a Virginia mother whose war diary is an eloquent testimony to wartime perseverance. Thanks also to Athena Angelos, our image researcher, who knows the Library of Congress photo database like the back of her hand. And to Doe Coover, our agent, for her expertise as well as her composure at difficult junctures, which was priceless. Thanks as well to Leslie D. Wells and Elisabeth Dyssegaard, our editors at Hyperion, for believing in this series and for their skills in bringing the book to fruition.

Dennis wanted to acknowledge that the book was largely written in Albany's libraries—at Sage College, the University at Albany, and at the Albany Public Library, all wonderful, quiet spaces. He also wanted to thank all the librarians who helped him find what he needed. Peter also wanted to thank Abbe Raven, President and CEO of A&E Television Networks, who taught him that history doesn't have to be dry and boring; Libby O'Connell, Chief Historian at History, for her guidance through this project; and Nancy Dubuc, President and General Manager at History, who encouraged him to pursue this project, introduced him to Hyperion, and who taught him that if you really want something, "just do it." Dennis and Peter would also like to thank each other, as well as their friends and families—especially Julia, Jason, Kathy, and Sophia—for just being there.

INTRODUCTION

This book started with an idea. My brother, Peter, an executive at the History Channel, knows that people love history, but have little tolerance for textbooks, multi-volume tomes, or obscure academic books. In these hectic times, he was convinced what most people want to read is reliable history broken down into manageable bites. That led him to a history book idea: one organized like a calendar, with 52 chapters, corresponding to the weeks in a year.

Each week would include seven related entries, like the days in a week. He even came up with a title: *The Seven-Day Scholar*. But my brother is neither a researcher nor a writer, and he had a full-time job. So he asked me, his brother, a writer and a history buff, if I wanted to pursue the book with him. I said no. It sounded like an encyclopedia, and I find them boring. But then I had my own "aha" moment: Why not write a book organized as Peter imagined, but full of historical stories?

We chose the Civil War as the first book in a series. We pursued good real-life stories, well-known or obscure. In the process, we've learned so much. We didn't know that the Rebel yell was born when Confederate commander "Stonewall" Jackson told his attacking troops at the Battle of Bull Run to "yell like furies!" We didn't know that landmines, submarines, and trench warfare were developed during the Civil War. Or that Jefferson and Varina Davis adopted a black child during the war to protect him from a cruel slave owner. Or that since the war ended, scholars have battled over why the Union won—or whether the Confederates lost.

We've kept each day's entry to a page or two. Seven related entries—mostly stories, but also historical debates, documents such as letters, and one image—make up each chapter. For those who want to learn more—budding scholars always do—we've recommended relevant books. Read this volume over a year or swallow it in a week. It's your pace and your journey.

Best,
Dennis Gaffney

ENGINE "NASHVILLE"
OF THE LINCOLN FUNERAL TRAIN

PRELUDE *to a* WAR: SPARKS *Before the* FLAME

INTRODUCTION

What Caused the Civil War?

Confederates, Unionists, scholars and soldiers, abolitionists and slaveholders have found the cause with different people, different places, and different historical forces. Was it caused by a fundamental disagreement between North and South over the morality of slavery? If so, why did the conflict erupt in 1860 and not at some other point during the 250 years that slavery was tolerated on the continent? And if Southern slavery was the cause, then why did the election to the presidency of an Illinois lawyer who accepted slavery in the South trigger secession?

And why were the compromises over slavery cobbled together by American politicians in 1820, 1850, and 1854 no longer possible in 1860? How much of the rupture was fueled by the competing cultures and interests of the industrializing North and the agricultural South?

Who were the true rebels in 1860—Northerners or Southerners— and who was ultimately responsible for the eruption of violence that would lead to the deaths of more than 600,000 men? Was the match that lit the conflagration the violence in "bleeding Kansas," or the slave insurrection attempted by a failed businessman and religious militant named John Brown, or the election of the "black Republican" Abraham Lincoln, or the cannonballs fired by South Carolinians at Fort Sumter in Charleston Harbor, or Lincoln's subsequent call for troops?

No one cause existed. Instead, a complicated, decades-long chain of events led to the violence that ripped the country apart and shaped American history. These are some of the links in that chain.

SLAVERY
AND ITS DISCONTENTS

WEEK 1

THOMAS JEFFERSON AND
THE CONFLICT BETWEEN FREEDOM AND SLAVERY

In June 1776, as the revolutionary urge for independence from England flared into violence in the American colonies, colonial leaders came together in Philadelphia to write a document declaring to the world who they were, what they were seeking, and why. "We hold these truths to be self-evident that all men are created equal, that they are endowed by their Creator with certain unalienable Rights, among them life, liberty and the pursuit of happiness." These, the most famous political words in American history, were written by Thomas Jefferson, a slave-owner.

African slaves came to the British colony of Virginia in 1619, a little over 150 years before the Declaration of Independence was written and a year before the *Mayflower* landed at Plymouth, when a Dutch frigate sold twenty slaves to English settlers in Jamestown, Virginia. Tens of thousands more Africans would make that dismal voyage, dragged across a sea and sold to plantations and forced to grow tobacco, rice, and cotton—as well as raise children of white families.

Thomas Jefferson at times denounced the slave trade and slavery, but his luxurious lifestyle was supported by it. When he wrote the Declaration of Independence, Jefferson owned one hundred slaves. He believed that African-Americans were "inferior to whites in the endowments of body and mind." But he also believed that slavery would gradually, and naturally, pass from the land.

But slavery would not fade. By the Fourth of July, 1826, the day Jefferson died, the slave population in America had grown to 2 million, many shipped to the Deep South and West to grow cotton that kept Europeans supplied with dresses, shirts, and bedsheets.

In his eighty-three years, Jefferson would free just three of his slaves. Five more would gain freedom in his will, all part of the Hemings family. Not mentioned in the will was Sally Hemings, a slave who is believed to have been the mother of some of Jefferson's children. Jefferson had worked hard to keep the slave families at his home together, but when he died, they were sold, and therefore scattered, to pay off his enormous debt. Jefferson was a man conflicted, in a nation conflicted, both caught between an urge to create a country that defended freedom and a desire to reap the benefits that came with the enslavement of other human beings.

HOW A YANKEE INVENTOR SAVED SLAVERY

When the U.S. Constitution was signed in 1787, many of the country's leaders expected slavery would fade quickly across their new country. But this expectation faded soon after June 1793, when Thomas Jefferson, then secretary of state and inspector of patents, received a request for a patent from a twenty-nine-year-old schoolteacher named Eli Whitney. It was for an engine—"gin" for short—to separate the cotton from the seeds. Jefferson, a patriot, a planter, and a slave-owner who grew cotton, wrote back an encouraging letter to the young man:

> *As the state of Virginia, of which I am, carries on household manufactures of cotton to a great extent, as I also do myself . . . I feel a considerable interest in the success of your invention for family use.*

The cotton gin used wire hooks to pull cotton fibers through a screen and away from seeds. It would prove to be the most important invention in the country's short history, revolutionizing the production of cotton—and resuscitating the business of slavery. The device made it possible to profitably grow short-staple cotton, which grew so well in the Deep South.

Before Whitney's cotton gin, a slave had to pick seeds for ten hours to produce just one pound of cotton. With the cotton gin, in the same time, a slave could produce fifty pounds. From 1795—the first year of the cotton gin's operation—to 1800, the American production of cotton went from 8 million pounds to 32 million pounds. All growers needed now to produce profitable cotton was the right climate—lots of rain and two hundred frost-free days—conditions found across the Deep South and west to Texas.

On January 1, 1808, fifteen years after granting that patent, Jefferson signed a law that banned the international slave trade, "I hope preparing," he said, "under auspices of heaven, for a total emancipation." But by mid-century, American cotton made up three-quarters of the world's supply and amounted to more than half the value of all United States exports. By 1860, to meet the exploding demand, a million slaves had been dragged into the Western states such as Alabama and Mississippi, which had become the greatest cotton-growing region in the world.

TWO PATHS: THE INDUSTRIAL NORTH
AND THE AGRICULTURAL SOUTH

Through much of the nineteenth century, people in the North and South prayed to the same God, spoke the same language, fought in the same wars, and even sang the same songs.

But as the century flowed toward 1860, the economies and cultures of the regions began to diverge. The North was becoming an urban culture fed by immigrants. Between 1844 and 1854, roughly 300,000 European immigrants, many of them Irish or German, poured annually into Northeastern cities such as Boston and New York City. Low-wage immigrants powered an industrial revolution, and in 1861, for the first time, the value of American manufactured goods outpaced the value of agricultural products. Only a tenth of those manufactured goods were produced in the South.

In 1800, half of Americans lived in the South; by 1850 it was just a third. Of the nine largest cities, only New Orleans was located in the lower South. Life there remained rural and largely agricultural, dominated by crops such as tobacco, sugar, and especially cotton.

Two competing aristocracies grew: a Northern one built on commerce and banking and industry, and a Southern one built on old wealth, plantations, and slavery. Northern businessmen wanted high tariffs to protect their manufactured goods from foreign imports; Southerners fought tariffs to keep down the cost of finished goods they had to import from the North or Europe. Northerners became more judgmental of slavery; Southern slave-owners became more defensive about the institution their wealth and their culture were built on.

"Every day [the North] grows more wealthy and densely populated," observed one French visitor to the country, "while the South is stationary or growing poor. . . . The first result of this disproportionate growth is a violent change in the equilibrium of power and political influence. . . . [And] [w]ealth, like population, is displaced. These changes cannot take place without injuring interests, without exciting passions."

NAT TURNER AND WILLIAM LLOYD GARRISON
REBEL AGAINST SLAVERY

In the summer of 1831, in southeast Virginia, the bloodiest slave uprising in American history erupted, led by a preacher named Nat Turner, a charismatic slave who believed he was acting on orders from God. Over three days, he and his black followers killed sixty white men, women, and children, many at night in their beds, using knives, hatchets, axes, and improvised clubs so as not to draw attention with gunfire. "[T]was my object to carry terror and devastation," Turner said after he was caught, "wherever we went."

The uprising intensified slave-owners' fears that their families could also become the victims of angry slaves, and the backlash came swiftly. White men killed between one hundred and two hundred black men, women, and children, many unrelated to the revolt. One innocent black traveler was shot to death and then decapitated, his head put on a post at a crossroads. In Raleigh, North Carolina, fearful officials arrested every free black in the city. In Virginia, the legislature debated banishing fifty thousand free blacks who lived in the state.

Just before Turner's revolt, a Boston newspaperman named William Lloyd Garrison launched a weekly antislavery newspaper named *The Liberator*, the nation's first newspaper dedicated to immediate emancipation. "I *will be* as harsh as truth, and as uncompromising as justice," he wrote in the first issue. "On this subject, I do not wish to think, or speak, or write with moderation. Tell a man whose house is on fire, to give a moderate alarm; tell him to moderately rescue his wife from the hands of a ravisher; tell the other to gradually extricate her babe from the fire into which it has fallen;—but urge me not to use moderation in a cause like the present. I am in earnest—I will not retreat a single inch—AND I WILL BE HEARD."

Over time, those who shared Garrison's views found each other, forming abolitionist groups consisting of whites and blacks, poor and rich, connected over the North and the South, all committed to ending slavery. Many of these abolitionists risked their reputations, their property, and sometimes their lives by helping fugitive slaves come North on secret routes, stopping at safe houses where they hid as they journeyed northward to free states or Canada. This informal route to freedom was called the Underground Railroad.

HARRIET TUBMAN ESCAPES SLAVERY
AND RIDES THE UNDERGROUND RAILROAD

Harriet Tubman was born as Araminta "Minty" Ross in 1822, the fifth of at least nine children, on Maryland's Eastern Shore, a flat land of water and marshes. She grew up almost as a feral child, "neglected like a weed, ignorant of liberty," she said later. When hungry, she sometimes fought the hogs for their feed. She was also beaten frequently, and bore visible scars the rest of her days. As a child, she witnessed two of her sisters being led away in shackles, and later said that "every time I saw a white man I was afraid of being carried away."

When she was eleven or twelve, she was in a general store when a white overseer hurled a lead weight at a slave who refused to do his work. The weight missed the man but hit Tubman in the head. For the rest of her life, she suffered from headaches, seizures, and fits of sleepiness, but also visions and abilities such as a "fluttering" that warned of danger.

In the spring of 1849, her owner died and she received word that she and her brothers would likely be sold. She and two of her brothers fled, but the group got lost and returned in defeat. Afterward, she had visions of horsemen coming for her and flying over the landscape like birds. In the fall, she tried again to escape. This time, white Marylanders helped her, hiding her in their homes. She later wrote of reaching Pennsylvania. "I looked at my hands to see if I was the same person. There was such a glory over everything; the sun came like gold through the trees and over the fields, and I felt like I was in Heaven. I had crossed the line."

Believing she was acting on God's behalf, she journeyed back to Maryland a dozen times over the next decade to free about seventy slaves. She would go under cover of winter nights, helped by a network of family, freed blacks, slaves, sympathetic whites, and her own wile. Although illiterate, she sometimes carried a book, which would deceive slave-hunters looking for field hands. Other times she played dumb, a friend explaining that "she could . . . look so stupid that nobody would suspect her of knowing enough to be dangerous."

And she was tough. When a fugitive slave became upset about being hidden in a swamp for a day without food, he threatened to back out of the escape, which would have endangered everyone. Tubman put a gun to his head, saying, "Move or die." He moved. When friends cautioned her to avoid "too much adventure & peril," she replied, "The Lord who told me to take care of my people meant me to do it just so long as I live, and so I do what he told me to do."

"GIVE US SLAVERY OR GIVE US DEATH"—THE HARDENING
OF THE PRO-SLAVERY POSITION IN THE SOUTH

At one time antislavery societies in the South outnumbered those in the North. In 1832, the Virginia legislature had debated a proposal for gradual, compensated emancipation that would have granted freedom to slaves in 1861. But as the cotton crop spread south and west, and with it the South's reliance on slavery, the defense of the institution hardened. Pro-slavery representatives were behind the Fugitive Slave law, part of the Compromise of 1850, which subjected citizens who helped escaped slaves to a $1,000 fine and six months in jail. Northern abolitionists condemned the law as a deal with the devil and Massachusetts philosopher Ralph Waldo Emerson called it a "filthy enactment."

Hatred spawned hatred, and Southerners, more and more defensive, dug in. What Southerners had seen as a temporary and imperfect institution, perhaps a necessary evil, was reinterpreted as a social good. Slaves liked slavery, they argued; slavery lifted African-Americans. Southerners used the Bible to justify the institution, and paraphrased Patrick Henry with the cry, "Give us SLAVERY, or give us death!"

Views on slavery colored the judgments of each region about the other. "The Southern planter's career," sputtered William Lloyd Garrison, the publisher of *The Liberator*, "is one of unbridled lust, of filthy amalgamation, of swaggering braggadocio, of haughty domination, of cowardly ruffianism, of boundless dissipation, of matchless insolence, of infinite self-conceit, of unequalled oppression, of more than savage cruelty." Southerners painted Northerners as hypocritical, condemning slavery but thinking nothing of underpaying wage-earners, and saw Yankees generally as avaricious and power-hungry.

The Democrats, whose candidates had occupied the White House for most of the previous forty years, were pulled apart by slavery-haters and slavery apologists. Religious groups splintered into antislavery Northern sects and pro-slavery Southern ones. Just as the abolitionists and the Republican Party ascended in the North, radical secessionists, so-called "fire-eaters" because of their fiery oratory, ascended in the South. The fire-eaters screamed for a country of their own—Southern, proud, and pro-slavery. Abolitionist William Lloyd Garrison burned the Constitution because it countenanced slavery. Such fierce emotions and symbolic deeds were prelude to the fiery actions that would follow.

THE COTTON GIN INCREASES
THE DEMAND FOR SLAVES

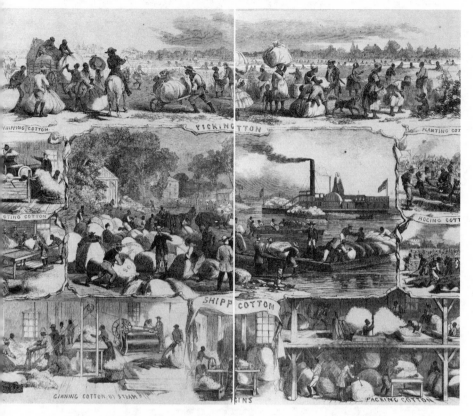

Before Eli Whitney invented the cotton gin, a slave had to pick seeds for ten hours to produce just one pound of cotton. With the "gin" (short for engine), a slave could remove seeds from fifty pounds in the same amount of time. This 1862 wood engraving shows the cotton production process in South Carolina, including the picking, transporting, and ginning of cotton.

GOING WEST,
PULLING APART

WEEK 2

THE CONQUEST OF MEXICO—
FREE STATES OR SLAVE STATES?

On the morning of September 14, 1847, a tired army of Americans in tattered uniforms—most of them from slave-owning states—marched into Mexico City and raised a bullet-holed American flag. The U.S. band played "Hail to the Chief" and "Yankee Doodle"—and General Winfield Scott, who would be the first Union general in the Civil War fourteen years later, formally accepted surrender of the city. Soon the U.S. envoy was negotiating a treaty that expanded the territory of the United States by over a million square miles, almost one-quarter again its size, and cut Mexico's territory in half.

The annexation of so much land would force the political fault line between antislavery Northerners and pro-slavery Southerners to rumble dangerously. Northerners saw a conspiracy of "the Slave Power" behind the conquest. Hadn't President James Polk pushed for the annexation of Texas, a slave territory, as part of his presidential platform, and started the war with Mexico too? Wasn't he a slaveholder? Weren't Southerners desperate to swallow more and more territories South of the Mason-Dixon Line, where slavery was allowed?

Southerners were just as suspicious of Northerners. "What do you propose, gentlemen of the Free Soil Party?" Senator Jefferson Davis of Mississippi once responded to a Northerner who opposed spread of slavery into the West. "It is not humanity that influences you . . . it is that you may have an opportunity of cheating us that you want to limit slave territory . . . it is that you may have a majority in the congress of the United States and convert the Government into an engine of Northern aggrandizement . . . you want by an unjust system of legislation to promote the industry of the United States at the expense of the people of the South."

Whether these territories would come in as slave or free states dominated the political discussion from 1846 to 1850. Thomas Hart Benton, Missouri's first senator, said the relentless intrusion of slavery into the national political discourse was like the pervasiveness of frogs in an Old Testament plague: "You could not look upon the table but there were frogs," he complained. "You could not sit down at the banquet but there were frogs, you could not go to the bridal couch and lift the sheets but there were frogs!"

A CARIBBEAN SLAVE STATE?

The struggle between the North and the South focused on midwestern territories such as Kansas and Nebraska. But some Southerners eager to increase the number of slave-holding states had long set their sights on a tropical land: Cuba. In 1848, shortly after the conclusion of the Mexican War, Senator Jefferson Davis of Mississippi, the future president of the Confederacy, said that the Gulf of Mexico was a "basin of water belonging to the United States" and that "Cuba must be ours" so as to "increase the number of slaveholding constituencies." Southern leaders wouldn't have to introduce slavery to the island because it was still permitted there under the Spanish.

The annexation was more than a notion: President James Polk approved an offer of $100 million for the island in the summer of 1848. The Spaniards refused. In 1849, a charismatic Cuban soldier named Narciso Lopez organized Cuban exiles to invade the island. He asked Davis to lead the adventure; when Davis turned him down, he knocked on the door of another Mexican War veteran, Robert E. Lee, who considered the offer but demurred as well.

Lopez eventually went to New Orleans for recruits, planning to "rest his hopes on the men of the bold West and chivalric South." He recruited six hundred men, and crowds on the docks cheered as they sailed to Cuba. The invaders captured the town of Cardenas, burned the governor's mansion, but no uprising of planters followed. They were lucky to outrace a Spanish warship to Key West. Lopez was indicted, but he was freed by a hung jury in New Orleans, where, one newspaper explained, "no jury could be impaneled to convict him because public opinion makes a law."

Lopez would organize another Cuban invasion in 1851, but it would also fail, the Spanish killing two hundred, capturing one hundred sixty more, and executing fifty, including Lopez. The desire to turn Cuba into another slave state would fade, but the battle would come home to less exotic places, like the sparsely populated land that would be the locus of a bloody prelude to the Civil War: Kansas.

COMPROMISES AND MORE COMPROMISES
TO PUT OFF THE CONFLICT

From the founding of the country until the Civil War, Northerners and Southerners fought over control of the government. Northern mercantile interests who supported free labor competed with Southern agrarian interests whose wealth was tied up in slavery. Again and again, when control threatened to shift North or South, senators and congressmen wrestled out a compromise that preserved the balance of power between slave states and free states.

In the Northwest Ordinance of 1787, Congress forbade slavery above the Ohio River but permitted expansion below it. But what to do when it came time to carve states from the Louisiana Purchase in 1803? "This momentous question," wrote an elderly Thomas Jefferson to a friend in 1820, "like a fire-bell in the night, [has] awakened and filled me with terror. I considered it at once the [death] knell of the Union." But the crisis was put off with the Missouri Compromise, which drew a line through the territories at the 36° 30' latitude to the Rocky Mountains. Above the line, new states would be free. Those below the Mason-Dixon Line would enter as slave states.

Passions for and against slavery grew hotter still, until another accommodation, the Compromise of 1850, was passed. It allowed people in the territories acquired as part of the Mexican War to vote to decide whether they came in as slave states or free states, which exacerbated tensions in territories such as Kansas. The compromise also included the Fugitive Slave Act, which required federal officials to help find runaway slaves and also subjected citizens in free states, who aided an escaped slave, to six months in jail and a $1,000 fine.

"I confess, I hate to see the poor creatures hunted down . . ." said former congressman Abraham Lincoln, "but I bite my lip and keep quiet." Many Northerners were outraged that they were required by law to defend slave interests in free states. One Northern woman implored her sister-in-law to write something to reveal the injustices of the Fugitive Slave Act. The relative she called on to write the tract was Harriet Beecher Stowe.

UNCLE TOM'S CABIN—THE STORY BEHIND THE BOOK

In Harriet Beecher Stowe's *Uncle Tom's Cabin*, runaway slave Eliza, clutching her baby, steps to the edge of the frozen Ohio River on a night as "dark as a wolf's mouth." Behind her are slave-catchers; across the river, freedom.

> *Right on behind her they came; and nerved with strength such as God gives only to the desperate, with one wild cry and flying leap, she vaulted sheer over the turbid current by the shore, onto the raft of ice beyond. With wild cries and desperate energy she leaped to another and still another cake;—stumbling,—leaping,—,slipping,—springing upwards again! Her shoes are gone,—her stockings cut from her feet,—while blood marked every step; but she saw nothing, felt nothing, til dimly, as in a dream, she saw the Ohio side.*

Eliza and her child barely make it across the river to safety. It's one of the most dramatic scenes in one of the most influential books in American history, but it pales next to the real-life slave escape, told to Stowe by a Reverend John Rankin, who took in the real "Eliza" on a bitterly cold night in 1838. The woman had escaped from a plantation, was forced onto the cracking ice of the Ohio River by dogs while clutching a wooden plank in one arm and her infant, swaddled in a shawl, in the other. She immediately broke through into the frigid water, but managed to scramble out and run over firmer ice toward the Ohio shore. She fell through again. She pushed her baby ahead onto ice and used the plank to clamber out, broke through again, and finally crawled onto the cold bank in a free state, exhausted.

A white man was waiting for her. He was not a friend, as in the book, but a slave-catcher. But when he heard her baby cry, he found he couldn't do it. He took her to Rankin's house, an Underground Railroad stop, saying, "No nigger has ever been got back from that house." The woman had become a human being, not just a slave.

Slave escapes such as this one hardly made a dent in the growing Southern slave population, but it may have hastened emancipation by confronting white Northerners with the reality of what slave-owners euphemistically called its "peculiar institution." *Uncle Tom's Cabin* amplified this message, selling 2 million copies in the United States and across Europe over the next decade, making it, in proportion to population, the best-selling novel of all time.

PASSIONS ARE INFLAMED BY THE LAST AMERICAN SLAVE SHIP—THE *WANDERER*

In 1858, just three years before the Civil War erupted, a group of investors led by Charles A. L. Lamar, a wealthy cotton-trader from Savannah, bought and outfitted a ship to go to Africa to import slaves—a practice that had been outlawed in 1807. The ship was called the *Wanderer*, and it would be the last ship ever to transport Africans to the United States to be sold as slaves.

The ship was an 1856 luxury racing yacht described by one historian as "the noblest of all sailing vessels," and included table linens, satinwood cabinets, a library, and "Brussels carpets." After its purchase, it was also fitted with extra-large water tanks below deck, an indication to all experienced seamen that the ship would serve as a slave ship.

The *Wanderer* arrived at the Congo River in the fall of 1858 and picked up 409 slaves, age thirteen to nineteen. They were packed into the hold, each one allotted a space twelve inches wide, eighteen inches high, and six feet long, less even than in the slave ships of old. On the return trip to Georgia, about 80 slaves died. The captives were sold quickly, but rumors spread, and the ship was confiscated, and several participants, including Lamar, were arrested and charged with slave-trading.

Lamar and his cohorts wanted their escapade to inflame passions in the North and South, thereby encouraging secession, and it did. During the trial, the *New York Times* wrote: "If they fail to hang the men, if their officials are so lax, or their juries so perjured, as to permit this trade to be carried on with impunity . . . they will suffer all the consequences of an actual complicity in the proceeding itself. . . . The entire population of the North will wage upon [the South] a relentless war of extermination."

The juries acquitted Lamar and others of the most serious charges. Lamar would participate in the Civil War. On April 16, 1865, in a skirmish outside Columbus, Georgia, Lamar would be caught and shot dead. It would happen a week after Robert E. Lee's surrender, and after a rumor—that the war was over—had circulated through the Confederate lines.

FIGHTING IN KANSAS LEADS TO A CANING
IN THE SENATE

In 1854, with the passage of the Kansas-Nebraska Act, Congress decided to let people in the territories decide whether they wanted their state to join the Union as a slave state or a free state. The battle over slavery moved to Kansas, and both sides knew that its outcome might shift the power to the North or South and decide the fate of slavery. The battle became violent, as the two sides clashed and the potential state became known as "Bleeding Kansas." Five thousand pro-slavery Missourians swept into the territory illegally, took over polling places, and created a legislature that made it a crime to even speak out against slavery. Henry Ward Beecher, a Brooklyn preacher who was Harriet Beecher Stowe's brother, sent what were called "Beecher's Bibles"— Sharps rifles—to arm antislavery Kansans. War broke out.

The violence bled back to the floor of the Senate. For two days in May 1856, Charles Sumner of Massachusetts, a leading antislavery politician, spewed against Southerners to packed Senate galleries in a speech he called "The Crime Against Kansas." He singled out South Carolina's senator Andrew P. Butler, who "had chosen a mistress to whom he has made his vows . . . I mean the harlot slavery." Sumner denounced all of South Carolina and "its shameful imbecility from Slavery."

Two days after the speech, Congressman Preston Brooks walked into a largely empty Senate chamber and approached Sumner, who was writing letters at his desk. Sumner's speech, spit Brooks, "is a libel on South Carolina, and Mr. Butler, who is a relative of mine." As Sumner began to rise, Brooks raised a gold-headed cane and beat him.

Southern supporters sent Brooks canes by the dozen to replace the one he had broken over Sumner's head, with inscriptions such as *Hit Him Again*. Southern supporters in the House of Representatives prevented the two-thirds majority needed to remove him. Sumner's injuries largely kept him away from the Senate for four years. Congressmen from both sides of the Mason-Dixon Line began coming into their chambers with pistols in their pockets.

One of the men most outraged by the caning was a fifty-six-year-old man who looked like he had stepped from the Old Testament world to demand an eye for an eye. His name was John Brown.

ELIZA,
HARRIET BEECHER STOWE'S
RUNAWAY SLAVE

Eliza, the fictional young mother who desperately fled across an icy Ohio River in *Uncle Tom's Cabin,* was based on a real runaway slave. This theatrical poster publicized one of the many stage productions of Harriet Beecher Stowe's novel produced after the Civil War.

JOHN BROWN—
METEOR OF THE CIVIL WAR

WEEK 3

AT AGE TWELVE, JOHN BROWN BECOMES
A "MOST DETERMINED" ENEMY OF SLAVERY

After the War of 1812 broke out, John Brown, the man Herman Melville would decades later call "the meteor" of the Civil War, went to work with his father, Owen Brown, who was a beef contractor with the army. John, just twelve, drove the wild steers and cattle through one hundred miles of forest to get them to the Michigan outposts. At the end of these cattle drives, John lodged in the home of a U.S. marshal who treated him like family, giving him presents and praising his intelligence and conversational abilities.

The marshal owned a serving slave about John's age. Owen Brown had always taught his children to fear God and to hate slavery, and at first, John felt pity for the boy, who was both "badly clothed" and "poorly fed."

But the two boys sought each other out, and despite their disparate worlds, they forged a quick friendship. John was aware that despite the praise the marshal had given him, his young friend was his superior— smarter, more agile, and also emotionally stronger, as he had borne the loss of his entire family.

One night, after some guests had left, John watched the marshal criticize the boy slave for some trivial fault in his dinner service. Then the man lifted an iron shovel from the fireplace and beat the boy around the head and shoulders. Long after the boys went to bed, John thought he could hear the slave boy's stifled sobs.

John would never forget the "wretched, hopeless condition" of that "Fatherless & Motherless" slave boy. It was that beating he witnessed, he would insist, that transformed him into a "most determined" enemy of slavery, a soldier who, nearly five decades later, would ultimately give his life to end the institution.

JOHN BROWN INVITES FREDERICK DOUGLASS
TO JOIN HIS RAID

Nearly half a century after John Brown witnessed the beating of a boy slave, he recruited allies for an attack against the institution of slavery. The day before Independence Day 1859, Brown rented a farmhouse near Harpers Ferry, Virginia. A small number of recruits hid there, assuming Brown would conduct a raid to free slaves.

But one night, Brown revealed that he would lead the men in a take-over of the federal arsenal at Harpers Ferry, which would spark a slave rebellion and provide arms for the rebels. Brown expected support from Virginia's 58,000 free blacks and some 491,000 slaves.

In mid-August 1859, John Brown met Frederick Douglass in Chambersburg, Pennsylvania. Brown told his friend that the attack would "serve as notice to the slaves that their friends had come, and as a trumpet to rally them." Douglass wasn't convinced. You are "going into a perfect steel trap, and once in, you will never get out alive." Worse yet, such an attack would "array the whole country against us."

Douglass, who was eighteen years younger than Brown, would later write that he felt wiser and more realistic than his idealistic friend, but also less devoted to the antislavery cause.

When Douglass finally stood to leave, Brown leaped up and put his arms around Douglass's neck. "Come with me," he whispered. "I will defend you with my life. When I strike, the bees will begin to swarm, and I shall want you to help hive them." Douglass, guided, he would recall, either by my "discretion or my cowardice," finally departed, and the two would never meet again.

FAILURE AT HARPERS FERRY

As night fell on the drizzly evening of October 16, 1859, John Brown addressed his raiders—eighteen idealists, free blacks, runaway slaves, and white college men. "Men," he said, "get on your arms; we will proceed to the Ferry." Each carried a knife and forty to fifty rounds of ammunition to supply a revolver and a rifle. Most of the men were under forty; John Brown was fifty-nine. The men walked two-by-two, but Brown rode alone in a farm wagon loaded with Sharps rifles, speared pikes, a sledgehammer, a crowbar, and a few torches.

By midnight, the men had occupied the two most important caches of weapons in the arsenal and the two major roads. Then Brown sent six men to the homes of two prominent slave-owners in the city to free their slaves and arm them. One of the slave-owners was Colonel Lewis Washington, who was forced to give up a sword that had belonged to his great-granduncle George Washington.

Then things began to fall apart. Two of the raiders confronted a night watchman for the railroad on the bridge over the Potomac. The raiders ordered the man to halt, but he fled. He got to the Wager House and told the clerk that two train robbers or perhaps worse had attacked. The first man killed in the raid was a baggage man, Shephard Hayward, a well-liked free black man from Harpers Ferry. As morning came, the raiders stopped a train and Brown told the conductor his plans. He then mysteriously let the train continue.

The train pulled into its next station and authorities informed the White House. Meanwhile, Brown waited for the uprising of slaves and the arrival of antislavery white men. But only armed white men came, incensed by the invasion of Northern abolitionists. The steel trap that Frederick Douglass had foreseen snapped shut.

President Buchanan sent marines to put down the uprising, and they arrived on Monday evening, October 17, under the command of Colonel Robert E. Lee. The next morning Lee sent another future Southern military leader, Lieutenant J. E. B. Stuart, to the brick building where the raiders had retreated. When Brown refused to surrender, Stuart swung his hat over his head, a signal for a bayonet assault by U.S. Marines. Brown was thrust with a light sword that almost lifted him off the floor, but it broke when it hit his belt or a rib bone, and he lived. If he had died that day, his words over the next two months, prophetic and incendiary, would never have been spoken.

JOHN BROWN'S TRIAL
TURNS HIM INTO A NORTHERN MARTYR

Ten of the men in John Brown's party were killed during the raid. Ten were executed after the New Year. Because of his injuries, John Brown lay on a cot during his trial, held at Charlestown, about ten miles from Harpers Ferry, in November 1859. His first act was to shout down his lawyer, who tried to present an insanity defense. Brown heard from visitors that abolitionists wanted to free him from jail, but he made it clear that he didn't want freedom. "I am worth inconceivably more to hang," Brown wrote, "than for any other purpose."

After deliberating just forty-five minutes, the jury found Brown guilty of treason against Virginia, murder, and inciting a slave rebellion. At his sentencing, Brown spoke with an eloquence that would lead Ralph Waldo Emerson to compare his speech to Lincoln's Gettysburg Address. Brown said,

> *I deny everything but what I have all along admitted—the design on my part to free the slaves . . . Had I interfered in the manner which I admit . . . in behalf of the rich, the powerful, the intelligent . . . and suffered and sacrificed what I have in this interference . . . every man in this court would have deemed it an act worthy of reward rather than punishment. . . .*
>
> *I see a book kissed here which I suppose to be the Bible, or at least the New Testament. That teaches me that all things whatsoever I would that men should do to me, I should do even so to them. It teaches me, further, to "remember them that are in bonds, as bound with them." I endeavored to act up to that instruction . . . I believe that to have interfered as I have done . . . in behalf of His despised poor was not wrong, but right.*
>
> *Now, if it is deemed necessary that I should forfeit my life for the furtherance of the ends of justice, and mingle my blood further with the blood of my children and with the blood of millions in this slave country whose rights are disregarded by wicked, cruel, and unjust enactments—I submit; so let it be done!*

PRAISE AND VILIFICATION—
JOHN BROWN DIVIDES THE COUNTRY

When Northerners heard news of John Brown's raid, Abraham Lincoln, a prominent antislavery politician, spoke for many others when he said that even though Brown was right to believe slavery wrong, "that cannot excuse violence, bloodshed, and treason." But Brown's reputation rose quickly. The philosopher and activist Henry David Thoreau praised Brown's actions and he delivered a speech two weeks after the raid, calling Brown a "crucified hero." In Boston on that same day, abolitionist William Lloyd Garrison gave up the torch of pacifism he had held for nearly three decades. "Give me, as a non-resistant, Bunker Hill and Lexington, and Concord," he said to the crowd, "rather than the cowardice and servility of a Southern slave-plantation." Henry Wadsworth Longfellow thought that Brown's raid and his death "will be a great day in our history; the date of a new Revolution,—quite as needed as the old one."

But Southerners were horrified by Brown's violent raid and feared it would spark slave revolts across the South. News spread of Brown's maps, which marked counties where slaves overwhelmingly outnumbered whites. Virginia governor Henry A. Wise received reports that slave plots all over the South were imminent. Reports spread of a "great slave agitation in Kentucky" and a "stampede of Negroes in Missouri." Discipline was ratcheted up on plantations. By December 2, an estimated four thousand men were under arms in Virginia and thousands more in other states.

Before the raid, the cause of secession "had almost died out in Virginia," reported the *Richmond Enquirer*, but the Harpers Ferry invasion had "advanced the cause of disunion more than any event that has happened since the formation of the government; it has rallied to that standard men who formerly looked upon it with horror; it has revived with tenfold strength the desires of a Southern Confederacy. . . . Thousands of men . . . who, a month ago, scoffed at the idea of a dissolution of the Union . . . now hold the opinion that its days are numbered."

JOHN BROWN'S HANGING
AND THE PROPHET'S PREDICTION

Fifteen hundred troops surrounded the gallows at Charles Town, Virginia (now West Virginia), on December 2, 1859. Many of the most important figures of the South came to watch the hanging. Virginia's governor Henry A. Wise sent down Thomas Jackson, a professor at Virginia Military Institute, who would earn the nickname "Stonewall" during the war. There, too, was the sixty-year-old Edmund Ruffin, a fire-eater who had been pushing the South to secede. Also on hand were Virginia militiamen who called themselves the Richmond Grays.

"Brown was a brave old man," said one twenty-two-year-old recruit, "a man inspired . . . the greatest character of this century." Yet he despised him as well, believing abolitionists like him to be "the *only* traitors in the land." The soldier was a young actor named John Wilkes Booth.

Brown stepped out of his cell at about eleven a.m., wearing a wrinkled black suit, a white shirt, a low broad-brimmed hat, and slippers. He was brought to the gallows in a wagon and sat on a large poplar box filled with a black walnut coffin made for him. "This is a beautiful country," he said to the jail keeper as they drove. "I never had the pleasure of seeing it before."

He stepped up on the platform, and a noose was placed around his neck and a white hood over his face. Many had thought that Brown would speak before the hanging, but he was silent, except the words to his guard, "Don't keep me waiting longer than necessary." A trapdoor under Brown's feet opened, and the old man fell three feet. The noose jerked, and the crowd could see his hands clench before they went slack. His body swayed in the wind.

No one spoke until Colonel Preston of the Virginia Military Institute faced the crowd. "So perish all such enemies of Virginia!" he yelled. "All such enemies of the Union! All such foes of the human race." The crowd dispersed, unaware Brown had slipped a piece of paper to a guard at the jail before he left. "I, John Brown," he had written, "am now quite *certain* that the crimes of this *guilty land* will never be purged *away,* but with blood."

JOHN BROWN
AND HIS LONG WHITE BEARD

John Brown (1800–1859) was steeped in the Old Testament—
and looked like an Old Testament figure when he grew a long white
beard in his last years.

LINCOLN IS ELECTED—AND THE DEEP SOUTH SECEDES

WEEK 4

LINCOLN IS ELECTED—
"GOD HELP ME, GOD HELP ME"

At sunrise on November 6, 1860, a cannon shot boomed over Springfield, Illinois. It did not mark the beginning of a battle but it might as well have, because it signaled the start of the most controversial election day in American history. If Lincoln slept at all the previous night, the cannon shot probably woke him in the second-floor bedroom of the house where he had lived with his family for sixteen years. As was his habit, he put on his black suit, punctuated by a white shirt and collar, and perhaps ate his usual breakfast, eggs with toast and coffee, joined by his wife, Mary, and their two younger sons, nine-year-old Willie and seven-year-old Tad. Their eldest, Robert, was at Harvard for his freshman year.

"A memorable day," wrote the diarist and patrician New York lawyer George Templeton Strong, a gung-ho Lincoln supporter. "We do not know yet for what. Perhaps for the disintegration of the country, perhaps for another proof that the North is timid and mercenary, perhaps for demonstration that Southern bluster is worthless. We cannot tell yet what historical lesson the event of November 6, 1860, will teach, but the lesson cannot fail to be weighty."

The Virginia fire-eater Edmund Ruffin also was behind Lincoln because he believed a Lincoln victory with the "Abolition Party of the North" would convince Southern states to resist "oppression and impending subjugation," secede, and strike out for "independence."

Lincoln spent most of the day at the city's limestone State House, but around three thirty p.m. he stepped leisurely to the Sangamon County Court House, surrounded by a small group of friends and protectors, to vote. From the dense crowd that surrounded him, people called out, "Old Abe!" "Uncle Abe!" "Honest Abe!" and "the Giant Killer," and even Democrats doffed their hats.

After nine p.m. Lincoln took up an invitation from the Illinois & Mississippi Telegraph Company to read the dispatches as soon as they came in. When a report arrived that he won Massachusetts by fifty thousand votes, he remarked that it was a "clear case of the Dutch taking Holland." After midnight, Lincoln and his friends went to a nearby ice cream saloon, where people took turns reading the results until the candidate read the results from Philadelphia. Eyewitness Newton Bateman remembered it this way: "All eyes were fixed upon his tall form and slightly trembling lips, as he read in a clear and distinct voice: 'The city and state for Lincoln by a decisive majority,' and immediately added in slow, emphatic terms, 'I think that settles it.'"

The election would be historic in many ways. While he received more votes than any president before him, he won only 40 percent of all the votes cast in this four-person race, the second-lowest percentage ever for a victor, behind John Quincy Adams. And Lincoln had had almost no support in the South. In Virginia, he won only 1,929 votes—just over 1 percent. He fared even worse in his home state of Kentucky, receiving only 1,364 votes of the 146,216 cast. Southern leaders kept Lincoln's name off the ballot in ten Deep South states. In the five slave-owning states where Lincoln did appear on the ballot, he received just 26,000 votes, and many of those came from St. Louis, with a high number of Republicans.

But in Springfield, people were reveling through the night. An hour past midnight, Lincoln bid adieu to his friends, saying that it was about time he "went home and told the news to a tired woman who was sitting up for him."

John Nicolay, who would be Lincoln's private secretary, said he saw the "momentary glow" of victory retreat to "the appalling shadow of his mighty task and responsibility. It seemed as if he suddenly bore the whole world upon his shoulders, and could not shake it off." Lincoln had once confided in his friend Ward Hill Lamon that from boyhood "my ambition was to be president." Now he was, and the final words his friends remember him saying before he left for home were, "God help me, God help me."

SOUTH CAROLINA IS THE FIRST TO JUMP

Most South Carolinians interpreted Lincoln's election as a revolutionary cannon shot aimed at their principles, their property, and their honor. "The tea has been thrown overboard," wrote the *Charleston Mercury*, owned by radical secessionist Robert Barnwell Rhett, of the election of Lincoln and the Republicans. "The revolution of 1860 has been initiated."

Abraham Lincoln believed the Constitution denied him the power to ban slavery where it existed. But most Southerners saw his election as an assault on slavery and the South. For seventy-five years, the federal government had been controlled by Southern slavery-supporters and Northerners deferential to slaveholders. Nine of twelve presidents were slaveholders from 1788 until 1850 and the Supreme Court had been pro-slavery since the day it was appointed. This new Republican government, Southerners believed, would encourage slave revolts and fight for emancipation and social equality for blacks. "A party founded on the single sentiment . . . of hatred of African slavery," wrote the *Richmond Examiner*, "is now the controlling power."

After word of Lincoln's election, the grand jury for U.S. District Court in Charleston refused to continue its work. Presiding Judge Andrew Magrath removed his judicial robe and announced he would resign his post. "As far as I am concerned," he said, "the Temple of Justice, raised under the Constitution of the United States, is now closed." He was the first paid federal official in South Carolina to give up his post, but many followed, including Senator James Henry Hammond, who later admitted privately, "I thought Magrath and all those fellows were great asses for resigning and have done it myself. It is an epidemic and very foolish. It reminds me of the Japanese who, when insulted, rip open their own bowels."

In mid-December, a South Carolina convention on secession was held amid marching bands, fireworks, and rallies of Carolinians waving their palmetto flag. In its Declaration of Causes of Secession, South Carolina's politicians called Lincoln "hostile to Slavery. . . . Because he has declared that 'Government cannot endure permanently half slave, half free.'" On December 20, after only a few hours of discussion, a vote was taken to dissolve "the union now subsisting between South Carolina and other States." The measure passed 169–0.

THE OTHER SOUTH—
SAM HOUSTON AND THE ANTI-SECESSIONISTS

In 1861, Sam Houston, sixty-eight years old, was governor of Texas. He had led successful Texas forces in the state's War of Independence against Mexico in the mid-1830s. When Lincoln was elected, he was one of many Southerners who disapproved of the fire-eaters' call for secession.

"Within ten years we would have ten or more separate confederate governments," Houston predicted, echoing Lincoln, who maintained that secession was the "essence of anarchy," which could lead to a never-ending splintering of the country. Houston argued further that slavery was safer within the Union. "The first gun fired in the war will be the knell of slavery," he said, noting that secessionists "forget or else are ignorant of the fact that the best sentiment of Europe is opposed to our system of negro slavery."

When Lincoln was elected, Houston refused to call a secessionist convention. When Texas secessionists went ahead anyway and voted to join the Confederacy, Houston challenged their right to do so, giving in only when Texans voted for secession by a three-to-one margin.

He also resisted the notion that the courage and abilities of Southern men exceeded those of Northern ones. "Never was a more false or absurd statement ever made by designing demagogues," said Houston, who expected secession would lead to a civil war. "When it comes," he predicted, "the descendants of the heroes of Lexington and Bunker Hill will be found equal to the patriotism, courage, and heroic endurance with descendants of the heroes of Cowpens and Yorktown.

"Let me tell you what is coming," he warned the secessionists. "Your fathers and husbands, your sons and brothers, will be herded at the point of bayonets. . . . You may, after the sacrifice of countless millions of treasure and hundreds of thousands of lives, as a bare possibility, win Southern independence . . . but I doubt it. . . ." Houston was pushed from his governorship and, after Fort Sumter, he acquiesced to the passions of Southern secessionists. "All my hopes, my fortunes are centered in the South," he admitted. "When I see the land for whose defense my blood has been spilt, and the people whose fortunes have been mine through a quarter of a century of toil, threatened with invasion, I can but cast my lot with theirs and await the issue."

THE DEEP SOUTH GOES OUT—AND THE FATHERS
OF THE CONFEDERACY MEET IN MONTGOMERY

After South Carolina seceded, Charleston publisher Robert Barnwell Rhett, who wrote South Carolina's resolutions of secession, called for a convention of seceded states in Montgomery, Alabama, in February 1861 to draw up a new government and constitution, creating an incentive for states to secede. The plan worked.

Mississippi seceded on January 9, 1861; Florida on January 10; Alabama on January 11; Georgia on January 19; Louisiana on January 26; and Texas on February 1. The average vote margin was four to one.

On the weekend of February 2 and 3, 1861, fifty Southern delegates and their entourages began arriving in Montgomery, Alabama, to establish a new country. The Montgomery Convention marked a changing of the Southern guard. The convention would never have happened without the efforts of the Southern radical "fire-eaters" such as Rhett, Congressman William L. Yancey of Alabama, and the slaveholder Edmund Ruffin, who had for years pressed for a new Southern Confederacy.

But most of the men who gathered in Montgomery were pragmatists. They revealed their conservatism in one of their first decisions, choosing as vice president moderate Alexander Stephens, the tubercular and intellectual Georgia politician, who had resisted secession but succumbed to his state's decision to secede.

For president, the delegates looked to Jefferson Davis, a U.S. senator who had resigned after Mississippi, his home state, had seceded. Well-spoken and well-educated, Davis had a political résumé as strong as any. He had served as a congressman and senator, and he was a West Point graduate, a veteran of the Mexican War, and had served as secretary of war.

He was also a Southern loyalist, a states' rights advocate, and a slave-owner who believed the institution was socially beneficial for all involved. Before and after Lincoln's election, Davis, too, had resisted secession. But when Mississippi seceded, Davis supported her. The night after he bid adieu to the Senate, his wife, Varina, heard her husband pacing, repeating, "May God have us in His holy keeping and grant that before it is too late, peaceful councils may prevail."

Told by Mississippi's governor J. J. Pettus that he was needed to command Mississippi volunteers, Davis returned to Brierfield, the family's plantation, to await an army to command. That's where he was when a messenger from the Montgomery convention arrived. The messenger found Davis with Varina in their garden, cutting roses.

JEFFERSON DAVIS GOES PALE WHEN INFORMED
HE WILL LEAD THE CONFEDERACY

The messenger sent from the Montgomery Convention to Davis's Brier-field Plantation, one hundred miles away, handed him a telegram. Davis stopped cutting roses and silently read the note. Varina thought her husband looked stricken. He read the note to her.

> *Sir:*
> *We are directed to inform you that you are this day unanimously elected President of the Provisional Government of the Confederate States of America, and to request you to come to Montgomery immediately.*

When he spoke of the note, Mrs. Davis would later say, he did so "as a man might speak of a sentence of death." He left for Montgomery the next day, and at the train's many stops, crowds gathered to see him. Davis talked confidently but gravely. Prepare for a war, he warned them, and a long one. The throngs, hardly dampened by his warning, cheered.

When Davis arrived at the convention in Montgomery on February 16, a crowd followed him from the train to the Exchange Hotel. There, William L. Yancey, the fire-eating orator from Alabama, quieted the crowd by raising his hand. He then pointed at Davis, declaring that "the man and the hour have met!" "Dixie," which would become the Confederate national anthem, was played; men wept. They also sang "Fare-well to the Star-Spangled Banner."

"The time for compromise has passed," Davis said. "The South is determined to maintain her position, and make all who oppose her smell Southern powder and feel Southern steel." To that end, the provisional Confederate government in Montgomery called for its member states to provide a hundred thousand men for an army. The war of words and political maneuvers was becoming one of guns and marching men.

WERE THE SECESSIONISTS REBELS OR CONSERVATIVES?

Secessionists believed that just as states had formed the United States, they had the right to leave the United States. As justification, many cited the preamble to the Declaration of Independence, which maintained "that whenever any Form of Government becomes destructive to these ends [Life, Liberty and the pursuit of Happiness], it is the Right of the People to alter or to abolish it, and to institute new Government." After states began to tumble out of the Union, one Confederate officer stated he "never believed the Constitution recognized the right of secession. I took up arms, sir, upon a broader ground—the right of revolution. We were wronged. Our properties and liberties were about to be taken from us. It was a sacred duty to rebel."

But was it really a revolution? The Rebels sometimes argued they were conservatives, inheritors and protectors of the revolution of 1776. It was no surprise that Jefferson Davis was inaugurated on George Washington's birthday—and that the Confederates put Washington's image on the Great Seal of the Confederate States. In his inaugural address, Davis said, "We hope to perpetuate the principles of our revolutionary fathers."

Like the Founding Fathers, the Confederates also formed a country and a Constitution that protected slavery. "What were the rights and liberties for which Confederates contended?" asks historian James McPherson in his book *Battle Cry of Freedom*. "The right to own slaves; the liberty to take this property into the territories; freedom from the coercive powers of a centralized government."

The real revolutionaries might have been Abraham Lincoln and the radical Republicans, who upset the political apple cart that had allowed slavery to thrive on the continent for two and a half centuries. Confederate President Jefferson Davis agreed, saying it was "an abuse of language" to call the Southern retreat from Union a revolution, adding that secessionists left the Union "to save ourselves from a revolution" that threatened to make "property in slaves so insecure as to be comparatively worthless."

EDMUND RUFFIN,
VIRGINIA'S RADICAL SECESSIONIST

Edmund Ruffin (1794–1865), a Virginia farmer and slave-owner, defended slavery and fiercely lobbied for the secession of Southern states. He predicted the Civil War in his book, *Anticipations of the Future, To Serve as Lessons for the Present Time.*

The COUNTRY EXPLODES, *the* CANNON *is* FIRED
(1860–1861)

INTRODUCTION

The Civil War approached like a fight that escalates between two angry brothers. An insult, an insult returned, one steps away, the other grabs, someone swings, and before it's done blood is spilled.

The dispute before the Civil War, between the North and the South, simmered over slavery. In 1860, the North elected Republican Abraham Lincoln, who, along with his party, was committed to keeping slavery from spreading to the Western territories. Southerners saw that election as a shift of power to the North and to a government they believed was determined to free 4 million slaves, thereby destroying their economy and their way of life.

Southern states, one by one, left the Union. Congress made some desperate attempts to appease the Southerners, but couldn't keep making the kinds of compromises that had held the country together over the last half-century.

The day after Lincoln was inaugurated, he learned that Fort Sumter, a federal fort in Charleston Harbor that was a lightning rod for both sides, might have to be abandoned to South Carolina within weeks. The president was plagued by headaches and insomnia as he tried to chart a course that would hold the country together. Guns were fired at Fort Sumter; Lincoln called for troops; and four more Southern states seceded.

Young men marched blindly into what they expected would be a bloodless war that would last just a few months. The first land battle in Virginia caused 4,500 casualties, numbers that shocked the country. By the time the war was exhausted, such casualties would hardly be noticed, minor losses next to a virtual river of blood.

THE CREATION OF
THE CONFEDERATE STATES
OF AMERICA

"DIXIE"—A SONG STOLEN FROM BLACK MUSICIANS BY AN OHIO WHITE SONGWRITER FOR A MINSTREL SHOW?

While many Northern and Southern leaders put slavery aside in their public declarations, the unofficial anthems that arose from the people—"Dixie" for the South and "John Brown's Body" for the North—did not.

The tune for "John Brown's Body" may have come from an English sea shanty borrowed from a Swedish drinking song or from a Southern African-American folk song. It was sung in America back in the early 1800s at Southern religious camp meetings with the words, "Say, brothers, will you meet us," and a "Glory, glory, hallelujah" chorus. In one version, sung in the Carolina low country, they sang, "Say, brothers, will you meet us? . . . On Canaan's happy shore?"—likely an allusion to a promised land following freedom from slavery.

The "John Brown" lyrics were written after word of John Brown's hanging in 1859 came to the Twelfth Massachusetts Regiment, where a Sergeant John Brown sang in the regiment's quartet. This led one soldier to reportedly deadpan, "But he still goes marching around." The joke became the lyrics "John Brown's body lies a-mouldering in his grave . . . But his truth goes marching on." The regiment sang it wherever it went, until June 1862, when Sergeant John Brown drowned while crossing the Shenandoah River. By that time, the rest of the Union army had taken it up, adding a more explicit verse: "We'll hang Jeff Davis to a sour apple tree."

The official story for "Dixie" is that it was written in 1859 by Daniel Decatur Emmett, originally from Mount Vernon, Ohio, who had written classic folk songs such as "Turkey in the Straw," "Blue-Tail Fly," and "Old Dan Tucker." He may have written it, or he may have simply learned the song from Ben and Lew Snowden, African-American musicians in his hometown. Either way, Emmett certainly popularized the song for a group he belonged to, called Bryant's Minstrels, white singers who blackened their faces with burned cork to entertain white audiences. "Dixie" swept the country—especially the South. The lyrics imagined a black man who yearned for the good life of the plantation. "I wish I was in de land ob cotton/Old times dar am not forgotten/Look away! Look away! Look away! Dixie Land."

When sung by Southern whites, especially soldiers during the Civil War, another line gained an emotional pitch: "In Dixie land I'll take my stand, to lib and die in Dixie." The song became so popular that it was sung at Jefferson Davis's inauguration in February 1861. Lincoln liked the song, too, and he would ask the band to play it when the war ended.

HOW TO HANDLE SLAVERY
IN THE CONFEDERATE CONSTITUTION?

The delegates at the Montgomery Convention drafted a provisional constitution so similar to the U.S. Constitution they almost could have copied much of the original onto a blank sheet of paper. Almost. Confederate presidents were allowed just one six-year term, and received a line-item veto and more power over appropriations. The delegates also gave states' rights a boost by noting that the "people" part of "We the people" in their Constitution consisted of "each State acting in its sovereign and independent character."

But what would the delegates do about slavery? The U.S. Constitution never mentions slavery by name, using instead the euphemism "person held to service or labor." The delegates at the Montgomery Convention called a slave a slave. "No . . . law," they wrote, "denying or impairing the right of property in negro slaves shall be passed." No state was permitted to bar slaves from being transported within the Confederacy. The drafters also extended the right to own and transport slaves to any future territory overseen by the Confederacy, a repudiation of Lincoln's stand against extending slavery into the territories.

The radicals also wanted to reinstitute the slave trade with Africa, to send a legal signal that there was no shame in the institution. But moderates wanted nothing to do with the slave trade. They didn't want to offend European powers, especially England, which they hoped would recognize their country and take their side if it came to war. They also resisted because they were still trying to entice the people of the Upper South and the border states into the Confederacy. Even slaveholders might object to the revival of the African slave trade, because it would depress the price of their slaves, and it would offend many Southerners who approved of slavery but not the brutal transport of slaves across the Atlantic.

What most secessionists wanted was separation, not revolution. "Confederates did not believe they needed to make new worlds," wrote Civil War historian Emory M. Thomas. "They were more than content with the world they already had."

SOME PREDICTED A BLOODLESS DISPUTE, OTHERS A COUNTRY "DRENCHED IN BLOOD"

The secession of Southern states was not a declaration of war, and many denied that a conflict was inevitable. In the South, it became fashionable to say that "a lady's thimble will hold all the blood that will be shed."

Cornelia Peake McDonald, a middle-class Virginian with nine children, would keep a journal during the war, often scribbling "between the lines of printed books" when paper couldn't be found, to record life "inside the house." During the war, she would lose her husband, fight to save her house from Union soldiers, have slaves sold away and escape, lose an infant to illness, and almost lose more children to starvation. In early 1861, politicians passed through the town. "Dinner parties were given and feasting went on as if we were not all standing on the brink of an abyss. . . . Everybody seemed to be frantic, bereft of their sober senses."

Yet a few leaders would come close to predicting the course of the war. Alexander Stephens, the future vice president of the Confederacy, warned that "revolutions are much easier started than controlled, and the men who begin them [often] . . . themselves become the victims." Robert E. Lee warned that "the war will last at least four years."

On Christmas Eve 1860, William Tecumseh Sherman was dining at the Louisiana State Military Academy, where he was superintendent, with a classics professor, when a servant came in with a newspaper proclaiming that South Carolina had seceded. Sherman declared,

> *This country will be drenched in blood, and God only knows how it will end. It is all folly, madness, a crime against civilization! You [Southern] people speak so lightly of war. . . . War is a terrible thing! Besides, where are your men and appliances of war. . . ? The North can make a steam engine, locomotive, or railway car; hardly a yard of cloth or a pair of shoes can you make. You are rushing into war with one of the most powerful, ingeniously mechanical, and determined people on earth—right at your doors. You are bound to fail. . . .*

WAS SLAVERY THE PRIMARY REASON FOR SECESSION?

What caused the Civil War? In his Second Inaugural Address, Abraham Lincoln said that slavery "was, somehow, the cause of the war," and few people from his time, Confederates or Yankees, would have argued with him.

But in the post–Civil War era, ex-president Jefferson Davis and other Confederate leaders asserted that they did not secede to preserve slavery, but to preserve the rights of states against a tyrannical federal government. After the war, Davis claimed that "the existence of African servitude was in no wise the cause of the conflict, but only an incident." This view became part of the Lost Cause ideology, expressed in South Carolina's 1965 monument erected at Gettysburg, which stated its soldiers fought for *"the sacredness of states rights. . . ."*

In their 1927 book, *The Rise of American Civilization,* Charles and Mary Beard argued that the conflict was not over slavery, but between a plantation system and industrial capitalism. Secession was an attempt to protect the agricultural South, they argued, from the industrial Leviathan in the North. "If the southern planters had been content to grant tariffs, bounties, subsidies, and preferences to northern commerce and industry," the Beards wrote, "it is not probable that they would have been molested in their most imperious proclamations of sovereignty." In this theory, Lincoln was less a "Black Republican" than the figurehead for oppressive Northern capitalists.

Yet almost all professional historians today agree with W. E. B. Dubois, who was astounded that "anyone who reads . . . the lives of contemporary statesmen and public characters, North and South, the discourses in the newspapers and accounts of meetings and speeches, [could] doubt that Negro slavery was the cause of the Civil War." An obvious example is Alexander Stephens, speaking in Savannah just a few weeks after the Deep South seceded. He stated that slavery was the "immediate cause of the . . . present revolution." He said that the United States had been founded on the false assumption that all men were created equal, and that the "cornerstone" of "our new Government is founded upon . . . the great truth that the negro is not equal to the white man. . . . This, our new government, is the first, in the history of the world, based upon this great physical, philosophical, and moral truth."

HARRIET TUBMAN HAS A VISION THAT THE SLAVES WILL BE FREED

As tensions grew between the North and South in the first months of 1861, Harriet Tubman, the powerful woman who had freed slaves on the Underground Railroad for a decade before the war, which earned her the title "Moses of her people," expected a long and bloody war to break out. After Abraham Lincoln's inauguration in March, she stayed with the prominent New York Presbyterian minister and radical abolitionist Henry Highland Garnet, famous for once calling on slaves to kill their slave masters.

Asleep in his home, she had one of those visions that guided and inspired her through her entire life. She came down to the main floor of the home, as if she were in an ecstatic trance.

"My people are free!" she sang. "My people are free!"

Garnet dismissed Tubman's vision. "You've come to torment us before the time. Do cease this noise! My grandchildren may see the day of the emancipation of our people," he said, "but you and I will never see it."

"I tell you, sir," she informed Garnet, "you'll see it and you'll see it soon." She brushed aside breakfast, absorbed in the power of her prophetic vision. "My people are free!" she sang out again. "My people are free!"

MONEY, MEN, AND MUNITIONS—
THE RISE OF THE CONFEDERATE NATION

In just six days, the delegates gathered at Montgomery, Alabama, had made themselves into a provisional government, established a provisional constitution, and elected a provisional president and vice president. And provisional was how it looked. The president's office was indicated with a piece of stationery pinned to a door, and the cabinet that Davis appointed met in a hotel room. The secretary of the treasury had to buy his own chair and desk. Without a printing press to do the job, the Confederacy had to hire a New York firm to print up its money.

Even after it reached its full complement of eleven states, the Confederacy had only 30 percent of the national wealth—most of it tied up in land and slaves—21 percent of the bank deposits, and 12 percent of the circulating currency.

But the coffers weren't completely empty, as the Montgomery Convention accepted a $500,000 loan in specie seized from a New Orleans mint and the United States Customs Office. The loan set the tone for a Confederate treasury that filled its vaults with gifts, loans, and quickly printed Confederate bills. Southern politicians avoided taxation as un-Southern. When the Confederates imposed a small direct tax on its states in August 1861, most paid it not by collecting a tax but by borrowing more money or printing state notes. They knew that such actions would eventually cause inflation, but they needed money for what they believed would be a limited emergency.

They also needed a military—both men and weapons—either to discourage the North from fighting a war or to wage one if necessary. In December, Davis had contracted with manufacturer Eli Whitney for one thousand rifles that would go to his home state of Mississippi. Bizarrely, the United States Army ordnance office in Washington also agreed to sell five thousand guns to Mississippi from its arsenal in Baton Rouge, despite the likelihood they would be used against the Union if war broke out. By mid-April, 62,000 Southerners had signed up as soldiers. But the question remained: Would war break out? And, if so, where?

JEFFERSON DAVIS ACCEPTS THE PRESIDENCY OF THE CONFEDERATE STATES OF AMERICA

Jefferson Davis (1808–1889) accepted the presidency of the Confederate States of America with much apprehension, well aware that war was likely.

FAILED COMPROMISES
TO SAVE THE UNION

WEEK 6

"HOPE TO THE WORLD FOR ALL FUTURE TIME"— LINCOLN CONNECTS TO THE FOUNDING FATHERS

On February 22, 1861, just weeks after Southern politicians gathered in Montgomery to put together their new government, Lincoln traveled from Springfield, Illinois, to Washington, DC. On the way, the president-elect stopped at Independence Hall in Philadelphia, where the Declaration of Independence had been signed in 1776. He spoke on the birthday of George Washington, a hero of Lincoln's, and said:

> I am filled with deep emotion at finding myself standing here, in this place, where were collected together the wisdom, the patriotism, the devotion to principle, from which sprang the institutions under which we live. You have kindly suggested to me that in my hands is the task of restoring peace to the present distracted condition of the country. I can say in return, Sir, that all the political sentiments I entertain have been drawn, so far as I have been able to draw them, from the sentiments which originated and were given to the world from this hall. I have never had a feeling politically that did not spring from the sentiments embodied in the Declaration of Independence (great cheering). . . .
>
> I have often inquired of myself what great principle or idea it was that kept this Confederacy so long together. It was not the mere matter of the separation of the Colonies from the motherland; but that sentiment in the Declaration of Independence which gave liberty, not alone to the people of this country, but, I hope, to the world, for all future time (applause). It was that which gave promise that in due time the weight would be lifted from the shoulders of all men (cheers). . . .
>
> [I]f this country cannot be saved without giving up that principle— I was about to say I would rather be assassinated on this spot than to surrender it (applause).

BUCHANAN FEARS A WAR,
BUT FREDERICK DOUGLASS WELCOMES ONE

Those who knew James Buchanan found the tall, ruddy, silver-haired gentleman genial, which served "Old Buck" well during his steady upward climb in the Democratic Party and in his posts as minister to Russia and Great Britain.

But the troubles of 1860—the election of Lincoln and then the secession of Deep South states—seemed to paralyze President Buchanan. He declared that secession was illegal but also made it clear he would not coerce the Deep South back into the country. It might have been the diplomat's attempt at preventing war, but such a contradictory policy led William Seward, Lincoln's future secretary of state, to reply that it was the same as saying "that no state has the right to secede unless it wishes to" and that "it is the President's duty to enforce the laws, unless somebody opposes him."

Buchanan feared that taking military action would initiate a cascading series of disasters that would drive more states into the Confederacy. If Virginia went out, and Maryland, both slave states, Washington, DC, would become an embattled capital, swallowed up between them. If Kentucky went, and Missouri, commerce along the Ohio and Mississippi Rivers might be taken away from the North. War might also mean banks in the North, closely tied to the Southern economy, could collapse. Buchanan's chief motivator seemed to be fear of starting a war before he could get out of office.

Unlike Buchanan and many other politicians in the months leading up to the war, freed slave Frederick Douglass welcomed the maelstrom. "I confess to a feeling allied to satisfaction at the prospect of a conflict between the North and the South," he recalled after the war. "Standing outside the pale of American humanity, denied citizenship, unable to call the land of my birth my country, and adjudged by the Supreme Court of the United States to have no rights which white men were bound to respect, and longing for the end of the bondage of my people, I was ready for any political upheaval which should bring about a change in the existing condition of things."

MAJOR ROBERT ANDERSON RETREATS
IN THE MIDDLE OF THE NIGHT TO FORT SUMTER

Major Robert Anderson, fifty-five years old, had once been an Illinois colonel to a gawky young captain named Abraham Lincoln; he had served in the Indian wars with Jefferson Davis, a friend. A lifetime soldier, he hated war. "I think," he said early in his career, "that killing people is a very poor way of settling national grievances." He had arrived in Charleston on November 19, 1860, and he knew his decisions would be the fulcrum on which war was weighed.

He immediately saw that Fort Moultrie, where he commanded Union troops in Charleston Harbor, was far too vulnerable. The wall at the fort was so low that sharpshooters could fire over it from sand hills and homes only a hundred yards away. "If attacked in force by any one not a simpleton," he wrote a friend, "there is scarcely a probability of our being able to hold out."

Anderson had begged for more troops to dissuade the South Carolinians from attacking, but President Buchanan was paralyzed. South Carolina's most famous secessionist, Robert Barnwell Rhett, warned: "If you send any more troops into Charleston Bay it will be bloody."

Anderson decided to move his troops, secretly, in small boats, to Fort Sumter, a tiny island in the harbor. Its walls were eight- to twelve-feet thick, and the fort boasted 146 guns. But the transfer to Fort Sumter was risky. South Carolina governor Francis Pickens had put steamboats in the harbor, probably armed, to prevent such a move. The indecisive President Buchanan might also disavow the action and court-martial Anderson. To prevent leaks, Anderson kept the plan secret until twenty minutes before the boats were launched. At seven p.m., two cannons boomed. Edmund Ruffin, one of the fiercest secessionists, was on a boat leaving the harbor for Florida to convince its representatives to join the Confederacy. He wrote in his diary that the cannon fire "must have been a signal for something." It was: two boats loaded with Union soldiers turned toward Fort Sumter.

"Anderson's course is universally approved and if he is recalled or if Sumter is surrendered . . ." wrote a prominent New York Democrat afterward. "Northern sentiment will be unanimous in favor of hanging Buchanan." But despite Anderson's popularity, a mounting problem—the dwindling of food at the fort—would soon put an end to his attempts to forestall a catastrophic war.

CRITTENDEN ATTEMPTS TO APPEASE THE SLAVE STATES

After Lincoln's election, American politicians scrambled to elude a severing of the nation, or perhaps worse, a war. In December 1860, John J.
Crittenden, a Kentucky senator, tried to do what a former Kentucky
senator, Henry Clay, had done in 1820 and 1850—find a compromise
over slavery. Crittenden cobbled together a series of amendments to the
Constitution that attempted to appease the South.

They protected slavery in the District of Columbia until the day
Virginia and Maryland outlawed the institution. They forbade Congress to interfere with slave trading between states and financially compensated slaveholders unable to retrieve runaway slaves. They assured
states that the national government would never interfere with slavery.
The compromise also revived the Missouri Compromise of 1820 by
forbidding slavery in territories north of 36°30' and protecting it south
of the line in territories "now held, or hereafter acquired." But Republicans maintained that such a compromise "would amount to a perpetual covenant of war against every people, tribe, and State owning a foot
of land between here and Tierra del Fuego." Yet some Republican businessmen, fearing war would trigger a panic on Wall Street, endorsed
the compromises and even William Seward, Lincoln's future secretary
of state, seemed sympathetic.

But President-elect Lincoln told Seward that Crittenden's compromise would "put us again on the high-road to a slave empire." Lincoln
noted that a territorial compromise "acknowledges that slavery has equal
rights with liberty, and surrenders all we have contended for. . . . We
have just carried an election on principles fairly stated to the people.
Now we are told in advance, the government shall be broken up, unless
we surrender to those we have beaten. . . . If we surrender, it is the end of
us. They will repeat the experiment upon us *ad libitum*. A year would
not pass, till we shall have to take Cuba [as a slave state] as a condition
upon which they will stay in the Union."

In a note to politicians, Lincoln wrote, "Entertain no proposition for
a compromise in regard to the *extension* of slavery." In another note, he
used a phrase that would be remembered long after his death: "The
tug," he wrote, "has to come & better now than later." On January 16,
1861, Crittenden's compromise was turned down by a vote of twenty-
five to twenty-three. All twenty-five no votes were Republican.

A THIRTEENTH AMENDMENT—TO *PROTECT* SLAVERY?

The Thirteenth Amendment to the Constitution, passed in 1865, reads, "Neither slavery nor involuntary servitude, except as a punishment for crime . . . shall exist within the United States. . . ." But early in 1861, an earlier Thirteenth Amendment, protecting rather than banning slavery, passed both the House and Senate by huge majorities.

In February 1861, U.S. congressmen were working desperately to keep the eight Upper South slave states from seceding. They knew that if these states joined the seven Deep South states, bringing them back into the Union, with or without a war, would be exceedingly difficult. And the matter was pressing: five had scheduled conventions to discuss secession. To keep these states, a conciliatory amendment was drafted, and on February 28, the House and Senate voted on a Thirteenth Amendment to the Constitution. It read, "No amendment shall be made to the Constitution which will authorize or give to Congress the power to abolish or interfere, within any State, with the domestic institutions thereof, including that of persons held to labor or service by the laws of said State."

William Seward, soon to be Lincoln's secretary of state, abandoned his strong antislavery views and publicly endorsed the amendment. His wife, Frances, was outraged. "Compromises based on the idea that the preservation of the Union is more important than the liberty of nearly 4,000,000 human beings cannot be right," Frances wrote her husband. "The alteration of the Constitution to perpetuate slavery . . . these compromises cannot be approved by God or supported by good men. . . ." President-elect Abraham Lincoln also gave the amendment his tacit approval.

"I hope to have God on my side," Lincoln was reported to have said regarding the border states, "but I must have Kentucky." But for the amendment to pass, it needed the approval of three-fifths of the states. Before that process could gain momentum, conciliation gave way to cannon fire.

LINCOLN DISGUISES HIMSELF TO ESCAPE FROM
FEARED ASSASSINS—AND REGRETS IT

For twelve days and nights in early February 1861, Lincoln would take eighteen railroads 1,904 miles on a circuitous ride from Springfield, Illinois, to Washington, DC. All along the way there were whistle-stops, with large crowds—perhaps sixty thousand in Columbus, Ohio— coming to listen to the bands, watch artillery fire a salute to the president-elect, and see and hear Lincoln in person.

Along the way Lincoln downplayed the crisis that had enveloped the nation, describing it as something "gotten up . . . by designing politicians." In Cleveland, he said, "Why all this excitement? Why all these complaints? . . . The crisis is all artificial." Lincoln believed that the South's commitment to secession and its saber-rattling, if ignored, would quiet. To many, this assumption was evidence that Lincoln did not understand the depth of the crisis.

As his train to Washington approached its destination, the Pinkerton National Detective Agency received reports that operatives in Baltimore were planning to assassinate the president. At first, the president ignored the warnings, refusing to speed up his schedule and slip through Baltimore at night. But as the train was leaving for Harrisburg, news came that both the future Secretary of State William Seward and General Winfield Scott believed the conspiracy was real. Allan Pinkerton, head of the Pinkerton Agency, proposed putting Lincoln on a special train from Harrisburg to Philadelphia and then slipping him through Baltimore in disguise to the Washington train.

Lincoln reluctantly agreed. That night, Lincoln quietly left his hotel wearing a soft felt hat someone had given him in New York rather than his signature stovepipe one. An overcoat was put over his shoulders. "I was not the same man," Lincoln admitted.

The press quickly twisted the details of the stealth arrival to mock the president. Cartoonists portrayed Lincoln's disguise as a tam and kilts.

Lincoln later regretted the decision to sneak into Washington disguised. He had spent much of the train trip trying to forge an image of a politician who was firm but not rash. Now that was replaced by an image of a fearful man. Where Northerners wanted a brave leader, some saw a weak one, even a coward—before he had even taken office.

THE INAUGURATION OF PRESIDENT ABRAHAM LINCOLN— MARCH 4, 1861

Crowds gather at the Capitol building—which the Lincoln administration continued to build through the war—for Abraham Lincoln's inaugural. "If people see the Capitol going on," Lincoln said, "it is a sign we intend the Union shall go on."

THE GUN IS FIRED—
FORT SUMTER

WEEK 7

WHAT TO DO WITH FORT SUMTER—
LINCOLN'S HARD CHOICES

Upon his election, Lincoln wanted time to organize his cabinet and to convince the secessionists that he wanted peace, not war. But on the morning after his inauguration, the first thing placed in his hands was a dispatch from Major Robert Anderson, commander of the Union garrison in Charleston Harbor. His supplies, he told Lincoln, would run out in a few weeks.

All of Lincoln's options were fraught with potential disaster. He could send all the soldiers and ships at his disposal and shoot his way into the bay to reinforce Anderson, but this would probably cause secession of the border states and perhaps saddle the president with the responsibility of starting a civil war. If this weren't deterrent enough, General Winfield Scott told him that reinforcing the fort, given the military buildup in the bay, would take 25,000 men and an armada—at a time when the navy was feeble and the entire United States Army comprised 16,000 ill-prepared soldiers.

Scott saw "no alternative but a surrender" of the fort. The secretaries of war and navy agreed. William Seward, Lincoln's secretary of state, argued that it would be a conciliatory move that would keep the border states with the Union. On March 15, five of seven of his cabinet members urged Lincoln to order an evacuation, and the Baltimore *American* thought the decision had been made, writing, "The cabinet has ordered the withdrawal of Major Anderson from Fort Sumter."

But Lincoln balked. To yield the fort would be to give up his pledge to "hold, occupy and possess" U.S. property. And it would alienate the Republicans who elected him, divide Northerners, and give implicit recognition to the Confederacy. That could lead England and France to recognize the Confederacy and even ally with it in a war. Montgomery Blair, Lincoln's postmaster general, said that giving up the fort was as good as giving up the Union.

For six weeks Lincoln agonized over what to do. Many days he was plagued by migraines; many nights he got little or no sleep. Meanwhile, one of Lincoln's cabinet members sent surreptitious notes to the Confederacy, telling them, reassuring them, nearly promising them, that the fort would be surrendered.

WILLIAM SEWARD CHALLENGES LINCOLN'S AUTHORITY

William Seward, Lincoln's secretary of state and a former Republican rival, told Lincoln that Fort Sumter should be given up as a gesture of good will to Southern states still in the Union. When Lincoln hesitated, Seward took it upon himself to secretly inform Southern leaders that the North would let the island fort go. One North Carolinian politician wrote to Seward, saying, "Unionists look to yourself, and only to you Sir, as a member of the Cabinet—*to save the country.*" Seward's insubordination was based on his assumption that he knew better than the president. Seward was so confident with his view that he leaked the story to the press, which reported the development during Lincoln's first week in office.

On March 28, General Scott again urged Lincoln to abandon Fort Sumter and Fort Pickens, a federal fort in Florida. But this time he gave political instead of military reasons, arguing these evacuations "would instantly soothe and give confidence to the eight remaining slaveholding states, and render their cordial adherence to this Union perpetual." Lincoln's cabinet, now doubting Scott's earlier argument that it was militarily impossible to fortify Fort Sumter, reversed itself, with a majority recommending reinforcement.

But not Seward. On April 1, he sent an extraordinary memo to Lincoln, titled "Some Thoughts for the President's Consideration." In addition to urging again that Fort Sumter be abandoned, he suggested that attention be deflected from the crisis by having the U.S. "demand explanations" from Spain and France for their meddling in Santo Domingo and Mexico. If their explanations didn't satisfy, he recommended declaring war on these countries to unite the North and South against a foreign enemy. He was urging a foreign war rather than a civil war to achieve Union. "Whatever policy we adopt," Seward wrote, "it must be somebody's business to pursue and direct it incessantly." He no doubt considered himself that somebody.

The next day, Lincoln wrote a firm note to Seward, ignoring his suggestion to provoke a war with foreign powers. He also wrote that he had pledged to hold, occupy, and possess federal property, and that included Fort Sumter. And whatever policy was pursued, Lincoln made clear, "*I* must do it."

CONFEDERATES DECIDE TO ATTACK FORT SUMTER

President Lincoln rejected the two options his aides had offered regarding Fort Sumter: abandon the fort to appease the South, or resupply it with warships, which could be seen as an act of war. Lincoln chose a creative third option, and on April 8 a message was sent to South Carolina's governor Francis Pickens: *"to expect an attempt will be made to supply Fort Sumpter with provisions only; and that, if such attempt be not resisted, no effort to throw in men, arms or ammunition will be made without further notice, or in case of an attack upon the Fort."*

It was a subtle move: Lincoln would supply the symbolic fort and try to keep it in Northern hands longer, but he would avoid the responsibility of starting a war. In Montgomery, Jefferson Davis and his cabinet chewed over possible responses. Curiously, Robert Toombs, the Southern planter who had pushed for secession, urged caution. "Mr. President," said the Confederate secretary of state, "at this time it is suicide, murder, and will lose us every friend at the North. You will wantonly strike a hornet's nest which extends from mountains to ocean, and legions now quiet will swarm out and sting us to death. It is unnecessary; it puts us in the wrong; it is fatal."

Davis and the others saw it otherwise. "The gage is thrown down," said the *Charleston Mercury* after hearing about Lincoln's decision to resupply Fort Sumter, "and we accept the challenge. We will meet the invader, and God and Battle must decide the issue between the hirelings of Abolition hate and Northern tyranny, and the people of South Carolina defending their freedom and their homes." On April 10, the Davis administration sent a message to Pierre Gustave Beauregard, who oversaw Confederate forces in the bay, to demand the fort's evacuation, "and if this is refused proceed, in such manner as you may determine, to reduce it."

Major Robert Anderson, the fort's commander, rejected the request, yet thanked Beauregard for the "fair, manly and courteous terms proposed. . . ."

At dawn on April 12, 1861, South Carolinian Mary Chesnut, wife of U.S. Senator James Chesnut, was awakened early the next morning by the booming of Confederate cannons—"I sprang out of bed," she wrote in her diary, "and on my knees, prostrate, I prayed as I have never prayed before."

Anderson surrendered a little more than a day after the bombardment began. On April 15, Lincoln issued a proclamation calling for 75,000 volunteers to put down the insurrection. Virginia seceded on April 17; Arkansas on May 6; North Carolina on May 20; and Tennessee on June 8.

WAS IT FORT SUMTER—
OR LINCOLN'S CALL FOR RECRUITS—
THAT LED TO SECESSION OF THE UPPER SOUTH STATES?

Cornelia Peake McDonald, the Virginian mother and diarist, spoke for many Southerners when she said it was not the guns of Fort Sumter but Lincoln's call for troops the day after that prompted the secession of Virginia and other states in the Upper South:

The Virginia Convention had been sitting for weeks in sad delibera-tion; for there were many of the best and truest men in it who thought secession fatal to the Southern interests, and had seen with sorrow the hasty action of South Carolina and the Gulf States. . . . The moder-ate men in the Convention and in the whole country hoped for peace, and opposed extreme measures; but when Lincoln's proclamation came, calling on Virginia to contribute her quota of 75,000 men, necessary to "put down the rebellion of the other states," what a change! Those who had been calm and moderate were now furiously indignant to the insult to Virginia. Not a dissenting voice was raised when the ordinance was passed that took her out of the company of the states which were ruled by the vulgar rail-splitter . . . who had the insolence to call on her for aid in crushing the sovereign states which had only acted as she believed she had the right to do. Some days before the proclamation was known, some friends requested me to go to Mr. Sherrard's to assist in making a Confederate flag . . . and as we were cutting out the white and red stripes Judge Parker came, and . . . begged us to relinquish the idea of making it, as there was a danger of an attack on the bank building . . . as the mechanics and trades-people were so opposed to secession that it would enrage them if they knew a flag was being made. We put it away, but at the end of a week, when the odious proclamation had decided Virginia's course, a change had come over the feelings of all classes; and the flag was brought out, and triumphantly unfurled to the sound of ringing of bells that announced the secession of Virginia.

DID LINCOLN PROVOKE THE SOUTH?

Did Lincoln intend to provoke war when he decided to provision Fort Sumter? Historians have debated that question ever since the day cannons boomed in Charleston Harbor in April 1861. In 1937, Professor Charles W. Ramsdell forwarded an argument long repeated in the South that Lincoln deliberately manipulated the Confederacy into firing the first shot.

"Lincoln," he stated, "having decided that there was no other way than war for the salvation of his administration, his party, and the Union, maneuvered the confederates into firing the first shot in order that they, rather than he, should take the blame of beginning bloodshed." The argument was not much different from the one made by Jefferson Davis in his 1881 book, *The Rise and Fall of the Confederate Government.* "He who makes the assault is not necessarily he who strikes the first blow or fires the first gun." Regarding Lincoln's decision to resupply Fort Sumter, he wrote: "To have awaited further strengthening of their position by land and naval forces, with hostile purpose now declared, would have been as unwise as it would be to hesitate to strike down the arm of the assailant, who levels a deadly weapon at one's breast, until he has actually fired."

In their ten-volume history of Lincoln, Lincoln's private secretaries John G. Nicolay and John Hay wrote that Lincoln knew just what he was doing when he ordered Fort Sumter to be resupplied. "[H]e was master of the situation . . ." they wrote, "master if the rebels hesitated or repented, because they would thereby forfeit their prestige with the South; master if they persisted, for he would then command a united North." Heads, Lincoln wins; tails, Jefferson Davis loses. He was, they argued, "looking through and beyond the Sumter expedition to the now inevitable rebel attack and the response of an awakened and united North."

It's fair to say that both Lincoln and Davis wanted peace, but on their own terms. Lincoln wanted peace with one united country. Davis wanted peace between two separate countries. "Both parties deprecated war," Lincoln later said, "but one of them would *make* war rather than let the nation survive; and the other would *accept* war rather than let it perish. And the war came."

CHOOSING SIDES—ROBERT E. LEE JOINS
THE CONFEDERACY

At the time Fort Sumter exploded, Robert E. Lee was fifty-four years old. He was the son of a Revolutionary War hero, and finished second in his class in West Point in 1829. He'd spent his entire life in the U.S. Army, and served admirably in the Mexican War, and as a superintendent of West Point. General Winfield Scott, the old general-in-chief of the Union army and a fellow Virginian, was convinced that Lee was the finest officer in the army. The Tennessee soldier Sam Watkins would see Lee in his camp later in the war and describe him as many saw him: "His whole make-up of form and person, looks and manner had a kind of gentle and soothing magnetism about it that drew every one to him and made them love, respect, and honor him."

At General Scott's urging, President Lincoln offered Lee field command of the Union army on April 18, 1861. On the same day, Lee learned that Virginia had seceded. Like many other Southern officers, he found his allegiance to his state stronger than his allegiance to his country. "I cannot raise my hand against my birthplace, my home, my children," Lee wrote a friend from the North.

"You have made the greatest mistake of your life," General Scott, a friend to Lee, told him, "but I feared it would be so."

As Virginia left the Union, Richmond became the new capital of the Confederacy, a nod to Virginia's primacy. Little did Virginians know that the choice would make the hundred-mile swath between their capital and Washington, one of the bloodiest battlefields in modern warfare.

After Virginia seceded, so, too, did Arkansas, North Carolina, and Tennessee. These states would supply many of the Confederate commanders, such as Thomas "Stonewall" Jackson, Joseph E. Johnston, Jeb Stuart, Albert Johnston, John Bell Hood, and Nathan Bedford Forrest.

But the North had more men and resources. The South had just half the mileage of railroad track as the North; it produced one-quarter the number of manufactured goods as the Northern states. The North had 22 million people; the Confederacy just 9 million, and nearly 4 million of them were slaves.

MAP OF THE NORTHERN AND SOUTHERN STATES

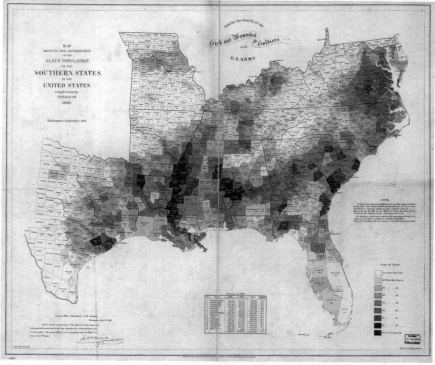

This is a *Harper's Weekly* map of the United States east of the Rocky Mountains that shows the split between the Confederacy and the Union as of early 1861. Note that Maryland, Kentucky, and Missouri are shown as Confederate states although all three had divided loyalties and were truly places where brother fought against brother.

INNOCENCE
BEFORE THE SLAUGHTER

WEEK 8

CLARA BARTON AIDS THE UNION'S FIRST RECRUITS, ATTACKED IN BALTIMORE

Clara Barton, who would later nurse the wounded in the Union Army, remembered being "indignant, excited, alarmed" when she heard that something horrible had happened to the Sixth Massachusetts Regiment on their way to Washington City. It was April 19, 1861, when the soldiers passed through Baltimore, seven days after cannon balls flew at Fort Sumter. A mob of Southern sympathizers attacked, shooting with revolvers, pelting the soldiers with bricks, and screaming "nigger thieves." A few Union soldiers fired back and by the time the melee was over, four soldiers and twelve citizens of Baltimore were dead. They were the first casualties of the Civil War.

Barton, too, was a Massachusetts native, as well as a strong Republican supporter. In a letter, Barton noted that the date of the riot was the anniversary of the Battle of Lexington and the "shot heard round the world" an "omen of evil import to those who have dared to raise the hand of rebellion against the common country."

As she thought about the riot and the "great national calamity," she wrote: "I look out upon the same beautiful landscape—the same blue sky, the same floating clouds—the face of nature is unchanged—nothing there indicates that the darkest page in our country's history is now being written in lines of blood! But I turn and one glance on the *face* of *man* reveals the terrible certainty of some dark impending war."

The Saturday after the attack, Barton visited the Sixth Massachusetts, which had moved into the Senate Chamber because no barracks were yet available. Noticing the regiment was largely without supplies, she went home to collect thread, needles, scissors, pins, strings, salves, and serving utensils, and went to the market to buy food. She then hired five black men to bring the supplies to the troops.

Secessionists destroyed railroad bridges and telegraph wires around Baltimore, which cut off Washington. Confederate campsites could be seen from Washington, and rumors spread that they were about to attack. "If it must be, let it come," Barton wrote a friend, "and when there is no longer a soldier's arm to raise the Stars and Stripes above our Capitol, may God give strength to mine."

NORTH AND SOUTH, ADVANTAGES AND DISADVANTAGES

When the war started, the South had less manpower and manufacturing, but it had a strategic advantage: it didn't have to win the war, just not lose it. That prospect was made likelier by its vast territory—750,000 square miles, making it as large as Russia west of Moscow. Jefferson Davis, a military man, imagined he could win the Civil War the way George Washington had won the Revolutionary War: by avoiding decisive battles and giving up land, thereby forestalling defeat until the enemy was weary of fighting and weaker, militarily and politically.

For the Union to win, it had to defeat the Confederacy, and many expected that would mean invading the states that had seceded. But Union general Winfield Scott disappointed almost all Northerners in the first few months of the war by resisting a ground invasion that he believed would produce "fifteen devastated provinces! [Slave states] not to be brought into harmony with their conquerors, but to be held for generations, by heavy garrisons. . . ."

Scott's alternative was to suffocate the Confederacy by putting up a blockade along the Atlantic and the Gulf of Mexico and then following up by sending troops and boats up the Mississippi River, a strategy that would bring it "to terms with less bloodshed than by any other plan." The "Anaconda plan," as newspapers dubbed it, was unpopular because it lacked drama and required patience.

Horace Greeley's *New York Tribune* demanded an invasion instead to prevent a scheduled Richmond session of the Confederate Congress on July 20, urging "Forward to Richmond!" Northerners set their sights on a railroad junction north of Richmond, which had spokes reaching down the Shenandoah Valley and into the Deep South. Lincoln thought that a victory there might finish the war quickly, avoiding the need for the protracted Anaconda plan or a protracted war. The name of the town was Manassas.

RHODE ISLAND'S ELISHA HUNT RHODES ENLISTS "WITH MINGLED FEELINGS OF JOY AND SORROW"

In late April 1861, the governor of Rhode Island called on young men to enlist for three years for the Union cause. A young man from Pawtuxet named Elisha Hunt Rhodes, just nineteen, wanted to join. "Saturday night I visited my home and laid the matter before my mother," Rhodes wrote in his diary account, *All for the Union.*

> *She at once refused her consent, and giving as a reason that I was her only support, I was forced to promise that I would remain at home until such time as she might consent to my enlisting. The next Sunday was a sorrowful one at our home. My mother went about with tears in her eyes, while I felt disappointment that I could not express and therefore nursed my sorrow in silence. Sunday night after I had retired, my mother came to my room and with a spirit worthy of a Spartan mother of old said: "My son, other mothers must make sacrifices and why should not I? If you feel that it is your duty to enlist, I will give my consent." She showed a patriotic spirit that much inspired my young heart. I did not sleep much that night and rose the next morning (which was in early May) and took the omnibus at six o'clock for Providence.*

Rhodes officially enlisted on June 5, and on June 19 the Second Rhode Island volunteers started for Washington. "The streets were crowded with people and we were observed continually," Rhodes wrote. "My knapsack was heavy; in fact it was so heavy that I could hardly stagger under the load. At the wharf an immense crowd had gathered and we went on board our steamer with mingled feelings of joy and sorrow."

DAY 4

SAM WATKINS—" 'HIGH PRIVATE' IN THE REAR RANKS OF THE REBEL ARMY"—AND OTHERS ENLIST

In April 1861, Cornelia Peake McDonald, the diarist from Winchester, Virginia, a city that would change hands numerous times, noted that young Virginia men from "all grades and pursuits" began to converge on Harpers Ferry, the federal arsenal that John Brown had raided a year and a half earlier. They included "farmers from their ploughs, boys from their schools came in companies which in sport they had formed for drilling, students from the colleges, all were full of ardour at the prospect of encountering the Yankees. . . ."

Later, she would watch Georgian recruits in her town drill, and "after it was over, the boys, for boys most of them were, began to play games, leap frog and others; so joyous they looked, so full of life and gaiety, that I could not help contrasting their happy looks with the melancholy face of their commander." Who in two months would be dead "over the dreadful field of Manassas."

One of the soldiers who signed up in the spring of 1861 was Sam Watkins. He would later, in his memoirs, describe himself as a " 'high private' in the rear ranks of the rebel army." Over four years, he would fight with the First Tennessee Infantry in Shiloh, Corinth, Murfreesboro, Chattanooga, Chickamauga, Missionary Ridge, Franklin, Nashville, and Atlanta. Instead of living as one of the "great men, who wear the laurels of victory; have grand presents given them," he lived the life of one of the "fellows who did the shooting and killing, the fortifying and ditching, the sweeping of the streets, the drilling, the standing guard . . . and who drew . . . eleven dollars per month and rations." In his book, Watkins describes the days after Tennessee joined the Confederacy:

> From that day on, every person, almost, was eager for the war, and
> we were all afraid it would be over and we not be in the fight. . . .
> Everywhere could be seen Southern cockades made by the ladies and
> our sweethearts . . . we wanted to march right off and whip twenty
> Yankees. But we soon found out that the glory of war was at home
> among the ladies and not upon the field of blood and carnage of
> death, where our comrades were mutilated and torn by shot and
> shell.

EVERYONE IS UNPREPARED FOR WAR

At the start of the war, the Union had old weapons, hardly a navy, an army of just sixteen thousand—much of it scattered in the Western territories—and a commander in chief, Winfield Scott, who was seventy-four years old, suffered from edema and vertigo, and was almost too large to get on a horse, much less ride one.

The South had it worse: no navy and just 3 percent of the country's firearms. Josiah Gorgas, chief of Confederate ordnance, sent men to England to purchase arms, ammunition, and even ships that could serve as blockade-runners. At the war's outset, cartridges and shells were in such short supply that one Confederate officer asked that "in every battle we fight we must capture as much ammunition as we use." They also would gather guns from abandoned battlefields as well. By scavenging, they collected 100,000 enemy weapons in 1862 alone. The Macon *Daily Telegraph* even published a short ditty that made light of the grim task of collecting weapons from dead enemy soldiers:

> *Want a weapon?*
> *Why, capture one!*
> *Every Doodle has got a gun,*
> *Belt and bayonet, bright and new;*
> *Kill a Doodle, and capture two!*

The women worked as well to make supplies. "We, the ladies," wrote Cornelia Peake McDonald, of Winchester, Virginia, "worked unceasingly making lint, rolling bandages, (alas! For limbs that then were sound and active) making jackets and trousers, haversacks and havelocks, and even tents were made by fingers that had scarcely ever used a needle before."

Southern newspapers also asked Confederate women to save their urine, which was collected and used to make niter ("chamber lye"), or saltpeter, a necessary ingredient in gunpowder the Confederacy lacked. The home brew was teased in one popular song, which included this verse:

> *We thought the girls had work enough*
> *Making skirts and kissing,*
> *But you have put the pretty dears*
> *To patriotic pissing.*

SOUTHERN SPIES GET NORTHERN PLANS
FOR THE ATTACK ON MANASSAS

The most important information about the first ground battle of the war at Manassas, an important railroad junction, came not from scouts or generals or maps but from a woman named Rose O'Neale Greenhow. She was a friend to Lincoln's predecessor in the White House, James Buchanan, and in the summer of 1861 she was a forty-four-year-old grande dame of Washington political circles and a passionate supporter of the Rebel cause.

On July 9, 1861, Greenhow sent a sixteen-year-old girl named Bettie Duvall to the village of Fairfax Court House, ten miles north of Manassas Junction, to meet Brigadier General Milledge Luke Bonham. At first, he refused to see her, but changed his mind when he was told that she was "very pretty." "I was very much startled," he wrote later, "at recognizing the face of a beautiful young lady, a brunette, with sparkling black eyes, perfect features, glossy black hair." When they met, Duvall reached up, pulled a comb from her hair, and shook her hair loose. A tiny black silk bag fell out. Inside, a sheet of white paper carried a coded message: "McDowell has certainly been ordered to advance on the sixteenth." It was signed "ROG," for Rose O'Neale Greenhow.

General Beauregard, the leader of Confederate forces at Manassas, would later say that he forwarded the message to President Jefferson Davis in Richmond, asking Davis to send General Joseph E. Johnston and his twelve thousand men from the Shenandoah Valley immediately. In the first use of trains to transport troops to a battlefield, the troops were moved and a telegram was sent back to Greenhow: "We are ready for them . . ."

But the attack wouldn't come nearly as quickly as Greenhow predicted, largely because the inexperienced Union army was slow-moving and inefficient. On the evening of July 20, rumors circulated in the Union camps that the attack would be launched at two a.m. "The sky is perfectly clear," wrote one Northern soldier stationed near a creek named Bull Run, "the moon is full and bright, and the air as still as if it were not within a few hours to be disturbed by the roar of cannon and the shouts of contending men."

The Sixth Massachusetts Regiment fired into the crowds on Pratt Street while passing through Baltimore to Washington on April 19, 1861. Four soldiers and twelve Baltimore civilians were killed, and many injured.

BULL RUN (MANASSAS)—
THE GREAT SKEDADDLE

WEEK 9

"BULLY FOR US"—WASHINGTON'S ELITES
WATCH THE BATTLE

The Battle of Bull Run was the first major land battle of the Civil War, but it also was the only battle that the Washington, DC, elite came out to watch. At Thomas's Bookshop in Washington, those eager to follow the combat could pick up battle maps for a nickel. Some stopped by Crandall's on the corner of M and First Streets to buy spyglasses or canes that could be converted into seats from which to watch the show.

When troops began to march out of the city, Washington's well-off grew excited. Many politicians as well as businessmen and ladies went to the offices of Major General Winfield Scott to get passes, gladly given out, for entrance into Virginia and the expected battlefield, a six-hour carriage ride away. Demand increased for celebratory picnic baskets that included cigars, good wine, and even silver flasks of bourbon to toast the victory.

"The French cooks and hotel keepers," wrote William Howard Russell, a correspondent for *The Times* of London, "by some occult process of reasoning, have arrived at the conclusion that they must treble the prices of their wines and of the hampers of provisions which the Washington people are ordering to comfort themselves at their bloody Derby."

On Sunday morning, black carriages rolled over the Aqueduct Bridge toward Manassas. Wrote one Massachusetts volunteer: "We saw carriages . . . which contained civilians who had driven out from Washington to witness the operations. A Connecticut boy said, 'There's our Senator' and some of our men recognized . . . other members of Congress. . . . We thought it wasn't a bad idea to have the great men from Washington come out to see us thrash the Rebs."

Russell was with the crowd near Centreville as the battle progressed and wrote that one officer galloped past on his horse, calling out, "We've whipped them on all points. We have taken all their batteries. They are retreating as fast as they can, and we are after them." The crowd cheered him along and the congressmen shook each other's hands and called out, "Bully for us. Bravo!" Some of the spectators headed back to Washington bringing news that the battle had been won.

THE BATTLE OF BULL RUN—THROUGH THE EYES
OF ELISHA HUNT RHODES

Just as many politicians went into war blithely, so, too, did the war's first recruits. In his diary entry on July 21, 1861, Elisha Hunt Rhodes, a private in Company D of the Second Rhode Island Volunteer Infantry, wrote about stumbling into his first fight—the Battle of Bull Run. The regiment had been ordered to clear a road during the wee morning hours before the battle. This is what happened next:

> *About nine o'clock in the forenoon we reached Sudley church, and a distant gun startled us, but we did not realize that our first battle was so near at hand. We now took a side road and skirted a piece of woods and marched for some distance, the men amusing themselves with laughter and jokes, with occasional stops for berries. On reaching a clearing . . . we were saluted with a volley of musketry, which, however, was fired so high that all the bullets went over our heads. [M]y first sensation was one of astonishment at the peculiar whir of the bullets, and that the Regiment immediately laid down. . . . Colonel Slocum gave the command: "By the left flank—MARCH!" and we commenced crossing the field. One of our boys by the name of Webb fell off of the fence and broke his bayonet. This caused some amusement, for even at this time we did not realize that we were about to engage in battle.*

Fighting broke out, and, "On what followed, I had very confused ideas." After caring for a wounded colonel, Rhodes was separated from his regiment.

> *About three o'clock in the afternoon the enemy disappeared in our front and the firing ceased. . . . The wounded were cared for and then orders came for us to retire to a piece of woods in our rear and fill our boxes with ammunition. We found the First Rhode Island in the woods with arms stacked and some of the men cooking. I met friends in the First Regiment and congratulated them on our victory, little expecting the finale of our day's fighting.*

THOMAS "STONEWALL" JACKSON AND THE REBEL YELL

Many of the men who fought in the Battle of Bull Run—or Manassas, as the Southerners called it—would go on to lead both armies. William Tecumseh Sherman and Ambrose Burnside would fight for the Union. Fighting for the Confederates were Joseph Johnston, Pierre Beauregard, Jubal Early, James Longstreet, Richard Ewell, and the flamboyant Jeb Stuart. But the man whose reputation was forged at Manassas was an artillery professor named Thomas Jackson, a devout Presbyterian who organized religion classes for black children before the war, ascribed Southern success to the Lord, and saw Yankees as devils.

During the morning, Confederate troops had retreated, and some Union soldiers were so confident of victory that they picked up as souvenirs swords and bayonets Confederates had left behind. At noon, many Confederates were taking flight over Henry House Hill, with a good portion of the six thousand troops disorganized and discouraged. Jackson placed his men behind the crest of the hill to wait for the charging Yankees. General Barnard Bee of South Carolina saw Jackson standing tall in his saddle and, in an attempt to rally his sagging men, shouted words that have become part of Confederate folklore: "There is Jackson standing like a stone wall! Rally behind the Virginians!"

Jackson's men held, Confederate reinforcements arrived, and the fighting pitched back and forth on the hill through the early afternoon. Jackson's men, fighting fiercely, would suffer more casualties than any other Confederate brigade that day.

At about four o'clock, Beauregard called for a massive counterattack against the Union forces and Jackson told his men that they should "yell like furies!" as they charged. What he got was the Rebel yell—a high-pitched yelp; part fox cry, part fury. "There is nothing like it this side of the infernal region," said one Union veteran many years later. "The peculiar corkscrew sensation that it sends down your backbone under these circumstances can never be told. You have to feel it, and if you say you did not feel it, and heard the yell, you have *never* been there."

The first battle of the war, the Battle of Bull Run, went to the Confederates. The general credited with turning the tide became known as Thomas "Stonewall" Jackson, and his men as "The Stonewall Brigade."

THE GREAT SKEDADDLE—SOLDIERS, CONGRESSMEN, AND PICNICKERS FLEE TO WASHINGTON

"What is all this about?" asked William Russell, the London *Times* journalist, when he saw the Union soldiers fleeing the battlefield back to Washington. "Why it means we are pretty badly whipped," replied a federal officer. When Thomas Jackson learned that the Union Army was scurrying back to Washington, he shouted, "They ran like sheep! Give me five thousand fresh men and I will be in Washington City tomorrow!"

The battle was fought for over seven hours, and was more a battle between armed mobs than disciplined soldiers. Men had not yet learned how to maneuver under fire. Over a quarter of the Union Army never was brought into the battle, true of at least the same proportion of Confederates. The battle also proved more bloody than spectators or officers expected. Over 600 Confederates were killed and 1,600 wounded. Over 600 Union men were also killed and 950 wounded, with 1,200 captured.

Confederates chased the retreating federal troops with cannon shot as they fled away on the turnpike to Washington. A "stampede commenced," wrote Elisha Hunt Rhodes, who had prematurely exchanged congratulations with his fellow soldiers earlier that afternoon. Old Edmund Ruffin, the fierce secessionist who had pulled the lanyard on one of the first cannons fired at Fort Sumter, happily pulled a lanyard here as well.

The Union soldiers, ambulances, and supply trains overflowed on the turnpike to Washington, competing with congressmen and picnickers to get away from the battlefield and the fierce Black Horse Cavalry that the Confederates were rumored to have. In the days ahead, newspapermen would find a name for the flight: The Great Skedaddle.

The Black Cavalry never did charge and the Confederate Army didn't follow. As General Johnston later explained, "Our army was more disorganized by victory than that of the United States by defeat." Rhodes fled through the night, thirsty and hungry, struggling on in a rainstorm.

"Many times I sat down in the mud determined to go no further, and willing to die to end my misery," Rhodes wrote. "But soon a friend would pass and urge me to make another effort, and I would stagger on a mile further. At daylight we could see the spires of Washington, and a welcome sight it was."

GLEE AND RECRIMINATIONS, NORTH AND SOUTH

Sam Watkins, the Tennessee enlistee, was disappointed to arrive after the Battle of Bull Run had ended. "Everyone was wild, nay, frenzied with the excitement of victory," he wrote. "We felt that the war was over, and that we would have to return home without even seeing a Yankee soldier. Ah, how we envied those that were wounded. We . . . would have given a thousand dollars . . . to have had our arm shot off, so we could have returned home with an empty sleeve."

In the weeks following the Confederate victory, though, proud Southern newspapers looked to blame someone for the failure to follow up on the triumph, though "the prospect of 'taking' Washington in July 1861," according to Civil War scholar James McPherson, "was probably an illusion." Confederate supplies of food were almost gone, the army was in disarray after the first major battle, and the weather turned bad, converting the roads into a pasty mush. The notion that a total victory had been squandered revealed a Southern hubris. A Georgia secessionist believed the battle had "secured our independence," calling it "*one of the decisive battles of the world.*" But Mary Boykin Chesnut, the South Carolina diarist, cautioned the South that its quick victory "lulls us into a fool's paradise of conceit" while it "will wake every inch of [Northern] manhood."

Recriminations echoed everywhere in the North as well. "We are utterly and disgracefully routed, beaten, whipped," wrote the *New York Tribune* editor Horace Greeley, who had just weeks before urged the Union attack. "On every brow sits sullen, scorching, black despair. . . . If it is best for the country and for mankind that we make peace with the rebels, and on their own terms, do not shrink even from that."

Lincoln wasn't thinking peace; he was preparing for a longer war. The day after Bull Run, he signed a bill that authorized the enlistment of 500,000 more men, and three days later, he authorized another 500,000. Northern soldiers began swarming Washington, DC, where Lincoln chose a young and charismatic general to whip them into shape. His name was George McClellan.

ROSE O'NEALE GREENHOW IS ARRESTED FOR SPYING

On August 23, 1861, Allan Pinkerton, who was directing counterintelligence for the Union, approached Rose O'Neale Greenhow at her residence in Washington, DC. "I have come to arrest you," said Pinkerton, to which Greenhow replied, "By what authority?"

"By sufficient authority," said Pinkerton, and he and another detective escorted her into her home. "I have no power to resist you," she noted coldly, "but had I been inside of my house, I would have killed one of you before I submitted to this illegal process." Greenhow and her daughter Rose were put under house arrest.

Lincoln avoided a trial, knowing it would provide a pulpit for the sharp-tongued Washingtonian. She managed to publicize her grievances anyway: a letter she sent Secretary of State William Seward found its way to newspapers in the Confederacy. "You may prostrate the physical strength, by confinement in close rooms and insufficient food," Greenhow wrote, "but you cannot imprison the soul. Every cause worthy of success has had its martyrs. My sufferings will afford a significant lesson to the women of the South, that sex or condition is no bulwark against the surging billows of the 'irrepressible conflict.'"

Richmond's papers condemned her treatment; New York papers dismissed her complaints. When she was suspected of sneaking out coded messages plotting an escape, Greenhow was transferred to the shabby Old Capitol Prison on First Street in Washington in January 1862.

There Greenhow complained that she and Rose lacked privacy and decent food and she had to use candles to burn vermin off the walls. But her most vociferous complaint was that she had to share the facility with black prisoners. "The prison-yard . . . was filled with them, shocking both sight and smell—for the air was rank and pestiferous with the exhalations from their bodies; and the language which fell upon the ear, and sights which met the eye, were too revolting to be depicted."

In the spring of 1862, she finally agreed, under protest, to a "banishment" to the South. In May 1862, after ten months of imprisonment, a Union ship took Rose to City Point, Virginia, whence she made her way by rail into Richmond. The second night she was there, her old friend Jefferson Davis paid her a visit and noted later in a letter to his wife how much Greenhow had aged. But on this night he thanked her and told her, "But for you, there would have been no Battle of Bull Run." Greenhow was moved, and in her memoir she wrote that she would remember the compliment "as the proudest moment of my whole life."

Rose O'Neale Greenhow and her daughter Rose are shown in a photo taken while they were imprisoned at the Old Capitol Prison in Washington, DC. A friend of President James Buchanan, Greenhow was a Washington socialite who would give her life to the cause of the Confederacy.

THE MAKING AND UNMAKING
OF SOLDIERS, SPIES, AND
MUNITIONS MANUFACTURERS

WEEK 10

McCLELLAN WINS, LEE LOSES, AND WEST VIRGINIA SECEDES—FROM VIRGINIA

On May 23, 1861, Virginia citizens voted to secede by a three-to-one margin, but many of the small independent farmers in the western part of the state talked of seceding from Virginia.

The thirty-five counties west of the Shenandoah Valley were mountainous with few plantations, and slaves and slaveholders were rare. These western counties had long resented the "tidewater aristocrats" of Virginia's lowland region who dominated Richmond politics. When the vote came for secession in April 1861, only five of these thirty-five western counties voted to leave the Union.

To support these dissidents, Lincoln sent General George McClellan, a handsome thirty-four-year-old from an upstanding Philadelphia family, to command forces in the region. He had graduated second in his West Point class, was schooled in warfare during the Mexican War, and was said to be able to bend a quarter with his fingers and lift a 250-pound man over his small frame. He was articulate, cultured, and confident as a rooster.

In July, McClellan led twenty thousand men in the western part of the state to defeat small Confederate forces twice, leading Northern newspapers to dub him the "Young Napoleon," a title he did not discourage. McClellan chased the Confederate forces from western Virginia, and Confederate leaders responded by sending the esteemed Robert E. Lee to western Virginia with ten thousand men. Richmond papers wrote in August that they expected Lee would drive the Yankees out of Virginia and across the Ohio River. But Lee's attack at Cheat Mountain was thwarted by sick, underfed troops; by a plan too complicated for his inexperienced officers; and by rains that turned the ground porridge-like. He called off the assault on September 15, causing Southern newspapers to call him names such as "Granny Lee" and "Evacuating Lee." A caustic editor at the *Richmond Examiner* declared Lee was "outwitted, outmaneuvered, and outgeneraled."

By the end of June, the western Virginia counties established their own rump state, West Virginia, and sent two senators and three representatives to the U.S. Congress. (Antislavery Tennesseans attempted a similar split, but failed.) "Western Virginia," explained a Clarksburg newspaper, "has suffered more from . . . her eastern brethren than ever the cotton states all put together have suffered from the North."

WHY SOLDIERS WENT TO WAR—AND CONTINUED TO FIGHT

Why did soldiers enlist? This much is certain: the three million men who fought were not professionals, the pay was bad, and in the first year, none were drafted. At first, expectations of glory and adventure enticed soldiers. Enlistees spoke of wanting to "see the elephant"—a phrase that referred to any adventurous experience. "I am absent in a glorious cause," wrote one Southern soldier to his family in June 1861, "and glory in being in that cause." Another Mississippi soldier echoed the sentiment, describing the fight against the Yankees as "all fun and frolic."

But James McPherson, who studied soldiers' letters and diaries in *For Cause & Comrades*, believes it was more than potential glory that motivated the men, noting that "ideological motifs almost leap from many pages" of soldiers' diaries and letters. The cause Northern soldiers most often gave was "fighting to maintain the best government on earth"—a democratic republic—a cause that Lincoln emphasized throughout the war. Southerners said they fought for self-government, states rights, and liberty. But among many Southern soldiers, the cause often seemed more territorial than ideological. "I'm fighting," one captured Southern soldier told his captors later in the war, "because you're here."

Did defending slavery or fighting for its abolition motivate soldiers? McPherson writes that early in the war, three in ten Northern soldiers understood that destroying slavery helped preserve the Union by destroying the South and the Confederate war machine, both dependent on slaves.

Southerners didn't believe Lincoln when he said that he did not intend to interfere with slavery in the South. As he was heading off to war, one Kentucky soldier wrote, "We are fighting for our liberty, against tyrants of the North . . . who are determined to destroy slavery." Some Confederate soldiers managed to cast themselves as the oppressed slaves in the story. "Sooner than submit to Northern slavery," wrote one South Carolina officer who was a slave-owner, "I prefer death."

ULYSSES S. GRANT FAILS BEFORE HE FIGHTS

Before the Civil War, Ulysses S. Grant showed little evidence that he could earn a stable living, much less command an entire army. He attended West Point only because his father insisted he do so. "If I could have escaped West Point without bringing myself into disgrace at home, I would have done so. . . . A military life had no charms for me, and I had not the faintest idea of staying in the army even if I should be graduated, which I did not expect."

He exceeded his own expectations, finishing in the middle of his West Point class in 1843, and might have ended up "a professor of mathematics in some college," but the Mexican War intervened. He was involved in a number of battles in a war he considered "one of the most unjust ever waged by a stronger against a weaker nation." "I never went into battle willingly," he said, "or with enthusiasm."

After the Mexican War ended in 1848, Grant married Julia Dent, and served in Michigan and New York before being transferred to a remote California post, which didn't pay enough to bring his family West. He missed Julia, who was pregnant, and his two-year-old son, and drinking problems or difficulties with his superiors—the truth is murky—led him to resign on April 11, 1854.

He worked as a farmer on land given by his father-in-law as a wedding present, but fared so poorly that in December 1857, he pawned his gold watch for money to pay for Christmas presents. The next year, bad weather destroyed his crops and he chopped down the trees on his property and sold firewood on a St. Louis corner in an old army overcoat to earn money. He failed at bill-collecting and selling real estate, and moved back to Galena, Illinois, to join the family business, a leather goods store, which was managed by his two younger brothers. His father hired him as a clerk. Grant was thirty-eight years old.

When the Civil War broke out, Grant looked for a way to contribute. "There are but two parties now," he wrote his father, "Traitors & Patriots and I want hereafter to be ranked with the latter. . . ." When a friend advised the future general to sign up as a colonel in the war, Grant's response was that "there are few men really competent to command a thousand soldiers, and I doubt whether I am one of them." He joined volunteers who went to Springfield, Illinois, and then went to seek a command position from George McClellan, whom he had met during the Mexican War. McClellan was too busy to see him. Grant became a military aide to Governor Richard Yates, partly through the influence of Elihu Washburne, an Illinois congressman who had befriended Grant in Galena and who later recommended him for a promotion to brigadier general.

INTIMATE ENEMIES—FIGHTING GENERALS WERE OFTEN FRIENDS

Many of the men who would fight each other throughout the Civil War were friends, their lives entwined as young men at West Point and soldiers fighting side-by-side in the Mexican War.

Two lieutenants who were acquaintances in the Mexican War, George McClellan and Pierre Beauregard, would become star generals of their respective armies. The defense of Fort Sumter was overseen by Robert Anderson, an artillery instructor at West Point who was so impressed by his student Pierre Beauregard that he got him a post as an assistant instructor. Beauregard oversaw the bombing of Fort Sumter.

At West Point, McClellan was classmates with George Pickett, who led the infamous Pickett's charge at Gettysburg ordered by Robert E. Lee. After the war began, Pickett wrote his wife, "[McClellan] was, he is, and he always will be—even were his pistol pointed at my heart—my dear, loved friend." When Grant's army was squeezing Richmond, the general and some other Union officers sent Pickett a silver service as congratulations for the birth of his son, accompanied by the note, "To our friend and classmate, George Pickett."

Confederate General Simon Bolivar Buckner lent Grant money before the war and thought their friendship might translate into favorable terms of surrender after the Battle of Fort Donelson in Tennessee in early 1862. (It wouldn't, as Grant demanded "unconditional and immediate surrender.")

Albert Sidney Johnston fought alongside Joseph Hooker at Monterrey in Mexico; James Longstreet and Winfield Scott Hancock fought next to each other in the battle of Churubusco; Lee and George Meade served together as engineers under General Scott.

At Gettysburg, General Lewis Armistead was mortally wounded leading Confederate troops over a stone wall, holding his hat high on his sword, during Pickett's Charge. Dying, he asked that General Hancock, one of his best friends, who led the corps that had decimated Armistead and his men, return his belongings to his family. And after Lee surrendered at Appomattox, Grant slapped General Longstreet, an old West Point friend, on the back and suggested "we have a game of [poker] as we used to."

DID SHERMAN GO INSANE?

In October 1861, William Tecumseh Sherman, commander of Union forces in Kentucky, met with Secretary of War Simon Cameron to discuss strategy for the western theater. Sherman spoke of the overwhelming strength of the enemy and said he needed 60,000 men to defend his territory and 200,000 to go on the offensive. When Cameron got back to Washington, he called Sherman's request for 200,000 men "insane." Soon, publications were repeating the charge that Sherman was "crazy, insane, and mad."

The assessment was probably accurate. After the Union defeat at Bull Run, Sherman, who was by nature high-strung, worked day and night, often refusing to sleep. While in Louisville, he would wait in the telegraph office until three a.m. and then pace the rest of the night in his hotel hallway. The *New York Times* duly reported that the general's "disorders" had "removed him, perhaps permanently from his command." Sherman wrote his wife, Ellen, on New Year's Day 1862: "Could I live over the last year I think I would do better, but my former associations with the South have rendered me almost crazy as one by one all links of hope [of averting war] were parted."

Three days later, Sherman would write his brother John. "I am so sensible of my disgrace in having exaggerated the force of our enemy in Kentucky that I do think I Should have committed suicide were it not for my children," he wrote. "I do not think that I can again be trusted with command." Ellen was so upset by the rumors and newspaper accounts that she went with her influential father, Thomas Ewing, to see the president. Lincoln calmed her, praised her husband, and said he didn't consider him crazy.

On February 13, Halleck reassigned Sherman to Paducah, Kentucky, Ulysses S. Grant's base. Grant saw not insanity in Sherman but competence. Later in the war, when a civilian badmouthed Grant, Sherman would defend him, saying, "General Grant is a *great general*. He stood by me when I was crazy, and I stood by him when he was drunk; and now, sir, we stand by each other always."

A GUN FOR HIRE—WEAPONS MANUFACTURERS
SELL THEIR WARES

In February 1861, a Connecticut arms maker, imagining that real armies would soon supplant the angry rhetoric of war, wired his factory superintendent in Hartford. "Run the armory night and day with double sets of hands," he wrote. "I had rather have an accumulation of our arms than to have money lying idle."

The dispatch was written by Samuel Colt, the man who invented the revolver. Until the Battle of Bull Run in July 1861, he sold hundreds of his revolvers to the Confederacy; afterward, he sold most of his guns to the Union. Over the course of the war, Colt would sell about 40 percent of the revolvers bought by the federal government—146,840 of them—and 75,000 Springfield Rifles as well, despite the fact a devastating fire on February 5, 1864, stopped production for over a year.

Many manufacturers capitalized on the sudden need for mass quantities of weapons. One New England axe manufacturer switched over to sabers and forged 7,500 of them a month. James Mowry, who oversaw a cotton textile factory in Norfolk, Connecticut, before the war, won a government contract to produce 30,000 muskets. He had one problem—he had no experience manufacturing weapons. So Mowry subcontracted different parts of the work to local machine shops and then assembled the parts at his converted textile factory, which was producing 1,200 muskets a week within a year.

Some businessmen were crafty enough to make war profits from weapons without manufacturing them. In the summer of 1861, a speculator named Arthur Eastman, from Manchester, New Hampshire, purchased a large number of old guns from the War Department arsenal in New York for $3.50 each. Eastman then sold the weapons to a middleman, Simon Stevens, for $12.50 each. Stevens rifled and rechambered the guns and sold the entire lot back to the Army Department in the West for $22 a rifle. The government ended up buying the guns back for 530 percent more than they had sold them for.

GENERAL GEORGE B. McCLELLAN POSES LIKE NAPOLEON

After George McClellan came to Washington, DC, to lead the Union Army, he visited Mathew Brady's studio to make a portrait that was suitable for sale across the North. Note that he put his right hand into his jacket, a pose meant to imitate Napoleon. In fact, the *New York Herald* and other newspapers began calling him the "Napoleon of America."

LINCOLN RESISTS
A WAR OF FREEDOM

WEEK 11

NO BLACKS NEED APPLY—
WHY BLACKS WERE KEPT OUT OF THE UNION ARMY

When the American Civil War began in 1861, Jacob Dodson, a free black man living in Washington City, wrote to Secretary of War Simon Cameron, offering "300 reliable colored free citizens" who were eager to enlist and defend the capital. Cameron replied unequivocally, writing that "this department has no intention at present to call into the service of the government any colored soldiers." Cameron was stating an old policy. Though an estimated five thousand blacks served in the Revolutionary War, after the passage of the National Militia Act of 1792, only white men could enlist.

Republicans considered arming African-Americans but they quickly rejected the idea, fearing it would fracture the delicate prowar coalition. Democrats strongly opposed the idea, as did slave states that had stayed with the Union—Missouri, Kentucky, Delaware, and Maryland. "If Kentucky was polled upon the proposition of placing arms in the hands of negroes," maintained Garret Davis, the U.S. senator from Kentucky, "I have no doubt to-day that nine hundred and ninety-nine out of every thousand . . . would vote against it." And white soldiers, too, he believed, would "feel themselves degraded fighting by their side," and Lincoln feared a mass desertion of Northern white soldiers if black men were armed.

Despite the ban, a few black men managed to join the army. Nicholas Biddle, an escaped slave who lived in Pottsville, Pennsylvania, joined the Washington Artillerists just two days after Lincoln's initial call for volunteers. Sixty-five years old, Biddle served as an aide, and moved with five companies in mid-April 1861 to protect Washington from an expected rebel attack. They arrived in Baltimore by train on April 18, and as they marched across the city to catch a connecting train to Washington, a mob harassed them, particularly Biddle, crying, "Nigger in uniform!" and "Kill that damned brother of Abe Lincoln!"

Biddle was smashed in the face with "a missile hurled by a rioter" and was cut "so severely as to expose the bone." Biddle returned to Pottsville. When he died in 1876, at age eighty-two, his friends engraved his tombstone: "His was the proud distinction of shedding the first blood in the late war for the Union . . ."

LINCOLN DISAPPROVED OF SLAVERY . . .

As a young politician, Abraham Lincoln had made it clear he was personally opposed to slavery, even repulsed by it. "I have always hated slavery," he said before the war, "I think, as much as any Abolitionist."

As a state representative in 1837, he refused to vote for a resolution to condemn abolitionists. He opposed the Mexican War as an attempt by Southerners to expand the number of slave states; supported the failed Wilmot Proviso, which forbade the introduction of slavery into land taken from Mexico; denounced the Supreme Court's infamous *Dred Scott* decision in 1857 for denying a black person's humanity; and supported the gradual abolition of slavery in the District of Columbia. In his Illinois Senate campaign against Stephen Douglas in 1858, he called the institution a "monstrous injustice."

At the start of the war, Lincoln was probably more sympathetic to the plight of African-Americans than most Northern whites. In 1860, just four states—Maine, Vermont, New Hampshire, and Massachusetts—allowed blacks to vote, and no state permitted blacks to serve as jurors. Lincoln's Illinois, as well as Ohio, Indiana, and Oregon, had passed "Black Laws" that discouraged blacks from settling in their states, and while many white Northerners disapproved of slavery, few disapproved enough to do anything to overturn it. Once the war began, Union general George McClellan announced he would squelch "any and all slave revolts" and even refused to let his troops sing antislavery songs.

. . . BUT THE PRESIDENT WAS NO ABOLITIONIST

While Lincoln was appalled by slavery, his prejudices against African-Americans were similar to those of many Northerners and Southerners of his day. During his debate with Stephen Douglas during the Illinois senatorial race in 1858, Lincoln revealed his limitations, stating,

I am not, nor ever have been in favor of bringing about in any way the social and political equality of the white and black races, that I am not nor ever have been in favor of making voters or jurors of negroes, nor of qualifying them to hold office, nor to intermarry with white people; and I will say in addition to this that there is a physical difference between the white and black races which I believe will for ever forbid the two races living together on terms of social and political equality. And inasmuch as they cannot so live, while they do remain together there must be the position of superior and inferior, and I as much as any other man am in favor of having the superior position assigned to the white race.

Such views separated him from the far more egalitarian abolitionists of his day. He committed to nothing more than stopping slavery from expanding into the territories, and called for gradual emancipation, with financial compensation to slave-owners—a solution he believed should take decades.

In the 1860 presidential election, abolitionist Frederick Douglass recommended a vote for Radical Abolitionist Party nominee Gerrit Smith, a wealthy philanthropist.

Ten thousand votes for Gerrit Smith . . . would do more . . . for the ultimate abolition of slavery in this country, than two million for Abraham Lincoln or any other man who stands pledged before the world against all interference with slavery in the slave states, who is not pledged to the abolition of slavery in the District of Columbia, or anywhere else the system exists, and who is not opposed to making the free states a hunting ground for men under the Fugitive Slave Law. . . . Let Abolitionists . . . vote in the coming election for [candidates] who believe in the complete manhood of the negro, the unconstitutionality and illegality of slavery, and are pledged to the immediate and unconditional abolition of slavery.

LINCOLN OVERTURNS A GENERAL'S PERSONAL EMANCIPATION PROCLAMATION

"We have passed the Rubicon. . . ." said abolitionist Wendell Phillips of Abraham Lincoln's election. "Not an Abolitionist, hardly an antislavery man, Mr. Lincoln consents to represent an antislavery idea." But Lincoln disappointed the abolitionists in 1861 by refusing to free Rebel slaves. In the summer of 1861, General John C. Frémont, a hero in the Mexican War and the Republican nominee for president in 1856, would challenge Lincoln's refusal by releasing a bold proclamation without the president's consent. On August 30, Frémont ordered his troops to confiscate slaves of Rebel supporters to be "declared freemen." It was his personal emancipation proclamation.

Lincoln found out about Frémont's edict by reading a newspaper, and Northern presses almost unanimously praised it. The president was furious. He wrote to Frémont that he saw "great danger" in "liberating slaves of traiterous owners," a move that would "alarm our Southern Union friends, and turn them against us—perhaps ruin our rather fair prospect for Kentucky." The president asked the general to rescind the proclamation. Frémont sent his wife, Jessie, on a three-day trip to hand-deliver his reply.

"She sought an audience with me at midnight," complained the president. Jessie Frémont said the president "bowed slightly" when they met but didn't ask her to sit down. She then handed Lincoln her husband's letter, which said he wouldn't retract the proclamation on "my own accord."

Jessie said that the president didn't understand the political complexities of Missouri, and that unless the war became a war of emancipation, European powers would support the Confederacy. "You are quite a female politician," the president responded, a comment that Mrs. Frémont interpreted as a rude one. Lincoln noted later that she "taxed me so violently with many things that I had to exercise all the awkward tact I have to avoid quarrelling with her."

Next, the president mailed "an open order" for Frémont to rescind his proclamation. Antislavery forces were exasperated by Lincoln's refusal to acquiesce to Frémont's order. "Many blunders have been committed by the Government at Washington during this war," said Frederick Douglass of Lincoln's decision, "but this, we think, is the largest of them all."

THREE SLAVES ESCAPE IN A CANOE—
AND BEGIN TO CHANGE WHAT THE WAR IS ABOUT

On a May night in 1861, three slaves who were working as laborers on a Confederate fortification near Fort Monroe, Virginia, slipped from their camp, and paddled a canoe to Union lines. The next morning, an indignant slave-master, suspecting where his slaves had gone, approached Fort Monroe. He was there, he told federal officers, to claim the three runaways under the Fugitive Slave Act, passed in 1850, which required the return of escaped slaves.

Two months earlier, eight runaway slaves who had arrived at Fort Pickens, Florida, had been returned to their master. But at Fort Monroe, Brig. General Benjamin Butler, an abolitionist, asked Washington for permission to keep the slaves. It was a revolutionary act.

Butler, a former courtroom lawyer, used shrewd logic to justify his action. Since Virginia and other Confederate states considered themselves a foreign country, the Fugitive Slave Act no longer applied, he argued. And didn't Confederates insist that slaves were property? In war, property was subject to confiscation, like enemy weapons or supplies. Butler called the escaped slaves not "fugitives" or "runaways" but "contrabands," a word that Northerners would thereafter use to describe slaves freed by Union troops. Then, Butler hired the escaped slaves to reconstruct a bakery.

In one day, Butler had undertaken three historic acts: he had had slaves freed by the military; he had established an innovative legal argument to justify it; and he had employed the slaves in the Union army.

By July, almost a thousand escaped slaves had fled to the safety of Fort Monroe, and wherever the Union line existed, slaves began to cross it. In August 1861, Congress passed the cautious Confiscation Act, which allowed the Union Army to liberate slaves if they had worked for the Confederate Army. Though limited, it was the first official government act—tacitly approved by Lincoln—that implied that the war was about more than the preservation of the Union. "Pre'dent Lincoln didn't free me," reported one freed slave later. "The General . . . tol' me I was free. Then he put me to work."

"The American people and the government at Washington may refuse to recognize it for a time," Frederick Douglass said, "but the 'inexorable logic of events' will force it upon them in the end; that the war now being waged in this land is a war for and against slavery."

FREDERICK DOUGLASS LOBBIES TO MAKE
BLACK MEN SOLDIERS

From the first shot of the war, black abolitionist Frederick Douglass believed that enlisting black men to fight as soldiers would swing the war to the Union. "We are striking the guilty rebels with our soft, white hand," wrote Douglass, "when we should be striking with the iron hand of the black man, which we keep chained behind us. We have been catching slaves, instead of arming them. . . ." In the September 1861 issue of *Douglass' Monthly*, Douglass blasted white Northerners who resisted employing blacks in the fight:

> *What upon earth is the matter with the American Government and people? Do they really covet the world's ridicule as well as their own social and political ruin? What are they thinking about, or don't they condescend to think at all? . . . They are sorely pressed on every hand by a vast army of slaveholding rebels, flushed with success, and infuriated by the darkest inspirations of a deadly hate, bound to rule or ruin. Washington, the seat of Government, after ten thousand assurances to the contrary, is now positively in danger of falling before the rebel army. . . . Our Presidents, Governors, Generals and Secretaries are calling, with almost frantic vehemence, for men.— "Men! Men! Send us men!" they scream, or the . . . life of a great nation is ruthlessly sacrificed, and the hopes of a great nation go out in darkness; and yet these very officers, representing the people and Government, steadily and persistently refuse to receive the very class of men which have a deeper interest in the defeat and humiliation of the rebels, than all others. . . .*
>
> *Why does the Government reject the Negro? Is he not a man? Can he not wield a sword, fire a gun, march and countermarch, and obey orders like any other?*

FREDERICK DOUGLASS UNDERSTANDS
WHAT THE WAR IS ABOUT

Frederick Douglass, one of the most eloquent activists in American
history, understood from the war's first shot that it wasn't about union
or independence, as many politicians claimed. Instead, he knew that
"the war now being waged in this land is a war for and against slavery."

A BLOODY WAR—
for FREEDOM
(1862)

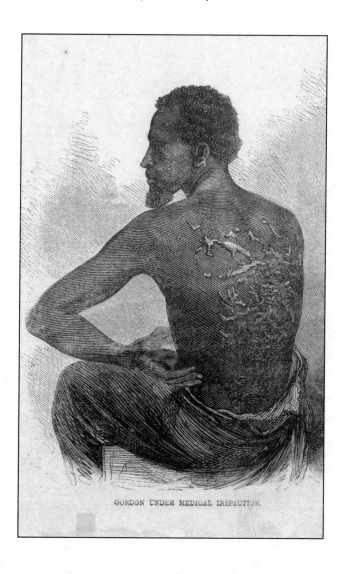

GORDON UNDER MEDICAL INSPECTION.

INTRODUCTION

As the winter of 1861–1862 approached, Union General George McClellan rested his massive army in winter quarters in Washington. During that lull, he wrote his wife about being "thwarted and deceived" by "incapables at every turn. . . . It now begins to look as if we are condemned to a winter of inactivity. If it is so the fault will not be mine." Lincoln's generals seemed intent more on avoiding failure than on pursuing success. When the president pushed for attacks in the West by generals Don Carlos Buell in Kentucky and Henry Halleck in Missouri, Halleck demurred. "I am not ready to cooperate," he wrote Lincoln on New Year's Day 1862. "Too much haste will ruin everything."

When McClellan came down with a case of typhoid fever in December 1861, he hid his spring battle plans from everyone and refused to take a visit from the man he referred to privately as "the gorilla"—Abraham Lincoln. "General, what shall I do?" President Lincoln asked Quartermaster General Montgomery Meigs. "The people are impatient; [Secretary of the Treasury Salmon P.] Chase has no money and tells me he can raise no more; the General of the Army has typhoid fever. The bottom is out of the tub. What shall I do?"

Throughout 1862, Lincoln would react to events more than propel them. McClellan would get close enough to hear the bells of Richmond—only to be beaten back by a promoted Confederate general named Robert E. Lee. Twice more—at the Second Battle of Bull Run and at Fredericksburg—Union attempts to get at Richmond would fail. In the fall, Lee would confidently take the war north into Maryland.

By the end of the year, the war would no longer be about just preserving or dissolving the Union. Now it became a struggle over the survival or extinction of slavery. The stakes raised, the fight became bloodier, with brutal battles in little-known places such as a creek named Antietam, a town named Fredericksburg, and ground near a church named Shiloh, a word that means "place of peace" in Hebrew.

THE WAR IS PRESSED

WEEK 12

THE "BATTLE HYMN OF THE REPUBLIC"—
AN ABOLITIONIST SONG?

On November 17, 1861, Julia Ward Howe arrived in Washington with her husband, Samuel Gridley Howe, who was sent by the governor of Massachusetts to inspect conditions among the troops. During the trip South, Julia said, "I thought of the women of whose sons or husbands were fighting our great battle; the women themselves serving in the hospitals [or] the Sanitary Commission. . . ." Howe wanted to serve as well, but she had a child not yet two, and "could not leave my nursery to follow the march of our armies."

The couple joined the soldiers as they returned on a crowded road back to Washington and sang songs, including "John Brown's Body." One of her companions suggested that Howe, a poet, write "some good words for that stirring tune."

Howe went to bed that night, slept soundly, but then, she wrote, "I awoke in the gray of the morning twilight; and as I lay waiting for the dawn, the long lines of the desired poem began to twine themselves in my mind." Careful not to wake her infant daughter, she "found in the dimness an old stump of a pen which I remembered to have used the day before. . . . I scrawled the verses almost without looking at the paper." In February 1862, the *Atlantic Monthly* printed her hymn, paying her five dollars. It soon became the anthem for the Union Army.

Howe took apocalyptic phrases and images from the Bible—the "terrible swift sword" and "trampling out the vintage where the grapes of wrath are stored" both came from Revelations. She and her husband were both abolitionists (he supported John Brown), and so her vision was not of reuniting the country but of freeing the slaves:

In the beauty of the lilies Christ was born across the sea,
With a glory in His bosom that transfigures you and me:
As He died to make men holy, let us die to make men free,
While God is marching on.

CHAMPAGNE AND OYSTERS NO MORE

In the Congressional session that opened on December 2, 1861, politicians debated the war effort—and General George McClellan's performance. To his Republican critics, the phrase "all quiet on the Potomac" became a sarcastic epithet for the general's inaction. Lincoln, too, was frustrated.

Pressure for military action came from all quarters. U.S. Attorney General Edward Bates wrote in his diary on the last day of 1861 that the war lacked direction. "I insisted," Bates wrote, referring to a conversation with Lincoln, "that being 'Commander in Chief' by law, he must command—especially in such a war as this. . . . If I was President . . . I would know what army I had, and what the high generals . . . were doing with that army."

Charles Francis Adams, minister to England, warned that foreign intervention by England loomed without quick action. In early January, Adams wrote that "one clear victory at home might save us a foreign war."

Lincoln pushed the general, stating at one White House war council, "If General McClellan does not want to use the Army I would like to borrow it for a time. . . ." Even Secretary of War Edwin Stanton, a friend of McClellan's, grew disillusioned. "The champagne and oysters on the Potomac must be stopped," he wrote. "I will *force* this man McClellan to fight."

Finally Lincoln did resort to force. On January 27, General War Order Number One required that McClellan's forces move by no later than February 22, Washington's birthday.

Many Union soldiers were just as eager as Lincoln to see the Army of the Potomac break the confines of Washington. "Mud, mud, mud," wrote Elisha Hunt Rhodes, the Rhode Island recruit, on January 31, 1862. "I am thinking of starting a steamboat line to run on Pennsylvania Avenue. . . . If I was owner of this town, I would sell it very cheap. Will the mud never dry up so the army can move? I want to see service and I want the war over so that I can go home." As nearly everyone urged McClellan to act, another general acted on his own. His name was Ulysses S. Grant, an unknown officer in the West.

ULYSSES S. GRANT REVEALS HIMSELF
AT FORT DONELSON

"Whatever nation gets . . . control of the Ohio, Mississippi, and Missouri Rivers," wrote William Tecumseh Sherman, "will control the continent." These rivers flowed north to south, into the very heart of the Confederacy, and were big enough to ferry vast invading armies and their supplies. Also crucial were the Tennessee and Cumberland Rivers, which flowed west through Kentucky and Tennessee. On February 6, 1861, Ulysses S. Grant stood by at Fort Henry on the Tennessee River while the river fleet, under Commodore Andrew Foote, bombarded the fort at close range. The Rebels surrendered and the Tennessee River was suddenly opened as a highway for the Yankee invaders.

Grant, never one to dally, set his sights next on Fort Donelson, twelve miles east of Fort Henry on the Cumberland River. The fort was a threat to Kentucky, which both Union and Confederate leaders wanted in their fold. This time, Foote's naval assault failed miserably. If the fort were to be taken, it would have to be done by Grant's army, which closed in.

Confederates knew they had to act before they were trapped. On the morning of February 15, while Grant was downriver conferring with Foote, Confederate Cavalry leader Nathan Bedford Forrest, the son of a blacksmith, who became a millionaire before the war selling land, cotton, and slaves, led a breakout. After Sumter, Forrest had recruited a battalion of men in Memphis by putting up posters asking who wanted to kill Yankees. He then equipped an entire battalion of cavalry out of his own pocket. "War means fighting," Forrest was fond of saying. "And fighting means killing."

The Rebels nearly broke through, but anxious Confederate leaders panicked, ordering a retreat at about the same time that Grant returned to find his troops in disarray. Grant was the perfect man for the situation—steady under fire.

Grant would show these qualities at Fort Donelson and again and again throughout the war. "Some of our men are pretty badly demoralized," Grant told his officers, "but the enemy must be more so, for he has attempted to force his way out, but has fallen back: the one who attacks first now will be victorious . . ." Grant led a counterattack, winning back in the afternoon the land his troops had lost in the morning. The Rebels were trapped.

THE DRAMATIC ESCAPE BY NATHAN BEDFORD FORREST
FROM FORT DONELSON

Nearly a thousand men were killed in the day's battle and three thousand more were wounded. Many of them died in the bitter cold of the night. That evening, the Confederate leaders were in disarray. The commander of the fort, Brigadier General Gideon J. Pillow, wanted the men to fight their way out the next day. But Brigadier Generals John B. Floyd and Simon Bolivar Buckner, believing that such attempted heroics would cost them most of their men, pushed for surrender.

Floyd, who was wanted by the North because he had supported secessionist activities while secretary of war under President James Buchanan, thought it might be better if *others* tendered the surrender. So, that night, he took fifteen hundred of his Virginian brethren on two steamboats downriver. Pillow, who had previously declared "liberty or death" as his slogan, voted for liberty when he escaped with his staff down the Cumberland in a skiff. Buckner, planning to surrender the next day, hoped his friendship with Grant would win him and his sixteen thousand men good terms.

As the Confederate generals bickered and bolted, Forrest, disgusted, planned an escape. "Boys, these people are talking about surrendering," he said to his cavalry, "and I am going out of this place before they do or bust hell wide open."

Before daybreak on February 16, Forrest gathered the seven hundred men in his cavalry, discovered a hole in the Union line, and led his men across an ice-cold Cumberland swamp. He took his men seventy-five miles to the safety of Nashville, but he would return again and again to haunt the Union Army.

"UNCONDITIONAL SURRENDER" GRANT

The next morning, Confederate Brigadier General Simon Bolivar Buckner asked Grant for terms of his surrender. Grant replied: "No terms except an unconditional and immediate surrender can be accepted. I propose to move immediately on your works." Buckner characterized the response as "ungenerous and unchivalrous," especially since he had lent Grant money to get home after he resigned unceremoniously from the army in 1854. Still, Grant held firm; Buckner surrendered his sixteen thousand men.

Northern cities celebrated the news of the first important Northern victory of the war by ringing church bells, and Lincoln promoted Grant to major general, putting him second in command to Henry W. Halleck in the West.

On February 23, Nashville was evacuated, the first state capital and industrial hub of the Confederacy to surrender. In eight months, Grant had risen from an ex-captain with a shadowy reputation to a hero celebrated across the North. A population eager for bold victories said Grant's initials—"U.S."—stood for "Unconditional Surrender."

It was after Donelson that Grant also acquired his life-long habit of chain-smoking cigars. "I had been a light smoker previous to the attack on Donelson," he later told his assistant, General Horace Porter. "In the accounts published in the papers I was represented as smoking a cigar in the midst of the conflict; and many persons, thinking, no doubt, that tobacco was my chief solace, sent me boxes of the choicest brands. . . . As many as ten thousand were soon received. I gave away all I could get rid of, but having such a quantity on hand I naturally smoked more than I would have done under ordinary circumstances, and I have continued the habit ever since."

THE LINCOLNS' SON WILLIE DIES
AND MARY BLAMES HERSELF

Just before General Ulysses S. Grant's first major successes at Forts Henry and Donelson, the Lincolns refurbished the White House under Mary's direction. Five hundred guests were invited to view it. Supreme Court justices, senators and representatives, medaled generals, and diplomats were greeted in the East Room by the Lincolns. Abraham wore a new black swallowtail coat. Mary wore an unusually low-cut white silk dress and listened to the United States Marine Band play a new piece, "The Mary Lincoln Polka."

But the couple was distracted. Shortly before the party, their son Willie had fallen ill with "bilious fever," which was most likely typhoid fever caused by polluted water. The source of contamination was probably the Potomac River: tens of thousands of soldiers were stationed along its banks without proper latrines. The Lincolns had considered calling the party off, but the doctor they called told them "there was every reason for an early recovery." Through the evening, Abraham and Mary slipped upstairs to comfort their son.

Willie grew sicker and finally delirious over the next two weeks. Then, at five p.m. on Thursday, February 20, Willie died. Lincoln burst into his office, his voice choked, and said to his secretary, "Well, Nicolay, my boy is gone—he is actually gone." Then he wept.

For three weeks, Mary stayed in bed. Her seamstress and confidante, Elizabeth Keckley, said Mary was "inconsolable"; Tad, also seriously ill, recovered. When Mary finally emerged from her room, she wore layers of black veils that made her almost invisible.

She thought that God had punished her for her vanity and worldly concerns. "I had become so wrapped up in the world, so devoted to our own political advancement that I thought of little else." That was her sin, and God must have "forsaken" her in stealing "so lovely a child." She would never again enter Willie's bedroom.

NATHAN BEDFORD FORREST—AS SKILLED AS ANY CAVALRYMAN

The Confederate cavalryman Nathan Bedford Forrest earned the nickname "Wizard of the Saddle" for his daring raids. He led an escape from Fort Donelson, fought at Shiloh, and also participated in the Chickamauga campaign. The one mark on his service record was the massacre by Forrest's troops of Union soldiers at Fort Pillow, Tennessee, in which many of the victims were African-Americans.

A BATTLE NAMED
AFTER A CHURCH—SHILOH

WEEK 13

A WIFE VISITS HER HUSBAND NEAR A CHURCH NAMED SHILOH

Just before dawn on Saturday, April 5, 1862, a steamer named the *Minnehaha* landed at Pittsburgh Landing, a port on the west bank of the Tennessee River. The boat brought Ann Dickey Wallace from Illinois to surprise her husband, Will, a Union general, whom she heard was sick. The day before, Will had written Ann a letter, saying how delicate the April leaves were and how much he wanted to be with her. "I must not think of it now," Will added, "I trust in God that it may not be long ere we are again united . . ."

Will Wallace was one of nearly forty thousand Union men under the command of Ulysses S. Grant, who had camped in this largely forested area, waiting impatiently for the arrival of General Don Carlos Buell and his Army of the Ohio. General Henry Halleck had ordered Grant and Buell to take Corinth, an important railroad hub twenty-two miles inland in Mississippi.

On Sunday, April 6, Ann put on her Sunday best, but her plans for a surprise reunion with her husband were interrupted by "the roar of cannon and musketry," she said, that "was almost deafening." Ann worried not only about Will but also about her father and two brothers, all soldiers here.

The battle she heard was initiated by the Confederate general Albert Sidney Johnston, the good-looking fifty-nine-year-old Kentuckian whom Grant believed to be the most capable general in the Confederate Army. He oversaw the western theater, which stretched from the Appalachian Mountains in the East to the Indian Territories in the West. A few weeks before the attack, President Davis had written Johnston: "My confidence in you has never wavered . . . I . . . feel that it would be worse than useless to point out to you how much depends on you." Johnston planned to destroy Grant's army before General Buell's troops arrived.

Grant and General William Tecumseh Sherman had been so confident the surrounding creeks protected them from attack that they had built no defenses at their river encampment. Besides, Confederate deserters had told them that "the great mass of the rank and file are heartily tired." This day, Grant would learn how misinformed he was.

"WE ARE ATTACKED!"—UNION OFFICERS ARE SURPRISED

William Tecumseh Sherman had taken his headquarters in a tent near a weathered one-room Methodist church built from logs. The church would give its biblical name—Shiloh—to the first grisly battle of the Civil War. In Hebrew, Shiloh means "place of peace."

Two days before the attack, Sherman received reports that at least two regiments of Confederate infantry were amassing cavalry and artillery nearby. "Oh, tut, tut!" Sherman replied to the messengers. "You militia officers get scared too easily."

On April 6, the morning of Johnston's attack, Sherman rode out on his horse to investigate encounters with the enemy. As he raised his field glasses to see what was happening, Rebels jumped out of the brush just fifty yards away and took aim. "The fire opened . . ." wrote Sam Watkins, the Tennessee soldier who was among the attacking Confederates, "a ripping, roaring boom, bang!" Sherman's right hand was hit by buckshot, and his orderly, riding at his side, was shot dead. "My God," Sherman cried. "We are attacked!"

That morning, at points all over the battlefield, Confederates attacked Union troops. "The order was given for the whole army to advance," Watkins recalled. "The air was full of balls and deadly missiles. The litter corps was carrying off the dead and wounded."

Through the day, wounded Union soldiers were brought in "by hundreds onto the boat," recalled Ann Wallace. The *Minnehaha* was floated into mid-river, so soldiers fleeing the battle wouldn't swamp it. By evening, she had transformed herself into a hospital ship from hell, Anne recalled. "The floor of the cabin was covered by men in tiers, like bricks in the brickyard . . . as the overtaxed surgeons went their fearful rounds."

In the evening, Ann's brother Cyrus Dickey came on board and told his sister that her husband, Will, had been leading his men back to the river when he was shot in the head. They had wanted to carry him to safety but feared the enemy would overtake them, and left him behind. Ann had little time to worry. "I spent much of [that awful] night bathing the fevered limbs and faces of [those] suffering about me."

AMBROSE BIERCE SEES MEN ROASTED AT SHILOH

Ambrose Bierce, a journalist and author who served in the Union Army's Ninth Indiana Infantry Regiment, wrote stories such as "An Occurrence at Owl Creek Bridge" based on his war experiences. He was known for his realistic accounts of the war, including these gruesome observations of the fate of the wounded from his memoir, *What I Saw at Shiloh.*

The dense forests wholly or partly in which were fought so many battles of the Civil War, lay upon the earth in each autumn a thick deposit of dead leaves and stems. . . . In dry weather the upper stratum is as inflammable as tinder. . . . In many of the engagements of the war the fallen leaves took fire and roasted the fallen men. At Shiloh, during the first day's fighting, wide tracts of woodland were burned over in this way and scores of wounded who might have recovered perished in slow torture. . . .

The fire had swept every superficial foot of it, and at every step I sank into ashes to the ankle. It had contained a thick undergrowth of young saplings, every one of which had been severed by a bullet, the foliage of the prostrate tops being afterward burnt and the stumps charred. Death had put his sickle into this thicket and fire had gleaned the field. Along a line . . . lay the bodies half buried in ashes; some in the unlovely looseness of attitude denoting sudden death by the bullet, but by far the greater number in postures of agony that told of the tormenting flame. Their clothing was half burnt away—their hair and beard entirely; the rain had come too late to save their nails. Some were swollen to double girth; others shriveled to manikins. According to degree of exposure, their faces were bloated and black or yellow and shrunken. The contraction of muscles which had given them claws for hands had cursed each countenance with a hideous grin. Faugh! I cannot catalogue the charms of these gallant gentlemen who had got what they enlisted for.

THE DEAD AND WOUNDED GATHER AROUND BLOODY POND

As darkness enveloped the Shiloh battlefield, soldiers on both sides collapsed where they were, exhausted. Eight of ten men who fought on that first day at Shiloh had never seen battle before. Many of the dead and wounded were left where they fell on the battlefield.

"Some cried for water," a Union veteran remembered. "Others for someone to come and help them. God heard them, for the heavens opened and the rain came." At ten p.m., a cold drizzle started; by midnight, it was a downpour, coupled by a cold wind that swooped down from the north. Many of the wounded men sought relief by dragging themselves to a large shallow spill of water near the peach orchard. In the morning, the water had gained a reddish tint and a name: Bloody Pond.

In twelve hours of fighting, Johnston's army had pried Union soldiers from every stand they had made, and had taken more than twenty cannon. Perhaps the only good news for the Union was that Confederate General Albert Johnston had been killed during the first day of battle. The Union army had been pushed back two miles. Almost an entire division had surrendered; the other four had been ripped apart. Before Confederate General Beauregard, who took over for Johnston, went to sleep, he wired Richmond that the army had won "a complete victory." He would say later that "I thought I had General Grant just where I wanted him and could finish him up in the morning."

That night, Grant couldn't sleep. He saw soldiers with "their wounds dressed, a leg or an arm amputated . . . ," he wrote in his memoirs. "The sight was more unendurable than encountering the enemy's fire and I returned to my tree in the rain."

Sherman found Grant standing under the tree, his coat collar up and his hat turned down. Grant leaned on a crutch because he had injured his ankle badly when his horse had fallen in the mud two days before. Sherman had been shot through his hat, had a spent minié ball hit his shoulder strap, received a wound to his hand, and had three horses shot from under him. He'd concluded that, even with the arrival of Union reinforcements, the Confederates would prevail, and was going to tell Grant that it would be best "to put the river between us and the enemy, and recuperate." But when he saw Grant, he was "moved by some wise and sudden instinct" not to mention retreat. Instead, he said, "Well, Grant, we've had the devil's own day of it, haven't we?"

"Yes," Grant replied. "Lick 'em tomorrow, though."

NATHAN BEDFORD FORREST—
THE LAST SOLDIER WOUNDED AT THE BATTLE OF SHILOH

Most of the Confederates fell asleep exhausted, and those who thought of the morning to come expected victory. "Now those Yankees were whipped, fairly whipped and according to all the rules of war they ought to have retreated," said Sam Watkins, the Tennessee soldier. "But they didn't."

That night eighteen thousand soldiers had begun streaming into Pittsburgh Landing from General Don Carlos Buell's Army of the Ohio. They were seen arriving by Confederate cavalry scouts sent out in the night by Nathan Bedford Forrest, the cavalryman who had slipped from the Union forces at Fort Donelson. Forrest woke General James Chalmers to tell him that the federal army was "receiving reinforcements by the thousands, and if this army does not move and attack them between this and daylight, it will be whipped like hell before 10 o'clock tomorrow."

Chalmers suggested he take the news to General Hardee, who thought it best that Forrest take the news to Beauregard, but Forrest couldn't find him. Forrest woke Hardee again, and was told to stay positive. Afterward, an aide said of Forrest: "He was so mad he stunk."

Grant attacked at dawn, believing, as he had at Fort Donelson, that "either side was ready to give way if the other showed a bold front." The Union Army now numbered over fifty thousand men, half of them fresh, to the South's thirty-five thousand battle-worn soldiers. By the afternoon, the Confederate Army, overwhelmed, retreated.

Protecting the rear of the retreating Confederates was Nathan Bedford Forrest and his cavalry. At one point, he led a charge at the chasing federal soldiers only to find himself surrounded by Union soldiers, who cried out, "Kill the goddamn Rebel! Knock him off his horse!" One Union soldier put the muzzle of a rifle into his side and fired, lifting Forrest from his saddle. Forrest spun his horse around and galloped away, suffering the last wound inflicted during the battle of Shiloh.

DAY
6

A WIFE SAYS GOOD-BYE TO HER HUSBAND—
AND GRANT ALMOST RESIGNS

On the morning of Monday, April 7, as Union troops swept the Confederates from the battlefield at Shiloh, Cyrus Dickey came upon the
spot where he had laid down his brother-in-law, Will Wallace, on the
first day of battle. To Dickey's surprise, Wallace was still breathing,
despite a bullet blown through his eye socket.

They moved him to a boat transport, where his wife, Ann, came to
see him; however, a few days later, Will died. He was one of the
100,000 men who had fought in the first monumental battle of the
Civil War. In two days, the armies suffered nearly 24,000 casualties.
That was more than the American casualties in the previous American
wars—the Revolution, the War of 1812, and the Mexican War—
combined.

"Up to the battle of Shiloh I, as well as thousands of other citizens,
believed that the rebellion against the Government would collapse suddenly and soon if a decisive victory could be gained over any of its
armies . . ." wrote Grant years later, "but [afterward] I gave up all idea
of saving the Union except by *complete conquest*."

After the battle, Grant was denounced by the press, some generals,
and even congressmen for being unprepared for the initial attack. General Henry Halleck, jealous of Grant's success at Fort Donelson, gave
him little to do. One day, Sherman found him gathering his possessions. "I inquired where he was going," Sherman wrote later,

*and he said, "St. Louis." I then asked him if he had any business
there, and he said, "Not a bit." I begged him to stay, illustrating his
case by my own. Before the battle of Shiloh, I had been cast down by
a mere newspaper assertion of "crazy"; but that battle had given me
new life, and now I was in high feather. I argued with him that, if
he went away events would go right along, and he would be left out.
Whereas, if he remained some happy accident might restore him to
favor and his true place.*

Grant stayed. The trial they had been through together for two days
at Shiloh had brought the men closer. Grant respected Sherman's bril-
liance; Sherman understood his friend's steadiness under fire and what
he called Grant's "simple faith in success." Over the spring of 1862,
Grant gained another supporter. It was the president, who refused calls
to relieve Grant. "I can't spare this man," Lincoln said. "He fights."

One of Grant's soldiers said he "habitually wears an expression as if he had determined to drive his head through a brick wall and was about to do it."

IRONCLADS

WEEK 14

A FEARSOME CONFEDERATE IRONCLAD—THE *MERRIMACK*

The South began the war with virtually no navy, but it did have a competent secretary of the navy, Stephen R. Mallory. What he wanted were ironclad ships that might decimate the wooden Union fleet. "Such a vessel at this time could traverse the entire coast of the United States, prevent all blockades, and encounter, with a fair prospect of success, their entire Navy," Mallory wrote after the firing on Fort Sumter. He first thought he might buy such ships from the European powers, but he soon learned that they were reluctant to step in blatantly on the side of the Confederates.

On June 3, 1861, Mallory asked one of his trusted advisors, Lieutenant John Mercer Brooke, whether the South could build its own iron ships. Brooke came up with a basic design and went to the Gosport Navy Yard in Virginia with William Williamson, the Confederate Navy's chief engineer, to find an engine and boilers to power a prototype.

There, they laid eyes on the remains of one of the most formidable ships in the Union Navy: the USS *Merrimack,* a 4,636-ton combination steam and sailing frigate built in 1854, which was almost as long as a football field. When Union forces were chased from Norfolk on April 20, they burned and sunk the ship to keep it out of the hands of the Confederate Navy, but the Confederates had raised its hull. Why not ironplate the Merrimack, asked Williamson.

On July 12, 1861, construction began. The ship housed ten guns. One gun could shoot a 100-pound shell 4 1/2 miles—a devastating punch at close range. Down to the waterline, it was encased with overlapping plates of two-inch armor from the Tredegar Works in Richmond. A four-foot iron ram protruded from its bow.

News of the floating fortress sent shudders through the Lincoln administration. The Union had converted merchant ships into warships and was building forty-seven new ones—but not one was an ironclad. Union leaders feared the Confederate ironclad might do more than destroy their naval blockade. "Who," asked Gustavus Fox, the assistant secretary of the U.S. Navy, "is to prevent her dropping her anchor in the Potomac. . . . And throwing her hundred pound shells into [the White House] or battering down the halls of the Capitol?"

"SHE SHALL LIVE IN IT LIKE A DUCK"—
THE NORTH BUILDS THE *MONITOR*

The man who was perhaps best prepared to design a ship that could match the *Merrimack* had been blackballed by the United States Navy. His name was Jon Ericsson and he was a Swedish wunderkind with an ego to match his talent. In 1844, he had designed a radical new ship that was fast, maneuverable, and had powerful guns. It also used a screw propeller the Swede had patented—the kind used on almost all seagoing vessels today—and a steam engine below the water line, protecting it from enemy fire. But when the boat was unveiled at a public ceremony, one of the guns on the ship—not designed by Ericsson— exploded, killing the United States secretaries of state and navy, among others. The navy blamed Ericsson and never paid him the $15,080 he was owed for his work.

In 1861, when the U.S. Navy called for ironclad ship designs, Ericsson didn't even submit a design he'd buried in a chest years earlier. But when a financier approached him, he revealed the plan, a radical one for an all-iron ship. It would have a revolving turret mid-ship that could turn its two powerful guns toward its target no matter where it was. "The sea shall ride over her," Ericsson explained, "and she shall live in it like a duck." It was probably the most innovative nautical warfare design of the nineteenth century.

Ericsson wrote Gustavus V. Fox, the assistant secretary of the navy, that the ship would "admonish the leaders of the Southern Rebellion . . . by the booming of the guns from the impregnable iron turret . . . The iron-clad intruder will thus prove a severe monitor to those leaders." Hence, its name: the *Monitor*.

Still wary of Ericsson, the navy offered an ungenerous contract. The ship had to be built in just ninety days, and if it didn't succeed, the government would get its money back. Some interpreted the clause to mean that the ship had to be successful *in battle*. If it failed, they suspected, Ericsson would get stiffed again.

MIGHT THE *VIRGINIA* ATTACK NEW YORK CITY?

On March 7, 1862, Confederate Secretary of the Navy Stephen Mallory wrote a letter to Franklin Buchanan, the captain of the *Merrimack*, renamed the *Virginia*, expressing his high expectations for the ship.

> *Can the* Virginia *steam to New York and attack and burn the city? . . . Such an event would eclipse all the glories of all the combats of the sea, would place every man in it eminently high, and would strike a blow from which the enemy could never recover. Peace would inevitably follow.*

Captain Buchanan, or "Old Buck" as they called him, had no plans to send the *Virginia* to New York City to wreak havoc, well aware his ship was hardly the marauding weapon that Secretary Mallory imagined her to be. Her engines were so unreliable and weak they had been condemned by the U.S. Navy when it owned the vessel. The guns hadn't been fired since they had been installed on the ship. And, rather than experienced sailors, nearly all the 260-man crew had been borrowed from the army. Catesby Jones, the officer who knew her best, said she was "unseaworthy, her engines were unreliable, her draft, over twenty-two feet, prevented her from going to Washington."

Instead, Buchanan planned to take the *Virginia* to Hampton Roads, a stretch of water where the James, Nansemond, and Elizabeth Rivers flow into Chesapeake Bay. It was also the northern terminus of the Union blockade, which the Confederacy hoped to destroy, giving Richmond access to the weapons and supplies they so desperately needed from Europe. About two miles out of Norfolk, on its way to Hampton Roads, it reached a turn in the Elizabeth River that revealed another problem: it didn't steer well. The *Virginia* took a tow from the far smaller wooden *Beaufort*, painstakingly turning toward what would be the most fateful naval battle of the Civil War.

THE CONFEDERACY RULES THE SEAS—FOR A DAY

The Confederate States Ship (CSS) *Virginia*, shiny and black, steamed from the Gosport Navy Yard on March 8, 1862, at eleven a.m., the waters calm. The ship's crew, thinking they were on a practice run, doffed their caps to gathering crowds on nearby wharves. But Franklin Buchanan, the captain of the CSS *Virginia*, secretly planned to attack the USS *Cumberland* and the USS *Congress*, the bulwarks of the United States blockade that were floating nearby at Hampton Roads.

March 8 was a Saturday, washday on the USS *Cumberland*. When they saw the black smoke from the *Virginia*, Union sailors snapped their clothes off the rigging. Sand was tossed on the deck to make sure footing remained secure if blood was spilled.

The *Virginia* churned forward, "weird and mysterious, like some devilish and superhuman monster, or the horrid creation of a nightmare," wrote a Boston newspaperman. Once the *Virginia* was in range, the *Cumberland*, the *Congress*, and shore batteries showered shots on her. But the shells bounced off harmlessly, having no more effect than "peas from a pop-gun," perhaps helped on their way by beef fat the *Virginia*'s crew had smeared on its armor.

The *Virginia* hammered the USS *Cumberland* with its guns and then rammed it. In an hour, the *Cumberland* was sunk and 121 of its men were dead.

The *Virginia* then turned its attention to the *Congress*. The *Congress* fired thirty-five guns, nearly one thousand pounds of iron, simultaneously, pounding the *Virginia* at one hundred yards, but the broadsides again bounced off the *Virginia* like "hail upon a roof." The *Virginia* replied with a broadside of explosive shell. By four p.m., 135 of her 434-man crew were dead. The survivors abandoned ship. In four hours, the *Virginia* had handed the U.S. Navy its most humiliating defeat in its eighty-six-year history, and its deadliest day of the war. The *Virginia* had lost twenty-one men, but its iron shell was intact after a pummeling by one hundred guns. "The *Merrimack* business came like a gleam of lightning," Mary Chesnut wrote in her diary, "illuminating a dark scene."

WILL THE *VIRGINIA* DESTROY NEW YORK AND BOSTON?— PANIC IN THE WHITE HOUSE

While the CSS *Virginia* was destroying the Union fleet at Hampton Roads, U.S. Secretary of War Edwin Stanton received a telegram telling of the destruction of the USS *Cumberland* and *Congress*, and predicting the imminent loss of the *Minnesota* and the *St. Lawrence*, which had both been run aground by the *Virginia*.

The morning after the attack—Sunday, March 9—Secretary of the Navy Gideon Welles was called to the White House for an emergency meeting. Welles arrived to find Lincoln, Secretary of State William Seward, Secretary of the Treasury Salmon Chase, and Secretary of War Edwin Stanton in a frantic discussion about the battle. The men asked Welles: What could be done to stop the *Virginia*?

Welles tried to calm them, saying that the *Monitor*, the only ship able to stop the *Virginia*, was on its way to Hampton Roads as they spoke. Stanton wasn't mollified; he strutted from room to room, waving his arms and ranting. "The *Merrimack* will change the whole character of the war," he declared. "She will lay all the cities on the seaboard under contrition!" He added that it was "not unlikely we shall have a shell or cannon-ball from one of her guns in the White House before we leave this room." Lincoln looked out a White House window toward the Potomac. Welles tried again to reassure them, pointing out that the deep draft of the *Virginia* would prevent it from coming up the Potomac.

Stanton wanted to telegraph the mayors of New York City and Boston to warn them about a potential attack. Welles tried to convince him that such cables would only spread panic, and that the iron ship couldn't be everywhere at once. "How many guns does [the *Monitor*] carry?" asked Stanton. Two, Welles replied. Stanton gave Welles a look that the naval secretary believed combined "amazement, contempt, and distress." Stanton did send telegrams to the mayors of Northern cities, suggesting they sink obstacles in their harbors. It was as if he was shouting a warning up the Atlantic Coast: The *Virginia* is coming, the *Virginia* is coming.

THE *MONITOR* NEARLY SINKS BEFORE
THE FIRST BATTLE OF IRONCLADS

On the second day of its maiden voyage from Brooklyn, New York, the crew of the *Monitor* hit a gale and troubled waters. Jon Ericsson had designed the turret to fit snugly in a brass ring on the deck, where its own weight would seal it. But instead, builders used old rope as a seal. The storm battered the turret, the rope dislodged, and water began to pour into the ship "like a waterfall." The ship threatened to sink.

Ericsson had also refused to build smokestacks taller than six feet from the deck, despite sailors' warnings. In the storm, waves broke over a six-foot smokestack and a four-foot air intake stack, pouring water into the fire in the engine room, where it produced poisonous carbon dioxide. Men began passing out.

Finally, the *Monitor*'s tug pulled her to calmer waters where the crew was able to restart the boilers, circulate the air, and pump out water. By three p.m. on March 8, the ship crossed the southern side of Chesapeake Bay's mouth, and saw black spots of smoke. Veterans knew they were watching exploding shells, evidence that the *Virginia* was decimating the Union fleet at Hampton Roads. The two ironclads, built six months and three hundred miles apart, arrived at the same watery battlefield within six hours of each other. For the Union, it was six hours too late.

The next day, March 9, 1862, Lieutenant Catesby Jones of the *Virginia* was eager to finish off the Union fleet he had devastated the day before. "We began the day," one crewmember later recalled, "with two jiggers of whiskey and a hearty breakfast." Breakfast for the crew on the *Monitor* was not so hearty: cold biscuits and cheese, the only food available. Many had been up the previous forty-eight hours, desperately working to keep their ship afloat.

At seven thirty a.m., the *Virginia* steamed right for the *Minnesota*. When the Confederate fleet spotted the *Monitor*, they were at first confused. One crewman called it "an immense shingle floating in the water, with a gigantic cheese box rising from its center; no sails, no wheels, no smokestack, no guns. What could it be?"

But the *Virginia*'s Lieutenant Jones, who had been following the *Monitor*'s progress in the press, knew exactly what it was. Before attending to it, he fired on the *Minnesota*, starting a fire. The captain of the *Monitor*, John Worden, then steamed his ship directly at the *Virginia*, and "the contrast was that of a pygmy to a giant," wrote one sailor.

The *Monitor* fired first, and a 180-pound projectile slammed into the *Virginia* and bounced off. The *Virginia* answered, hitting the *Monitor*'s turret again and again, creating a deafening clang inside it. But Union sailors were relieved to discover that their ship was impregnable. At times, the ships shot at each other from no more than a few yards away.

Sometime after ten a.m., the pilots aboard the *Virginia* mistakenly ran their ship aground. While Ramsey struggled to get the ship free, he noticed that his gunners had stopped firing. Peeved, he asked why. "Our powder is very precious," came the reply from one gunner, "and after two hours' incessant firing I find I can do [the *Monitor*] about as much damage by snapping my thumb at her every two minutes and a half." Jones figured he'd try an ancient naval tactic that he'd successfully used the day before: a ramming, this time without a ramming rod. But the *Virginia*, "as unwieldy as Noah's ark," according to one of its junior officers, was unable to poke its spry rival.

Finally, Jones gathered men to board the smaller ship, providing them with tarpaulins to cover the gun-slits of the *Monitor* and blind the crew, and iron crowbars to jam her turret and pry open her hatch. But every time the *Virginia* plodded forward, the *Monitor* slipped away. The battle ended when the *Monitor* slipped into shallow water to resupply its guns and the *Virginia* retreated to Norfolk so as not to get stuck in the falling tide.

When it received news of the battle, Britain's Royal Navy, still the world's preeminent fleet, cancelled the construction of all wooden warships. The *Times* of London ran an editorial that would have pleased Ericsson: "Whereas we had available for immediate purposes one hundred and forty-nine first-class war-ships, we have now two, those two being the *Warrior* and her sister *Ironside* [Britain's only iron ships]. There is not now a ship in the English navy apart from these two that it would not be madness to trust to an engagement with that little *Monitor*."

THE *MONITOR*—DENTED BUT ALIVE

This is the deck and turret of the USS *Monitor* on the James River, as
seen from the bow. Note the battle damage on the turret, caused during
the close-up battle with the CSS *Virginia*. Commissioned in 1861 and
completed in a little over three months, the *Monitor* was the first
ironclad built for the U.S. Navy.

THE NAVAL WAR

WEEK 15

NO CONTEST—
THE UNION NAVY ESTABLISHES A BLOCKADE

On April 19, 1861, Abraham Lincoln issued a proclamation deeming it "advisable to set on foot a blockade" of the states that were in rebellion. The blockade was the essence of General-in-Chief Winfield Scott's so-called Anaconda Plan, which called on the Union Navy to squeeze the South to death. But calling for a blockade was different from enforcing one. The area along the Atlantic Ocean and the Gulf of Mexico included over two hundred rivers, harbors, and inlets that stretched 3,500 miles from the Potomac River to the Rio Grande. To enforce a blockade, the Union had just forty-one ships—about half of them obsolete.

The man charged with imposing the blockade was Gideon Welles, an ex-Democrat with little experience in naval matters, who had made his name as a New England newspaper publisher. He sported a long white beard and, to hide his baldness, an obvious wig. Lincoln affectionately called his secretary of navy Father Neptune.

But Welles proved himself resourceful. His first major initiative was to build or buy sailboats, yachts, ferryboats, and tugboats, and then fit them with guns to intimidate—and, if necessary, sink—merchant ships trying to trade with Confederates. By 1862, the Union Navy had grown nearly tenfold, with 427 federal ships patrolling Southern ports. To man all these ships, Welles recruited green sailors who had never seen an ocean. The navy, which had never prevented blacks from serving, expanded the number in their ranks. Of the 3,220 casualties in the navy, 800 would be black sailors.

How could the Confederacy compete? Confederate Secretary of Navy Stephen Mallory, a naval expert and former senator, resorted to underdog tactics and technological innovations. He authorized the laying of mines in harbors and in river mouths to keep Union boats out, and pushed for "torpedo" boats—small, cigar-shaped vessels, forerunners of submarines. And if those tactics failed, he used one more classic underdog maneuver for beating blockades: sending fast boats on adrenaline-pumping dashes right through them.

BOREDOM AND EUPHORIA—BLOCKADE AND BLOCKADE RUNNING

The Confederacy responded to the Northern blockade by buying blockade-runners, mostly built in Liverpool, England. Nearly all were side-wheel steamers, built for speed, with shallow drafts that made them difficult to spy.

By the end of 1862, the ports along the Eastern Seaboard, except for Charleston and Wilmington, had been taken by the U.S. Navy, so international goods destined for Southern states were often diverted to ports along the Gulf of Mexico, New Orleans, and Mobile. Two or three successful runs could pay for a ship, the rest contributing to the fortunes of sea captains and traders.

At the beginning of the war, blockade-runners carrying luxury goods such as cigars, wines, and silks could bring profits of 500 to 600 percent. After Confederate leaders imposed restrictions on luxury goods, half the cargoes had to be reserved for military supplies. Blockade-runners would eventually bring 600,000 rifles into the Confederacy.

Some blockade-runners achieved eighteen knots, or twenty miles per hour, a phenomenal speed at the time. These ships ran the blockade on moonless nights, in fogs, or under cover of bad weather. The ships used anthracite coal, which burned less visible smoke; smokestacks were shrunk; and hulls were painted gray so they'd blend in with the sea and fog. Sometimes one blockade-runner would play the decoy. As the Union ships converged, a gap for a companion runner would open, and they'd shoot through.

The squeeze of the Anaconda blockade grew tighter as the war continued. Runners had a 90 percent chance of getting through at the beginning of the war; by the end, the odds had dropped to about one in two. About 1,500 blockade-runners were captured, sunk, or burned. But the real measure of the blockade's success was how much transatlantic ships were discouraged from traveling to and fro Southern ports. During the four years prior to war, twenty thousand vessels came in and out of Southern harbors, compared to only eight thousand during the war. And the smaller blockade-runners carried much less than the larger ships before the war. The result was constant shortages of military and consumer goods, and a debilitating inflation. Still, the supplies that did make it through heartened Southerners. "An iron steamer has run the blockade at Savannah," wrote the diarist Mary Chesnut. "We raise our wilted heads like flowers after a shower."

WHY DIDN'T KING COTTON BRING EUROPE TO ITS KNEES?

The common wisdom in the Confederacy in the early part of the war was that a blockade might help as much as hurt the South by keeping "King Cotton" out of Europe. "The cards are in our hands!" proclaimed the *Charleston Mercury*, "and we intend to play them out to the bankruptcy of every cotton factory in Great Britain and France for the acknowledgement of our independence." In July 1861, Confederate Vice President Alexander Stephens stated that unless the blockade was broken and England gets its cotton, "there will be revolution in Europe. . . . Our cotton is . . . the tremendous lever by which we can work our destiny."

Textiles were the dominant British industry at the beginning of the war, and the British textile manufacturers imported three-quarters of their cotton from Southern states. To make sure Europeans felt the loss of cotton, Confederate leaders and cotton merchants agreed to embargo it. Planters should "keep every bale of cotton on the plantation," advised an editor of the *Memphis Argus*. "Don't send a thread to New Orleans or Memphis till England and France have recognized the Confederacy—not one thread." At first, the power of the cotton embargo looked promising. One English newspaper pronounced that "England must break the Blockade, or Her Millions will starve" and French and English diplomats discussed a joint action to break it and considered recognizing the Confederacy.

But it never happened. Why? One reason was that England was never really deprived of cotton. Because of bumper crops in the years before the war, manufacturers still had cotton inventories that took them to the end of 1862. By this time, many Confederates, desperate for foreign military and consumer goods, were selling cotton to pay for them. English manufacturers also turned to cheaper Egyptian and Indian cotton. Overall, the Confederates' attempt to use cotton as a diplomatic weapon proved a bust.

THE CSS *ALABAMA*, THE CONFEDERACY'S FIERCEST MERCHANT RAIDER

In June 1861, the Confederacy turned to commerce raiders to sink Union merchant ships and undermine its foreign trade. The most famous raider was the CSS *Alabama*, a ship that was built secretly in England and then christened in international waters on August 24, 1862, as its crew struck up "Dixie." Engraved in bronze on the ship's wheel was the crew's motto—"God helps those who help themselves."

The ship was commanded by Raphael Semmes, who had served in the U.S. Navy for three decades. The ship was sleek, three-masted, and fast-moving, equipped with eight guns and a three-hundred-horsepower coal-burning steam engine to drive its propeller when winds were idle. In just two weeks in the Azores, the *Alabama* robbed and burned ten ships. By October, the Union press and ship owners demanded that the *Alabama* be destroyed, and more than a dozen warships went hunting for her.

To escape, the *Alabama* traveled the world, sailing 75,000 miles from Singapore to South America. The "Greyhound of the Seas" never stopped merchant traffic to the United States, but it did disrupt it, destroying sixty-six ships in two years, the highest number of conquests by one ship in the history of high-seas raiding.

After two years at sea, Semmes brought the worn *Alabama* into Cherbourg, France, for repairs. The captain of the USS *Kearsarge*, which had been hunting the *Alabama* for a year, got word of its arrival and steamed to Cherbourg's harbor. Semmes let it be known that "my intention is to fight the *Kearsarge*. . . . I beg she will not depart until I am ready to go out."

On June 19, 1864, the *Alabama* and the *Kearsarge* spiraled around each other eight times about seven miles off Cherbourg, and pounded each other for an hour. The more maneuverable *Kearsarge* got the better of it, and the *Alabama* went down, its crew scooped up by an English yacht and carried back to England. That was the beginning of the end of the Rebels' commerce raiders, with the notable exception of the *Shenandoah,* the ship that fired the last shot of the Civil War.

DAY
5

DAVID FARRAGUT RUNS THE GAUNTLET AND
TAKES NEW ORLEANS

One part of the Union Anaconda strategy was to take the Mississippi River. That meant taking New Orleans, the Confederacy's largest city and busiest port.

Fleet commander for the New Orleans mission was David Glasgow Farragut. The sixty-year-old Farragut was older than almost any other commander and had first served as a midshipman at age nine, and in the War of 1812, the twelve-year-old Farragut had captained a captured British ship. He was respected, energetic, and experienced.

Confederate leaders thought any approach to New Orleans could be stopped by a line of chains strung together with ship hulls tied across the river, and by two mighty ironclads the Confederacy was building. Or, if those failed, an attack would be repelled by Forts Jackson and St. Philip, located seventy-five miles below the city on the Mississippi.

But construction of the ironclads sputtered when Confederate funds ran short. They were weeks from completion when Farragut steamed up the river. Union mortar ships battered the two forts for six days, but to little effect. Farragut, growing impatient, had two gunboats cut the river chain, and at two a.m. on the morning of April 24, 1862, Farragut's warships squeezed, single-file, through the hole. When they steamed past the two forts, they were pounded with ninety or so guns, but responded with twice that number.

The cross-bombardment was one of the most spectacular naval artillery exhibitions in American history. Farragut remembered passing the forts as "one of the most awful sights and events I ever saw or expect to experience. . . . [It] seemed as if all the artillery of heaven were playing upon the earth." He lost 37 men and 149 more were wounded, but before dawn, the ships were anchored safely out of range of the fort's guns.

When Farragut's fleet approached New Orleans, a future Louisiana novelist George Washington Cable observed that "the crowds on the levee howled and screamed with rage. The swarming decks [of Farragut's fleet] answered never a word; but one old tar on the *Hartford*, standing with lanyard in hand beside a great pivot-gun, so plain to view that you could see him smile, silently patted its big black breach and blandly grinned."

THE *HUNLEY*—A DARK AND DANGEROUS CONFEDERATE SUB

In April 1862, George E. Dixon, a twenty-three-year-old private in the Twenty-first Alabama Infantry, was shot in the left thigh at the Battle of Shiloh. Legend had it that Dixon was given a $20 gold coin as a good-luck charm by Queenie Bennett, his sweetheart from Mobile, and that when he was shot at point-blank range, the gold coin blocked the bullet.

While recuperating in Mobile, Alabama, Dixon crossed paths with men who were building a long, cigar-shaped submarine. It was just four feet high, giving a seven-man crew enough room to sit on a long bench single-file and turn a crank that spun an iron propeller. The eighth man steered.

Confederate General Pierre Beauregard, stationed at Charleston, hoped the new sub might destroy the Union fleet blockading and bombarding the city. In August 1863, it was shipped to Charleston. But later that month, an accident on a practice run killed five men, and in October, another accident killed eight more. Beauregard now had severe doubts about the *Hunley*, but Dixon convinced him to salvage the ship and was given command of a third crew. On the night of February 17, 1864, Dixon and six others propelled the *Hunley* through dark tides toward a Union steam sloop called the *Housatonic*. Hunley's crew drove a spar torpedo into the ship's hull under the water line, exploding a massive hole in the ship. The *Housatonic* was the first ship ever sunk by a submarine. A panicked message was sent to U.S. Navy officers, but it was for naught. The *Hunley* and its crew never returned to port.

In 1995, the remains of the *Hunley* were found four miles from shore, buried in mud. Five years later, it was raised, and among the remarkable finds was a bent $20 gold coin that George E. Dixon had taken with him on his last journey. It was a $20 gold piece, minted in 1860. On the side with the image of Lady Liberty, they found traces of lead. The back of the coin was engraved by hand in cursive:

Shiloh
April 6th 1862
My Life Preserver
G.E.D.

THE *HUNLEY*—SHAPED LIKE A LARGE CIGAR

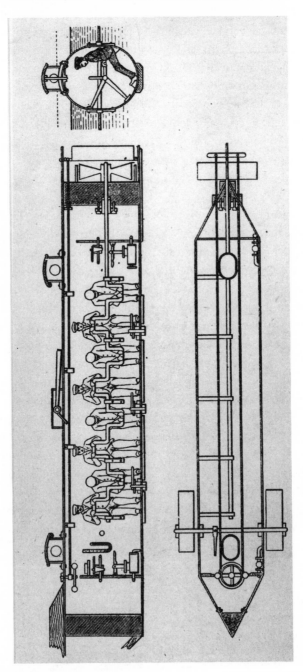

These are cutaway drawings of the *H. L. Hunley,* the first submarine to sink an enemy warship in battle. The *Hunley* was forty feet long and tapered into a wedge at each end, making it easier for its crew to propel it through the water. The Confederate sub was hand-powered by nine men, eight to crank the propeller and one to steer.

THE FIRST CRACKS
IN THE INSTITUTION
OF SLAVERY

WEEK 16

SLAVERY IS ABOLISHED IN THE DISTRICT OF COLUMBIA

In the movement to free the slaves, Lincoln was largely led by Congress, dominated by Republicans who were freed from the constraints of the now-absent Southern politicians. On April 16, 1862, Congress voted by a 2–1 majority in both houses to abolish slavery in the District of Columbia. There was some worry that Lincoln wouldn't sign the bill, so the abolitionist senator Charles Sumner hurried to the White House to speak with him. "Do you know who at this moment is the largest slaveholder in this country?" Sumner asked him. "It is Abraham Lincoln for he holds all of the 3,000 slaves of the District, which is more than any other person in the country holds."

Lincoln signed the bill. One million dollars was placed in it to compensate slave-owners; a three-man board would eventually approve payout on 966 slaveholder petitions regarding 3,100 slaves. The bill also included $100,000 to assist freed slaves who "may desire to emigrate," a small crumb offered to Lincoln, who advocated for the colonization of freed slaves abroad.

History was taking a new direction, and many noticed. Clement Vallandigham, the Ohio congressman and war critic, voted against the measure, suspecting it was the first step in a grand "scheme of emancipation." The lawyer and diarist George Templeton Strong wrote: "Only the damnedest of 'damned abolitionists' dreamed of such a thing a year ago. John Brown's soul's a-marching on, with the people after it." Frederick Douglass called the freeing of the capital's slaves "the first step toward a redeemed and regenerated nation."

Blacks in the capital, once sold at public auctions, were now able to work freely for business and government—and were no longer hampered by a black curfew. Congress also established schools for black children, who had previously been forbidden to learn to read. In June, Congress expanded emancipation by forbidding slavery in the territories, deciding the issue that had stoked the fires of secession in the 1850s.

Lincoln hoped that the compensated emancipation plan in Washington would lead the Union border states, where slavery was legal, to adopt a similar measure, but they balked. Congress and the president would stomp out slavery in varying degrees in various regions, but its ultimate trampling would come from the marching of soldiers.

MARY TODD LINCOLN'S SEAMSTRESS HELPS
BLACK REFUGEES IN WASHINGTON

Elizabeth Keckley was a slave who had purchased freedom for herself and her son and moved from St. Louis to Washington to ply her trade as a dressmaker. She made dresses for Varina Davis, wife of Jefferson Davis, and other society women before the war, and eventually became Mary Todd Lincoln's seamstress.

The city had an established community of well-educated African-Americans such as Keckley, but as the Union Army began to make headway in the South, the city filled with refugees. "In the summer of 1862, freedmen began to flock into Washington from Maryland and Virginia," Keckley wrote in her autobiography. "They came with great hope in their hearts and with all their worldly goods on their backs," thousands of "poor dusky children of slavery." A year after slavery was banned in Washington, about ten thousand crowded the city and its environs.

Many were corralled into Camp Barker, a block of military barracks, tents, and stables that provided makeshift shelter to refugees. Built next to a swampy excavation, it was hardly habitable, and Maryland slave-owners often roamed the shantytown to steal back fugitives. The "bright joyous dream of freedom to the slave faded," Keckley noted, and one day, seeing a fund-raising party for Union soldiers, she decided that "well-to-do colored people" should do the same for Washington's refugees.

She brought the idea up at her church, and within two weeks, the Contraband Relief Society was organized with Keckley as its president. The first lady immediately contributed $200 and encouraged cabinet wives to do the same. When Mrs. Lincoln went to Harvard to see her son Robert, she took Keckley along, and in Boston and then New York on the return trip, abolitionists such as Wendell Phillips, African-Americans such as Frederick Douglass, and ordinary citizens such as black dining-room waiters, contributed to the cause.

At the same time, the federal government also took steps to dismantle the fetid Camp Barker and move the ex-slaves to a former plantation outside of Washington where they could enjoy "the salutary effects of good pure country air." It was no accident the property chosen was the prewar property of Mary Custis Lee and her husband, Robert.

ONE SLAVE FAMILY
SEEKS REFUGE WITH THE UNION ARMY

As the Union army captured more and more Southern land, hundreds and then thousands of slaves fled to them for refuge. The former slave Mary Barbour, age eighty-one, was interviewed in Raleigh, North Carolina, in 1937, as part of a Federal Writers' Project, which recorded the accounts of 2,300 former slaves. In this account, Barbour recalls the night her family stole away, seeking the safety of the Union Army.

'Fore de war, I doan know nothin' much 'cept dat we lived on a big plantation an' dat my mammy wucked hard, but we wuz treated pretty good.

We had our little log cabin off ter one side, an' my mammy had sixteen chilluns. Fas' as dey got three years old, de marster sol' 'em till we las' four dat she had wid her durin' de war. I wuz de oldes' o' dese four; den dar wuz Henry an' den de twins.

. . . I 'members . . . my pappy wakin' me up in de middle o' de night, dressin' me in de dark, all de time telin' me ter keep quiet. . . .

We snook out o' de house . . .

I reckons dat I will always 'member dat walk, wid de bushes slappin' my laigs, de win' sighin' in de trees, an' de hoot owls an' whippoorwhils hollerin' at each other frum de big trees. I wuz half asleep an' skeered stiff, but in a little while we pass de plum' thicket an' dar am de mules an' wagin.

Dar am er quilt in de bottom o' de wagin, an' on dis dey lays we youngins. An' pappy an' mammy gits on de board cross de front an' drives off down de road. . . .

De Yankees tells pappy ter head fer New Bern an' dat he will be took keer of dar. . . . My pappy wuz a shoemaker, so he makes Yankee boots an' we gits 'long pretty good.

WHICH SIDE ARE YOU ON? NOT ALL SLAVES FLED THE PLANTATIONS

Many idealistic Union soldiers expected that all Southern slaves, whether field hands or house servants, would welcome them, readily turn on their masters, and immediately abandon their homes and plantations.

But slaves didn't always react so predictably. Sometimes fear and ignorance kept them from leaving. "What I see'd of slavery," said Oliver Bell, a slave from Livingston, Alabama, "was a bad idea, I reckon. But everybody thought they master was the best in the land. Us didn't know no better. A man was growed plum green before he knew the whole world didn't belong to his old master."

Some slaves were closely bound to the land they lived on, sometimes for generations, and many resented the sheer destruction the Union Army wrought. Union soldiers often stole livestock and crops from a plantation and, especially later in the war, burned down the mansion and destroyed the fields. The contraband camps that formed on the outskirts of Union armies were populated by slaves who *wanted* to flee, but also by those who *had* to flee properties that could no longer support them.

Some slaves also identified with their masters. Lee Randall, a slave from South Carolina, explained, "I thought what was my white folks' things was mine too." Slave John Love said that in his region of Alabama, many young slaves escaped to the Union lines, but "the oldest ones . . . was faithful, and these are the ones that kept the homes from being broken up, and the land all gone to waste. They is the ones that folks knows stood true to the trust the master put in them." A Mississippi slave named Prince Johnson said he "couldn't leave" his plantation during the war because "I had to stay and protect the women folks."

One slave named Beverly in Troup County, Georgia, remembered the day a Yankee soldier pointed a revolver at the wife of the slave-owner, demanding to know where the valuables were hidden. Beverly stepped in front of the soldier. "If you have to shoot," he said, "shoot me, not my mistress." The soldier retreated.

FINALLY, CONGRESS LETS AFRICAN-AMERICANS
FIGHT IN THE WAR

By late 1862, the rush of war had faded, and Northern governors were having trouble meeting their troop quotas. Recruiting blacks was thought to be a way to take the pressure off.

While Lincoln hesitated, afraid of the political backlash abolitionist measures would cause, a Republican Congress led the way. In July 1861, the Congress resolved that it was "no part of the duty of the soldiers of the United States to capture and return fugitive slaves." In March 1862, Congress took a bolder step, threatening military leaders with a court-martial if they returned fugitive slaves to their owners. Then, in July 1862, in the Second Confiscation Act, Congress freed the slaves in Union-occupied areas of the rebelling states and allowed the employment of black men in the army. The same day, Congress took another leap forward in its passage of the Militia Act, authorizing "persons of African descent" to serve as soldiers. Congress was so far in advance of the president that the Emancipation Proclamation freed no slave who hadn't already been granted freedom by Congress.

The abolitionists knew that to press their case on only moral grounds would hardly convince the majority of Northerners, since many were racist and others thought that slavery was protected by the Constitution. Instead, antislavery leaders argued that the freeing of the slaves was a "military necessity." Freeing slaves took away workers from the Confederacy and transferred them to the Union Army.

Among those who disliked the new policies was Union General George McClellan. On July 8, when Lincoln visited Harrison's Landing to review the condition of McClellan's army, the general gave the president a memorandum outlining his opposition to emancipation. "Neither confiscation of property . . . [n]or forcible abolition of slavery should be contemplated for a moment. . . ." McClellan wrote. "Military power should not be allowed to interfere with the relations of servitude. . . . A declaration of radical views, especially upon slavery, will rapidly disintegrate our present armies." Lincoln read the memorandum in McClellan's presence, but didn't respond. His views were moving away from McClellan's, and he had already begun drafting a proclamation about the freeing of slaves and their conscription as soldiers, a proclamation about emancipation.

HARRIET TUBMAN LEADS A FREEDOM RAID

As slaves began to come to Union lines, Harriet Tubman arrived at the headquarters for the Department of the South at Port Royal, South Carolina. Tubman was one of the first blacks to participate in the "Port Royal Experiment," in which Northern abolitionists provided freed blacks with guidance and education. She served as a nurse and also established a "wash house," where she taught newly freed women to cook, sew, and wash, skills that could earn them wages with the Union Army.

She soon met General David Hunter, a vigorous abolitionist, who in May 1862 declared all slaves free in his jurisdiction, which included South Carolina, Georgia, and Florida. Hunter even started training black soldiers until Lincoln stopped him, as he had stopped Frémont's effort to free slaves in Missouri, rebuking him as well.

Tubman criticized the president, arguing that without black soldiers the war would go on and on "till they are *tired* of sending, or till they use up all the young men. . . . Master Lincoln, he's a great man, and I am a poor negro; but the negro can tell master Lincoln how to save the money and the young men. He can do it by setting the negroes free."

Tubman started gathering information about the countryside from the contrabands at the camp. Before long, she was scouting up rivers and streams in the region to find out about enemy whereabouts and supplies. On June 1, 1863, she became the first woman to execute a raid in the Civil War. In the night, Tubman steamed into the interior with three hundred black soldiers led by Colonel James Montgomery. They captured supplies of rice and corn that Tubman had located, and then, at dawn on June 2, black troops landed and swept through nearby plantations, burning homes and barns. The gunboats sounded whistles to let the slaves know they were there.

Tubman never forgot what followed. Slave men, women, and children came streaming from the surrounding countryside to the gunboats. She was reminded of "the children of Israel, coming out of Egypt."

The boats soon became overwhelmed with slaves, and Montgomery felt they'd be sunk, as people clung to the ships' sides for fear they'd be left behind. He called on Tubman to "speak a word of consolation to your people." Tubman improvised a solution. ". . . I didn't know what to say. I looked at them about two minutes, and then I sung to them." People along the banks began punctuating her singing with cries of "Glory!" The slaves let go of the boats, and the evacuation continued, the gunboats shuttling the escaped slaves, until 727 people had been taken to freedom. In a single two-day raid, Tubman freed ten times the number of slaves she had freed in the ten years of toil on the Underground Railroad.

BLACK SOLDIERS FINALLY GET BLUE UNIFORMS

This illustration from the July 4, 1863, edition of *Harper's Weekly* shows a slave named Gordon who escaped across Union lines to freedom. The illustration shows the scars from a whipping, a kind of brutality that *Harper's* only depicted on its pages after the Civil War began. On the right, Gordon is shown in his Union Army uniform.

OF PRIVATES AND
GENERALS—
THE MEN WHO FOUGHT

WEEK 17

WHO WERE THE SOLDIERS WHO FOUGHT THE WAR?

Despite homes on opposite sides of the Mason-Dixon Line, and different reasons for fighting, the backgrounds of the men in blue and in gray were surprisingly similar. Most were farmers, and most were young. The average age of the Civil War soldier was twenty-one; most of the 600,000 who died hadn't reached their mid-twenties.

As many as 76,000 soldiers who fought in the war were under eighteen. Recruits sometimes wrote the number 18 on a piece of paper and put it in their shoe so they could say without lying that they were "over 18," the minimum age for enlistment. Walt Whitman, the poet who cared for wounded soldiers in Washington, met one wounded soldier who had been through several battles, who was just fifteen years old. The next day he saw the boy marching down Pennsylvania Avenue. "My boy was . . . stepping along with the rest. . . ." Whitman wrote in 1863. "There were many boys no older. . . . They all had the look of veterans—worn, stained, impassive . . ."

The vast majority of men enlisted through their states, which had quotas they had to meet set by the national government. Initially, most joined up expecting that the war would last just a few months, and many worried that it would end before they had a chance for action.

Often, an entire town of young men would go off to war together. Such company provided comfort for men away from home, but it also spelled disaster when most of the men from an entire town were wiped out in one of the war's many brutal battles.

Most soldiers were native-born, but immigrants also signed up, especially in the North. Irishmen fought in the Irish Zouaves, the Irish Volunteers, and the St. Patrick Brigade. Italians joined with the Garibaldi Guard and the Italian Legion. Germans signed up with the Steuben Volunteers, German Rifles, Turner Rifles, and the DeKalb Regiment. Many of the immigrants shared one handicap: they often couldn't understand English commands.

SOUTHERN CONSCRIPTION—
THE FIRST IN AMERICAN HISTORY

In April 1862, with Union General George McClellan and his men pressing toward Richmond, Jefferson Davis signed into law the first draft on the North American continent, the first of three conscription acts the Confederates would institute during the war. Men between the ages of eighteen and thirty-five (the age would be raised to forty-five in September) were drafted to serve for three years—or less, if the war ended sooner. Many Southerners bristled, grousing that the measure undermined one of the tenets of their new country: states' rights. Georgia's governor Joe Brown went so far as to pad the number of exemptions and challenged the federal conscription in state court; when it upheld national conscription, Brown resisted sending Georgians.

Some Southern fire-eaters, bitter at having been overlooked for high office, used the measure to paint Davis a despot. Many soldiers objected to the draft for more practical reasons. In his memoirs, Sam Watkins, the Tennessee soldier, chafed at the conscription act, which forced soldiers to stay on beyond their twelve-month enlistment. Men who had "done their duty faithfully and well [and] wanted to see their families," he wrote, "in fact, wanted to go home anyhow."

> From this time on till the end of the war, a soldier was simply a machine, a conscript. It was mighty rough on rebels. We cursed the war . . . we cursed the Southern Confederacy. All our pride and valor had gone, and we were sick of war and the Southern Confederacy.

Watkins was also upset by an addendum to the Confederate law passed in October 1862 that exempted from service slave-owners who oversaw twenty or more slaves. "It gave us the blues," wrote Watkins, "we wanted twenty negroes. Negro property suddenly became very valuable, and there was raised the howl of 'rich man's war, poor man's fight.'"

"POLITICAL GENERALS" APPOINTED
NEXT TO MILITARY ONES

The U.S. military is often thought of as an independent professional organization, where soldiers rise through the ranks based on their abilities. In the Civil War, though, the selection of generals was often a political decision. Both Abraham Lincoln and Jefferson Davis felt obliged to appoint generals based on party allegiance, connections, and their home state. Davis had more men with military training to choose from: seven of the eight military colleges in the country in 1860 were in slave states; a third of Virginia's field officers alone were alumni of the Virginia Military Institute. But he still found room for civilian generals such as Leonidas Polk—an Episcopal bishop.

Lincoln seemed more inclined to appoint "political generals"—a term that became a pejorative. Wanting to nurture Democratic support for the war, he appointed well-known Democrats to generalships, including John A. Logan, John A. McClernand, Benjamin F. Butler, and Daniel E. Sickles. Sickles had been censured for escorting a prostitute into New York's State Assembly; he had also shot and killed his wife's lover in a scandalous affair. As part of his political comeback, Sickles got a commission from the governor of New York to raise volunteers. He eventually raised five regiments—the Excelsior Brigade—and financed their training with his own money, at one point hiring a circus tent from P. T. Barnum to house a few hundred recruits-in-training. He would rise to corps commander before Gettysburg.

The controversies that accompanied Butler, a Massachusetts man, came after his appointment. There was, for example, the time he decreed that any New Orleans woman who insulted Northern soldiers "be regarded and held liable to be treated as a woman of the town plying her avocation"—a prostitute.

Soldiers often paid for the inexperience of their political generals. Sickles claimed he won the Battle of Gettysburg for the Union—but many argued that he almost single-handedly lost it.

"It seems but little better than murder to give important commands to such men as [Nathaniel] Banks, Butler, McClernand, Sigel, and Lew Wallace," wrote Henry Halleck, a West Pointer, "yet it seems impossible to prevent." For all their faults—and the political generals had many—few did worse than professional military men such as Braxton Bragg, Ambrose Burnside, John Pope, or Joseph Hooker.

AN ORDER WAS AN ORDER—
UNLESS SOLDIERS DISLIKED IT

Presidents Lincoln and Davis appointed generals, but in both armies, the selection of lesser officers, such as captains and lieutenants, was left to the common soldier. It was an American tradition that citizens who became citizen-soldiers held on to their voting rights. So why shouldn't they elect officers as well? Since companies and entire regiments often came from the same town, officers were often elected because of their popularity rather than their military skills. Elections included campaigning and speeches, and afterward, the winner hosted a party supplied with good food and drink.

As with civilian elections, officer elections sometimes included shady practices. "In the evening Col. Cumming meets us in our barracks," wrote one Illinois soldier, "and tells us . . . that an election was only a matter of *form* (!) then put it to us by word of mouth, whether or not we would sustain him, and no one daring to object, he was sustained— This was called an election! What a farce!"

Power arising from below undermined the authoritarian structure of many armies, as did the familiarity of soldiers and their officers. Why hand over power to a man who was a miller back home because he wore the epaulets of an officer? An order was more like a request to be considered—and sometimes refused. The inspector-general of the Army of Northern Virginia complained of "the difficulty of having orders properly and promptly executed. There is not that spirit of respect for and obedience to general orders which should pervade a military organization."

Sometimes regiments refused to step into battle if they thought the charge suicidal. Sometimes the rebellions were over more minor matters. "We have tite Rools over us," wrote one Georgia soldier. "The order was Red out in dress parade the other day that we all have to pull off our hats when we go to the coln or genrel. You know that is one thing I wont do. I would rather see him in hell before I will pull off my hat to any man and tha Jest as well shoot me at the start."

NEVER ENOUGH SHOES—SCAVENGING FOR CLOTHES IN THE CONFEDERATE ARMY

The Confederate Army often lacked shoes. Before the war, Southerners bought shoes from Northern manufacturers; after Fort Sumter, they had to rely on fledgling Tennessee tanneries. By spring 1862, even these supplies shriveled up. Hard-marching campaigns that summer tore apart the shoes they had, and the Confederacy had difficulty finding new supplies. During the Antietam campaign of 1862, as much as 80 percent of General Robert E. Lee's army was shoeless. When the Army of Tennessee retreated from the Battle of Perryville in late 1862, they left a trail of blood from their bare feet. Shoes were often the first objects taken from dead Union soldiers; one Confederate soldier said he once looked over a field with hundreds of dead Yankees—all missing shoes.

Confederates were reduced to taking clothes off dead Yankees on the battlefield. "Saw Sgt. Alex Clemency of Company G wearing an officer's cap with a slot of his brains sticking to it," said one soldier from the Army of Northern Virginia. "Sgt. Bridges of Company M wears a frock coat with a ball hole in the waist of it, and the tails covered in blood where the fellow was shot in the back." Some Confederate units appropriated so many uniforms that the gray ones in their ranks barely outnumbered the blue.

The Confederate soldiers' lack of clothing was often life-threatening. The Tennessee soldier Sam Watkins recalled going out with his regiment in the winter of 1862 to relieve soldiers from the Fourteenth Georgia and Third Arkansas.

> *We went to the place that we were ordered to go to, and when we arrived there we found the guards sure enough. . . . There were just eleven of them. Some were sitting down and some were lying down; but each and every one was as cold and as hard frozen as the icicles that hung from their hands and faces and clothing—dead!*

THE SONGS THEY SANG WERE OFTEN SENTIMENTAL

Some of the songs soldiers sang were patriotic and inspirational, such as "The Battle Cry of Freedom," in which the men in blue proclaimed, "We'll rally round the flag; Boys, we'll rally once again. Shouting the battle cry of freedom."

Most songs, though, especially as the soldiers suffered on, acknowledged harder truths, such as the soldier's homesickness, loneliness, and fear of death. A Rebel favorite was "All Quiet Along the Potomac," a poem about a picket's lonely death, which was put to music by a Southern musician in 1863:

"All quiet along the Potomac," they say,
Except now and then a stray picket
Is shot, as he walks on his beat, to and fro,
By a rifleman hid in the thicket.

'Tis nothing—a private or two, now and then,
Will not count in the news of the battle;
Not an officer lost—only one of the men,
Moaning out, all alone, the death rattle.

Many of the songs were sad-hearted ballads that alluded to loves, real or imagined, back home. They included "Aura Lee," "Lorena," and "The Yellow Rose of Texas." Perhaps the most popular Northern song of the war, "When This Cruel War Is Over," was also its saddest, often drawing tears from the men who sang it around the campfire.

Dearest love, do you remember,
When we last did meet,
How you told me that you loved me,
Kneeling at my feet?
Oh, how proud you stood before me
In your suit of blue,
When you vowed to me and country
Ever to be true.

Weeping, sad and lonely,
Hopes and fears how vain!
Yet praying, when this cruel war is over,
Praying that we meet again.

NEW YORK SOLDIERS SIT OUTSIDE A TENT

This unusually casual portrait is of soldiers in Company G of the Seventy-first New York Volunteers. The average Civil War soldier was about twenty-one years old, and of the 600,000 soldiers who died, most didn't reach their mid-twenties.

"ON TO RICHMOND!"—
THE PENINSULA
CAMPAIGN BEGINS

WEEK 18

MAGRUDER'S BATTLEFIELD THEATRICS
DECEIVE McCLELLAN

After Lincoln ordered General George McClellan to mobilize his army before Washington's birthday, McClellan came up with a plan of his own. Instead of attacking Richmond directly, he would transport his army by water in the spring of 1862 from Washington to the tip of the Virginia Peninsula, between the York and James Rivers. He would then march his men northwest up the peninsula to attack Richmond. Rains slowed McClellan's progress up the peninsula, but it was grand theater that stopped him.

The theatrics were provided by a Confederate major general named John B. Magruder, in his early fifties and a lifetime officer in the U.S. Army. He was tall, dark-haired, and mustachioed, and he cultivated an aristocratic air. His friends called him Prince John.

Magruder's most dramatic flourish came in his defense of Yorktown. When he got word of the armada of ships that were dropping Union soldiers off at Fort Monroe, at the tip of the Virginia Peninsula, Magruder telegraphed Richmond. "The enemy are evidently concentrating forces along this line," he wrote. He had only eleven thousand men defending his line against a Union army of over one hundred thousand. He called for reinforcements, but General Robert E. Lee, still unsure of McClellan's plan of attack, refused to provide them. Magruder worriedly cabled Lee: "The enemy's pickets [have] advanced in sight of Yorktown, but it is now raining, and I think there will be no attack today. I have made my arrangements to fight with my small force, but without the slightest hope of success."

To delay the progress of the Union Army until General Joseph Johnston's army could arrive to help him, Magruder designed to make his force look larger by moving his soldiers in a large circle over and over again.

"The way Magruder fooled them," as Lieutenant Robert Miller of the Fourteenth Louisiana put it, "was to divide each body of his troops into two parts and keep them traveling all the time for twenty-four hours, till reinforcements came." Miller's regiment marched from Yorktown back to the James River six times.

The ruse was amplified by sound effects: Magruder kept his drum and bugle corps playing, had officers shout fake orders loud enough so Union officers could hear them, and periodically had soldiers on the front lines burst out shooting.

GEORGE McCLELLAN'S HABIT OF MISCALCULATING EVERYBODY'S TROOP STRENGTH

One of General George McClellan's habits throughout his command was to overestimate the enemy's troop strength and underestimate his own. He was not the only general in the Civil War to do so, but he managed to deceive himself more consistently than any other general on either side.

During the Peninsula Campaign, McClellan told Lincoln and other Union leaders he could field only 85,000 soldiers. They responded by noting he had 128,000 soldiers, of which 102,000 were equipped to fight at any time. The difference in numbers came from McClellan's habit of counting only enlisted men and only those present that day for assignment. He then reduced that number by one-sixth, accounting for those not on the front lines. It was one way to calculate the figure. The problem, though, was that he didn't use the same formula to figure his enemy's troop strength.

At Yorktown, only 11,000 Rebel troops were on the ground. McClellan imagined a far more formidable foe. "It seems clear that I shall have the whole force of the enemy on my hands," he wrote in one telegram to Lincoln, "probably not less than 100,000 men, and possibly more."

When McClellan sent a longer telegram to Secretary of War Edwin Stanton, explaining he would begin a siege of Yorktown rather than an attack and that he also needed 40,000 more men to win the battle, Stanton exploded. "If he had a million men he would swear the enemy had two millions," he said to an aide, "and then he would sit down in the mud and yell for three." All the dawdling earned McClellan a new nickname: "The Virginia Creeper."

AERIAL RECONNAISSANCE AND THE YORKTOWN BALLOONS

When General George McClellan began a siege in April against Confederate troops stationed at Yorktown, he probed enemy positions by experimenting with one of the innovations of warfare that intrigued Abraham Lincoln most: the hot-air balloon. The pilot was Thaddeus S. C. Lowe, the "aeronaut of the Army of the Potomac," a former magician's assistant. At first, the professor and military officers would go up in one of two balloons—the *Intrepid* or the *Constitution*—to conduct aerial surveillance.

Then Lowe taught ballooning skills to one of McClellan's friends, the enthusiastic General Fitz John Porter. At dawn one morning, Porter decided to go up on his own. He was in the basket to the balloon when the rope securing it snapped, and he floated off. A reporter witnessed the scene.

> *It was a weird spectacle—that frail fading oval, gliding against the sky, floating in the serene azure, the little vessel swinging silently beneath, and a hundred thousand martial men watching the loss of their brother-in-arms. . . . The south wind held mastery for a while, and the balloon passed the Federal front amid a howl of despair from the soldiery. It kept right on, over sharpshooters, rifle pits, and outworks, and finally passed, as if to deliver up its freight, directly over the heights of Yorktown. . . . None of their great guns could be brought to bear upon the balloon; but there were some discharges of musketry that appeared to have no effect. . . . Then, as all looked agape, the aircraft plunged and tacked and veered, and drifted rapidly toward the Federal lines again. . . . and the balloon fell like a stone, so that all hearts once more leaped up, and the cheers were hushed.*

After the Porter incident, McClellan wrote to his wife, Ellen, "You can rest assured of one thing: you won't catch me in the confounded balloon, nor will I allow any other generals to go up in it."

LINCOLN TO McCLELLAN—"YOU MUST ACT"

On April 9, 1862, as McClellan hesitated at Yorktown, urging Washington to send more troops, Lincoln sent the general a telegram imploring him to attack at Yorktown. "I think it is the precise time for you to strike a blow." Lincoln wrote,

> By delay the enemy will relatively gain upon you—that is, he will gain faster by fortifications and reinforcements than you can by reinforcements alone. And once more let me tell you, it is indispensable to you *that you strike a blow. I am powerless to help this.* You will do me the justice to remember I always insisted that going down the bay in search of a field instead of fighting at or near Manassas was only shifting and not surmounting a difficulty; that we would find the same enemy and the same or equal entrenchments at either place. The country will not fail to note—is now noting—that the present hesitation to move upon an entrenched enemy is but the story of Manassas repeated. I beg to assure you that I have never written you or spoken to you in greater kindness of feeling than now, nor with a fuller purpose to sustain you, so far as, in my most anxious judgment, I consistently can. But you must act.

The advice went unheeded. "In a few days, the object of his delay was apparent," said Magruder. "In every direction in front of our lines, through the intervening woods, and along the open fields, earthworks began to appear." McClellan was digging in for a siege of Yorktown. But the delay led to just what Lincoln feared.

General Joseph Johnston rushed his army through Richmond, leading one Richmond woman to note: "All felt that this splended army must prove invincible." When Johnston arrived at Yorktown on April 12, he saw how thin the lines were along the peninsula and how meager Magruder's troops were, noting: "No one but McClellan could have hesitated to attack."

A DEADLY INNOVATION—LAND MINES

The night before the Union planned its bombardment of the Southern troops at Yorktown, Confederate General Joseph Johnston retreated, leading Union General George McClellan to announce, "Our success is brilliant." But one government official remarked to a friend that General McClellan "has let the rat escape, after having it fairly in a hold; . . . he is no rat-dog."

Confederates had left the advancing federal army an unexpected surprise: land mines, called torpedoes at that time, another weapon innovation of the Civil War. They were devised by General Gabriel J. Rains, who believed that there were "vast advantages to our country to be gained from this invention." They consisted of artillery shells buried in the ground and rigged to go off under pressure or when hidden wires were tripped.

One Yankee soldier, Richard Derby, wrote of wandering into a fortification at Yorktown to examine a cannon, only to see another soldier "on the same errand trod on a torpedo, and the shell exploded, throwing him ten feet into the air, tearing off one leg, and burning him black as a negro!"

The Confederates, under the direction of Rains, had buried "subterra shells," or land mines, along the town's roads and beaches. Afterward, McClellan estimated that the mines killed four or five men and injured a dozen or so. Rains believed land mines were the perfect way to slow down pursuing troops, but some of his men placed mines around wells and flour barrels, which struck both Yankees and some Southerners as uncivilized. McClellan accused the enemy of "the most murderous & barbarous conduct"—and then made Confederate prisoners disarm the mines.

Both Yankees and Confederates, Jefferson Davis included, charged that the land mines were unethical, and Rains was transferred to James River, where his mines were used to blow up Union warships, which was considered a far more acceptable use of the weapon.

UNION TROOPS COME ACROSS THE GRANDDAUGHTER OF MRS. GEORGE WASHINGTON—MRS. ROBERT E. LEE

After the Confederate retreat at Yorktown, the Union Army kept pushing the Confederates back toward Richmond. At White House Landing on the Pamunkey River, the Union Army came upon a plantation where George Washington had courted the widow Martha Custis. On the house, the soldiers found a note nailed to the door:

> *Northern soldiers who profess to reverence Washington forebear to desecrate the home of his first married life,—the property of his wife, now owned by her descendants.*
>
> *A Grand-daughter of Mr. Washington*

The granddaughter referred to was Mary Custis Lee. Her husband, Robert E. Lee, had settled her on the plantation, owned by William H. F. "Rooney" Lee, their son, to keep her out of harm's way. She left a few days before the Union Army arrived. Instead of occupying the house, McClellan pitched a tent on its front lawn and placed guards to protect the grain and livestock on the plantation. When a captain paid a slave two dollars to shoot a pig, McClellan had him arrested. But his care was for naught: when the Union Army left the site, a federal straggler burned down the house.

Mary Lee had fled to the Pamunkey River plantation belonging to the Virginia radical Edmund Ruffin. When Yankees overcame Ruffin's plantation, Mary was still there, and McClellan had guards posted inside the house. Mrs. Lee complained bitterly about their presence. On June 10, a makeshift white flag was placed in the whip stand of a plantation carriage and Mary was escorted over a bridge on the Chickahominy River to Confederate lines. She was met by her husband and by cheers from his troops. She then took up residence in Richmond, the city McClellan still expected to conquer in the coming weeks.

MEN CONTROL THE CLIMB OF
AN OBSERVATIONAL BALLOON

The men in the photo are controlling the climb of the balloon *Intrepid* used for reconnaissance at the Battle of Seven Pines on May 31 and June 1, 1862. In the balloon is Thaddeus S. C. Lowe, the "aeronaut of the Army of the Potomac."

THE PENINSULA CAMPAIGN
AND THE RISE OF
ROBERT E. LEE

WEEK 19

RESIDENTS FLEE RICHMOND AS McCLELLAN'S ARMY APPROACHES

Through April and May 1862, the Army of the Potomac, commanded by General George McClellan, had moved cautiously up the Virginia Peninsula, drawing close enough to Richmond to hear its church bells. "The negroes are delighted to see us," wrote Elisha Hunt Rhodes, "but the whites look as if they would like to kill us." Just outside the city, McClellan waited for reinforcements from General Irvin McDowell's corps, which would give him 135,000 men, about twice as many as General Joseph Johnston had on hand to stop him.

"It is distressing to see how many persons are leaving Richmond apprehending that it is in danger," wrote Judith White McGuire, the wife of a Richmond minister, in her diary on May 3. Wagons piled with family belongings rolled from the city; others left by railroad; still others took boats out the James River Canal. Secretary of War George Randolph had the Confederacy's gold reserves packed and the War Department archives boxed and readied for shipment. President Jefferson Davis sent his wife, Varina, and their four children to North Carolina.

The impending attack on Richmond seemed the last in a chain of setbacks suffered by the Confederacy. Ulysses S. Grant had shown his eagerness to fight and had won two battles the previous winter—one at Fort Henry on the Tennessee River and the other at Fort Donelson on the Cumberland River. In April, Union forces had also taken the Mississippi River fortress of Island No. 10, Fort Pulaski at Savannah and Fort Macon outside Beaufort Harbor in North Carolina, and controlled Hampton Roads and Norfolk, Virginia—two important seaports. That same month, a Confederate army couldn't stop the federal troops along the Tennessee River in the Battle of Shiloh, where Confederate General Albert Johnston was killed.

Perhaps the worst news for the Confederates had come on April 25, when federal troops had captured New Orleans, the Confederacy's largest city and busiest port. When the Richmond resident Sally Putnam wrote her wartime memoirs, she would list these Southern defeats under the title "Accumulating Disasters."

But just as the Confederacy looked as though it would lose its capital, the tide of war turned, not in Richmond but to the west, where a general named Thomas "Stonewall" Jackson took command in the Shenandoah Valley.

THE ECCENTRIC "STONEWALL" JACKSON ATTACKS IN THE SHENANDOAH VALLEY

The Union victory that many expected at Richmond would turn into a series of stumbling defeats, in large part because of a general with piercing blue eyes running roughshod in the Shenandoah Valley to the west: Thomas "Stonewall" Jackson, a fervent Christian and warrior.

Jackson would prove one of the Confederacy's greatest generals, but many who knew him considered him strange, even mad. He refused to use pepper, because, he said, it made his left leg ache. He would sometimes raise one hand in the air while in the saddle to improve circulation, and preferred standing to sitting to prevent putting his internal organs "out of alignment."

His own troops often feared him. The Tennessee soldier Sam Watkins recalled: "He would have a man shot at the drop of a hat, and he'd drop it himself." In fact, the first order Watkins heard after joining Jackson's men was to put to death two soldiers who had interrupted an attack to carry off a wounded soldier.

His men put up with his idiosyncrasies and his twenty-five-mile-a-day marches—his infantry was called "foot cavalry"—because he brought them victories. In the Shenandoah Valley, from mid-March to mid-June, Jackson came close to invincibility. His pace picked up after he received a telegram from Robert E. Lee, who, hoping to keep federal troops from reinforcing Richmond, urged Jackson to attack and "do it quickly." The two Union generals that Jackson faced—John C. Frémont and Nathaniel Banks—had far more men than Jackson, but he confused and rattled them by disappearing and then reappearing repeatedly on the Union flanks. At Winchester, Front Royal, Cross Keys, Port Republic, and half a dozen other places, they thought they'd finish him. But, armed with a detailed map of the area, which stretched eight feet long, he'd hit and run, and hit again, using roads, bridges, and mountain passes.

In Winchester, Jackson beat Banks's division and chased it north over the Potomac River. "Stop, men!" shouted Banks at his retreating soldiers. "Don't you love your country?" "Yes, by God," one answered, "and I'm trying to get back to it just as fast as I can!"

Lincoln, fearing that Jackson would be bold enough to shoot eastward to take Washington and its officials, sent Irvin McDowell to deal with Jackson rather than join McClellan. But Jackson eluded him. The Union Army finally gave up the chase, and Jackson marched his men to the Virginia Peninsula, where he knew the war was turning.

DAY
3

"THE BEST [SHOT] EVER FIRED FOR THE CONFEDERACY"—
LEE TAKES OVER AFTER JOHNSTON IS WOUNDED

As did many battles of the war, the battle begun on May 31, 1862, on the banks of the Chickahominy River, had two names. The Confederates named the battle Seven Pines, after a crossroads where they had done their best fighting. Union forces named it Fair Oaks, for the area where *they* had succeeded most.

The attack by Joseph E. Johnston, aimed at an isolated segment of the Union Army, turned out to be a bloody stalemate, with the North losing five thousand men and the South losing six thousand. The most significant casualty during the battle was Johnston himself, who was shot in the shoulder and then blasted with a fragment from a shell that hit him in the chest and threw him from his horse, breaking his ribs and damaging a lung.

When he arrived in Richmond on a stretcher, an elderly man from vintage Virginian lineage said that his wounding was a "national calamity." Johnston disagreed. "The shot that struck me down was the best ever fired for the Confederacy, for I possessed in no degree the confidence of the government, and now a man who does enjoy it will succeed me and be able to accomplish what I never could."

The man he referred to was Robert E. Lee, who had been advising President Davis in Richmond since March. McClellan crowed at the change in command. "I prefer Lee to Johnston—[Lee] is too cautious and weak under grave responsibility—personally brave and energetic to a fault, he yet is wanting in moral firmness when pressed by heavy responsibility and is likely to be timid and irresolute in action." It was a description that many—including Lee—believed described McClellan himself.

Lee would prove himself a fighter. Loyal to Virginia as much as the Confederacy, he renamed his fighting force the Army of Northern Virginia, and was personally angered by McClellan's invasion. That spring, President Davis asked Lee where their army should make a stand once Richmond fell. Lee mentioned the Staunton River, a hundred miles to the south, but then quickly added, "Richmond must not be given up. It *shall* not be given up."

JEB STUART CIRCLES McCLELLAN'S ARMY— AND IS PROUD TO DO SO

Lee intended to attack McClellan's troops, but first, he sent James Ewell Brown Stuart—or "Jeb" Stuart—a brigadier general cavalry commander, to explore McClellan's right flank north of the Chickahominy River. Stuart was willing, but he had a bolder ambition: to circle McClellan's army.

The bold move fit with Stuart's character. One of Stuart's officers once described him as "a gallant figure to look at. The gray coat buttoned to the chin; the light French saber . . . the cavalry boots above the knee, and the brown hat with its black plume floating above the bearded features, the brilliant eyes, and the huge mustache which curled with laughter at the slightest provocation—these made Stuart the perfect picture of the gay cavalier."

But he was also "a soldier from the feathers in his hat to . . . his spurs," said General Robert E. Lee's nephew Fitzhugh Lee, who served under Stuart. "His Bible and tactics were his textbooks. He never drank liquor. . . . Once when on the eve of an expected battle he was telegraphed that his child was dying and urged to go to her, he replied, 'I shall have to leave my child in the hands of God; my duty requires me here.'"

After his reconnaissance of McClellan's right flank, Stuart told his twelve hundred cavalrymen what he desired, expressing his "hope of striking a serious blow at a boastful and insolent foe which would make him tremble in his shoes." When the Army of the Potomac discovered that Confederate soldiers were behind their lines, rumors circulated that the force included up to forty thousand men under "Stonewall" Jackson. The three-day circling, which covered a hundred miles from June 12 to June 15, became part of Southern folklore. Stuart's men captured one hundred seventy prisoners and three hundred horses and mules, destroyed telegraph poles and a rail line.

Stuart's men were welcomed as heroes when they arrived in Richmond. One enterprising paper boy from Richmond found his way through federal lines and sold an armful of *Richmond Examiner*s to Yankee soldiers as eager as anyone to find out what had happened. An officer in Stuart's cavalry apparently read many of the triumphant newspaper stories, remarking that they "were filled with accounts of the expedition, none accurate, and most of them marvelous."

LEE BEATS BACK McCLELLAN IN
THE SEVEN DAYS' BATTLES

With Jeb Stuart's reconnaissance complete, General Robert E. Lee hit the Union right at Mechanicsville on June 26. Lee lost fifteen hundred men in the first attack, yet he kept coming at McClellan over the next week at Gaines' Mill, Savage's Station, Frayser's Farm, and Malvern Hill, in what became known collectively as the Seven Days' Battles. Federal artillery finally stopped the Confederates, slaughtering many of the attackers. A Union soldier woke up to see five thousand Confederates on the battlefield. "A third of them were dead or dying, but enough of them were alive and moving to give the field a singular *crawling* effect."

The North had lost only one of the battles badly—two were near-stalemates and two more were Union victories—but McClellan was so unnerved by the assault he kept retreating south until he had reached the protection of federal gunboats stationed at Harrison's Landing on the James River. Confederates had twenty thousand casualties, the Union fifteen thousand, but Lee had eviscerated McClellan's plans to lay siege to Richmond, and was hailed as the hero who had saved the Confederate capital. "McClellan driven back, driven away!" wrote Cornelia Peake McDonald, the Winchester diarist, on July 4. "The whole town is rejoicing. . . . The hateful, boasting enemy are driven away."

McClellan arrived at Harrison's Landing on July 2, and a week later, Lincoln came to see him. McClellan said he hadn't lost, but had "failed to win" and needed fifty thousand or even a hundred thousand more men. Lincoln told him there were no more. McClellan was soon ordered to take his army back to Washington. "Today we took a steamer," Elisha Rhodes of Rhode Island wrote in his diary on September 3, "and went up the Potomac past Washington . . . and landed at Georgetown. . . . It is hard to have reached the point we started from last March, and Richmond is still the Rebel Capital."

If McClellan had succeeded in taking Richmond, the war might have ended and the Confederacy returned to the Union as it was. But by defeating McClellan, Lee extended the war until it became a total war that destroyed Southern society—including the institution of slavery.

"OUR FLORENCE NIGHTINGALE"—SALLY TOMPKINS TENDS THE WOUNDED IN RICHMOND

From the Seven Days' Battles, the Confederate wounded, many of whom would soon die from their injuries, came streaming into Richmond—on a wagon, on the shoulder of a fellow soldier, or stumbling back as best they could on their own. The Confederate Medical Department had begun to build the Chimborazo Hospital on a hill on the east side of the city, but by the summer of 1862, the hospital was still small and was overwhelmed by the wounded men. Over fifteen thousand wounded Confederates were brought into Richmond during the week, and many Confederates ended up dying in the streets.

The men who knew Richmond asked to go to the Robertson Hospital established by Sally Louisa Tompkins. At the beginning of the war, Tompkins, the daughter of a wealthy Richmond politician, could have fled to Europe, but her patriotism kept her in the capital. After the Battle of Bull Run, a Richmond judge left the city and offered Tompkins his two-story home as an infirmary. She equipped the hospital herself and took no pay. On July 31, 1861, Tompkins opened the twenty-two-bed hospital to care for sick and wounded Confederate soldiers, working with four slaves and numerous volunteers. Tompkins would carry a Bible and her medicine bag from soldier to soldier.

They called her "Captain Sally," and Mary Boykin Chesnut, a frequent visitor to the hospital, wrote in her diary: "Our Florence Nightingale—is Sally Tompkins." One of the traits that Tompkins shared with Nightingale was what one woman called her "obsession" with sanitation. She demanded military discipline and the highest standards of cleanliness. Robertson Hospital would become known for one of the most remarkable medical achievements of the war: of the 1,333 soldiers that came through the door, only 73 died. It was the lowest mortality rate of any military hospital during the Civil War.

GENERAL ROBERT E. LEE

The Tennessee soldier Sam Watkins would see General Robert E. Lee in his camp and describe him as many saw him: "His whole make-up of form and person, looks and manner had a kind of gentle and soothing magnetism about it that drew every one to him and made them love, respect, and honor him."

WOMEN TO THE RESCUE—
MEDICAL CARE
AND CLARA BARTON

WEEK 20

DISEASE KILLS TWICE AS MANY MEN AS WEAPONS

In 1861, as armies in the North and South massed, men who were once protected from contagion by their isolation in rural communities marched shoulder to shoulder and slept side by side in unventilated tents. Such close quarters became breeding grounds for what would kill at least twice as many men as bullets and cannon shot during the war—disease.

Childhood diseases such as mumps, chicken pox, and measles ran rampant through both armies. One million Union soldiers contracted malaria. When the armies began to move and fight, resistance was crippled further by chronic malnutrition, fatigue, and exposure to the extremes of weather. Epidemics were common. Nobody yet understood the connection between unsanitary conditions and disease and infection, and by May 1861 about a third of all the troops in the Union Army had been sick at least once, most with "acute diarrhea." In 1862, one Southern doctor said: "All complainants were asked the same questions: 'How are your bowels?' If they were open, I administered a plug of opium, if they were shut, I gave a plug of blue mass."

At this time, in France, Dr. Louis Pasteur was on the verge of grasping the role played by microorganisms, but not yet. Doctors didn't understand the connection between bad water and typhoid or between mosquitoes and yellow fever. The common assumption was that malaria was caused by "bad air" or "noxious vapors" that rose from marshes or rotting vegetation. Some doctors still prescribed leeches to heal soldiers' ailments.

In July 1861, Mary Boykin Chesnut, the Richmond diarist, wrote about the convalescing men she saw waiting to be transported on a train:

Yesterday as we left the cars we had a glimpse of war. It was the saddest sight. The memory of it is hard to shake off. Sick soldiers—not wounded. There were quite two hundred lying about as best they might on the platform . . . [T]hese pale, ghastly faces. So there is one of the horrors of war we had not reckoned on.

WITH HER FATHER'S BLESSING, CLARA BARTON BECOMES A NURSE

In March 1862, a former teacher and patent office clerk named Clara Barton went back to her family home in Massachusetts to care for her dying father. As a child, Clara had listened "breathlessly to his war stories" from the Indian Wars. As she sat with him now, she confessed that she wanted to nurse wounded Union soldiers, but was worried that the soldiers would treat her, a forty-year-old unmarried woman, like a prostitute and that her reputation as a lady would be ruined.

Later, Barton recalled in a letter what her father told her: "I know soldiers, and they will respect you and your errand." As a daughter of a Mason and a member of the Universalist Church, he said, she was duty-bound to "seek and comfort the afflicted everywhere" calling on her to "serve and sacrifice for my country in its peril and strengthen and comfort the brave men who stood for its defense." When her father died, Barton embarked upon the role for which she would become famous: nurse to wounded soldiers.

On June 26, 1862, Clara wrote to her sister Julia about her experiences in Washington treating Union soldiers injured in McClellan's Peninsula Campaign. "I cannot make a pleasant letter of this," she wrote. "Everything is sad, the very pain which is breathed out in the atmosphere of this city is enough to sadden any human heart. 5000 suffering men, and room preparing for 8000 more, poor fevered, cut up wretches, it agonizes me to think of it."

BARTON'S PRACTICAL RULES FOR PACKING BOXES

While still working at the patent office in Washington, Clara Barton filled her spare time by seeking and distributing donations for hospitals, filling warehouses with supplies, often handmade, sent by friends and others. In a letter to her friend Mary Norton, she gave advice as to what was needed and how to box supplies. Small packages were preferred, she said, as they were treated more gently than large ones. She recommended against stewed foods that could explode in transit. "Lemons are very nice," she wrote, "but best by the whole box—they keep much better before disturbing.—Soldiers eat them like apples, they get so little acid and crave it so."

Boxes should be labeled, so they could be sorted quickly. "Knowledge is *time* you know—" she wrote, "and it used to be said that it was *money*, but it is a great deal more than that." At the battle of Antietam, in September 1862, she would learn another lesson. Food had run out during the battle. "Open the wine and give that," she told an assistant, "and God help us." When the box was opened, the women discovered it was packed not with the usual sawdust, but with cornmeal, which she cooked into gruel and fed to the wounded. Afterward, she directed all suppliers to pack boxes not with sawdust but with cornmeal or bran.

But Barton knew that less practical supplies could lift soldiers' spirits. "Your pillows are a great luxury," she wrote in another letter to Mary, adding that the pillowcases should be made from old colored calico dresses. "If a calico case gets greasy and soiled, the man if able can take it off and soap and wash it, and replace it, and it will smell clean, and not look badly. A white case would be a perfect fright."

FILTHY HOSPITALS, "GUILLOTINE" AMPUTATIONS, AND DEADLY INFECTIONS

In August 1862, in the field hospitals serving the battle of Cedar Mountain in Virginia, Clara Barton learned for the first time that a wound was often a death sentence. Photos of the dead on the field often depicted them with their clothes ripped open, as wounded soldiers scrambled to see if they were gut-shot, aware that such a wound almost always meant death.

If a doctor was presented with a soldier who had a broken arm or hand, leg or foot, he would almost always amputate, as the most common culprit, the minié ball, crushed and shattered bones. To perform an amputation, a wounded soldier would be put on a table. Preferably, the medical staff would put him to sleep using ether or chloroform, but if there was none, a patient might get a swig of whiskey or a hunk of leather or a bullet to chomp on to help him bear the pain. Then they would perform a "guillotine" amputation, consisting of cutting the flesh with a razor-sharp blade, cutting the bone with a toothed saw, and then snipping any bone splinters with clippers. The arteries would be clamped and tied closed, and the wound would be coated with a styptic to stop the bleeding, before it was dressed.

Surgeons didn't clean their hands or surgical instruments from one amputation to the next. At best, they'd dip their tools into a bucket of water. The result was rampant infection. If an "odorless creamy pus" appeared, surgeons considered it a *good* sign, the body's attempt to rid itself of harmful flesh. But doctors didn't welcome the "hospital gangrene" that turned flesh black, green, purple, and yellow and filled the air with a sickeningly sweet stench. Doctors threw nitric acid, turpentine, charcoal, and chlorine at it, but they didn't help (bromine proved a successful treatment later in the war). According to one authority, about one-quarter of all Civil War amputations resulted in death, "almost always of surgical fevers."

HOSPITAL CLEANLINESS IMPROVES
AS WOMEN BECOME NURSES

At the start of the Civil War, nursing was a male profession North and South, as many disapproved of exposing ladies to strangers of the opposite sex and the gory horrors of war, death, and disease. Change, though, had been seeded by the work of Englishwoman Florence Nightingale during the Crimean War, and by her popular book, *Notes on Nursing*, published in 1860. As war came, women such as Clara Barton in the North and Sally Louisa Tompkins in Richmond broke the gender barrier. For many women, the job of nursing soldiers would be a first foray out of the home, changing how others perceived them and how they perceived themselves.

With so many men at the battlefront, women nurses became a necessity. Dorothea Dix was named superintendent of female nurses for the U.S. Army, nicknamed "Dragon Dix" for her stern ways and her requirement that nurses be over thirty, Presbyterian, and "plain in appearance." Mary Ann Bickerdyke, called "Mother Bickerdyke" by appreciative soldiers, started cleaning, feeding, and nursing Union soldiers at an Illinois field hospital in June 1861. She worked for the Northwestern Sanitary Commission, and one soldier said she meant more to the men "than the Madonna to Catholics." Her harsh discipline led one officer to complain to General William T. Sherman, who wouldn't intervene. "She outranks me," Sherman said.

In June 1862, Northern civilians formed the United States Sanitary Commission to provide medical supplies, get quality food to soldiers, recruit medical staff, and pushed for reforms in medical care to reduce disease among soldiers. That same year, the Women's Central Relief Organization began training nurses. In July 1862, when Union Surgeon General William A. Hammond heard rumors that physicians were organizing a boycott of female nurses, he ordered that at least one-third of all nurses at hospitals be women. In September 1862, the Confederate Congress allowed women to serve as hospital matrons to tend to "the entire domestic economy of the hospital." Many women pushed for new standards of hygiene at the hospitals.

While treating the wounded after the battle at Cedar Mountain in Virginia on August 13, 1862, Barton spent much of her waking hours cleaning blood, slime, and excrement from the floors. She and her assistants would move the men from one side of the room to scrub, and then reverse the process. It was probably as effective as any effort they could make to prevent infections at the hospital.

TO TREAT THEIR WOUNDED, CONFEDERATES BUILD CHIMBORAZO HOSPITAL IN RICHMOND

Richmond's proximity to the war's largest battles and the five railroad lines that passed through it convinced Confederate leaders to build what was probably the largest military hospital in the world in 1861 and one of its best-organized. It was called Chimborazo and stood on a hill on the eastern edge of the city.

The hospital soon grew into a city within a city. As many as 4,000 patients stayed in its 250 buildings at one time; approximately 75,000 injured or sick men came through its doors during the war to convalesce. The facilities included five soup houses, five icehouses, and a bakery that put out 10,000 bread loaves every day at its peak. It had its own carpenters, shoemakers, apothecaries, and cooking staff. A farm with 200 cows and several hundred goats supplied the hospital with milk.

In her memoir, Phoebe Pember, a widow who came to work at Chimborazo as a nurse, said she didn't let her emotions succumb to the "scenes of pathos [that] occurred daily. . . . There was, indeed, but little leisure to sentimentalize . . . there was too much work to be done, too much active exertion required. . . ." When one soldier asked Pember to write a letter, she said she would do so if he cut his nails, which looked "like claws," as well as the "dirty hair." He refused, saying he used his nails as spoons and that he had "promised my mammy that I would let [my hair] grow till the war be over. Oh, it's onlucky to cut it!"

"Then I can't write any letter for you," Pember responded. The patient relented, and commented on the four-page letter that Pember transcribed for him.

> *"Did you writ all that?"* he asked, whispering, but with great emphasis.
> *"Yes."*
> *"Did I say all that?"*
> *"I think you did."*
> Then the soldier asked, *"Are you married?"*

CLARA BARTON, ANGEL OF THE BATTLEFIELD

"In my feeble estimation, General McClellan, with all his laurels, sinks into insignificance beside the true heroine of the age, the angel of the battlefield."
—Dr. James Dunn, surgeon at the Battle of Antietam, on Clara Barton

THE BLOODIEST DAY
IN AMERICAN MILITARY
HISTORY—ANTIETAM
(Sharpsburg)

WEEK 21

SECOND BATTLE OF BULL RUN—
JOHN POPE BOTCHES THE BATTLE

By the end of May 1862, the Union Army was twenty miles from Richmond and the Confederate Congress was fleeing its capital. By mid-August, General Robert E. Lee, the new commander of the Confederate forces, had sent General George McClellan and his army back to Washington, and the Rebel army was lurking—no one knew just where—about twenty to twenty-five miles west of the capital. With McClellan's army off the battlefield, the responsibility in northern Virginia rested squarely on the shoulders of General John Pope, brought from his successes along the Mississippi River. A bombastic man, Pope alienated his new troops as soon as he took command. His harsh treatment of civilians in Virginia also galled Confederate officers; even the usually discreet Robert E. Lee called him "a miscreant who must be suppressed."

Confronting an invisible enemy, Pope began to panic. "His whole force," Pope said in a cable on August 25, "as far as can be ascertained, is massed in front of me." He called for troops. McClellan wouldn't send them, as he wanted to keep them in Washington to prepare for the attack everyone feared was coming.

Then, on August 26, Pope's telegraph link to Washington went dead. The wires had been cut by the soldiers of "Stonewall" Jackson, who had swooped fifty-six miles around Pope's army, destroying rail and telegraph communications. Pope headed north to find Jackson, who dug in along Stony Ridge, overlooking the same Bull Run battlefield where he had earned his name and reputation. Three days later, McClellan suggested "to leave Pope to get out of his scrape, and at once use all our means to make the capital perfectly safe." Pope was not only facing the best commanders of the Confederacy—"Stonewall" Jackson, Robert E. Lee, and James Longstreet—but he was facing them with less than his full army.

Early Saturday, August 30, Pope sent word that a "terrific battle" had been fought the day before on the same field as the first Bull Run battle, and that while he had lost eight thousand men, the Rebels had probably suffered twice that and been "badly used up" and were "driven from the field, which we now occupy."

On the second day of battle, Pope had imagined that the Rebels were in retreat, when actually the other half of Lee's divided army, commanded by James Longstreet, had arrived at Bull Run. Pope had been warned of the presence of thirty thousand men, but he didn't believe it, and a crushing blow on his left flank sent the Union Army reeling. Many in Washington were reminded of another gloomy Sunday, thirteen months earlier, when the Union Army was sent fleeing the same battle-field.

On the windy morning of September 2, Pope sent a telegram, full of defeat, to Washington. "We had another pretty severe fight last night. . . . Unless something can be done to restore tone to this army it will melt away before you know it." The Confederate Army was now twenty miles from Washington, and threatening the Union capital. Lincoln's cabinet, blaming McClellan for refusing to reinforce Pope, called for his dismissal. But Lincoln reached another conclusion: Pope, hated by his troops, beaten in battle, had to be replaced. The president walked to McClellan's quarters on H Street and asked him to take command of Pope's army and Washington's defenses.

"Everything is to come under my command again!" wrote an ecstatic McClellan to his wife after he was given the news. He might have tempered his enthusiasm if he knew of the battle to come.

A CHILD'S DEATH AND DEVASTATION COME TO WINCHESTER'S CORNELIA PEAKE McDONALD

By August 1862, the euphoria that had swept Winchester after "Stonewall" Jackson's victories in the Shenandoah Valley that spring had disappeared. Without her husband, Angus, who signed up with Jackson's brigade, Cornelia Peake McDonald was left alone to manage a large family. In the summer, McDonald's three-year-old daughter became sick and died in her mother's arms. McDonald wrote about what happened next:

> On Tuesday night, August 26th, after she was buried, I was lying in bed with a feeling only of indifference to everything, a perfect deadness of soul and spirit. If I had a wish it was the world . . . could come to an end. Suddenly the house was shaken to its foundations, the glass was shivered from the windows and fell like rain all over me as I lay in bed; a noise, terrific as of crashing worlds, followed, prolonged for some fearful moments.
>
> I could not move, but lay fixed and paralyzed. Then a cry, and my room door was burst open. "The town is on fire!" screamed Betty, rushing in. I got up . . . and then saw the whole eastern sky lighted by the blaze of burning buildings. . . . We learned the next day that the enemy had evacuated during the night, and had fired the depot, and the buildings where were government stores and army supplies. . . . The great magazine had been blown up, which had caused the fearful noise. . . .
>
> My boys in looking over the field for whatever they could find of arms or any thing else left behind in the haste of the fugitives, came across the mutilated remains of the poor creature who had been sent back to see if the fuse was burning. One foot was found in our garden.

LEE'S BOLD PLANS TO INVADE MARYLAND
AND MARCH TO WASHINGTON

In the spring of 1862, General Robert E. Lee had stopped the Union Army within earshot of Richmond and sent General George McClellan backpedaling down the Virginia Peninsula. General Lee then shifted his focus to northern Virginia, where in the summer and fall he beat the Union Army at Cedar Mountain, the Second Battle of Bull Run, and then Chantilly. In each of the battles, Lee had fought to protect Southern soil. But come fall, he imagined a bolder strategy: an invasion of the North.

Lee believed that such a move might improve the prospects in the midterm elections of Northern "Peace Democrats," who saw the recent string of Northern defeats as evidence that the South could not be conquered. "After a year and a half of trial," wrote one such Democrat, "and a pouring out of blood and treasure, and the maiming and death of thousands, we have made no sensible progress in putting down the rebellion . . . and the people are desirous of some change." What they wanted was what Confederate leaders sought: an armistice, followed by peace negotiations, which would lead to recognition of the Confederacy as an independent country.

Lee hoped to encourage that result by ripping up the Baltimore and Ohio Railroad, destroying the Pennsylvania Railroad bridge over the Susquehanna, thereby cutting the Union's two east-west rail lines. "After that," a confident Lee concluded, "I can turn my attention to Philadelphia, Baltimore, or Washington, as may seem best for our interests." He and President Davis also knew that more successes in the field might convince British and French leaders, who sympathized with the Confederacy, to grant the South official recognition.

On September 4, the Army of Northern Virginia crossed the Potomac. Lee ordered the Confederate bands to play "Maryland, My Maryland," hoping to inspire the Marylanders to rise up against the Union, but instead these residents hid behind closed doors. Lee, expecting McClellan to pursue him slowly, decided to divide his army, sending orders to "Stonewall" Jackson to take military supplies at Harpers Ferry. As usual, McClellan slowly dragged his massive army northwest toward Lee. But along the way, his men made a discovery that might have altered the course of American history.

TWO UNION SOLDIERS FIND GENERAL ROBERT E. LEE'S BATTLE PLANS WRAPPED AROUND THREE CIGARS

General George McClellan's army arrived in Frederick, Maryland, on September 13, and settled down on the same land that the Rebel army had left a few days earlier. During a morning lull, a few of the men were drinking coffee in a field, when two of them, a Corporal Barton W. Mitchell and his friend First Sergeant John McKnight Bloss, noticed a long, bulky envelope in some trampled grass. Mitchell, curious, rolled over and reached for the folder. Inside, the two men found a long piece of paper wrapped around three cigars. The men began to search for matches when Mitchell unfurled the paper, nudged his friend, and the two started reading.

The page, dated three days earlier, read "Headquarters, Army of Northern Virginia," with the title "Special Orders No. 191." The document was filled with names of officers the Union soldiers recognized, such as Jackson, Longstreet, and McLaws. It was signed by an "R. H. Chilton, Assist. Adj.-Gen." The men showed the paper to their captain, and it marched quickly up the chain of command to General George McClellan. He wondered: Could the orders be real, or were they a ruse, meant to fool him and the Union Army?

One of the officers in McClellan's army had worked closely with Chilton, knew his handwriting, and was certain that Chilton had written the orders. Fortune had handed the Union Army the war plans of Robert E. Lee.

The paper became known as the Lost Order, and it probably was the greatest security leak in American history. It spoke of Lee's decision to split his army and send generals Jackson and A. P. Hill to take the isolated garrison at Harpers Ferry and then come north and join Lee at Boonsboro or Hagerstown. McClellan said of it, "Here is a paper with which if I cannot whip Bobbie Lee, I will be willing to go home." He then sent a telegram to President Lincoln: "I have all the plans of the rebels, and will catch them in their own trap if my men are equal to the emergency. My respects to Mrs. Lincoln. . . . Will send you trophies."

THE ARMIES CONVERGE AT A CREEK CALLED ANTIETAM

When Robert E. Lee received word that George McClellan was approaching, he called for his troops to gather in Sharpsburg, Maryland, about a mile from the Potomac. He could have retreated, but to do so would be to lose face and lower the chances of winning foreign recognition for the Confederacy. Besides, he had won each time he had faced the Union Army, and he planned to do so again.

On September 15, 1862, Lee planted his 18,000 men along a three-mile ridge east of Sharpsburg, his army backed by the Potomac, a precarious position. On the same day, General McClellan's army of 95,000 began to mass across a small creek called Antietam. Confederate Major General James Longstreet would later recall the sight:

> [T]he blue uniforms of the Federals appeared among the trees that crowned the heights on the eastern bank of the Antietam. The number increased, and larger and larger grew the field of blue until it seemed to stretch as far as the eye could see, and from the tops of the mountains down to the edges of the stream gathered the great army of McClellan.

If McClellan had hurled his army against Lee's small force that day or the next, he might easily have destroyed Lee's army and ended the war. Instead, he waited, giving General "Stonewall" Jackson enough time to bring his troops from Harpers Ferry and join Lee. It would be one of many critical mistakes the cautious general would make at Antietam.

The battle began at six a.m. Wednesday, September 17, when Union troops under Major General Joseph Hooker came down the Hagerstown Turnpike to attack a forty-acre cornfield where "Stonewall" Jackson's men lay in waiting. A mist blanketed the ground. As the Yankees came, "the sunbeams falling on their well-polished guns and bayonets gave a glamour and a show at once fearful and entrancing," one of the soldiers waiting in Jackson's brigade remembered later. Neither he nor his fellow survivors would ever forget the chaotic violence that followed.

THE BLOODIEST DAY OF WARFARE IN AMERICA'S HISTORY

The Battle of Antietam began when Union General Joseph Hooker's men came down the Hagerstown Turnpike. His batteries opened fire on what came to be known as The Cornfield and the Confederates hidden within it, their goal a modest whitewashed German Baptist church on a plateau where the Rebels had planted artillery. "Every stalk of corn in the greater part of the field was cut as closely as could have been done with a knife," Hooker recalled of the initial assault, "and the slain lay in rows precisely as they had stood in their ranks a few moments before."

That morning, a group of Texans under John Bell Hood, forced to abandon their first real meal in a week, blasted their way back into the cornfield. Then the Texans, in their turn, were blasted by Union reserves and artillery waiting in the rear.

Clara Barton had stationed herself at a farmhouse near The Cornfield with some surgeons. The artillery fire from both sides was so fierce "the tables jarred and rolled until we could hardly keep the men on them," Barton remembered. Outside the farmhouse, Barton lifted the head of a wounded man. When she brought a cup of water to his lips, she felt the right sleeve of her dress twitch. The soldier fell back, quivering. A bullet had pierced her dress and then the soldier's chest, killing him instantly.

Fifteen times The Cornfield was taken and lost. By ten a.m., eight thousand men lay dead or wounded there. Corporal Barton W. Mitchell, the man who had found Lee's Lost Order, was wounded, and the man he had first brought the order to, Captain Kopp, was killed.

Another fierce battle rose along a sunken road at Lee's center that would soon be called the Bloody Lane. After the battle, one Union soldier took it upon himself to determine the number of bullet holes in a Confederate soldier doubled over a fence. He counted fifty-seven. A third fierce battle within the larger battle would take place on Lee's right flank, at a stone bridge over Antietam Creek. By the end of the day, over 12,000 Union soldiers were killed, wounded, or missing. Roughly 10,300 Confederates were killed or wounded, more than a quarter of the army.

During the battle, Lee brilliantly moved troops in his line to defend against poorly coordinated Union attacks. Again and again, McClellan refused to send in reinforcements that might very well have crushed the Confederate forces. "O, why did we not attack them and drive them into the river?" asked Rhode Island's Elisha Hunt Rhodes. "I do not understand these things. But then I am only a boy." An aide to General Lee would later say that the Confederates had only "a single item in our advantage." He was referring to the general who faced them: the hesitant, fearful George B. McClellan.

THE DEAD IN FRONT OF DUNKER CHURCH IN ANTIETAM, MARYLAND

Antietam was the first battle in American history that photographers reached before the dead had been buried. In October 1862, Mathew Brady's New York City studio ran a graphic and gruesome exhibit called "The Dead of Antietam." The photos undermined the image of war as glorious and gallant, and a *New York Times* reporter wrote that "if [Mathew Brady] has not brought the bodies and laid them in our door-yards and along the streets, he has done something very like it."

APPROACHING
THE EMANCIPATION
PROCLAMATION

WEEK 22

SLAVES ESCAPE TO FREEDOM IN THE WAKE OF THE UNION ARMY—OR ARE SOLD SOUTH

As the armies of the North invaded the slave states of the Confederacy, many slaves took the opportunity to flee the plantations and the homes of their masters and travel in roving refugee camps with the Union Army. In March 1862, Congress voted to forbid military personnel to return fugitive slaves—or risk court-martial. Then in July 1862, against Lincoln's wishes, Congress officially approved what General John Frémont had tried to do in Missouri the year before: free slaves of owners who supported the rebellion. To prevent the confiscation of their slave "property," slave-owners in the Upper South sent or sold their slaves farther South.

Cornelia McDonald, the Winchester mother, rented a slave, Lethea, from a slave-owner to help with cleaning, cooking, and childcare. In October 1862, that owner wanted to sell her. McDonald wrote in her diary:

> *The owner of Lethea has been several times to persuade me to give her up. He wants to sell her to prevent her leaving with the Yankees.*
>
> *She has already been tried and found faithful, for she never offered to leave me when [Union soldiers] were here before. . . . I have refused to give her up, but am not sure that I have the right to do it, or that if she is lost we will not have to pay the owner for her. . . . I cannot endure the thought of her grief; to be torn from her husband and perhaps from her children. Her image will always be associated with that of my lovely [deceased] baby. She held her in her arms when she was first born, she fed and cared for her, and my darling loved her.*

The next week, wrote McDonald, "Poor L. [w]as gone. When she saw there was no hope, she submitted humbly and quietly. . . . Margaret was with her, but her other child was not to go." Lethea's owner had sent her South, away from the war—and from possible freedom.

LINCOLN ADVOCATES SENDING FREED SLAVES ABROAD

On August 14, 1862, three weeks after Abraham Lincoln told his cabinet about his decision to issue an Emancipation Proclamation, he called a group of five black ministers to the White House, the first time a U.S. president had addressed a solely black audience. The men weren't prominent antislavery spokesmen; they were local preachers, four of them former slaves. Instead of listening, Lincoln lectured his visitors on race and the benefits of voluntary colonization, the movement to send freed slaves abroad.

"We have between us a broader difference than exists between almost any other two races," Lincoln argued. With slavery, blacks had, he said, suffered "the greatest wrong inflicted on any people." Slavery had also provoked whites into a war in which they were "cutting one another's throats." Lincoln concluded: "Better for us both, therefore, to be separated."

Lincoln then espoused black emigration to Central America—he was enamored with an idea to send blacks to Panama to mine coal for the navy—rather than to Liberia. He argued that the strong resistance to emigration could be overcome if one hundred, or fifty, or even twenty-five black leaders led the way. He needed men who were educated and intelligent—such as the men he gathered—to promote the opportunity. The delegates first replied that the president had reduced their hostility to the idea, but they concluded that it was "inexpedient, impolitic and inauspicious to agitate the subject of the immigration of the colored people of this country anywhere."

Did Lincoln really believe in 1862 that black colonization was a good idea, even though almost all the 4 million slaves in the country had been born in the United States, and almost all abolitionists and African-American leaders were opposed to black emigration? Most historians, especially those sympathetic to Lincoln, have minimized Lincoln's support for black emigration, arguing it was his way of deflecting attacks against "Black Republicans." He invited five black ministers to the White House, they argue, with a reporter in tow to publicize his views, to signal to Northerners that freed black men would not inundate Northern communities and compete with white laborers—they'd go abroad, forever. Lincoln's meeting was a matter of public relations, not policy.

But in his essay "Lincoln and Colonization," Eric Foner points out that Lincoln had been a sincere and ardent supporter of colonization since the early 1850s, long before he was president. "No plan of emancipation," observed one *New York Times* reporter, "unless accompanied by a practical scheme for colonization, will ever meet the President's assent."

ABOLITIONISTS BLAST LINCOLN'S
COLONIZATION PROPOSAL

After the publication of Lincoln's colonization proposal in July, his views were denounced by abolitionists, black and white. "This is our native country," wrote a group of blacks from Newtown, Long Island, "we have as strong an attachment to our native hills, valleys, plains, luxuriant forests, flowing streams, mighty rivers, and lofty mountains, as any other people." *The Liberator*, the abolitionist newspaper founded by William Lloyd Garrison, found it pathetic that the president of a country "sufficiently capacious to contain the present population of the globe," a nation that "proudly boasts of being the refuge of the oppressed of all nations," should consider sending "the entire colored population . . . to a distant shore."

Lincoln didn't seem deterred, and in late September asked Secretary of State Seward to send a letter to European powers about creating a "refuge for the colored people" in Latin American countries, but the letter elicited little interest. That same month, Frederick Douglass attacked the logic behind Lincoln's colonization proposal: "Mr. President, it is not the innocent horse that makes the horse thief, not the traveler's purse that makes the highway robber, and it is not the presence of the Negro that causes this foul and unnatural war, but the cruel and brutal cupidity of those who wish to possess horses, money and Negroes by means of theft, robbery, and rebellion. Mr. Lincoln . . . ought to know at least that Negro hatred and prejudice of color are . . . merely the offshoots of that root of all crimes and evils—slavery. . . ."

In his annual message to Congress just weeks before he signed the Emancipation Proclamation, Lincoln called for a Constitutional amendment authorizing Congress to pay for colonization, and another that would provide gradual emancipation through the year 1900, with a provision to compensate slave states and slave owners. But the final Emancipation Proclamation said nothing about colonization, and declared immediate emancipation, without compensation. Lincoln's views on race had shifted fundamentally, and he would make no more public statements supporting colonization for the rest of his life.

LINCOLN'S LETTER TO HORACE GREELEY—
UNION, NOT EMANCIPATION, IS HIS CAUSE

On August 19, 1862, Horace Greeley, the influential *New York Tribune* editor, published a critique of Lincoln, called "Prayer of Twenty Millions." In it, Greeley criticized the policy Lincoln seemed "to be pursuing with regard to the slaves," which failed to recognize that "all attempts to put down the Rebellion and at the same time uphold its inciting cause [slavery] are preposterous and futile."

In his oft-quoted reply, Lincoln wrote that if Greeley's editorial had an "impatient and dictatorial tone, I waive it in deference to an old friend, whose heart I have always supposed to be right." Lincoln continued:

> As to the policy I "seem to be pursuing" as you say, I have not meant to leave any one in doubt.
>
> . . . My paramount object in this struggle is to save the Union, and is not either to save or to destroy slavery. If I could save the Union without freeing any slave I would do it, and if I could save it by freeing all the slaves I would do it; and if I could save it by freeing some and leaving others alone I would also do that. What I do about slavery, and the colored race, I do because I believe it helps to save the Union; and what I forbear, I forbear because I do not believe it would help to save the Union. . . .
>
> I have here stated my purpose according to my view of official duty; and I intend no modification of my oft-expressed personal wish that all men everywhere could be free.

Lincoln was perhaps trying to soften the impact of the soon-to-be released Emancipation Proclamation by declaring that it wasn't about emancipation but about aiding victory on the battlefield. "Here was something for all viewpoints," writes James McPherson in *Battle Cry of Freedom*. "A reiteration that preservation of the Union remained the purpose of the war, but a hint that partial or even total emancipation might become necessary to accomplish that purpose."

WHY DIDN'T LINCOLN PROPOSE
TO FREE ALL THE SLAVES?

Why didn't Abraham Lincoln propose to free all the slaves, rather than just those under control of the Rebels, as he did in the Emancipation Proclamation?

At least part of the reason was Lincoln's concern that if the war became a full-fledged war of abolition, the war coalition in the North would fall apart. To declare all slaves free, some feared, would alienate the Union border states of Maryland, Tennessee, Kentucky, and Missouri, where slavery was still intact, and drive them into the Confederacy. To take such a bold step also would risk the Republicans their majority in Congress in the fall election.

Westerners might also bolt from the Union. Many in the West followed the political line that Lincoln held in the 1850s, wanting to prevent slavery from extending into the territories, but willing to tolerate it in the South. Many Westerners were Democrats who lived in the southern parts of Ohio, Indiana, and Illinois, territories that shared borders and commerce with Southern states. They were fighting for the Union—Lincoln's original rallying cry—not for emancipation. Many in these states feared that freeing 4 million slaves in the South would send a flood of cheap labor north, bringing unwelcome competition for jobs.

"Ohio will be overrun with negroes," one Western politician predicted, "they will compete with you and bring down your wages, you will have to work with them, eat with them, your *wives* and *children* will be degraded to their level."

ANTIETAM CHANGES THE WAR—AND MAKES THE EMANCIPATION PROCLAMATION POSSIBLE

Vicksburg and Gettysburg have entered the American consciousness as the key battles of the Civil War, but Antietam was at least as pivotal.

After the war, the insightful Porter Alexander, in charge of ordnance for the Army of Northern Virginia, called Lee's decision to fight at Antietam the general's "greatest military blunder," maintaining that Lee could have easily retreated across the Potomac "with good prestige & a very fair lot of prisoners & guns, & lucky on the whole to do this, considering the accident of the 'lost order.'" The battle cost Lee a quarter of his men, losses that would dog his army the rest of the war. The casualties were so high that the Confederate government in Richmond balked at publishing the names of the more than ten thousand Confederate casualties, fearing the despair such a list would trigger.

Antietam also produced a dismal political failure for the South. With the repulse of General Lee's army, Lincoln and the Republicans held on to their majority in the Congress in the 1862 midterm elections against the Peace Democrats, who were agitating for an armistice and recognition of the Confederacy. Antietam also gave Abraham Lincoln the battlefield success he was waiting for to release his Emancipation Proclamation. That document made it clear that to recognize the Rebels was to support slavery, something that many antislavery British, especially the working class, could not stomach.

After Antietam, the Confederacy no longer had the option, which Lincoln held out during the first phase of the war, of coming back into the Union with slavery intact. The war was no longer over one country or two, united or divided, but over an issue as old as the first European settlers in America and as contentious as any in American history: slavery. The Confederacy would win the war and hold on to slavery—or lose the conflict and its way of life.

LINCOLN'S FIRST READING OF THE EMANCIPATION PROCLAMATION BEFORE THE CABINET, JULY 22, 1862

This depiction of Lincoln reading the Emancipation Proclamation was published in 1866, and is one of many artistic depictions of the reading. From left to right, are Lincoln and members of his cabinet, including Edwin M. Stanton, Salmon P. Chase, President Lincoln, Gideon Welles, Caleb B. Smith, William H. Seward, Montgomery Blair, and Edward Bates.

SIGNING
THE EMANCIPATION
PROCLAMATION

WEEK 23

"IF MY NAME EVER GOES DOWN INTO HISTORY
IT WILL BE FOR THIS ACT"—
LINCOLN'S EMANCIPATION PROCLAMATION

On July 22, 1862, Abraham Lincoln called his cabinet together to review a draft of a proclamation he had written, freeing slaves in Rebel states. Secretary of State William Seward urged the president to wait to issue it until the Union had scored a military victory, for fear the proclamation would "be viewed as the last measure of an exhausted government." Lincoln agreed.

The awaited victory came two months later, on September 17, when the Union Army beat back Robert E. Lee's army at Antietam Creek, near Sharpsburg, Maryland. Lincoln convened his cabinet five days later and told them, "When the rebel army was at Frederick I determined, as soon as it should be driven out of Maryland, to issue a proclamation of emancipation. . . . I said nothing to anyone; but I made the promise to myself and"—he hesitated here—"to my Maker. The Rebel army is now driven out, and I am going to fulfill that promise." The preliminary proclamation gave the Confederate states a hundred days to lay down their arms. If they refused, the United States would "thenceforward" consider all the slaves in the Confederacy free. Lincoln couched the historic document in legalistic language. It proclaimed that as of January 1, 1863,

all persons held as slaves within any State or designated part of a State, the people whereof shall then be in rebellion against the United States, shall be then, thenceforward, and forever free; and the Executive Government of the United States . . . will recognize and maintain the freedom of such persons, and will do no act or acts to repress such persons, or any of them, in any efforts they may make for their actual freedom.

After two and a half centuries of slavery in North America, Lincoln had issued a document that marked the beginning of the institution's end. It was a remarkable turnaround for the president. During his senatorial debates with Stephen Douglas in 1858, Lincoln said the "ultimate extinction" of slavery would not occur in "less than a hundred years at the least." Eighteen months before he issued it, Lincoln had promised he would never interfere with slavery in the states where it was entrenched. Only months earlier, he was pushing for gradual, compensated emancipation. Now he'd committed the country's political, military, and financial strength to its immediate demise. Lincoln had, in the words of Julia Ward Howe, "sounded forth the trumpet."

THE EMANCIPATION PROCLAMATION MOBILIZES
FREED SLAVES TO SERVE AS SOLDIERS

Lincoln defended the Emancipation Proclamation as a war measure—and it was. In spite of economic and cultural leanings toward the South, the people of England and France would prevent their leaders from taking up arms with the Confederacy against a country that had pledged itself against slavery.

The proclamation did something else that Douglass and abolitionists had been long pleading for Lincoln to do: mobilize the potential power of black soldiers.

"Persons of suitable condition," Lincoln wrote in an often overlooked part of the proclamation, "will be received into the armed service of the United States to garrison forts, positions, stations, and other places. . . ." For the first time in more than half a century, blacks would be permitted to enlist in the U.S. Army.

Douglass believed arming freed slaves would also improve their status as Americans. "Once let the black man get upon his person the brass letters, 'U.S.,'" said Douglass, "let him get an eagle on his buttons and a musket on his shoulder and bullets in his pocket, and there is no power on earth which can deny that he has earned the right to citizenship in the United States."

"THE MOST EXECRABLE MEASURE RECORDED IN THE HISTORY OF GUILTY MAN"— REACTION TO THE PROCLAMATION

Many Southerners saw the Emancipation Proclamation as a legal invitation for their black slaves to rise up against their masters and murder them. Confederate President Jefferson Davis called it "the most execrable measure recorded in the history of guilty man" that was "tempered by profound contempt for the impotent rage it discloses." The foreign press was puzzled, at best, by the proclamation. "The Government liberates the enemy's slaves as it would the enemy's cattle," an editorialist in the *London Spectator* wrote, "simply to weaken them in the coming conflict. . . . The principle asserted is not that a human being cannot justly own another, but that he cannot own him *unless he is loyal to the United States.*"

But abolitionists celebrated the signing. While they recognized that it did little that the Congress had not already done, they saw it as a sign that Lincoln knew the war had become an emancipation war. Frederick Douglass spoke for many when he said he "saw in its spirit a life and power beyond its letter." Douglass, who days before had called Lincoln "passive, cowardly, and treacherous to the very cause of liberty," was ecstatic. "We shout for joy that we live to record this righteous decree," he said. Lincoln himself reflected on the proclamation while speaking to a portrait painter in February 1865, calling it the "central act of my administration, and the greatest event of the nineteenth century."

"It was no longer the Union as it was that was to be reestablished," said one Unionist. "It was the Union as it should be. That is to say, washed clean of its original sin. We were no longer the soldiers of a political controversy. We were now the missionaries of a great work of redemption. The armed liberator of millions. The war was ennobled. The object was higher."

WOULD LINCOLN COME THROUGH?—ABOLITIONISTS WAIT IN BOSTON FOR THE SIGNING OF THE PROCLAMATION

New Year's Day 1863, the day the Emancipation Proclamation was to be signed, featured two celebrations, each attended by about three thousand people. One was a Jubilee Concert organized by poet Henry Wadsworth Longfellow at Boston's Music Hall. It was dominated by literary luminaries, including Oliver Wendell Holmes, John Greenleaf Whittier, and Ralph Waldo Emerson, who spoke.

Meanwhile, black leaders organized an all-day event at the Tremont Temple. In the morning, the proclamation was read, and William C. Nell, the black leader presiding over the event, pointed out that the first of the year had been the traditional day slaves were sold. "New Year's day," he said, "proverbially known throughout the South as 'Heart-Break Day,' from the trials and horrors peculiar to sales and separations of parents and children, wives and husbands—by this proclamation is henceforth invested with new significance and imperishable glory in the calendar of time."

Harriet Tubman was there, as was Harriet Beecher Stowe and abolitionists Wendell Philips and William Lloyd Garrison. But as the sun rose and then faded, no word came. "We were waiting and listening as for a bolt from the sky, which should rend the fetters of four millions of slaves," wrote Frederick Douglass in his autobiography, ". . . Eight, nine, ten o'clock came and went, and still no word. A visible shadow seemed falling on the expecting throng, which the confident utterances of the speakers sought in vain to dispel."

The doubters had their reasons. All in attendance knew that Lincoln's Republican Party had been severely challenged in the midterm elections in November. Mary Lincoln had slaveholders in her family.

"At last, when patience was well-nigh exhausted, and suspense was becoming agony, a man . . . with hasty step advanced through the crowd," Douglass recalled, "and with a face fairly illumined with the news he bore, exclaimed in tones that thrilled all hearts, 'It is coming! It is on the wires!!'" Lincoln's words were read: "I do order and declare that all persons held as slaves within said designated States and parts of States are, and henceforward shall be, free. . . ." The crowd stomped, applauded, shouted, and all joined Douglass's rich baritone in singing John Brown's favorite tune, "Blow Ye the Trumpet, Blow."

"The effect of this announcement was startling beyond description," Douglass remembered, "and the scene was wild and grand. Joy and gladness exhausted all forms of expression, from shouts of praise to sobs and tears. . . ." Said Douglass: "I never saw Joy before."

LINCOLN'S HAND SHAKES AS HE SIGNS THE PROCLAMATION

On the morning of January 1, 1863, ushers threw open the doors to the White House to let ordinary citizens mix with government officials, a New Year's tradition at the president's home. Abraham Lincoln was there, "his blessed pump handle working steadily," as one journalist put it, shaking the hands of hundreds of visitors.

In the early afternoon, the president left the East Room and went upstairs to his office on the second floor. Secretary of State William Seward was waiting for him, as well as some of Lincoln's assistants. Sitting on the large table in the middle of the room was a vellum manuscript that Lincoln had corrected a few hours before. He sat down at the table, ready to sign one of the most important documents not just of his administration but of American history. Lincoln dipped a steel pen into an inkwell but put the pen down when he noticed his hand was shaking.

The shake in his hand had nothing to do with nerves. "I never in my life felt more certain that I am doing right than I do in signing this paper," he said at the time. "I have been shaking hands since nine o'clock this morning, and my hand is almost paralyzed. If my name ever goes into history it will be for this act and my whole soul is in it. If my hand trembles when I sign the proclamation, all who examine the document hereafter will say, 'He hesitated.'" He picked up the pen again and tried to still his hand.

In large letters, at the bottom of the document, he wrote, "Abraham Lincoln." Then he let out a laugh, and stated, "That will do."

AFTER THEY ARE READ THE PROCLAMATION,
BLACK SOLDIERS SING "MY COUNTRY 'TIS OF THEE"

At a camp near Washington, ex-slaves gathered on the first day of 1863 to celebrate the signing of the Emancipation Proclamation. "I shall rejoice that God has placed Mr. Lincum in de president's chair," said a former slave named George Payne, "and dat he woudn't let de rebels make peace until after dis new year." In an account by African-American abolitionist William Wells Brown, another ex-slave stood and recounted the time he cried all night when he learned his daughter was to be sold away. "Dey can't sell my wife and child any more, bress de Lord! (Glory, glory! From the audience.) No more dat! No more dat! No more dat, now! (Glory!) Preserdun Lincom have shut de gate."

In Harrisburg, Pennsylvania, blacks passed resolutions declaring that "the hand of God" had guided the proclamation, adding that the day had come "when American soil shall no more be polluted with that crime against God, American slavery; but all will be able to say, 'Glory to God in the highest, on earth peace and good will to man.'"

At Camp Saxton on the Sea Islands, the First South Carolina Volunteers, a regiment of ex-slaves commanded by the abolitionist Thomas Wentworth Higginson, and other blacks gathered to celebrate "the greatest day in the nation's history," wrote a free Northern black woman, Charlotte Forten. The proclamation was read, "cheered to the skies," and as a chaplain rose, the crowd broke into a spontaneous version of "My Country 'Tis of Thee."

Then, in the evening, sitting on a wall of an old fort, Forten and others listened to the army band play the tune "Home, Sweet Home." Forten wrote of the night: "The moonlight on the water, the perfect stillness around, the wildness and solitude of the ruins, all seemed to give new pathos to that ever dear and beautiful old song. It came very near to all of us—strangers in that strange Southern land."

A UNION SOLDIER READS THE EMANCIPATION PROCLAMATION TO A ROOM OF SLAVES

Although Abraham Lincoln signed the Emancipation Proclamation on January 1, 1863, it was months, if not years, before the news reached many slaves, frequently isolated by their owners.

FREDERICKSBURG—
NORTHERN EXASPERATION
AS LEE TRIUMPHS AGAIN

WEEK 24

AN EXASPERATED LINCOLN FIRES McCLELLAN

After the Northern victory at Antietam on September 17, President Lincoln urged General George McClellan to finish off the Army of Northern Virginia with an attack that General Robert E. Lee, outnumbered three to one, expected the next day. But McClellan, hesitant as always, wouldn't attack, instead letting the Confederates limp back across the Potomac to safety.

Lincoln visited McClellan at Sharpsburg on October 1, and came away thinking he'd convinced the general to move at once, but once Lincoln was back in Washington, all he heard were more excuses. General Henry Halleck, the general-in-chief of the federal army, was appalled.

"I am sick, tired, and disgusted [by McClellan's inaction]," Halleck wrote in October. "There is an immobility here that exceeds all that any man can conceive of."

McClellan argued that his men needed better shoes and more food if they were expected to march twenty miles a day. Lincoln wrote him, "Are you not over-cautious when you assume that you can not do what the enemy is constantly doing? . . . If we can not beat the enemy where he now is, we never can. . . . If we never try we shall never succeed."

When all Lincoln got in response from McClellan were telegrams citing broken-down horses, Lincoln sent an uncharacteristically sarcastic telegram. "Will you pardon me for asking what the horses of your army have done since the battle of Antietam that fatigue anything?" The steady pressure from his superiors led McClellan to assert his own superiority—at least in a letter to his wife. "The good of the country requires me to submit to all this from men whom I know to be my inferior! . . . There never was a truer epithet applied to a certain individual than that of the 'Gorilla.'" That "certain individual" was the president.

When McClellan dawdled into November, the president finally decided it was time for a change. In November 1862, Lincoln replaced McClellan with General Ambrose Burnside.

McClellan told his troops, "Stand by General Burnside as you have stood by me, and all will be well." But he was wrong. Burnside had had successes along the coast of North Carolina, but he was convinced that he was not qualified to lead the Union Army. His first engagement, which came in December in Fredericksburg, would prove him right.

REFUGEES FLEE FREDERICKSBURG AS UNION FORCES CONVERGE ON THE TOWN

In the winter of 1862–1863, newly appointed Union General Ambrose Burnside decided to do what his predecessor had stubbornly refused to do—take the initiative. Burnside was handsome and likable, but also an anxious man. "Few men . . ." a Massachusetts colonel wrote, "have risen so high upon so slight a foundation as [Burnside]." His plan was to take on the eastern half of the Army of Northern Virginia by crossing the Rappahannock quickly and taking the hills that overlooked Fredericksburg before the Southern general and his troops arrived. After victory there, he planned to march back to Richmond, just fifty-five miles away.

It was a good plan, but it was one of the rare cases in the war where the supply lines failed the Union. Pontoons needed to cross the Rappahannock arrived seventeen days late. By the time they arrived, Lee had half of his 78,000 men entrenched along a seven-mile stretch of hills that overlooked Fredericksburg. As the armies massed on either side of the river, the residents of Fredericksburg fled, "thousands houseless, shelterless and starving," wrote Cornelia McDonald, "wandering in the woods, there to abide the frost and cold of the winter days and nights."

While the two sides prepared for the battle, Union soldiers traded sugar, coffee, and newspapers with Confederate troops for Southern papers and tobacco on makeshift boats floated across the river.

Finally, on December 11, Union forces began pounding Fredericksburg with artillery and then crossed the Rappahannock on six bridges. A full month had passed since the president told Burnside to move fast, and it had been three weeks since Union troops had first arrived on the river. Union officers and soldiers wondered why the resistance from the Rebels was soft. "They want to get us in," said one veteran. "Getting out won't be quite so smart or easy."

THE SLAUGHTER AT MARYE'S HEIGHTS

Union General Ambrose Burnside ordered the attack on Fredericksburg on December 13, 1862. The battle plan included an assault on Marye's Heights that overlooked the city. Confederate artillery was placed so it could hit the men directly and on both flanks. If artillery didn't keep the charging Union soldiers at bay, Rebel leaders expected they'd be put off by the 2,500 Confederates lined up four-deep behind a four-foot-high stone wall that was a quarter-mile long. Union generals couldn't believe Burnside would consider a direct assault on the Heights; one called it "murder, not warfare." From the top of the Heights, General Lee couldn't believe it, either. "A chicken could not live on that field," a Confederate artilleryman said on the morning of the Union assault, "when we open on it."

Through the day, nearly half of the Union Army would take part in the waves of soldiers who swept up toward the Heights. General James Longstreet compared the falling of those who did come to "the steady dripping of rain from the eaves of a house."

When it was time for General "Fighting Joe" Hooker to send his men toward the Heights, he sent back a protest to Burnside, and when that didn't work, he protested in person, and was rebuffed again. The troops Brigadier General Andrew A. Humphreys sent up the hill at twilight were faced with another handicap. The Union men in the field, injured or just cowering, tried to stop the next wave of soldiers by grabbing at their legs and feet, until they faltered.

Fourteen assaults on Marye's Heights failed, and 12,653 Union soldiers were killed, wounded, and missing at Fredericksburg, almost as many as at Antietam. Most were killed charging up Marye's Heights on December 13. The Confederates lost 5,309, but most of them had not been wounded or killed, but had gone home for the holidays. Not one Union soldier got within a hundred feet of the wall at Marye's Heights. Looking down on the carnage on the hill, General Lee observed, "It is well that war is so terrible—we should grow too fond of it."

NEW RECRUITS—MAINE'S JOSHUA CHAMBERLAIN
AND OTHERS SIGN UP

On one of the first days of September 1862, a slim, thirty-four-year-old professor with a bushy mustache was honored at a ceremony held at the parade ground at Maine's Bowdoin College in Brunswick, Maine, where he taught rhetoric. The professor had volunteered for the Union Army, and the school had given him, as a parting gift, a granite-gray stallion dappled white. The man's name was Joshua Chamberlain.

He and many new Maine volunteers were responding to Lincoln's request that governors send 300,000 more men to serve for three years. The first blush of war, accompanied by impassioned speeches and patriotic songs, had attracted many young soldiers. But, after battles like Shiloh, Antietam, and Fredericksburg, more men were needed. If a Maine town or city did not reach its quota, local leaders were required to establish a draft.

"I have always been interested in military matters," Chamberlain wrote the governor when he was appealing for an officer's position, "and what I do not know in that line, I *know how to learn*."

> *But, I fear, this war, so costly of blood and treasure, will not cease until the men of the North are willing to leave good positions, and sacrifice the dearest personal interests, to rescue our Country from desolation, and defend the National existence against treachery at home and jealousy abroad. This war must be ended, with a swift and strong hand; and every man ought to come forward and ask to be placed at his proper post.*

He would receive the post of lieutenant colonel and command these so-called boys of Maine—farmers, clerks, sailors, fishermen, carpenters, age eighteen to forty-five, many left over from other new regiments in the state. At the end of the year, some of the men would be lost at the Union debacle at Fredericksburg. In ten months, they would defend a hill at Gettysburg, and "the Twentieth Maine" would give its name to history.

"THE LIVING AND THE DEAD WERE ALIKE TO ME"— JOSHUA CHAMBERLAIN'S HELLISH NIGHT AT FREDERICKSBURG

The Twentieth Maine, led by Joshua Chamberlain, was one of the last units to charge up Marye's Heights at Fredericksburg, and got pinned down as night fell. They would spend one of the most unsettling nights of their lives on the field below Marye's Heights. Chamberlain later recalled:

> *Out of that silence . . . a smothered moan . . . as if a thousand discords were flowing together into a key-note weird, unearthly, terrible to hear and bear . . . some begging for a drop of water, some calling on God for pity; and some on friendly hands to finish what the enemy had so horribly begun; some with delirious, dreamy voices murmuring loved names, as if the dearest were bending over them. . . .*

The temperature dropped below freezing. Chamberlain pressed himself between two dead men to stay warm, and used a third for a pillow. At one point, a face, "half vampire-like," approached his, and Chamberlain would later say of that night, "the living and the dead were alike to me." The next day, the bullets of the Confederates would pound dully into a grisly wall of dead comrades that the men from the Twentieth built to protect themselves.

On the second night, the boys from Maine were distracted by a natural wonder rare as far south as Virginia. "An aurora borealis, marvelous in beauty," Chamberlain would write. "Fiery lances and banners of blood, and flame, columns of pearly light, garlands and wreaths of gold—all pointing and beckoning upward. . . . Who would die a nobler death, or dream of more glorious burial?" The Confederates who looked up toward the same ethereal lights saw it as a God-sent approval of their victory.

The next day, Burnside wanted to take his old Ninth Corps on one last charge against Marye's Heights but was talked out of it. As he withdrew his men back across the Rappahannock in the night, one aide called for three cheers for their new leader, but not one was given.

LINCOLN CONSOLES A DAUGHTER OF A SOLDIER KILLED

Abraham Lincoln knew death personally. He lost his mother when he was nine years old, and his beloved older sister, Sarah, when he was almost eighteen. He and Mary lost their son Edward at age three, and their favorite son, Willie, at age eleven.

Just before Christmas Day 1862, Lincoln wrote this letter to Fanny McCullough, the daughter of a Union soldier, William, who was killed in Mississippi. Lincoln knew William from Illinois, and he wrote the letter to Fanny after he had heard that the family feared the young girl might be driven insane by the loss of her father. He wrote:

Dear Fanny

It is with deep grief that I learn of the death of your kind and brave Father; and, especially, that it is affecting your young heart beyond what is common in such cases. In this sad world of ours, sorrow comes to all; and to the young, it comes with bitterest agony, because it takes them unawares. The older have learned to ever expect it. I am anxious to afford some alleviation of your present distress. Perfect relief is not possible, except with time. You can not now realize that you will ever feel better. Is not this so? And yet it is a mistake. You are sure to be happy again. To know this, which is certainly true, will make you some less miserable now. I have had experience enough to know what I say; and you need only to believe it, to feel better at once. The memory of your dear Father, instead of an agony, will yet be a sad sweet feeling in your heart, of a purer, and holier sort than you have known before.

Please present my kind regards to your afflicted mother.
Your Sincere Friend
A. Lincoln

UNION PONTOON BRIDGES USED AT THE BATTLE OF FREDERICKSBURG

The components of these two pontoon bridges, used to cross the Rappahannock River, arrived seventeen days late, delaying the Union attack at Fredericksburg.

An ALL-CONSUMING BATTLE
(1863)

INTRODUCTION

If Confederate President Jefferson Davis could have stopped the war at any point, it might have been after the winter of 1862–1863. General Robert E. Lee had shown his total command of the battlefield, chasing Union General George McClellan from Richmond during the spring of 1862 and then crushing his replacement, General Ambrose Burnside, at Fredericksburg in December. "If there is a place worse than hell," said Lincoln, wringing his hands, grief-stricken, after Fredericksburg, "I am in it."

The stakes of the war rose after Lincoln signed the Emancipation Proclamation on January 1, 1863. All understood the conflict could no longer be resolved with the country reuniting as it had been. "[The war] will be one of subjugation," Lincoln said to an official after the proclamation was issued. "The [old] South is to be destroyed and replaced by new propositions and ideas." Black soldiers, finally recruited into the Union Army in 1863, were one of the "new propositions."

After a brilliant victory at Chancellorsville in the spring, a confident Lee took the fight to Northern soil a second time in early summer. If it worked, it would be brilliant—he might send the Lincoln administration scurrying, force Ulysses S. Grant's army to pull back from the besieged Vicksburg, the key city on the Mississippi River, and destroy Northern morale. Success might even convince England and France to join the Confederacy in its war of independence.

Lee's Army of Northern Virginia crossed the Potomac into Pennsylvania, until some of his troops stumbled upon federal cavalry outside a small crossroads named Gettysburg. Within hours, 165,000 men converged. For the first three days in July, they would make devastating war in a battle that would become the largest ever fought in the Western hemisphere, producing suffering and death that exceeded anything Americans have experienced before or since.

A BROTHER'S WAR,
A BITTER WAR

WEEK 25

STONES RIVER, TENNESSEE—ENEMIES SING TOGETHER IN THE NIGHT AND BUTCHER EACH OTHER IN THE MORNING

For some time, Abraham Lincoln had been prodding William S. Rose-crans to march his Army of the Cumberland, with its 43,000 soldiers, from Nashville, Tennessee, and attack Braxton Bragg's Army of Tennessee at Murfreesboro. The idea was for Rosecrans's army to brush the 38,000 Rebs in Bragg's army aside, gain control of central Tennessee, and provide a supply base for attacks on Chattanooga and Atlanta. Rosecrans's army left Nashville on December 26, and four days later his men settled in for the night a few hundred yards from Bragg's.

Through the night, soldiers from both camps listened as bands from each army took turns playing their favorite tunes into the icy darkness. Northern bands played "Yankee Doodle" and "Hail Columbia," and then Southern bands countered with "Dixie" and "The Bonnie Blue Flag." Then one of the bands began to play the sentimental strains of "Home Sweet Home," a song that expressed a longing that transcended the Mason-Dixon Line. Soon tens of thousands of Confederate and federal soldiers, some of them raised in the same towns and the same families, began to sing the same words into the bitter cold. *Mid pleasures and palaces though we may roam, Be it ever so humble, there's no place like home.*

The next morning, New Year's Eve, the Confederates fired first, catching the federal troops while they were still eating breakfast. In a few hours, the Union forces had been beaten back three miles. Resistance by the division under Philip Sheridan, the compact cavalryman who would later gain fame sweeping through the Shenandoah Valley, prevented a Union disaster. He had awakened his men at four a.m., anticipating the attack, and so they were waiting after Bragg had crumpled two other Union divisions. In less than four hours of fighting, a third of Sheridan's men were killed, wounded, or missing. Illinois troops called the place they made their stand the "Slaughter Pen," because they said the blood-covered boulders reminded them of the floors of meat-processing plants back home.

That night, Bragg fully expected the federal troops to retreat, and telegraphed Richmond that "God had granted us a happy New Year." On January 2, Bragg ordered another attack. This time, the federal troops were waiting, and massed federal artillery destroyed the attacking brigades. On January 3, Bragg's army retreated, but neither side could claim a clear victory. Both sides had a third of their men killed, wounded, or missing, making it the deadliest battle of the war in proportion to the number of men who fought. From the soldier's perspective, the future looked bleak. "I see no prospects of peace for a long time," confessed one sobered Confederate veteran of Stones River. "The Yankees can't whip us and we can never whip them."

A BRUTAL WINTER CAMP

The winter months often meant a break in the military campaigns of the war and the killing, and as the winter of 1863 approached, many of the soldiers in the Army of the Potomac expected a respite, especially after the carnage of Fredericksburg. In the five weeks after the battle, they found themselves in Falmouth, Virginia, along the northern shore of the Rappahannock River, enduring frigid temperatures with inadequate supplies. One Wisconsin officer compared the encampment to the "Valley Forge of the war." Elisha Hunt Rhodes, the Rhode Island enlistee, forced himself to make an entry in his diary. "This morning we found ourselves covered with snow that had fallen during the night. It is too cold to write. How I would like to have some of those 'On to Richmond' fellows out here with us in the snow."

Soldiers' thoughts turned to grim survival. "The phrensy of soldiers rushing during an engagement to glory or death has, as our boys amusingly affirm, *been played out*," wrote one observant chaplain. Confidence in their leadership had evaporated. One Massachusetts soldier concluded: "Our poppycorn generals kill men as Herod killed the innocents."

The soldiers swarmed into the forests and felled trees to make homes warmer than any tent. Soon they'd built a small city made of logs and canvas arranged by regiments. New recruits put on all their clothes, including their overcoats, before bed. But veterans would take off their clothes and use them as blankets, which they were convinced kept them warmer.

An inspector from the Sanitary Commission reported that the winter quarters were "littered with refuse, food and other rubbish, sometimes in an offensive state of decomposition. . . ." Diseases such as scurvy, dysentery, typhoid, diphtheria, and pneumonia would kill two soldiers to every one downed on the battlefield. "One of the wonders of these times was the army cough . . ." one Union soldier recounted later. "[It] would break out . . . when the men awoke, and it is almost a literal fact that when one hundred thousand men began to stir at reveille, the sound of their coughing would drown that of the beating drums."

CORNELIA McDONALD LOSES A CHRISTMAS TURKEY AND FIGHTS FOR HER HOME

Cornelia McDonald, the Winchester mother, had struggled for almost two years to keep her family fed and housed, despite frequent intrusions by the Union Army. On Christmas Eve 1862, Union soldiers stole her Christmas turkey. The day after Christmas, soldiers came through her windows, she recalled later, to take "a cut glass decanter full of wine . . . butter and everything that could be carried off, including the remains of the Christmas dinner." Later in the month, Union soldiers would dismantle her hen and turkey houses for firewood.

On January 10, 1863, a Union soldier, a "vulgar looking man," knocked on the door of her large house and "informed me that he had orders to take my house for a hospital, or at least part of it. I felt almost too helpless and wretched to resist, but as nothing was left to do but resist, as we had only the roof over our heads left us, I resolved to defend it, as I could not consent to share it with sick men, and the alternative was to leave it." As she left to protest at Union headquarters, "there was already a wagon full of sick men drawn up before the front door. . . ."

She spoke with Union Major General Milroy. "I came to him for protection," she wrote later, as "he had the power. . . ." He asked where her "natural protectors" were. She told him they were in the Confederate Army.

"Yes," he said, "they leave you unprotected and expect us to take care of you."

"We would not need your care, if we were allowed to take care of ourselves," said I. "It is only from the army you command that we want protection."

Finally, Milroy gave in. When McDonald returned to her home, the men were poised to install a cooking stove for the army in her house. "They were soon all cleared out," McDonald wrote, "and we were once more at peace."

CHANCELLORSVILLE I

After the drubbing General Ambrose Burnside received at Fredericksburg in December, Lincoln replaced him with "Fighting Joe" Hooker. General Hooker had shown courage during the Peninsula Campaign and Antietam, and he quickly won over his troops by improving the food, providing amnesty to deserters, and cleaning up the camps.

Hooker set out to meet Lee with more than twice as many soldiers—130,000 to Lee's 60,000. Wanting to avoid Burnside's mistake of a direct attack at Fredericksburg, Hooker feinted there with a third of his army to fool Lee, and moved the rest of his army along the Rappahannock to get on Lee's unprotected left and rear. The troops there and at Fredericksburg would then squeeze Lee's army in a pincer movement.

On April 27, some of the Union troops crossed pontoon bridges below Fredericksburg, with the bulk of the army fording upriver, finding itself in a sixty-four-square-mile woods that included tangled undergrowth, marshes, and fallen trees that locals called the Wilderness. By April 30, fifty thousand Union troops had crossed upriver, but then Hooker would make one of his first of many fatal decisions during the battle. Instead of pressing eastward to get clear of the Wilderness and into open territory where his larger army and additional artillery could wield their advantage, he waited for more troops.

Confederate cavalry saw what the Union Army was up to and relayed the plans to Lee. What would Lee do? Conventional military wisdom recommended retreat when a general faced a force twice his army's size. It also said that a general should never divide his forces when face-to-face with the enemy, much less one of superior size. Lee, though, divided his forces, leaving only ten thousand troops under Major General Jubal Early to hold the Fredericksburg entrenchments. He sent the bulk of his army, led by Thomas "Stonewall" Jackson, to deal with Hooker's superior numbers upriver.

Jackson and his men left Fredericksburg at three in the morning on May 1, picked up two divisions on the way, and took a position on a ridge on the Turnpike and Plank Road east of the Wilderness. The Union forces came east that morning to escape the Wilderness, but before they got out, Jackson's experienced fighters hit like a pile-driver. Hooker panicked, calling all the men to retreat to a defensive position in Chancellorsville. "To tell the truth," Hooker admitted later, "I just lost confidence in Joe Hooker."

That night, cavalry leader Jeb Stuart, who had surveyed Union positions, rode up to the campfire where Lee, Jackson, and the rest of the high command were discussing plans while sitting on abandoned

Union cracker boxes. He had crucial intelligence: The Union right flank, he said, was "in the air," meaning that it was vulnerable, unprotected by any natural or manmade barriers.

In one of the riskiest moves in American military history, General Jackson convinced Lee to split the army a second time. Lee would stay behind with 14,000 soldiers to occupy Hooker, as Jackson would snake 28,000 men in his Second Corps on a twelve-mile trip on country roads and through woods to get at the Union's right flank. All day on May 2, anxious Union soldiers and officers warned their commanders that huge numbers of Confederate troops were moving to their right flank, but Hooker became increasingly convinced it was Lee's army in retreat.

It wasn't. At about five thirty in the evening, Confederate bugles sounded, deer bounded toward the Union's right flank, and the Rebel yell went up. Jackson's 28,000 battle-hardened men, in a formation two miles wide and four divisions deep, ran, firing, at the federal army's undermanned right flank.

CHANCELLORSVILLE II—LEE'S GREATEST VICTORY AND HIS GREATEST LOSS

In early evening on May 2, Thomas "Stonewall" Jackson's 28,000 men hammered the right flank of Union General Joseph Hooker's army west of Chancellorsville. Almost immediately, 2,000 men on the Union right were enveloped, killed, captured, or sent fleeing. One Union soldier later recalled, "Along the road it was pandemonium, and on the side of the road it was chaos." Union troops fell back two miles, their flight stopped only by Union artillery and the arrival of nightfall.

Wanting to continue the battle into the night, Jackson and a few officers rode their horses out in front of the Confederate lines to do reconnaissance. Union pickets fired on the general, and he pivoted his horse back toward his own front lines. A North Carolina regiment mistook the shadowy figures coming at them for Union cavalry, and fired. Two of Jackson's aides were killed, and Jackson was hit twice in his left arm. Shattered, it was amputated in the morning. Lee was devastated. "He has lost his left arm," Lee told Jackson's chaplain, B. Tucker Lacy, "but I have lost my right."

Hooker started the next day by abandoning key high ground at Hazel Grove, which Confederate cavalryman Jeb Stuart immediately took with thirty-one cannon, showering the Union Army below with fire. At one point, Hooker was leaning against a pillar on the porch at his headquarters at the Chancellorsville mansion when a Confederate shell hit it, knocking him to the ground, groggy. Yet he refused to turn over command, and went through the day far more dazed than daring. The Union soldiers retreated back through the Wilderness. Confederates followed, lobbing shells at the beaten Union soldiers. Dry as tinder, the woods ignited a fire that killed many men. By May 5, Hooker ordered his men to retreat back across the river under the cover of darkness.

Lincoln, his hopes once again undermined by poor generalship, exclaimed, "My God! My God! What will the country say?" The battle ended, Lee waited nervously on the fate of his wounded top general, Thomas "Stonewall" Jackson.

GENERAL "STONEWALL" JACKSON FADES AWAY

After "Stonewall" Jackson was shot at Chancellorsville on the night of May 2, 1863, General Lee had him transported on an ambulance wagon twenty-seven miles behind the lines to recuperate. He was put in a makeshift bed in an outbuilding on a 740-acre plantation named Fairfield. His wife, Mary Anna, arrived at the house on May 7 with their baby daughter, Julia, just three weeks old. Mary Anna said the visit was made more poignant because of "the additional charm and the attraction of the lovely child that God had given us."

In the first few days after the injury, Jackson seemed to be healing. "God will not take him from us," General Lee said, "now that we need him so much." Jackson, always devout, believed the same: "I am persuaded the Almighty has yet a work for me to perform." But just before Anna arrived, he contracted pneumonia and he was soon wandering in and out of consciousness. On Sunday, May 10, a surgeon told Anna that he would be gone by the end of the day. She told her husband, and he addressed the surgeon.

"Doctor," Jackson said, "Anna informs me that you have told her I am to die today. Is it so?" The doctor nodded. "Very good, very good," replied Jackson. "It is all right. It is the Lord's day; my wish is fulfilled. I have always desired to die on Sunday."

In the afternoon, his breathing became shallow as he gave commands to absent soldiers. "Order A. P. Hill to prepare for action! Pass the infantry to the front. . . . Tell Major Hawks—" Then he smiled, closed his eyes, and spoke his last words: "Let us cross over the river and rest under the shade of the trees."

When Confederate President Jefferson Davis heard the news of Jackson's death, he declared a day of mourning for the Confederate nation. In Winchester, Virginia, Cornelia McDonald wrote: "In every great battle fought in Virginia he has been a leader, and has never known defeat. . . . 'The Mighty has fallen,' but he carries to his grave the hopes, and is followed by the bitter tears of the people in whose defense he lost his life, and who loved him with grateful devotion."

GENERAL THOMAS "STONEWALL" JACKSON

This is called General Thomas "Stonewall" Jackson's "Chancellorsville Portrait," taken at a Spotsylvania farm on April 26, 1863, seven days before he was mortally wounded at the Battle of Chancellorsville.

FOOD AND DRINK—
THE EDIBLE, INEDIBLE,
AND COFFEE, ALWAYS

WEEK 26

HARD *TACK* COME AGAIN NO MORE

Early in the war, a filling, inexpensive staple for both Northern and Southern armies was fresh bread—healthy and easy to bake in large quantities. But fresh bread did not travel well. In the South, the Confederate leaders supplied men on the move with cornmeal, an all-purpose ingredient in biscuits, bread, stews, and Confederate cush, a mix of bacon fat, beef bits, water, and cornbread. In 1863, one Mississippi soldier wrote his sister that "I want Pa to be certain and buy wheat enough to do us plentifully [because] I never intend to chew anymore cornbread."

The traveling staple for the Union was hardtack, long familiar to sailors and despised by all. Hardtack was a cracker made by combining flour and water and usually shaped into three-inch squares about a half-inch thick. Soldiers used it to thicken stews and to stop "weak bowels" and, if they had to, as food.

In his classic work, *Hardtack and Coffee*, John Billings, the veteran of the Union Army, writes that hardtack came in "three conditions." In its original state, it was "so hard it could not be bitten" and would require "a very hard blow of the fist to break." Its second condition was "mouldy and wet." Its third was "infested with maggots or weevils," although Billings added that he believed these insects "never interfered with the hardest variety."

CARRYING IT, FINDING IT, MISSING IT—
FOOD ON THE MOVE

Once the armies left their winter quarters to seek out the enemy, their nutrition usually suffered. "On the march," wrote Rhode Island enlistee Elisha Hunt Rhodes in his diary, "salt pork toasted on a stick with hard bread and coffee is our principal diet." They'd pack dried vegetables and rice for the road as well. But often soldiers were reluctant to carry the food on long marches and into battle. "If as was sometimes the case, three days' rations were issued at one time and the troops ordered to cook them, and be prepared to march," wrote Confederate soldier Carlton McCarthy, "they did cook them, and eat them if possible so as to avoid the labor of carrying them. . . . To be one day without anything to eat was common. Two days fasting, marching and fighting was not uncommon and there were times when no rations were issued for three or four days."

Confederates suffered starvation diets more often than their Northern foe, and more so as the war dragged on, after the Southern landscape had been ravaged and supply lines cut by Yankees. During the retreat from Antietam, Southern officer C. Irvine Walker noted that he "frequently saw the hungry Confederate gather up the dirt and corn where a horse had been fed, so that when he reached his bivouac he could wash out the dirt and gather the few grains of corn to satisfy in part at least the cravings of hunger."

The men would often be forced to live off the land. Rhodes wrote of marching in Downsville, Maryland, in September 1862 and finding a tree "well stored with honey." Southern infantryman Sam Watkins and some of his fellow infantrymen filled their sacks with shelled mussels they found on the Duck River in Tennessee.

[W]e tried frying them, but the longer they fried the tougher they got. They were a little too large to swallow whole. Then we stewed them, and after a while we boiled them, and then we baked them, but every flank movement we would make on those mussels the more invulnerable they would get. . . .

SOLDIERS QUENCH THEIR THIRST WITH DIRTY WATER AND HOMEMADE HOOCH

More men died in the Civil War from disease than from battle wounds, and one of the primary culprits was dirty water. When the armies of the North or South arrived somewhere, the water they found was usually clean. But with tens of thousands of men, many of them sick, and horses and mules as well, what was clean was soon fouled. Neither army followed the basic rules of sanitation—separating lavatories from drinking water. Neither side had purification kits, and they regularly ignored the advice of medical authorities to boil water before drinking it. Henry T. Johns of the Forty-ninth Massachusetts Volunteers wrote:

> [W]e have drunk water that your farmers would hardly wash their hogs in. . . . The water being so poor and warm having no snap to it we use coffee to excess hence diarrhoea. O! For one glass of Berkshire water. I long for nothing so much. . . .

Coffee was one alternative to dirty water. Liquor was another. Officers were permitted to imbibe, but enlisted men were forbidden, a stricture that was often sidestepped. There are many jovial Civil War stories about the drinking of homemade hooch, such as the soldier who hid his liquor by pouring it into the barrel of his gun or another soldier who hid it inside a scooped-out watermelon. The soldiers didn't know it, but the alcohol in liquor killed bacteria, and while it may have muddied their minds, it killed water-borne diseases.

But drinking could cost lives when drunken officers or the troops that served under them made bad battlefield decisions. "We have lost more valuable lives at the hands of whiskey sellers," wrote Confederate General Braxton Bragg, "than by the balls of our enemies."

REAL COFFEE AND NEAR COFFEE

For Civil War soldiers, the antidote to hardtack, brick-hard cornbread, rancid meat, and withered vegetables was the drink prized more than alcohol: coffee. It was drunk after drilling, marching, eating, and even fighting, a drink to warm a cold body, to wake a tired one, and to wash away a perpetually bland or distasteful diet.

The Confederates didn't get as much as they wanted, on account of the Union blockade. As substitutes, the Southerners brewed coffee impostors from bark, sweet potatoes, peas, dried apples, grains, nuts, corn, and rye.

Union soldiers were luckier. They were sporadically issued rations consisting of eight pounds of ground-roasted coffee or ten pounds of green coffee beans. When they were lucky enough to get the beans, they'd roast them underground in pots and then smash them into grinds in the morning. When on the move, soldiers who would leave behind their equipment and food to lighten their load would almost never abandon their coffee.

When the coffee was gone, it was a major loss. One soldier, Samuel Saltus, wrote a letter describing a mock funeral when it was finished:

> On one side a coffee pot pierced with an arrow, words "no more grounds for complaint." Other side—coffee mill—words "the last rind." Pall bearers followed, then priest. . . . They marched through the camp, halted; a sort of funeral ceremony was performed, preaching and singing, in German, and a bonfire made and the last grounds burnt.

ONE-POT COOKING, TURTLE-SHELL PLATES, AND STICKS FOR FORKS

At the beginning of the war, food preparation in the Army of the Potomac was rudimentary. Provisions such as flour, pork, beans, rice, sugar, and coffee were issued to groups of five to ten men, who were told to cook it up themselves. The army soon figured out that company cooks could prepare better food, although they learned on the job.

One exception was the Fifty-fifth New York, which had Frenchmen serving as cooks. President Lincoln once dined with them when they were near Washington, and told them they would do well if they fought as well as they cooked. As the war went on, contraband slaves, some of them cooks, took on the job. The Twenty-first Massachusetts acquired one such cook, whom they named Jeff Davis. He'd take up collections from the men to supplement their army-issued meals with fresh eggs, butter, and produce. He might have been the best-liked man in the regiment.

The Rebels complained about the lack of food, and sometimes about the lack of cookware. In the fall of 1863, one Confederate colonel wrote up the chain of command:

> For God and the country's sake, make your fair-promising but never-complying quartermaster send me skillets, ovens, pots or anything that will bake bread or fry meat. . . . I cannot fight any more until I get something to cook in.

The men improvised plates and even corn graters from canteens they collected from the battlefield and cut in half. They mixed ingredients for bread in emptied turtle shells or hollowed-out pumpkin shells.

Necessity was the mother of handmade kitchen utensils, made from sticks, pocketknives, and bare hands. Corn was roasted in its husk, and red and white potatoes were tucked straight into the embers to cook. One-pot or one-skillet meals became the norm.

BEGGING, BUYING,
AND STEALING FOOD FROM CIVILIANS

Repelled by their own rotted rations and often moving faster than their supply lines, Union soldiers begged, bought, or stole food from civilians. Early in the war, fertile Southern farmlands not yet stripped clean by the war provided tasty fare for the Union Army. The soldiers were supposed to pay for their food—or at least leave receipts for food taken, to be paid later—but they'd often sweep through areas like rapacious locusts.

A Massachusetts recruit on the coast of North Carolina described the habitual thievery in a letter to his parents in late 1862:

> *Whenever we neared a town where we were to halt, our approach was marked by a spattering fussilade, amid which the last dying squeaks of the unfortunate pigs far and near were heard, and then we would see soldiers and sailors coming forth from the barnyards bearing their game impaled on a bayonet & dangling over their shoulders . . . When we first started the colonel tried to prevent our foraging but he quickly found out that all that was nonsense & before we got back we were as expert at it as any of the old hands.*

Pillaging was not just a Yankee approach. One Vermont soldier remembers offering to buy food from a Southern farmer: "Buy?" the farmer muttered. "Soldiers buy? They've stole all I've got that they could carry away. . . . [W]e can hardly live between the two armies."

NEW YORK SOLDIERS SHARE A MEAL

Timothy O. Sullivan's photograph depicts New York soldiers, part of
General George Meade's army, sharing a meal at a makeshift table
in 1863.

FIRE IN THE REAR— LINCOLN AND ANTIWAR POLITICIANS DUKE IT OUT

WEEK 27

LINCOLN SUSPENDS THE WRIT OF HABEAS CORPUS

Soon after the war began, the Lincoln administration arrested Confederate sympathizers and war dissenters. One was the grandson of Francis Scott Key, the composer of "The Star-spangled Banner," and another was John Merryman, who was allegedly involved with the burning of the bridges and tearing down of telegraph wires in Baltimore in April 1861.

Merryman challenged the case in court, and Judge Roger B. Taney, the Supreme Court Justice who had decided the controversial *Dred Scott* decision, called on the commanding officer at Fort McHenry to show cause for the arrest. The officer refused, noting that President Lincoln had suspended the writ of habeas corpus in parts of Maryland. Taney ruled the president had no right to suspend the writ, which protects people from being thrown in jail without a charge or a trial.

These were the first legal shots fired over civil liberties in the North. Lincoln ignored Taney's ruling, and on September 24, 1862, the president suspended the writ of habeas corpus across the North. Often, local military officials or police would arrest Southern sympathizers on flimsy counts, such as "being a noisy secessionist" or "hurrahing for Jeff Davis." One Virginia minister was arrested because he didn't lead a prayer for the president. An overzealous Illinois marshal arrested nearly forty suspected dissidents, including several judges and a Democratic congressman.

At three thirty a.m. on August 14, 1862, Dennis Mahony, a Peace Democrat and the outspoken editor of the *Dubuque Herald,* was woken by soldiers who had a War Department warrant for his arrest. They dragged him onto a train to Washington and, at a hotel stop along the way, he recorded his destination. "Bound for hell," the editor wrote, "sent there by the devil for speaking the truth." Ten weeks in the rank Old Capitol Prison would pass before he was told the charges. The New York lawyer and diarist George Templeton Strong declared, "Not one of the many hundreds illegally arrested and locked up for months has been publicly charged with any crime. All this is very bad—imbecile, dangerous, unjustifiable."

THE "FIRE IN THE REAR"—NORTHERN DISSENTERS
WANT TO END THE WAR

During the bleak winter of 1862–1863, Lincoln's attention turned away from the battlefields, worried that "the enemy behind us is more dangerous to the country than the enemy before us." Lincoln confessed to Massachusetts Senator Charles Sumner in January 1863 that he feared a "fire in the rear," his phrase for the Northern dissenters to the war. They included Mayor Fernando Wood, New York City's antiwar demagogue who suggested that the city declare its independence and pull out of the war; antiwar societies such as the Knights of the Golden Circle; and Copperheads—Democrats who were lobbying for peace without victory.

The resistance arose as it became clear that the Confederates would not fold easily, and battles such as Antietam had produced a level of carnage that few had imagined possible. Lincoln's signing of the Emancipation Proclamation, which made the war one of emancipation, also led to further political backlash in the West, and in states such as Michigan, Ohio, Iowa, Indiana, and Illinois. Nearly the entire regiment of the Illinois 128th deserted over emancipation, issuing a statement that they would "lie in the woods until moss grew on their backs rather than help free the slaves." The Democratic war dissenters were called Copperheads, which referred, depending on one's point of view, either to the copper pennies they wore on their lapels, showing "Lady Liberty," or to the poisonous snake.

These Copperheads, or Peace Democrats, called for a repeal of the Emancipation Proclamation and an armistice. They maintained the proclamation would bring freed slaves North, where they would take jobs from working-class white men. Politicians at Democratic state conventions spoke angrily against Lincoln's "wicked abolition crusade against the South" and urged others to "*resist* to the *death* all attempts to draft any of our citizens into the army." Democratic newspapers went beyond encouraging resistance; many editorials recommended soldiers desert. "I am sorry," wrote one Midwestern father to his son, "[that] you are engaged in this unholy, unconstitutional and hellish war . . . which has no other purpose but to free the negroes and enslave the whites. Come home. If you have to desert, you will be protected."

OHIO POLITICIAN CLEMENT VALLANDIGHAM IS JAILED FOR SPEAKING AGAINST THE WAR

Much of the dissent in the North came from the Midwest—particularly from the states of Ohio, Illinois, and Indiana. Many Midwesterners came from the South or traded with Southern states up and down the Ohio, Wabash, and Illinois Rivers. Newspaper readers throughout the North became familiar with the names of the dissenters, including Indiana Congressman Daniel Voorhees and Ohio Congressman Alexander Long, and editors such as Dennis Mahony and Samuel Medary. But the most vocal dissenter was a politician, Democratic Congressman Clement L. Vallandigham, of Dayton, Ohio, a handsome and eloquent minister's son.

Vallandigham, forty years old when the war began, opposed it from beginning to end. "I know that I am right," he said in April 1861, "and that in a little while the sober second thought of the people will dissipate the present sudden and fleeting public madness." "Valiant Val," as his friends called him, championed states rights and asserted that the federal government could not interfere with slavery, which he believed was protected by the Constitution.

In 1861, Vallandigham sponsored a series of Congressional resolutions that called for a censure of the president for what the congressman called the "illegal arrests" of dissidents, the suspension of the writ of habeas corpus, the smothering of free press, and the usurpation of Congress's power to declare war and raise troops. In 1862, Vallandigham introduced a measure to imprison Lincoln for what he believed was the president's reckless disregard of the Constitution. Republicans and War Democrats responded by labeling Vallandigham a "friend of Jeff Davis," with one calling him "worse than a Judas." The congressman's grocer, a Republican, called Vallandigham a traitor and refused to provide him credit. When the congressman threatened to beat him up, the grocer pulled out a pistol. The congressman retreated.

But Vallandigham embraced the role of a martyr. Campaigning for reelection in 1862, he referred to himself as "the prophet," and said, "I may die for the cause, but the immortal fire shall outlast the humble organ which conveys it." He narrowly lost reelection, but would battle Lincoln again, igniting a political firestorm that would confront the president in May 1863.

VALLANDIGHAM IS BANISHED TO THE SOUTH—
YET STILL DISSENTS

Early in 1863, Lincoln gave General Ambrose Burnside, demoted after badly bumbling the Fredericksburg battle in December, the job of keeping the West loyal to the Union. He soon proved himself as inept off the battlefield as he had been on it.

On April 13, Burnside issued General Order No. 38. The order promised that anyone committing "treason, expressed or implied" would be arrested and brought in front of a military tribunal. Clement L. Vallandigham, the former congressman from Ohio seeking the Democratic nomination for governor, responded defiantly to the order with a speech that railed against a failed war and argued that the conflict would end only if soldiers deserted and the people decided to "hurl King Lincoln from his throne."

After reading a transcript of the speech, Burnside sent soldiers to the politician's home at two a.m. on May 5. Vallandigham fired a few shots out the window when the soldiers appeared. When he refused to answer the door, the soldiers kicked it in. The officer in charge demanded that "Mr. Vallan*dig*ham"—emphasizing the third syllable of the name—come downstairs.

"My name is not Vallan*dig*ham," the politician corrected. (It's pronounced Velan'-digham.)

"I don't care how you pronounce it," the officer replied. "You are my man." His supporters responded by taking to the streets with torches and attacking the pro-Republican Dayton, Ohio, newspaper, the *Daily Journal*. Burnside dragged Vallandigham before a military commission the next day, but he was not cowed. "I am a Democrat—for the constitution, for law, for the Union, for liberty—this is my only 'crime.'" Vallandigham applied for a writ of habeas corpus to challenge his imprisonment, but a federal court denied it, reminding him, unnecessarily, that Lincoln had suspended the writ. The commission found Vallandigham guilty and sentenced him to prison for the rest of the war.

Lincoln learned of Burnside's actions by reading the morning newspaper. The *New York Atlas*, a partisan Democratic newspaper, pronounced that "the tyranny of military despotism" exhibited in the arrest of Vallandigham demonstrated "the weakness, folly, oppression, mismanagement and general wickedness of the administration at Washington." At a huge rally held in New York City, one speaker declared that if Vallandigham's arrest was allowed to stand, "free speech dies, and with it our liberty, the constitution and our country." Another noted that Vallandigham's critique of Lincoln and the war at hand paled against Lincoln's own critique of President Polk during the Mexican War. Even Lincoln's supporters, such as the *New York Tribune*'s Horace Greeley and George William Curtis, editor of *Harper's Weekly*, expressed displeasure, and in a rare show of unanimity, Lincoln's entire cabinet opposed the arrest of Vallandigham.

The president immediately had to make a decision: Should he support his general or somehow commute the sentence of the popular Ohio politician? As he often did, Lincoln found a third option. He publicly supported Burnside's arrest, but commuted Vallandigham's prison sentence, banning him to the Confederacy for the duration of the war. Vallandigham was placed on a federal gunboat to Louisville, transferred to a train to Nashville, and then escorted beyond the Confederate picket lines under a flag of truce. When a Confederate soldier approached, Vallandigham recited a prepared statement. "I am here within your lines by force and against my will," he said. "I therefore surrender myself to you as a prisoner of war."

On June 12, Lincoln sent a public letter to a group of New York Democrats who had protested the arrest. He said that he was "pained that there should have seemed to be a necessity for arresting" Vallandigham, and said he would free him "as soon as . . . the public safety will not suffer by it." In the letter's most memorable passage, he wrote, "Must I shoot a simple-minded soldier boy who deserts while I must not touch a hair of a wiley agitator who induces him to desert? I think that in such a case to silence the agitator and save the boy is not only constitutional but withal a great mercy."

LINCOLN MUZZLES THE PRESS

In June 1863, the *Chicago Times*, the city's leading Democratic news-paper, wrote a scathing editorial charging the Lincoln administration with replacing the rule of law with military despotism. The charge was made by editor Wilbur Storey, furious over the arrest of war critic Clement Vallandigham. The *Times* criticism was similar to that ex-pressed by many in the brutally frank Northern press, shrill even in peacetime.

Some considered the press's fierce antiwar stance to be treasonous. The *Newark Evening Journal,* responding to Lincoln's call for 500,000 more troops in 1863, wrote: "Those who wish to be butchered will please step forward. All others will please stay at home and defy Old Abe and his minions to drag them from their families." Were these words undermining the draft and the war effort? One judge thought so, and arrested and fined the editor.

During the war, the Lincoln administration closed more than twenty Northern and border newspapers. Between 1861 and 1863, more than thirteen thousand people were arrested, some for spying but many for simply criticizing Lincoln and the war. Secretary of State William Seward, who oversaw domestic security early in the war, once boasted that all he had to do to send a citizen to jail was to ring a bell on his desk. The remark was denounced for its arrogance—and its truth.

In the case of the *Chicago Times*, General Ambrose Burnside retali-ated, shutting it down for two days. Civic leaders asked Lincoln to overturn Burnside's decision, and he did. The *Times* reopened as bel-ligerent as ever, and Storey brought in muskets to protect the offices in case government agents invaded them again.

After the *Times* controversy, Lincoln relaxed restraints on the press. Secretary of War Edwin Stanton told Burnside, "The irritation pro-duced by such acts is likely to do more harm than the publication would do." Lincoln later directed another general, "You will only sup-press newspapers when they may be working palpable injury to the military in your charge. In this you have a discretion to exercise with great caution, calmness, and forbearance."

TO FIGHT THE WAR—OR ABANDON IT?
OHIO'S BELLWETHER MIDTERM ELECTION

War critic Clement L. Vallandigham escaped from his exile in the Confederacy and continued his vitriol against Lincoln from Canada. The Emancipation Proclamation, he charged during his election campaign as the Democrat running for Ohio governor in the fall of 1863, was unconstitutional and abolitionists were traitors. He suggested that the war's purpose was to free blacks and enslave whites. George Pugh, Vallandigham's running mate, suggested that if Vallandigham didn't win the election, Ohioans might want to "sell your goods and chattel and emigrate to some other country, where you can find freedom."

Republicans and War Democrats nominated John Brough, president of the Madison & Indianapolis Railroad, with a platform that backed Lincoln and the war. It was a heated contest: both sides charged the other with treason, and in Dayton, Vallandigham's hometown, a Democrat and a Republican were shot to death because of their political views.

A worried Lincoln gave Ohio troops furloughs and federal clerks fifteen-day leaves to return home to Ohio and vote. Lincoln's fears were for naught. On the night of the election, Salmon Chase, in Cincinnati, telegraphed that Vallandigham's defeat had been "complete, beyond all hopes."

"Glory to God in the highest," Lincoln wired the victorious Brough. "Ohio has saved the nation." The news elsewhere in the midterm election had also been good for the war effort, as most of the wins were for moderate Republicans and War Democrats. Pennsylvanians reelected Governor Andrew Curtin over a Democrat who supported peace and who had earned General George McClellan's support. Iowa, Massachusetts, Maine, and Wisconsin also reelected Republicans, and politicians read the results as a rejection of a negotiated peace. As one bitter Copperhead put it: "The people have voted in favor of the war."

The *Chicago Tribune*, which had so often clawed at the president and his administration, predicted: "Were an election for President to be held tomorrow, Old Abe would, without the special aid of any of his friends, walk over the course, without a competitor to dispute with him the great prize which his masterly ability, no less than his undoubted patriotism and unimpeachable honesty, have won." But the presidential election was a year away, and Lincoln would soon discover that his support was as shaky as the next Union victory.

LINCOLN IS CHASED BY "COPPERHEAD" OPPOSITION

This anti-Lincoln cartoon from 1863 shows the president and African-Americans menaced by giant "Copperheads," Democrats who were opposed to Lincoln and the war.

MORE DISSENT AT HOME— THE RICHMOND FOOD RIOT AND THE NEW YORK CITY DRAFT RIOT

WEEK 28

CORNELIA McDONALD FEARS STARVATION
AND LOSING HER HOME

Throughout the war, Cornelia McDonald feared she would lose her Winchester, Virginia, home. In May 1863, her worries became more intense:

> *I have had so many startling visits, and been so often summoned to surrender the house, and so often intruded upon by rude men, that if I hear a step on the porch my heart palpitates and flutters in a way to frighten me. It is often long before I can quiet its beatings. I am growing thin and emaciated from anxiety and deprivation of proper food and am weak; and now have become faint-hearted. So I fear if they make many more demands I must give up and leave all, for I do not think I can much longer continue the struggle.*

An estimated 200,000 Southerners became refugees, most women and children, pushed from their homes by poverty, hunger, disease, and the Union Army. From the Atlantic Coast, many fled to cities such as Raleigh, North Carolina, and Columbia, South Carolina. By 1862, Richmond's population had doubled, swelled by migrants. In the Deep South, Atlanta became a refuge until it fell to the Union Army in September 1864 and burned to the ground, spilling out more refugees.

Some county and state governments provided relief for soldiers' families, but if they left their homes, relief was hard to find. Some took refuge in churches, tents, and even caves. Some considered crossing into Union-occupied territory, where jobs and food were often more available. When one woman suggested going to Union-occupied New Orleans, her husband replied: "Prepare for a divorce. . . . I will never associate with you again."

FOOD RIOTS ERUPT IN RICHMOND

Bad economic policies, a tightening blockade, and disruptions in the food supply caused by voracious armies and war itself effected food shortages throughout the South. Matters were made worse by Confederate laws, which allowed commissary agents to collect food from farmers to feed Confederate armies. They figured what *they* thought was a fair price, and left the "seller" with IOUs. Half a billion dollars worth of these Confederate IOUs would remain unpaid.

Shortages caused inflation that spread like dry-tinder fires through the South, exacerbated by speculators who sometimes withheld food from the market to make a killing. It cost $6.55 to feed a family for a week before Fort Sumter; in mid-1863, it cost $68.25. Inflation pressed hard on the people of Richmond, which refugees had swollen to several times the city's 1860 population. In the fall of 1863, Richmond civilians paid $70 for a barrel of flour, but by year's end it would cost them $250. "You take your money to the market in the market basket," wrote a South Carolina judge, "and bring home what you buy in your pocketbook."

In the spring of 1863, angry women in Richmond marched on Capitol Square demanding that the government open the doors of its warehouses and sell them food at cost. One leader was Mrs. Jackson, a widow of a butcher in the city, who armed herself with one of her former husband's meat cleavers and a pistol that poked conspicuously from her belt. Many of the women's husbands worked at the Tredegar Iron Works or other Confederate factories, where pay hadn't kept up with inflation.

The women gathered at the monument depicting George Washington on horseback. Then they marched through Richmond's muddy streets, chanting "Bread or blood!" Several eyewitnesses remember one woman raising her emaciated arm and screaming, "We celebrate our right to live! We are starving!" The women broke into stores and government warehouses, taking food, clothing, wagons, shoes, and even jewelry from about a dozen merchants along a ten-block stretch. The rioting crowd of women in Richmond ignored commands from troops to stop, until finally President Davis came out to confront them.

JEFFERSON DAVIS CONFRONTS HUNGRY WOMEN
ON THE STREETS OF RICHMOND

"You say you are hungry and have no money," Confederate President Jefferson Davis told the rioters he faced in Richmond on the morning of April 2, 1863. "Here is all *I* have." He tossed the crowd a handful of change. He urged them to blame the Yankees, "the authors of all our troubles," for their deprivations. Davis then gave them an ultimatum: disperse within five minutes, or troops would open fire. Two minutes, three minutes, four minutes ticked by. Nobody moved. "My friends," he said, "you have one minute left."

The crowd went home. The riot had lasted only two hours, but it unnerved Confederate leaders. The next day, officials rolled cannon into the city's streets and Confederate soldiers stood guard at businesses throughout the city. Richmond created special markets where the "meritorious poor" (those not taking part in the riots) could obtain provisions, including food and fuel, at significantly reduced prices.

As for the rioters, sixty people were arrested, mostly women, a mix of poor and middle-class, young and old. Close to twenty were fined or jailed. Confederate Secretary of War James A. Seddon urged Richmond newspaper editors to keep the event quiet in order not to "embarrass our cause [or] to encourage our enemies." The *Examiner* did provide an account of the riot, but dismissed the rioters as "prostitutes, professional thieves, Irish and Yankee hags, gallows birds. . . ."

In 1863 and 1864, similar food riots occurred elsewhere: in Salisbury and High Point, North Carolina; in Petersburg, Virginia; in Mobile, Alabama; and in Atlanta, Augusta, Columbus, and Macon, Georgia.

Richmond would have no more riots, but prices continued to climb. By September 1863, shoes were $60, wood $40 a cord, butter $4 a pound, and tomatoes $1 each. By October, the *Richmond Examiner* wrote that the city's residents were being reduced to a "point of starvation." One woman asked a shopkeeper charging $70 for a barrel of flour, "How can I pay such prices? I have seven children; what shall I do?"

"I don't know, madam," the merchant reportedly replied, "unless you eat your children."

THE IRISH IN NEW YORK CITY OPPOSE LINCOLN, THE WAR, AND ABOLITION

As the war dragged into its third year, Irish-American New Yorkers, Catholic immigrants, grew angrier at Abraham Lincoln and the war. After the terrible losses suffered by the Irish Brigade in the battle of Fredericksburg in December 1862, they suspected that the Lincoln administration was using them as cannon fodder.

Irish animosity and racism, fueled by the city's Democratic newspapers, grew further after the passage of the Emancipation Proclamation. In their view, liberated slaves would compete with them for jobs and social respectability in American society. They thought they would be "degraded to a level with negroes," as the newspaper *New York's Day-Book* put it.

But nothing would outrage the Irish so much as conscription. On March 3, 1863, Lincoln and the Republican Congress instituted the North's first federal draft. Previously, the Union had relied on states to meet quotas for enlistees. But many enlistments were ending and new recruits had dropped off in the face of war's brutal reality. Blacks were beginning to join the ranks, but they couldn't make up for the overwhelming troop losses caused by death, disease, and desertion. The law also included a clause that allowed draftees to pay $300, nearly the annual salary of an average New York worker, for an exemption from the draft.

Many rich men, including Jay Gould, J. P. Morgan, Andrew Carnegie, and John D. Rockefeller, took advantage of the escape clause. Fathers of Theodore Roosevelt and Franklin Roosevelt hired substitutes. So did two future presidents: Chester Arthur and Grover Cleveland.

The draft law also created a police arm under the secretary of war that allowed the arrest of deserters, spies, and anyone else believed disloyal to the war effort. Democrats in New York were infuriated by the draft, the costly buyout clause, and the crackdown on resistance to the war. On July 4, 1863, as news began to trickle in over the telegraph wires from the battle at Gettysburg, New York Governor Horatio Seymour spoke at a meeting of Democrats at the Academy of Music. "Is it not revolution which [the Administration is] thus creating when you say that our person may be rightfully seized, our property confiscated, our homes entered?" Seymour said. "Remember this that the bloody and treasonable and revolutionary doctrine of public necessity can be proclaimed by a mob as well as by a government." Seymour's speech was incendiary, and what it lit was the most devastating mob violence in American history.

MOBS ATTACK AFRICAN-AMERICANS, THE RICH, AND REPUBLICANS

Draft lottery drawings began in New York City on a Saturday, July 11, 1863. On Monday morning, thousands of workers from the city's railroads, machine shops, shipyards, and foundries marched up Eighth and Ninth Avenues, banging copper pans and carrying NO DRAFT signs. The largely Irish mobs moved downtown in a hunt for guns, brushing aside policemen, militia, and even federal troops. They targeted Republicans and the wealthy, breaking into homes along posh Lexington Avenue and stealing or destroying "pictures with gilt frames, elegant pier glasses, sofas, chairs, clocks, furniture of every kind." Lawyer George Templeton Strong concluded that "the beastly ruffians were masters of the situation and of the city."

Late that afternoon, another crowd took out its wrath on African-Americans, burning down their homes and lynching half a dozen men from lampposts. They attacked the home of Robert Simmons, a black soldier in the Fifty-fourth Massachusetts, and stoned his seven-year-old nephew to death. They also ransacked an orphanage for black children on Fifth Avenue and Forty-fourth Street, screaming "kill the niggers' nest." The 237 children, most of whom were under twelve, escaped out the back door as a young Irishman named Paddy McCafferty shepherded them to the Twentieth Precinct House, bigger children carrying smaller ones on their backs. Mobs torched the orphanage and tenements, hotels, restaurants, dance halls, brothels, bars, and boardinghouses that catered to black workingmen.

By Thursday, six thousand troops, many from the recent Gettysburg battle, were patrolling the streets, crushing the riots. Other, smaller draft riots broke out in Jersey City; Portsmouth, New Hampshire; Blackford County, Indiana; Hartford, Connecticut; and Toledo and Cleveland, Ohio.

In New York, at least a hundred people were killed and five thousand African-Americans lost their homes. The riots would prove to be the largest civil insurrection in the history of the United States except for the Civil War. The riots had one positive result: the bare-knuckled hatred that erupted against African-Americans drew sympathy from white Northerners toward the cause of black freedom where there had before been only indifference, if not hostility.

LINCOLN PERSISTS WITH A NEW YORK CITY DRAFT

Despite the riots, Lincoln moved forward with plans for a New York draft in August. About 10,000 federal troops and the three batteries of artillery were brought from the Virginia front to keep the peace. More important was a compromise that was worked out with Democrat Tammany boss William Tweed. The federal quota of draftees in the city was reduced from 26,000 to 12,000 men. A New York City committee overseen by Boss Tweed allocated $2 million in city funds to pay the $300 exemptions for the city's draft resisters, including many of those who had rioted the previous month. Both sides got what they wanted: Lincoln was able to assert federal authority and establish a draft, and the Democrats reaped the political benefits of protecting their own from conscription.

Overall, few men were drafted, because conscription inspired many to volunteer so they could collect a bounty. This payout sometimes led to what was referred to as "bounty jumping." After the fall of 1863, Union soldiers received a $300 government payment to serve for somebody else. Some slippery enlistees volunteered over and over again. One man substituted for thirty-two draft avoiders before he was caught.

THE NEW YORK CITY
DRAFT RIOTS

Police battle New York City rioters, most of them working-class Irishmen, outside the *New York Tribune,* a newspaper rioters targeted for its antislavery slant.

MORE THAN GLORY—
THE FIFTY-FOURTH
MASSACHUSETTS
VOLUNTEER REGIMENT
IS BORN

WEEK 29

SHOULD WE JOIN? BLACKS QUESTION WHETHER THEY SHOULD FIGHT FOR THE NORTH

After Abraham Lincoln signed the Emancipation Proclamation, Massachusetts Governor John Andrew, a devoted abolitionist, began to recruit one of the country's first regular army units of free blacks: the Fifty-fourth Massachusetts. The effort was begun despite persistent opposition from many Northerners who argued that blacks were too cowardly to join, much less fight; that they would demoralize white soldiers who didn't need help putting down the rebellion; and that their presence would spur greater resistance from the Confederacy.

Many free blacks also had doubts the war was worth their sacrifice as soldiers. "This is a *white* nation," one black activist complained, "white men are the engineers over its . . . destiny; every dollar spent, every drop of blood shed and every life lost, was a *willing* sacrifice for the furtherance and perpetuity of a white nationality." Many free blacks demanded that a Massachusetts law requiring a "whites only" militia be stricken before blacks enlist. "Equality first," argued black abolitionist and author William Wells Brown, "guns afterward."

But George E. Stephens, the thirty-one-year-old black Philadelphia cabinetmaker who would join the Fifty-fourth and write about his experiences in letters to New York's *Anglo-African* newspaper, believed that blacks would tip the balance in the bloody stalemate for the North. "Black Unionists will have to step in at last," he wrote, "and settle the question." Frederick Douglass agreed, recruiting throughout the Northeast for the Fifty-fourth, calling on men to slay "the power that would bury the Government and your liberty in the same hopeless grave."

Once let the black man get upon his person the brass letters, U.S.; let him get an eagle on his button, and a musket on his shoulder and bullets in his pocket, and there is no power on earth which can deny that he has earned the right to citizenship in the United States.

Douglass proved his commitment by signing up his sons Lewis and Charles, the first two New York recruits for the Fifty-fourth. While the call of liberty brought in some enlistees, the notion of revenge brought in others. "They whipped my mother down South; they whipped my sister down South," said one black Pennsylvania recruit. Now he was ready "to go down and whip them."

WOULD A BOSTON PARADE BY THE FIFTY-FOURTH MASSACHUSETTS INCITE A RIOT?

To the question—Would they fight?—free black men responded by signing up all over the North in the first months of 1863, filling up the ranks of the first black regiment, the Fifty-fourth Massachusetts. Robert Gould Shaw, the well-connected white officer chosen to lead the regiment, at first doubted the abilities of the black soldiers, but soon his men changed his mind, and he wrote to his future wife, Annie, that the "men are very satisfactory. . . . [and] will be more soldierly" than most volunteers. On May 28, 1863, they were to parade through Boston before they shipped off to South Carolina.

When presenting flags to the regiment ten days earlier, Massachusetts Governor John Andrew, an abolitionist, told the men, "I know not . . . when, in all human history to any given thousand men in arms there has been committed a work at once so proud, so precious, so full of hope and glory as the work committed to you."

But Governor Andrew and others feared a parade would incite a race riot, especially among the Irish, who were threatened by black equality. Officers for the Fifty-fourth heard that "the roughs in Boston proposed to attack us as we pass through" the city. In case of violence, Andrew provided the soldiers with "six rounds of ball cartridges," and the rear guard of the regiment was ordered to march with fixed bayonets.

The parade day was warm and cloudless. Patrick Gilmore's marching band blared out "John Brown's Body." About twenty thousand Bostonians came to see the regiment, some purchasing a remembrance for the day that included a line written by Lord Byron, "Those who would be free, themselves must strike the blow." Family members broke into the ranks of soldiers to kiss their men, and one observer noted that even Irish women waved their handkerchiefs. At one point, some men did attack the rear of the column but police stopped them before a fight could break out. One reporter, watching the African-Americans marching behind the Union flag, wrote, "Can we believe our own eyes and ears? Is this Boston? Is it America?"

BLACK SOLDIERS GIVEN HALF PAY
AND FEW PROMOTIONS

George E. Stephens, the African-American correspondent during the war, had proudly signed up for the Fifty-fourth Massachusetts and was impressed with the bearing of his commander, Robert Gould Shaw, and the respect he showed the men. But two issues dampened his enthusiasm: the lack of promotion opportunities and less pay for blacks.

Black soldiers expected equal pay, but the War Department determined that the 1862 Militia Act requiring "contraband" laborers be paid $10 a month also applied to soldiers. Blacks were further insulted when they were charged a $3 monthly fee for clothing, bringing their pay down to $7. White soldiers were paid at least $13—more for officers. That meant that the lowest-paid white soldier received almost twice as much as the highest-paid black one.

The issue wasn't just pay; it was justice. "Because I am black," stated Stephens, "they tamper with my rights."

The pay disparity and the lack of promotions for blacks were two issues abolitionist Frederick Douglass took up during his first meeting with the president in August 1863. Douglass also urged Lincoln to authorize Northern officers to kill Confederate prisoners in retaliation for the murder of black prisoners.

[Lincoln] began by saying that the employment of colored troops at all was a great gain to the colored people . . . that the wisdom of making colored men soldiers was still doubted . . . that the fact that they were not to receive the same pay as white soldiers seemed a necessary concession to smooth the way to their employment at all as soldiers, but that ultimately they would receive the same.

Lincoln told Douglass that he would "sign any commission to colored soldiers whom his Secretary of War should commend to him." (Only 130 or so black soldiers would be commissioned as officers during the entire war.) As far as retaliating against Confederate soldiers for the execution of black ones, Lincoln told him that "if once begun, there was no telling where it would end . . . [and] the thought of hanging men for a crime perpetrated by others was revolting to his feelings. . . . In all this I saw the tender heart of the man rather than the stern warrior and commander-in-chief of the American army and navy, and, while I could not agree with him, I could but respect his humane spirit."

GLORY—A DOOMED ASSAULT IN CHARLESTON HARBOR

Of all the cities the Union Army wanted to take in 1863, none had more symbolic import than Charleston, South Carolina, the cradle of the Confederacy. On July 11, Union forces attacked Fort Wagner on Morris Island, which protected the southern approach to Charleston Harbor, but failed miserably: 330 Union soldiers were killed or wounded, compared to only 12 Confederates.

Afterward, commanding officer Quincy A. Gillmore asked Colonel Robert Gould Shaw, of the Fifty-fourth Massachusetts, if he wanted to lead a second assault on July 18. Shaw, who'd been married for just over two months, said yes. "If I could only live a few weeks longer with my wife," he told a fellow officer, "and be at home a little while, I might die happy, but it cannot be. I do not believe I will live through our next fight."

Before the attack, Shaw reminded the men that the entire world would know how they fared. He then led them out across six hundred yards of beach. After four hundred yards, the Confederate batteries blew flesh-tearing iron and lead balls at them.

A Union soldier wrote that "our men fell like grass before a sickle." Shaw somehow made it to the top of the parapet and then was shot dead. In just two hours, the Confederates lost 174 men, while the Union lost 1,515. Almost one in two men in the Fifty-fourth had been killed, wounded, or captured. The attack had been a military disaster, but the news soon spread: the black soldiers had fought, and fought fiercely.

"[N]ot a man flinched, though it was a trying time," one of the soldiers wrote to his fiancée after the battle. ". . . A shell would explode and clear a space of twenty feet, our men would close up again, but it was no use we had to retreat. . . . How I got out of that fight alive I can not tell, but I am here. My Dear girl I hope again to see you. . . . Remember if I die I die in a good cause. I wish we had a hundred thousand colored troops we would put an end to this war."

The letter was signed by Sergeant Major Lewis Douglass, Frederick Douglass's oldest son.

BRAVERY, SACRIFICE, AND RESPECT—
THE EFFECTS OF FORT WAGNER

While the Fifty-fourth Massachusetts was being recruited, many white officers refused to join for fear it would damage their careers. But after the assault at Fort Wagner, Colonel Robert Gould Shaw, the regiment's leader, was hailed as a martyr throughout the North. In a letter to Shaw's father, the Boston abolitionist Edward Pierce wrote, "With the opening of the war, your son gave himself to his country, and he has now laid down his life for a race." Abolitionist William Lloyd Garrison called Shaw "the martyred hero of the downtrodden of our land."

When Union soldiers asked for the body of Colonel Robert Gould Shaw after the battle at Fort Wagner, they were reputedly told by the Confederates, "We have buried him with his niggers." Some in Boston started to agitate that Shaw be exhumed from the mass grave and his body returned, but Shaw's father stopped them, saying there was "no holier place" than the grave where his son was buried.

The racial landscape in the North shifted. What Bunker Hill was to white Americans, the *New York Tribune* wrote, Fort Wagner would be to black Americans. White soldiers who once resisted serving with black soldiers now praised their courage. One sergeant wrote that the Fifty-fourth had been "the last to leave the Field" and another eyewitness wrote that "had it not been for the glorious Fifty-fourth Massachusetts, the whole brigade would have been captured or annihilated." The *Boston Commonwealth* quoted a Union soldier at Fort Wagner as saying, "We don't know any black men here, they're all soldiers." The Massachusetts Adjutant General's Office declared that after the battle opposition to black troops dissipated and that "many of their fiercest enemies have become their fastest friends."

By the end of 1863, sixty more black regiments had formed, and unlike the black men brought into the army in the first two years of the war, their job was not to dig ditches, cook meals, or move equipment. Now it was understood: They were there to fight.

DESPITE GLORY, THE MEN STILL MUST FIGHT
FOR FULL WAGES

Their ordeal at Fort Wagner in Charleston Harbor had earned the Fifty-fourth Massachusetts respect and even glory, but not the white soldiers' pay. As a protest, the Fifty-fourth and other black regiments refused to take their lesser pay. On September 30, 1863, two months after the Fort Wagner assault, the U.S. paymaster visited the Fifty-fourth and suggested that the men accept the $7 under protest, which would at least give the men money to send home to their families. They refused.

Without any earnings from their husbands, sons, and fathers, the families of the Fifty-fourth suffered. In the winter of 1863, a friend of soldier George Stephens found his family in Philadelphia—including his wife, Susan, his mother-in-law, and his three stepchildren—destitute. One soldier in the Fifty-fourth received a letter from his wife begging him to send fifty cents home.

Men in the Fifty-fourth discussed refusing to fight until they received their full pay; in February 1864, other soldiers took that very step. Sergeant William Walker of the Third South Carolina Volunteers, an African-American regiment, told his men to abandon their arms in front of a colonel's tent as a protest against the half-pay. Though he was warned he would be shot for mutiny, Walker refused to back down. On February 29, 1864, he was stood in front of the regiment and executed by a firing squad.

Massachusetts Governor John Andrew, disgusted, became convinced the federal government was committed to making black soldiers "in the eyes of all men 'only a nigger.'" Failing to convince the Union to provide his men equal pay, Andrew and others succeeded in getting Massachusetts to pay the men the differential. Once again, the men refused to take the money, unwilling, as one abolitionist editor put it, "that the Federal Government should throw mud upon them, even though Massachusetts stands ready to wipe it off."

Finally, pressure from abolitionist congressmen and the courage the black soldiers had shown in combat convinced the Congress. At the end of September 1864, nearly a year and a half after they had enlisted, the men of the Fifty-fourth finally received their full pay retroactive to their enlistment. It was a day of jubilation, and soldier after soldier sent money home, relieved to be respected at last.

BLACK SOLDIERS OF THE FIFTY-FOURTH
MASSACHUSETTS STORM FORT WAGNER

The black soldiers of the Fifty-fourth Massachusetts storm Fort Wagner
in Charleston Harbor. While the assault failed to take the fort, Northerners
gained a newfound respect for the regiment—and all black soldiers—
because of the valor they showed in the fight.

THE VICKSBURG CAMPAIGN

WEEK 30

"THE SPINAL COLUMN OF AMERICA"—NORTH AND SOUTH FIGHT FOR THE MISSISSIPPI RIVER

The transportation network that dominated America before railroads was the Mississippi River and its tributaries. Journalist Lloyd Lewis called the Mississippi of the nineteenth century the "spinal column of America . . . the trunk of the American tree, with limbs and branches reaching to the Alleghenies, the Canadian border, the Rocky Mountains." As the nation grew, the Mississippi, which ran through over a million square miles, brought the nation's rich Midwestern harvest to the world, and brought the world's products on flatboats and steamers to the country's fast-developing interior—North and South.

Once Louisiana and Mississippi seceded, they had the power to sever all commerce between non-coastal Northern states and the world. Discussing military strategy with his top leaders, around a map of the nation, Lincoln stressed the importance of the river and Vicksburg in particular. "I am acquainted with that region and know what I am talking about," he told the men, "and, as valuable as New Orleans will be to us, Vicksburg will be more so. . . . We can take all the northern ports of the Confederacy, and they can still defy us from Vicksburg. It means hog and hominy without limit, fresh troops from the States of the far South, and a cotton country where they can raise the staple without interference. . . . See what a lot of land these fellows hold, of which Vicksburg is the key. The war can never be brought to a close until the key is in our pocket."

Confederate President Jefferson Davis called Vicksburg the "nailhead that held the South's two halves together" because through it flowed supplies, soldiers, and food from Texas, Arkansas, and western Louisiana to the eastern states of the Confederacy.

In 1862, the Union Army and Navy would push up the river from New Orleans and down the river from Cairo, Illinois, in a pincer movement meant to take riverside Confederate forts and gain control of the Mississippi. "To secure the safety of the navigation of the Mississippi River I would slay millions," said William Tecumseh Sherman, one of the commanders involved in this campaign. "On that point I am not only insane, but mad."

"MISSISSIPPIANS DON'T KNOW . . . HOW TO SURRENDER"—FAILED ATTEMPTS TO TAKE VICKSBURG

By the end of June 1862, only one fortress remained on the Mississippi: Vicksburg, Mississippi.

The first threat to Vicksburg came from the ocean fleet led by David G. Farragut, the gutsy sixty-year-old commander of the blockading Union fleet in the Gulf. In May, his seagoing ships chugged upriver and anchored below the bluffs at Vicksburg. Farragut called for the city to surrender. "Mississippians don't know, and refuse to learn, how to surrender," retorted Vicksburg's military commander ". . . If Commodore Farragut . . . can teach them, let [him] come and try."

Farragut bombarded what became known as the "Gibraltar of the Confederacy" with his warships, but he finally concluded that he could only take the guns on the bluffs if he had a ground invasion to complement a river attack. Then, during a summer drought, the Mississippi dropped, and Farragut ran his ships back downriver to New Orleans to avoid a mass grounding. One Vicksburg resident, watching the fleet depart, gloated: "What will they say [in the] North now about opening the Mississippi River; huzzah for Vicksburg." The Mississippi, from Vicksburg to Port Hudson, Louisiana, a stretch of 250 miles, was again controlled by the Confederacy.

In October 1862, Lincoln gave General Ulysses S. Grant, commanding the Army of Tennessee, the task of taking Vicksburg by land. In December, Grant sent his friend William Tecumseh Sherman and his men to take Chickasaw Bayou, five miles northeast of Vicksburg. But Sherman lost seventeen hundred men to the Confederates' two hundred. "I reached Vicksburg at the time appointed," wrote Sherman in his report, "landed, assaulted, and failed."

During the winter of 1862–1863, Grant tried "experiments" to find an alternative approach to Vicksburg, including building a canal to get south of the city and finding a way through wetlands to the north, but all failed. Worse yet, his troops were devastated by pneumonia, malaria, dysentery, and other diseases. Many Northerners pilloried the general for foundering in the swamps around Vicksburg through the entire winter. Rumors started again about his drinking, and a Congressional party came to Lincoln asking for Grant's dismissal. He refused. "I can't spare this man," Lincoln said, "he fights."

WAS GRANT A DRUNKARD? AND DID LINCOLN CARE?

During the early months of 1863, with Grant's army bogged down around Vicksburg, newspaper editors and congressmen began to talk about Grant as an incompetent—and repeated rumors about his drinking. Were they true? Historians such as Kenneth P. Williams have refuted or at least questioned whether Grant had a drinking problem. Others, such as Benjamin Thomas, William McFeely, and Shelby Foote, have accepted the rumors as true. The only detailed account of a Grant drinking binge was written by Sylvanus Cadwallader, a Chicago newspaper correspondent who spent two years with Grant's army. But he wrote his account three decades after the war, and the account is suspect, as he probably wasn't with Grant when he said the drinking occurred. Civil War writer Bruce Catton, who originally gave credence to the drinking stories about Grant, concluded that Cadwallader's story was "but one more in the dreary Grant-was-drunk garland of myths."

In March 1863, the president allowed Secretary of War Edwin Stanton to investigate whether Grant had a drinking problem. To find out, Stanton sent Charles A. Dana, a former editor at the *New York Tribune*, under the pretext that he was checking on contracting issues, but Grant was aware of his real purpose. Grant welcomed him, and Dana sent back only favorable dispatches to Washington (although he wrote much later that he saw Grant in a drunken stupor one night). Dana called the general "thoughtful, deep and gifted with courage that never faulted" and "the most modest, the most disinterested and the most honest man I ever knew, with a temper that nothing could disturb."

Despite continued rumors, Lincoln refused to give up on Grant. "I think Grant has hardly a friend left, except myself," said the president. But "what I want . . . is generals who will fight battles and win victories. Grant has done this, and I propose to stand by him." Another story—perhaps apocryphal—describes Lincoln's reply to a delegation of officials who demanded that Grant be relieved. He said if he could find the brand of whiskey Grant drank, he would send a barrel to each of his generals.

"I WAS NOW IN THE ENEMY'S COUNTRY"—GRANT CROSSES THE MISSISSIPPI TO GET AT VICKSBURG

After Grant's failed water approaches to Vicksburg, in March 1863 the general resolved to march his men south through Louisiana on the west side of the river, ferry them across the Mississippi below Vicksburg, and then come north and storm the city by land.

It was a bold plan, as Union boats would have to run the gauntlet past the formidable artillery at Vicksburg to transport troops across the river south of the city. Once he crossed the river, he would have much more difficulty getting supplies and reinforcements. Retreat would be difficult, and destruction of his army a real possibility. Almost everyone, including Lincoln, advised against it. Grant later wrote that William Tecumseh Sherman, one of the generals involved in the campaign, warned "that I was putting myself in a position voluntarily which an enemy would be glad to maneuver a year—or a long time—to get me."

But Grant marched ahead anyway. As Union vessels steamed past Vicksburg, Sherman had oarsmen pull rowboats into the Mississippi south of the city to pick up survivors of destroyed boats. The fleet might have been destroyed, if not for a ball many of the Vicksburg artillerymen attended that night, letting precious minutes—and many Union boats—pass before they would return to their guns. Then David Dixon Porter, the man charged with moving the ships downriver, noticed that the guns firing at him from Vicksburg were angled to shoot too high. Porter responded by moving the ships closer to the Vicksburg shoreline to sail underneath the cannon fire. Many vessels were hit, but all survived and only twelve sailors were wounded.

At Bruinsburg, Union soldiers were ferried to the eastern shore of the Mississippi. "I felt a degree of relief scarcely ever equaled since," Grant wrote in his memoir. "I was now in the enemy's country, with a river and the stronghold of Vicksburg between me and my base of supplies. But I was on dry ground on the same side of the river with my enemy."

THE VICKSBURG CAMPAIGN—
GRANT OUTGENERALS PEMBERTON

Once Grant's army crossed the Mississippi River, he was forced to bring nearly everything his army needed. Soldiers carried ammunition boxes, and supplies were transported by carriages, buggies, and sturdy farm wagons pulled by a ragtag herd of mules and horses. Men stuffed their knapsacks and pockets with rations and sixty rounds of ammunition. They speared hunks of meat to their bayonets. The moving army would also "requisition" beef, poultry, and pork—take it, that is—from the numerous barns and smokehouses in its path.

Instead of moving directly at Vicksburg, a route that had a number of natural defenses that could stall his forces, Grant's men marched more than two hundred miles in what is sometimes called the blitzkrieg of the Vicksburg Campaign. He marched northeast along the Big Black River and then back toward Vicksburg in seventeen days, winning battles at Port Gibson, Raymond, Jackson, Champion Hill, and Big Black River Bridge, outgeneraling the Confederates and preventing Generals John Pemberton and Joseph E. Johnston from combining their forces. Grant's casualties numbered 4,300, compared to 7,200 for the Confederates. The beaten Rebels, under Pemberton, limped back into Vicksburg.

"I shall never forget the woeful sight," wrote one Vicksburg woman on May 17. "Wan, hollow-eyed, ragged, footsore, bloody, the men limped along unarmed . . . humanity in the last throes of endurance." General Joseph E. Johnston, whose army lay to the east of Vicksburg, urged Pemberton that "instead of losing both troops and place, we must, if possible, save the troops." Pemberton polled his senior officers about whether to stay in Vicksburg or abandon the city. They agreed that it would be "impossible to withdraw the army from this position with such *morale* as to be of further service to the Confederacy."

Grant's fifty thousand troops had trapped Pemberton's thirty thousand troops against the Mississippi. So began the first and only true siege of a major American city. "What is to become of all the living things in this place . . . shut up as in a trap," wrote Emma Balfour, wife of a prominent Vicksburg physician, "God only knows."

"THE APPROACHES . . . WERE FRIGHTFUL"—
VICKSBURG'S FORMIDABLE DEFENSES

Vicksburg was well protected from an attack by land. On the interior bluffs were mounted 115 cannon. The earthen walls in front of the dugout trenches were as thick as thirty feet. There were two rings of ditches, and ditches that connected the ring, leaving an elaborate spiderweb of trenches with Vicksburg at the center. The city boasted probably the most formidable breastworks of the war.

The bluffs around the edge of the city fell off into deep ravines that complicated the approach of an attacking army. The Confederates had also chopped down hundreds, perhaps thousands, of trees on the approaches to the bluffs to make it easy to spot attacking soldiers. They also built a sprawling abatis, a nineteenth-century fortification that consisted of felling trees toward the potential approaches of an attacking army. The branches of the trees were cut and then sharpened, and some of the branches were strung with telegraph wire—all to slow and tangle up potential attackers. "The approaches to this position were frightful," observed one of General Grant's officers. But the truth was that Pemberton's men were also trapped.

Meanwhile, President Jefferson Davis searched for ways to pull away Grant and his army from a besieged Vicksburg, and the man he thought could do it was Robert E. Lee.

ADMIRAL PORTER'S FLEET RUNS PAST REBEL GUNS AT VICKSBURG

Admiral David D. Porter's river flotilla, including low-draft ironclads, run past Vicksburg on the Mississippi River on April 16, 1863, to get to Union troops and transport them across the Mississippi River.

THE SIEGE OF
VICKSBURG

WEEK 31

LEE'S GAMBIT TO PULL GRANT AWAY FROM VICKSBURG BY INVADING THE NORTH

What could the Confederates do to save the besieged Vicksburg? Confederate President Jefferson Davis suggested sending General James Longstreet's army to take on General Grant. But Robert E. Lee dismissed that strategy, concluding, "It becomes a question between Virginia and Mississippi."

At a strategy meeting in Richmond on May 15, 1863, Lee laid out a far bolder plan. He wanted to take his Army of Northern Virginia, Longstreet included, on a daring dash North, into Pennsylvania. An attack into the Northern states would relieve the pressure on the South, especially Virginia, now war-spent, and supply his army with the harvests of Pennsylvania's lush fields and farms. Grant might also be forced to come North to repel the invasion, relieving pressure on Vicksburg. If Lee was successful, an invading Confederate Army would march through Philadelphia, and even into Washington, where they would send President Lincoln and his cabinet fleeing.

"If we can battle them in their various designs this year, next year there will be a great change in public opinion in the North," Lee wrote his wife in April 1863. "The Republicans will be destroyed & I think the friends of peace will become so strong as that the next administration will go in on that basis. We have only therefore to resist manfully . . . [and] our success will be certain." Lee believed such success might also lead to support from England and France.

Lee's grandest dream was the final annihilation of the Union Army. Once the Army of the Potomac was located, a subordinate remembers Lee saying, "I shall throw an overwhelming force on their advance, crush it, follow up the success, drive one corps back on another, and by successive repulses and surprises create a panic and virtually destroy the army. [Then] the war will be over and we shall achieve the recognition of our independence."

Southern leaders were largely persuaded by Lee, "whose fame," noted one Confederate cabinet member, "now filled the world." They believed that Lee's victories in places such as Chancellorsville and Fredericksburg were prelude to a glorious victory. "There never were such men in an army before," said Lee proudly. "They will go anywhere and do anything if properly led."

GRANT COMES AT VICKSBURG FROM THE EAST

On May 18, 1863, the Union Army cautiously approached Vicksburg from the east. General William Tecumseh Sherman looked at the field of Chickasaw Bayou, where his men had been defeated in December 1862, and told his friend Ulysses S. Grant, "Until this moment I never thought your expedition a success. I never could see the end clearly till now. But this is a campaign; this is a success if we never take the town." But Grant did intend to take Vicksburg, and the Rebels braced for an attack. On the evening of May 18, William Foster, a chaplain in the Thirty-fifth Mississippi Infantry, described his dread:

> *None but those who have had the experience can tell the feeling of the soldier's heart on the night before the approaching battle—when upon the wings of fond imagination his soul visits the loved ones at home—and while he thinks of a lonely & loving wife whose face he may never look upon again & who may never see his form any more on earth, his heart bleeds & dark forebodings fill his mind. Then when he lies down upon the cold ground & looks up to the shining stars above, the gloomy thought crosses his mind, that it may be the last time he will ever look upon the shining heavens & that those same stars which now look down so quiet upon him, may behold him on the morrow night a lifeless, mangled corpse.*

The Confederates had built fortifications on the bluffs around the outskirts of the city, crowning them with eighty-nine artillery positions that included two hundred twenty guns. On May 19 and 22, the Union troops hurled themselves at Vicksburg's defenses, losing over three thousand men, compared to less than five hundred for the Confederates. The Gibraltar on the Mississippi had held off a land-based attack as it had held off earlier attacks from the river. Grant decided to "outcamp" the Confederates. The explosive violence of battle now gave way to the gradual suffering of a siege.

"CUT OFF FROM THE WORLD"—VICKSBURG STRANGLES DURING THE SIEGE

As Grant's troops settled along the perimeter of Vicksburg, one Confederate soldier said the city was so thoroughly surrounded that "a cat could not have crept out . . . without being discovered." The Confederates were ordered to hold their fire to conserve ammunition. But for forty-seven days, more than two hundred guns from Grant's army and Union gunboats on the Mississippi shelled Vicksburg every day and night. The only times the Confederates seemed to get respite was at eight a.m., noon, and eight p.m., when the Union artillerymen took a break to eat. A Vicksburg woman wrote in her journal:

> *June 25. A horrible day. We were all in the cellar when a shell came tearing through the roof, burst up-stairs, tore up that room and the pieces coming through both floors down into the cellar, tore open the leg of [my husband's pants]. On the heels of these came Mr. J. to tell us that young Mrs. P. had her thighbone crushed. When Martha went for milk, she came back horror-stricken to tell us that the black girl had her arm taken of by a shell. For the first time I quailed.*

To protect themselves, Vicksburg civilians hired blacks to build hundreds of caves in the soft loam and then dragged rugs, beds, and chairs into their underground abodes. Caves were soon bought and sold, those considered safest fetching the highest prices. Union troops began referring to Vicksburg as a "prairie dog village," but the caves worked: fewer than twenty civilians were killed during the siege.

Safety outside the caves was hard to find. During one intense bombing, Margaret Lord, the wife of the rector at Christ Church, comforted her daughter Lida as the family huddled in the church's basement. "Don't cry my darling," she told her daughter, "God will protect us."

"But Momma," said Lida, "I's so 'fraid God's killed too."

GENERAL JOSEPH E. JOHNSTON WILL NOT COME— VICKSBURG IS ALONE

As the weeks progressed from May through June, the rations of the Vicksburg soldiers were reduced to three-quarters, to half, and then to a quarter. When the coffee ran out, the Confederates used a substitute made from sweet potatoes, blackberry leaves, and sassafras. When flour was gone, ground peas and cornmeal replaced it, a "nauseous composition," according to one soldier, with "the properties of India-rubber" and "worse than leather to digest." At the end of June, skinned rats began appearing for sale on the street, and on the last few days of the siege, the army distributed mule meat.

Water was also rationed, and dysentery, malaria, and diarrhea began to thin the ranks of the trapped Confederate Army. The only hope was that Confederate General Joseph E. Johnston would march his men to the city from the east and attack Union General Ulysses S. Grant's army from the rear. Confederate Secretary of War James A. Seddon counseled Johnston to do so, arguing that "the eyes and hopes of the whole Confederacy are upon you, with the full confidence that you will act, and with the sentiment that it is better to fail nobly daring, than, through prudence even, to be inactive."

The local Vicksburg newspaper, reduced to printing on wallpaper, went from declaring "Johnston Is Coming!" to asking "Where Is Johnston?" General John C. Pemberton, commanding the troops at Vicksburg, asked Johnston, "What aid am I to expect from you?" Johnston would only complain about his lack of men, horses, and weapons, and replied bluntly: "I am too weak to save Vicksburg." On June 15, Johnston cabled Confederate leaders in Richmond with an unambiguous message: "I consider saving Vicksburg hopeless." Pemberton came to the slow realization that his men and Vicksburg would soon succumb to a "new general," as one soldier put it: "General Starvation."

VICKSBURG SURRENDERS ON THE FOURTH OF JULY

On June 28, 1863, Confederate General John Pemberton received a letter signed anonymously by "Many Soldiers." It asked him to supply his men with "one small biscuit and one or two mouthfuls of bacon per day," concluding thus: "If you can't feed us, you had better surrender, horrible as the idea is, than suffer this noble army to disgrace themselves by desertion. . . . This army is now ripe for mutiny, unless it can be fed." The general considered a suicidal breakout from the city, the "only hope of saving myself from shame and disgrace." He decided instead "to sacrifice myself to save the army which has so nobly done its duty to defend Vicksburg."

A week later, on the morning of July 4, the same day that General Robert E. Lee began his retreat from Gettysburg, General Pemberton surrendered Vicksburg to General Grant. Fourteen months had passed since Farragut's fleet had first attacked Vicksburg. "I am a northern man," Pemberton said. "I know my people. I know we can get better terms on the fourth of July than on any other day of the year." On that day, 29,500 Confederate troops, many emaciated, raised white flags, stepped out of their trenches, laid down their rifles, and handed over their cartridge boxes and flags. It would be the largest number of soldiers surrendered on any day in American history. The Confederacy would also lose a weapons cache that it could not replace: 172 pieces of artillery, 38,000 artillery projectiles, 58,000 pounds of black powder, 50,000 firearms, and 600,000 rounds of ammunition.

Upon entering Vicksburg, the Union troops did what the residents of Vicksburg had wanted to do for weeks—break into the stores of speculators to distribute food and other essentials. A Louisiana sergeant wrote that Northern troops would shout, " 'Here rebs, help yourselves, you are naked and starving and need them.' What a strange spectacle of war between those who were recently deadly foes."

WAS VICKSBURG THE MOST IMPORTANT
VICTORY OF THE WAR?

The campaign to take Vicksburg was as long as any in the Civil War, and included an assortment of military operations, including attacks by riverboats and oceangoing vessels, the attempted dredging of a canal, cavalry raids, diversionary thrusts, and, finally, a siege. By taking the "Fortress on the Hill," the federal troops had achieved their aim of controlling the Mississippi River from one end to the other. Two weeks after the surrender at Vicksburg, a merchant steamship named *Imperial* would finish the twelve-hundred-mile passage from St. Louis to New Orleans undisturbed. "Thank God," Lincoln wrote. "The Father of Waters again goes unvexed to the sea."

The Confederacy was now divided in two, its eastern half severed from the supplies of its western lands. Combined with the blockade along the Atlantic and the Gulf, war supplies would now only trickle into the Confederacy, which meant the Anaconda Plan envisioned by old Union General Winfield Scott at the beginning of the war was finally realized.

Almost overnight, Grant's reputation changed from ineffectual drunkard to war hero. After Grant's victory at Chattanooga, Lincoln promoted him to commander of the entire U.S. Army. "Grant is my man," Lincoln said on July 5, "and I am his the rest of the war." In Grant's wake rose General William Sherman, who succeeded Grant as commander of the Army of Tennessee.

Southerners sensed the sudden reversal of fortunes. "Events have succeeded one another with disastrous rapidity," Confederate ordnance chief Josiah Gorgas wrote in his diary at the end of July. "One brief month ago we were apparently at the point of success. Lee was in Pennsylvania, threatening Harrisburg, and even Philadelphia. Vicksburg seemed to laugh all Grant's efforts to scorn. . . . It seems incredible that human power could effect such a change in so brief a space. Yesterday we rode on the pinnacle of success—today absolute ruin seems to be our portion. The Confederacy totters to its destruction."

UNION TROOPS LAY SIEGE TO VICKSBURG

Union General Ulysses S. Grant decided to lay siege to Vicksburg after he discovered the "City on the Hill" was too well-defended for a direct assault.

STUMBLING INTO BATTLE—
GETTYSBURG UNFOLDS
AS ANOTHER
CONFEDERATE VICTORY

WEEK 32

ROBERT E. LEE INVADES THE NORTH AGAIN

In the second week of June, Robert E. Lee moved his Army of Northern Virginia into Pennsylvania through the Shenandoah Valley, using the Blue Ridge Mountains to his east as cover against the Union Army. Before his army, refugees fled eastward, clouds of dust rising as white and especially free African-American Pennsylvanians took to the road. In Harrisburg, families swarmed onto departing trains "with trunks, boxes, bundles; packages tied up in bed-blankets and quilts; mountains of baggage" and were "rushing here and there in a frantic manner; shouting, screaming, as if the Rebels were about to dash into the town and lay it in ashes."

Lee had never adhered to William Tecumseh Sherman's notion of all-out war, and forbade arson, yet his army did take available food from homes and farms. "My friends," asked one Confederate officer addressing a crowd gathered at the town square in York, Pennsylvania, "how do you like *this* way of coming back into the Union?"

Many of the African-Americans in front of the rolling Confederate Army—including many of the 190 of those who lived in a town called Gettysburg—fled, and they had good cause. Those who were caught— whether long-free African-Americans or escaped slaves—were transported South and sold into slavery.

Panic swept east to Washington, DC, and Union General Abner Doubleday said, "People began to feel that the boast of Senator Robert Toombs of Georgia, that he would [one day] call the roll of his slaves at the foot of Bunker Hill Monument, might soon be realized."

DID LEE APPROVE OR DISAPPROVE OF SLAVERY?

Robert E. Lee has often been portrayed as a tragic hero of the Civil War, a general leading the Confederacy's defense of slavery, although he didn't support the institution. Those who make this case often quote a letter he wrote to his wife, Mary, in 1856, in which he calls slavery "a moral & political evil in any country." They also cite Lee's testimony to Congress after the war, in which he asserted, "I have always been in favor of emancipation—gradual emancipation."

But Elizabeth Brown Pryor, in her biography of Lee, *Reading the Man*, argues that his attitudes about slavery were typical of Virginia's aristocracy and consistent throughout his life. He believed slavery was an "unfortunate historical legacy," writes Pryor, and also believed Southerners had the right to have slaves in the territories—the issue that triggered the war. In that same 1856 letter, Lee writes that "blacks are immeasurably better off here than in Africa, morally, socially & physically. . . . How long their subjugation may be necessary is known & ordered by a wise and Merciful Providence." Pryor writes: "Lee may have hated slavery, but it was not because of any ethical dilemma. What Lee disliked about slavery was its inefficiency, the messiness of its relationships, the responsibility it entailed, and the taint of it."

Lee owned slaves at least until 1852 and used slaves as servants while in the Confederate Army. He offered financial rewards for the return of his escaped slaves, and one of them, Wesley Norris, accused Lee of encouraging a constable to "lay it on well" when the captured Norris was whipped. Lee also sold away many slaves from his estate, despite the pain the separation inevitably caused.

As the war came to a close in January 1865, a Virginia politician asked Lee whether African-Americans should serve in the Confederate Army. Lee said they should serve and eventually gain their freedom, but he also declared that "the relation of master and slave [is] the best that can exist between the white and black races while intermingled as at present in this country."

JEB STUART WANDERS OFF—AND LEE IS LEFT BLIND

On June 5, 1863, Jeb Stuart's cavalry, ten thousand strong, staged one of the most impressive reviews in cavalry history. Special trains on the Orange & Alexandria line brought in spectators, mostly women. Trumpeters heralded Stuart's arrival. As always, he wore the uniform of the dashing cavalier—knee-high boots, gauntlets that rode up to his elbows, and a red-lined cape with a yellow sash, topped with a felt hat from which rose his signature ostrich-feather plume. Women threw flowers as cavalrymen drew their sabers in a staged charge.

A few days later, however, Yankee cavalry, led by Major General Alfred Pleasonton, "came near surprising us in bed," wrote a Rebel artillerist. Before the day was over, federal troops got behind Stuart's men at Brandy Station, leading one officer to comment that it was the first time in fourteen months "that [Stuart] seemed *rattled.*"

After the largest cavalry battle of the Civil War, Pleasonton's cavalry retreated back over the Rappahannock River. Stuart, as usual, claimed victory, congratulating his cavalry on a "glorious day." Yet the *Richmond Examiner* spoke of the "puffed up cavalry" of the Army of Northern Virginia.

Perhaps wishing to reshine his image, Stuart suggested a circling of the Union Army, which he had done during McClellan's Peninsula Campaign and again after Sharpsburg. These showboat maneuvers had won him adulation from both generals and the public.

Lee gave his permission for another roundabout, provided that Stuart remain in contact with Lee's infantry and be able to return to the army at any time. On June 24, Stuart left to collect information about the whereabouts of the Union Army, disrupt enemy lines, and bring back supplies. He quickly ran into the Union's Second Corp moving northward. Instead of turning back, Stuart went farther afield, and skirmished his way over the next week, heading farther and farther east until he was at times closer to the Atlantic Ocean than to Lee's army. On June 28, nearly a hundred miles from the nearest Confederate foot soldier, he said he would have "marched down the 7th Street Road—took Abe & Cabinet prisoners" if not for his weary horses.

The grand circling of the Union Army had turned into a stumbling adventure. On July 1 and 2, 1863, as the greatest battle ever in the Western hemisphere unfolded, Lee repeatedly asked about Stuart's whereabouts, needing his cavalry for reconnaissance. But he was too far afield to be found. Lee would fight the most crucial battle of the war without the eyes and ears of his army, blind and deaf to the enemy's strength and movements.

DID CONFEDERATES COME TO GETTYSBURG ON A SEARCH FOR SHOES?

On the morning of July 1, 1863, as the mist rose from the surrounding farmland, a finger of the Confederate Army, moving through southern Pennsylvania, entered a market town named Gettysburg, seventy-five miles north of Washington and just north of the Mason-Dixon Line.

What brought them there?

Generations of historians and battlefield guides have repeated the story that the Rebels marched blindly into Gettysburg in search of shoes. The theory was bolstered by the assumption that the Confederate Army was almost always short of shoes, which was true. On June 28, Confederate officers demanded two thousand pairs of shoes from the residents of York, Pennsylvania, and a committee of citizens came back with fifteen hundred. Commanding officer General Henry Heth (pronounced Heath) strengthened this theory when he wrote after the war that he was on his way to "get those shoes."

But recently, historians have suggested this shoe story might be one of the many myths that have been spun around the battle. Heth's account, they say, might have been an excuse for bumbling into a firefight despite Lee's order that all battles be avoided until the entire Confederate Army had come together. The revisionists also point out that there were no shoes manufactured or stashed in Gettysburg. But some Rebel soldiers who fought in the battle later said they *thought* Gettysburg had shoes.

The larger point, which neither side disputes, is that the battle was unexpected and unplanned.

ACTIONS AND REACTIONS—TWO HUGE ARMIES
STUMBLE INTO BATTLE

On the morning of July 1, 1863, Major General Henry Heth marched into the prosperous town of Gettysburg on the Chambersburg Pike. Unfortunately for the Confederates, they bumped into the battle-tested General John Buford, a businesslike cavalry leader who had helped shake up Jeb Stuart at Brandy Station three weeks earlier.

Buford had arrived at Gettysburg the day before and, aware of Confederate troops several miles to the northwest, had evaluated the potential battle that might unfold, putting his men along high ground west and northwest of the town. The night before, Buford told a brigade commander: "They will attack you in the morning and they will come booming. . . . You will have to fight like the devil until supports arrive."

He was right. The Rebels came on aggressively with a three-to-one advantage in troops. Buford's men fought dismounted, hiding behind trees and farm fences, and delayed the Confederates for a crucial two hours, while couriers from both sides sent for reinforcements.

That same morning, as Robert E. Lee approached a gap in the mountains at Cashtown, eight miles northwest of Gettysburg, he was upset by the sound of artillery. Having learned that the Union Army might be near, he had told his commanders not to engage the enemy until his entire army had converged. "I cannot think what has become of Stuart," said Lee, referring to his cavalry commander. Without the cavalry, "I am in ignorance of what we have in front of us here. It may be the whole Federal army, it may be only a detachment. If it is the whole Federal force, we must fight a battle here."

By early afternoon, some 24,000 gray coats were battling some 19,000 bluecoats in a semicircle north and west of Gettysburg. In the afternoon, the Rebels overwhelmed the federal troops and chased them through the streets of Gettysburg. After the first day, it appeared that Lee's men would have another devastating victory.

Lee quickly understood that the key to the battle would be not the fields where the troops had met, or the crossroads town, but the high ground south of it. He called on Corps Commander Richard S. Ewell to attack Cemetery Hill, to which Union forces were retreating, "if practicable." But Ewell's corps was scattered, and the Union position was strong, so he didn't attack, creating a great "what if" of the battle. Through the night, Union Commander George Meade arrived, sent reinforcements to the formidable high ground, and told his men to brace for an attack in the morning.

THE DEATH OF AMOS HUMISTON, SOLDIER, HUSBAND, FATHER OF THREE

Late in the first day of battle, as Rebels swept Union forces through the town itself, a sergeant in the 154th New York was told to take arms in a brickyard a few blocks east of Pennsylvania College (now Gettysburg College). He was sent there to help delay the Confederates so Union troops had enough time to retreat to the safety of Culp's and Cemetery Hills, high ground south of town.

A few days later, his body was found with no identification other than a photograph his frozen hands held closely to his chest. The ambrotype showed three children—a girl and two boys. The children sat side by side, with serious expressions. The photograph and its story circulated after the Battle of Gettysburg, when a Philadelphia physician, Dr. John Francis Bourns, took the photo to the *Inquirer* and the *Press* and asked them to print a version of the photograph.

The woodcut illustrations were printed and circulated in Northern newspapers until about four months later, when the image made its way into a Presbyterian religious weekly in Portville, New York, Humiston's hometown. Philanda Humiston feared that the three young children in the paper were her Alice, Frank, and Fred. Dr. Bourns sent her a copy of the photo, which confirmed that her husband, Amos Humiston, missing since the Battle of Gettysburg, was dead. She now was a widow and her three children fatherless.

On the first day of July 1863, the day Humiston was killed, 9,000 of the 19,000 Union soldiers were lost: 5,500 of them killed or wounded and another 3,500 captured.

THE LAST THOUGHT OF A DYING FATHER

A New York soldier was found dead at the Battle of Gettysburg
clutching a photo of his three children. When the image was circulated
in Northern newspapers, *Philanda Humiston* identified the three children
as hers, thereby discovering her husband was dead.

THE BATTLE TURNS—
DAY TWO AND
DAY THREE OF GETTYSBURG

WEEK 33

LEE CONTAINS HIS RAGE AS JEB STUART RETURNS

General George Meade had served as commander of the Union Army for only five days when the second day dawned on the Gettysburg battle, but he knew enough to see the necessity of holding the high ground south of town. He issued a severe directive to his officers: "Corps and other commanders are authorized to order the instant death of any soldier who fails in his duty at this hour."

Lee, too, saw the necessity of the high ground. On the second day, he ordered Commander Richard Ewell to take Culp's Hill, on the Union's right flank, and for General James Longstreet to attack the Union left flank, purported to be in the shallow valley north of the Round Tops.

As Confederates prepared for the assault, a tired, dusty Jeb Stuart rode up to Lee. One officer remembered Lee raising his right hand as if he would strike Stuart. "I have not heard from you in days," he told Stuart, "and you are the eyes and ears of my army."

"I have brought you 125 wagons and their teams, General," Stuart replied.

"Yes and they are an impediment to me now," Lee said. Then, when he saw how distraught Stuart had become, Lee changed his tone. "We will not discuss this matter further. Help me fight these people."

DANIEL E. SICKLES STEPS FROM LITTLE ROUND TOP— AND INTO HISTORY

If not for the troop movements he directed on the second day of the Battle of Gettysburg, Daniel E. Sickles would have been best known for the murder of his wife's lover. In 1856, Sickles, a New York city politician known for his philandering and his shady politics, was elected to Congress. His wife, Teresa, began an affair with Philip Barton Key, son of the composer of "The Star-spangled Banner." In February 1859, in Lafayette Park, directly across from the White House, Sickles shot Key with a revolver. The trial became a cause célèbre. Sickles's team of lawyers, including Edwin M. Stanton, used a temporary-insanity defense— the first time it was ever used. Sickles was freed, in large part because of the unwritten law of the day that permitted a man to murder his wife's lover.

Sickles, a Democrat, at first defended the right of the South to secede, but after the bombardment of Fort Sumter, he began recruiting thousands of volunteers for the Northern cause. To resuscitate his ruined reputation, he raised not one regiment, as many men did, but four—an entire brigade. The patriotic politician was awarded with an appointment as brigadier general. By the Battle of Gettysburg, Sickles had risen to the position of corps commander.

At Gettysburg, Sickles's eleven thousand men held the south end of Cemetery Ridge, just north of Little Round Top, which was near the end of the Union Army's left flank. Sickles saw his position as exceedingly vulnerable, and moved his two divisions a half-mile out of the Union line, creating a V-shape, or salient, with the forward-most point situated in what would go down in history as the Peach Orchard. Detached now from the Union line on Cemetery Ridge, Sickles's line was thin and each flank of his Third Corp hung naked and vulnerable. Little Round Top, the primary hill on the Union's left flank, was undefended.

General George Meade was horrified when he learned what Sickles had done. But before Meade could call the troops back, General James Longstreet and his 15,000 men dashed from the woods along Seminary Ridge, shooting into the Union troops at places that soon entered American folklore: Rose Woods, the Wheatfield, Devil's Den, the Valley of Death, Little Round Top, and the Peach Orchard.

DID DANIEL E. SICKLES WIN THE BATTLE OF GETTYSBURG—OR ALMOST LOSE IT?

General James Longstreet's assault against Daniel Sickles and his soldiers on the Union's left flank came at four o'clock in the afternoon, and it almost immediately pierced holes in the Union lines. But Union General Meade skillfully moved in three corps of reinforcements to plug the gaps. Watching the battle while mounted on his horse, Sickles suddenly felt a sharp pain shoot through his right leg. A cannonball had crushed his lower leg. To counteract rumors of his death, he had an aide light a cigar and place it in his mouth. He puffed away as he was carried from the field. Each side won ground, lost it, and gained it again, buckling back and forth in what became a hellacious fight. One Massachusetts private remembered not the sights of battle but its sounds:

The hoarse and indistinguishable orders of commanding officers, the screaming and bursting of shells, canister and shrapnel as they tore through the struggling masses of humanity, the death screams of wounded animals, the groans of their human companions, wounded and dying and trampled underfoot by hurrying batteries, riderless horses . . . a perfect hell on earth . . . It has never been effaced from my memory, day or night, for fifty years.

At the end of the day, Sickles's corps had been driven from the Peach Orchard, retreating back to Cemetery Ridge, where they had started the day. Of Sickles's 10,000-man corps, 4,200 would be killed, wounded, or captured. Sickles would assert for the rest of his life that he'd saved the day at Gettysburg by taking the Peach Orchard. For decades afterward, Sickles charged that Meade was planning to retreat from Gettysburg and argued he was responsible for forcing the action—and winning the battle. But many have argued that by leaving Little Round Top undefended, the colorful general almost lost the battle. It's a debate that will probably live as long as the battle is remembered.

THE BOYS OF MAINE—AND NEW YORK AND MICHIGAN— DEFEND LITTLE ROUND TOP

As General James Longstreet's assault began on the afternoon of July 2, the second day of battle, Union General George Meade heard some "peppering" at a hill called Little Round Top, the smaller of two hills at the extreme left flank of the Union Army, and he sent Brigadier General Gouverneur K. Warren to take a look. Warren discovered that the crucial position was unguarded, since Sickles's Third Corps had moved into the Peach Orchard.

Warren immediately saw that if the Confederates took Little Round Top, Confederate soldiers and artillery might crumble the Union line that stretched north along Cemetery Ridge. Warren had a battery fire a shot in the trees on the ridge line. "The motion," Warren wrote later, "revealed to me the glistening of gun-barrels and bayonets of the enemy's line of battle. . . ." The Confederates were massed and ready to charge.

Desperate, Warren sent for reinforcements. Strong Vincent's brigade, which included the Forty-fourth New York, and the Sixteenth Michigan, climbed Little Round Top and took positions amid the boulder-strewn outcrop. The last of Vincent's regiments to ascend the hill was the Twentieth Maine, composed largely of lumberjacks and fishermen, and led by Colonel Joshua Chamberlain, a professor from Bowdoin College. "This is the left of the Union line," Vincent told Chamberlain. "You understand. You are to hold this ground at all costs."

About ten minutes later, at seven p.m., the Fifteenth Alabama infantry came up the southern slopes of Little Round Top. It was a brawl along the rocky, wooded slope, Chamberlain would remember, that "lasted with increasing fury for an intense hour. . . . "

Between attacks, the Maine soldiers hunted desperately through the cartridge boxes of the wounded and dead, their ammunition nearly gone. A third of Chamberlain's men went down.

Chamberlain would later say that he ordered his men to fix bayonets and to sweep across the field of battle; others said that the men attacked spontaneously. Either way, the soldiers of the Twentieth Maine swept across the hill like a swinging gate, and the Alabamians, shocked and exhausted—they had marched almost eighteen miles to get to the battlefield—surrendered.

At the day's end, the Union's left flank, and its right, had held. But the cost had been horrific: each side suffered roughly ten thousand casualties, making it, behind Antietam, the second bloodiest day of the war.

DAY THREE: JAMES LONGSTREET WANTS
NO PART OF PICKETT'S CHARGE

During the second night at Gettysburg, Union General George Meade met with his corps commanders in the living room of a little farmhouse, listened, and predicted that General Robert E. Lee, having failed to break both flanks, would strike a blow at the center of the Union line.

Meade was right. Lee, aware that the Union Army had reinforced its flanks on the second day, planned to launch a concentrated blow at its now-vulnerable center. He would take a fresh division, five thousand strong, commanded by General George Pickett, strengthen it with another eight thousand to ten thousand, and strike at the northern end of Cemetery Ridge.

But General James Longstreet looked across the yawning field and feared disaster. At the battle at Fredericksburg, Virginia, Longstreet's soldiers, protected by a stone wall, threw back sixteen Union assaults, inflicting six thousand to eight thousand casualties while suffering only twelve hundred. He feared that this time the roles would be reversed and *his* charging Confederate men would be slaughtered.

In his autobiography, *From Manassas to Appomattox*, Longstreet wrote that he pointed out that the Confederates "would have to march a mile under concentrating battery fire, and a thousand yards under long-range musketry; that the conditions were different from those in the days of Napoleon, when field batteries had a range of 600 yards and musketry about 60 yards."

"General Lee," Longstreet remembered telling the general, "I have been a soldier all my life. . . . It is my opinion that no fifteen thousand men ever arrayed for battle can take that position." Longstreet wanted to slide around the Union forces and occupy high ground between them and Washington, forcing the Northern commanders to attack. But Lee was not convinced, replying testily that his army had overcome similar odds in battles such as Chancellorsville, a battle Longstreet had missed—and could do it again. "That day at Gettysburg," Longstreet recalled, "was the saddest of my life."

At 1:07 p.m., the calm along the center of both lines exploded as 150 Confederate guns began to fire from Seminary Ridge, hoping to debilitate the Union center before the infantry assault. It was the heaviest bombardment ever seen in North America. The Union guns replied for about an hour, and then stopped to conserve ammunition. Lee and his generals assumed they'd obliterated the Union artillery. It was an assumption that the Confederate troops would pay for dearly.

PICKETT'S CHARGE

The Confederate charge on July 3, aimed at the Union center at Gettysburg, would become known as Pickett's Charge, after General George E. Pickett, who led one of three divisions that took part in the attack commanded by General James Longstreet. On this day, he hoped to lead his men to glory. "General," Pickett asked Longstreet in mid-afternoon, "shall I advance?" Longstreet feared that if he uttered the command, he would reveal his lack of confidence in the plan. He nodded instead. Pickett then shouted, "Up men, and to your posts! Don't forget today that you are from old Virginia."

Remembered one captain: "[We] obeyed with alacrity and cheerfulness for we believed the battle was practically over, and we had nothing to do but march unopposed to Cemetery [Hill] and occupy it." A Union officer remembered the sight, twelve thousand men coming as a line a mile wide, coming through the fields of grain, corn, and hay, "magnificent, grim, irresistible." Another said, "It was the most beautiful thing I ever saw."

The Confederates had assumed the Union cannon on Cemetery Ridge and Little Round Top had been disabled, but now they learned otherwise. Union artillery blasted the Confederate lines, but the men continued to march forward, as if on parade. "We could not help hitting them at every shot," remembered one officer. A dozen men might be felled by one bursting shell.

When the Confederates reached the Emmitsburg Road, Union cannon stationed behind the stone wall switched to firing canister—tin cans filled with iron and lead balls, which turned cannon into giant shotguns. As Confederate troops approached "the Angle," the center of the Union defense, Union troops behind the wall splattered the oncoming Confederates with deadly volleys. Vermont, Ohio, and New York regiments stepped out from the main line and shot at both flanks of the doomed columns.

All thirteen regimental commanders in Pickett's division were killed or wounded. Nearly half of the 12,000 Confederate men who stepped into the field that afternoon didn't make it back. In about an hour, 6,500 Confederates were dead or wounded—to roughly 1,500 Union soldiers. As the Confederate troops ran and stumbled and crawled back across the field, many Union soldiers at the Angle remembered a previous battle, where the positions had been reversed and Union forces decimated. "Fredericksburg!" they chanted. "Fredericksburg!"

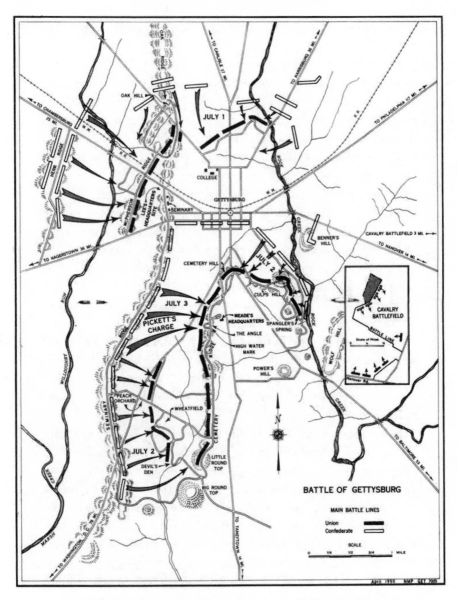

This 1950 map of the Battle of Gettysburg shows Confederate General Robert E. Lee's three failed attempts to break the Union lines on the first three days of July, 1863.

GETTYSBURG—
THE AFTERMATH

WEEK 34

WHO WAS TO BLAME FOR THE DEFEAT AT GETTYSBURG?

After the war, it became clear that Gettysburg was the turning point for Robert E. Lee's Army of Northern Virginia, and probably for the entire Civil War. In the late 1860s and 1870s, those who lionized Lee as the greatest general of the Civil War and perhaps one of the greatest generals ever, began to confront the nagging question: How did he lose this decisive battle?

On January 19, 1872—what would have been Lee's sixty-fifth birthday—former Confederate general Jubal A. Early gave an address at Washington & Lee University in which he put much of the responsibility for the loss at Gettysburg on cavalry leader Jeb Stuart, whose weeklong jaunt left him too far afield to bring vital military information to Lee as the Battle of Gettysburg unfolded. Early also blamed General James Longstreet, arguing that he ordered the failed attacks on the Round Top Hills and was too slow to execute the assault on the Union left flank on the second day of battle.

Southerners had another reason to blame Longstreet for the defeat. After the war, Longstreet supported Republicans and their Reconstruction plans for the South. His views were so despised that residents of New Orleans would snub him on the street when he passed.

Early's charges have not held up. Longstreet had urged Lee to move the army to a strategic location between the Army of the Potomac and Washington, DC, establish a defensive position, and then brace for a Yankee attack. It's true that Longstreet didn't attack Round Tops until late in the afternoon on the second day, but he was waiting for his two divisions to be fully deployed for the assault.

The decisions to fight at Gettysburg and launch Pickett's Charge were the kinds of bold decisions that won Lee success in other battles. But this time, Lee's gambit had failed. "It's all my fault," Lee was heard mumbling to himself after the battle. "It is I who have lost this fight. . . ." Writer Shelby Foote perhaps put it best when he said, "Gettysburg was the price the South paid for having Robert E. Lee."

General Robert E. Lee rode along Seminary Ridge on his horse, Traveler, as the survivors of Pickett's Charge ran, hobbled, or crawled back across the field just an hour after they had attacked. Lee told General Pickett, who had dreamed of glory that day, to "place your division in the rear of this hill, and be ready to repel the advance of the enemy should they follow up their advantage."

"General Lee," Pickett replied, distraught. "I have no division now."

General George Meade, commander of the Union Army, did not order a counterattack, though the Confederates were vulnerable: nearly 23,000 had been killed, wounded, or captured in three days, more than a third of Lee's army. Critics would say Meade could have finished the war if he had deployed the 13,600 fresh troops of the Sixth Corps.

But Meade's army had been battered, too. The day before had been the second bloodiest day in Civil War history. When a cavalry officer pushed for a counterattack, Meade, perhaps speaking for many of his nerve-shattered troops, said, "We have done well enough." The Army of the Potomac had stood up against the man many had considered invincible: Robert E. Lee. Later, Meade would explain that he wished not to repeat the "bad example [Lee] had set me, in ruining himself attacking a strong position."

By the end of the battle, 11,000 men were killed or died soon after, and 29,000 more were wounded. Another 10,000 were missing, most of them captured by Union forces. It was the largest battle ever fought in the Western hemisphere, the number of casualties nearly ten times those of American casualties on D-Day.

Folklore held that the thunder of the artillery elicited thunderstorms, and the next morning, rain began to fall around Gettysburg. The rains washed the spilled blood of the dead horses and men into the ground. But it didn't wash away the putrid stench of death and decay that hovered for many weeks over the fields and streets of Gettysburg.

"THE BEST FOURTH OF JULY SINCE 1776"—REACTION TO VICTORIES AT VICKSBURG AND GETTYSBURG

At Gettysburg, Northerners had finally proven to themselves that Robert E. Lee was not invincible. And the day after Pickett's Charge, in Vicksburg, Confederate General John Pemberton surrendered 31,000 "worn men in gray." With the fall of Vicksburg, the last Confederate position on the Mississippi, the North controlled the river that cut the Confederacy in two.

"Victory!" shouted one Philadelphia newspaper. "WATERLOO ECLIPSED." The Copperheads' antiwar momentum faltered, Lincoln's stature rose, and the emancipation policy gained support. The twin victories also echoed across the Atlantic Ocean. "The disasters of the rebels are unredeemed by even any hope of success," wrote young Henry Adams from London, where he served as secretary to his father, the American ambassador to England. "It is now conceded that all idea of [British] intervention is at an end."

"July 4, 1863. Was ever the Nation's Birthday celebrated in such a way before?" Rhode Island soldier Elisha Hunt Rhodes wrote in his diary. "I wonder what the South thinks of us Yankees now! I think Gettysburg will cure the Rebels of any desire to invade the North again." The next day he wrote, "Glorious news! . . . Vicksburg has fallen! We have thousands of prisoners and they seem to be stupefied with the news." Union General William Tecumseh Sherman was more succinct. "Glory hallelujah!" he declared after he heard the news. "The best Fourth of July since 1776."

GENERAL MEADE FAILS TO FOLLOW UP ON GETTYSBURG

When the telegraphs brought news of General George Meade's success at Gettysburg and General Ulysses S. Grant's at Vicksburg, Lincoln was thrilled. "Now, if General Meade can complete his work," Lincoln wrote on July 7, 1863, "so gloriously prosecuted thus far [at Gettysburg], by the literal or substantial destruction of Lee's army, the rebellion would be over."

On July 4, 1863, General Robert E. Lee ordered his shaken army to retreat to the Potomac. With them went an ambulance train several miles long, over muddy, rutted roads, an agony for the ten thousand injured soldiers they wheeled away. Meade trailed Lee, but was slowed by the rains that turned the roads into thick rivers of mud. Union General-in-Chief Henry Halleck kept pressing Meade to attack until the short-tempered Meade finally telegraphed on July 12 that he planned "to attack them tomorrow, unless something intervenes." Lincoln's humor evaporated: "They will be ready to fight a magnificent battle when there is no enemy to fight." Union forces had intercepted Lee's pontoons and had the Confederates pinned against an overflowing Potomac River. But Lee's men scavenged wood from nearby barns, patched together a bridge over the river, and retreated to their home country. They got away the night before Meade's attack was scheduled.

Meade, hearing of Lincoln's disappointment, offered to resign, but Lincoln didn't accept his resignation. Instead, he sat down to write a mollifying letter praising Meade for his "magnificent success." But as he wrote, his anguish emerged. He wrote that he was "distressed immeasureably" by the "magnitude of the misfortune involved in Lee's escape. . . . He was within your easy grasp, and to have closed upon him would, in connection with our other late successes, have ended the war. As it is, the war will be prolonged indefinitely." Lincoln put a letter in an envelope, on which he wrote, "To Gen. Meade, never sent, or signed."

A month after Gettysburg, Lee also offered his resignation. "I cannot even accomplish what I myself desire," he wrote to Confederate President Jefferson Davis. "How can I fulfill the expectations of others?" Davis kept on with the general he trusted above all others.

The war would continue for nearly two more years.

AFTER THE BATTLE—A LANDSCAPE OF FILTH AND DEATH

The 2,400 men, women, and children of Gettysburg were largely spared the overwhelming violence of bullets and bombs in the surrounding fields and hills. But on July 4, they woke to a landscape of filth and death. Upward of ten thousand dead bodies were left behind, many buried in shallow graves, others left, rotting and bloated, where they were killed. Thousands of horses and mules, also victims of the battle, were left "steaming in the sun."

Farmers dragged dead horses into piles, doused them with kerosene, and burned them. The smell of burning meat passed, but the smell of rotting flesh persisted for weeks. Residents closed the windows of their homes and walked the streets with handkerchiefs to their noses. Sarah Broadhead, a wife and mother, worried that "we shall be visited by a pestilence." But no epidemic descended.

About 21,000 wounded men, Confederates and Yankees, were left behind. By July 13, Broadhead's house was boarded by three wounded soldiers and twenty visitors, army officials and family members checking on the fate of soldiers, "strangers filling every bed and covering the floors." All over town, the brick homes, churches, and public buildings were turned into makeshift hospitals. Eliza Farnham, a volunteer nurse from Philadelphia, described "a man and his son lying beside him, each having lost a leg; other men with both legs gone. But the most horrible thing was to see these limbs lying, piled up like offal. . . ." A medical officer would proclaim that the battle and its aftermath led to "the greatest amount of suffering known in this nation since its birth . . ."

A CEMETERY IN GETTYSBURG IS DEDICATED

In the weeks and months following the battle, the people of Gettysburg slowly buried the dead and tended the thousands of wounded soldiers. By fall, they embraced a new mission: to improve the condition of the graves and create a cemetery for a place that had "become historic."

To design the cemetery, they chose the celebrated landscape architect William Saunders, who had created the Mount Auburn Cemetery in Cambridge, Massachusetts—the first major rural cemetery in the country. He planned a graveyard that gave no special distinction to officers' graves, and mixed the men regardless of their home states. But pressure from state politicians led him to give in on this point, and he organized the graves by the men's respective states in a semicircular design.

In October, the graves were reinterred and the dead men were identified as well as possible. Rebel bodies were left where they were; Yankee remains were moved to the new cemetery.

The townspeople wanted celebrated speakers to inaugurate the cemetery, and they invited the poet Henry Wadsworth Longfellow, but he declined. Edward Everett, though, the most famous orator of his day, accepted the role of the keynote speaker. Lincoln was expected to come, but he committed to attend only two days before the ceremony. Mary, still mourning the death of their son Will the previous year, wanted her husband to stay home because she was worried about their ten-year-old son, Tad, who was ill.

But Lincoln came. The president wanted to be there, to explain again his evolving reasons for this war, and to explain why the killing, so overwhelming at Gettysburg, would need to continue until the cause was won.

CONFEDERATE SHARPSHOOTER
KILLED AT GETTYSBURG

Timothy O'Sullivan's photo shows a crumpled Confederate
sharpshooter who was killed at Devil's Den at Gettysburg on the
second day of battle.

THE GETTYSBURG ADDRESS

WEEK 35

DID LINCOLN WRITE THE GETTYSBURG ADDRESS
ON THE BACK OF AN ENVELOPE?

The story goes that Lincoln wrote the Gettysburg Address on the train from Washington, in pencil on a scrap of brown paper, and that the crowd who heard it met it with mute silence. A *Scribner's* magazine piece in 1906 embellished the story, saying Lincoln crumpled up that scrap of paper, threw it on the ground, and then picked it back up again. The piece describes him reading his almost discarded words to an unappreciative audience.

A few things are known. Lincoln read his speech from a written copy because he didn't have time to memorize it. He probably did not write it on the train, according to his White House secretary John Nicolay, who joined him on the trip, as "the rockings and joltings of the train, [rendered] writing virtually impossible." Besides, no surviving copy shows the wobbly script you might expect from someone writing on an 1863 train.

Lincoln probably gave some thought to the speech before he arrived, well aware that a poor speech would not do on the national stage of the Gettysburg dedication. David Wills, the local lawyer who had organized the push for a cemetery and was Lincoln's host in Gettysburg, stated that Lincoln completed the speech the night before the dedication. Nicolay remembered Lincoln copying it over in the morning. And Liberty Hollinger, a sixteen-year-old girl who lived in Gettysburg at the time, remembered years later watching Lincoln come to the window to look at the crowds, holding a paper in his hands. Perhaps he was giving the address a last-minute read-through. The excitement of the people parading to the cemetery, Hollinger recalled, contrasted with the "inexpressible sadness" she saw on the president's face.

Despite all the evidence, the story persists of the hurried draft, perhaps because we like to believe Lincoln was a genius who divined his words from God rather than a public figure who worked hard to find the right ideas and the right words to express them.

LINCOLN IS NOT THE SHOW AT THE "GETTYSBURG SOLEMNITIES"

Rain fell early on the morning of November 19, 1863, but by the time the dedication ceremony began, the sun shone on a crowd of perhaps fifty thousand, pressed forward to get close enough to hear the music and speeches to come.

The "Gettysburg Solemnities," as the event was billed, began with a prayer (itself four times longer than Lincoln's address) and music by the Marine band, which was followed by Edward Everett's oration, the main event of the day. Everett was not, as the legend goes, a windbag who went on too long. Speaking was the entertainment of the day, and Everett was a rare storyteller; a scholar who could hold a crowd's attention.

Everett spoke for two hours, recounting the Gettysburg battles a day at a time, referencing Athens, attacking the Confederates' right to secession, and recounting the exhausting work done by the Gettysburg nurses. He ended by saying: "Down to the latest period of recorded time, in the glorious annals of our common country there will be no brighter page than that which relates the Battles of Gettysburg." The crowd enjoyed it, as did Lincoln. A song followed, and then Lincoln came to the podium dressed in black for what the program called his "Dedicatory Remarks." Circling his stovepipe hat was a white mourning band, worn in memory of his son Will, who had died the previous year. The president also wore formal white gloves. When he got to the podium, he put on his steel-rimmed spectacles and held his address in his hands.

His voice was high and shrill. He read the address slowly, so it could be heard by as many in the crowd as possible, including the reporters, who would take down every word for their newspapers. Everett had mostly memorized his two-hour speech; Lincoln read his two-minute one. He began with a formal phrase, which had biblical echoes, and finished just a couple of hundred words later with a sentence that recalled a sacred American text, the Declaration of Independence.

THE GETTYSBURG ADDRESS

Four score and seven years ago our fathers brought forth upon this continent, a new nation, conceived in liberty, and dedicated to the proposition that all men are created equal.

Now we are engaged in a great civil war, testing whether that nation, or any nation so conceived and so dedicated, can long endure. We are met on a great battlefield of that war. We have come to dedicate a portion of that field, as a final resting-place for those who here gave their lives that that nation might live. It is altogether fitting and proper that we should do this.

But, in a larger sense, we can not dedicate—we can not consecrate—we can not hallow—this ground. The brave men, living and dead, who struggled here have consecrated it, far above our poor power to add or detract. The world will little note, nor long remember what we say here, but it can never forget what they did here. It is for us the living, rather, to be dedicated here to the unfinished work which they who fought here have thus far so nobly advanced. It is rather for us to be here dedicated to the great task remaining before us—that from these honored dead we take increased devotion to that cause for which they gave the last full measure of devotion—that we here highly resolve that these dead shall not have died in vain—that this nation, under God, shall have a new birth of freedom—and that government of the people, by the people, and for the people, shall not perish from the earth.

DID LINCOLN'S GETTYSBURG ADDRESS
DISAPPOINT HIS AUDIENCE?

As important as what Lincoln said in his Gettysburg Address is what he didn't say. He didn't mention the Confederacy or the Union. He didn't address slavery directly or emancipation, as Edward Everett had in his opening speech. He didn't mention the carnage at Gettysburg, the trials of its people, or even Gettysburg by name. Instead, Lincoln talked in universals, using just 279 words to speak about what the men at Gettysburg died for and why the nation was fighting a civil war.

His first sentence and the phrase "new nation, conceived in liberty and dedicated to the proposition that all men are created equal" was a reference to the Declaration of Independence, and it meant different things to different people. To many, "all men" assumed white men, and their civic, economic, and social birthright to freedom. But to Northern abolitionists and Lincoln, "all men" now included African-Americans as well.

The crowd would applaud after the opening line as they would five more times before he would finish . . .

We have come to dedicate a portion of that field as a final resting place for those who here gave their lives that that nation might live. It is altogether fitting and proper that we should do this. But in a larger sense, we cannot dedicate, we cannot consecrate, we cannot hallow this ground. The brave men, living and dead who struggled here have consecrated it far above our poor power to add or detract. The world will little note nor long remember what we say here, but it can never forget what they did here.

A soldier at the front of the crowd, one of about forty or fifty wounded veterans present, raised his remaining arm to his face and sobbed audibly. Then he raised his eyes and said, in a low, solemn way, "God bless Abraham Lincoln." Applause followed.

It is for us the living rather to be dedicated here to the unfinished work which they who fought here have thus far so nobly advanced. It is rather for us to be here dedicated to the great task remaining before us—that from these honored dead we take increased devotion to that cause for which they gave the last full measure of devotion— that we here highly resolve that these dead shall not have died in vain . . .

This homage to the soldiers again drew applause. Some have characterized the words in this speech as vernacular, a precursor of Twain's language. But this speech is not colloquial; it's far more formal and spare than Twain's. Perhaps his abbreviated prose was influenced by the telegram or the lawyerly appreciation of the simplest argument. Lincoln then finished reading his last sentence, the longest of the nine in his speech.

> . . . *that we here highly resolve that these dead shall not have died in vain—that this nation under God shall have a new birth of freedom, and that government of the people, by the people, for the people shall not perish from the earth.*

When the president stopped speaking, "the assemblage stood motionless and silent," recalled George Gitt, who was fifteen at the time. It was only after the president turned and began to walk back to his chair that the applause began.

Ward Hill Lamon said the president turned to him when he was seated and said, "Lamon, that speech won't *scour!*" The word "scour" was a reference to a plow that cuts smoothly through the ground. "It is a flat failure, and the people are disappointed."

But if the crowd held back its applause, it might have been because of the solemnity of the speech, which honored the dead soldiers. Wild applause would have been inappropriate, as it would be today.

LINCOLN MAKES THANKSGIVING A NATIONAL HOLIDAY

For years, the popular women's magazine *Godey's Lady's Book* had called for a holiday of thanksgiving. The editor, Sarah Josepha Hale, wrote the president in September 1863 that she wanted "our annual Thanksgiving made into a national and fixed Union festival."

Spurred by victories at Gettysburg and Vicksburg, the president issued the Thanksgiving Proclamation, establishing a national holiday on the last Thursday of November. It received far more attention than Lincoln's Gettysburg Address. "The year that is drawing towards its close, has been filled with the blessings of fruitful fields and healthful skies," it began.

In the midst of a civil war of unequaled magnitude and severity . . . peace has been preserved with all nations, order has been maintained, the laws have been respected and obeyed, and harmony has prevailed everywhere except in the theatre of military conflict. . . .

Needful diversions of wealth and of strength from the fields of peaceful industry to the national defense, have not arrested the plough, the shuttle or the ship; the axe has enlarged the borders of our settlements, and the mines, as well of iron and coal as of the precious metals, have yielded even more abundantly than heretofore. Population has steadily increased . . . and the country, rejoicing in the consciousness of augmented strength and vigor, is permitted to expect continuance of years with large increase of freedom.

. . . [We] commend to His tender care all those who have become widows, orphans, mourners or sufferers in the lamentable civil strife in which we are unavoidably engaged, and fervently implore the interposition of the Almighty Hand to heal the wounds of the nation and to restore it as soon as may be consistent with the Divine purposes to the full enjoyment of peace, harmony, tranquility and Union.

Does the prose sound a bit flowery for Lincoln? That's because Secretary of State William Seward, who cosigned it, wrote the document.

TIME'S ASSESSMENT:
WHY THE GETTYSBURG ADDRESS HAS LASTED

While newspapers in the days after the Gettysburg Solemnities focused on Edward Everett's speech, some did praise Lincoln's Address in the months and years that followed. Ralph Waldo Emerson said the "brief speech at Gettysburg will not easily be surpassed by words on any recorded occasion." Harriet Beecher Stowe, author of *Uncle Tom's Cabin*, listed the president's Farewell to Springfield, the Second Inaugural, and the Gettysburg Address as Lincoln's most eloquent speeches. "Perhaps [in] no language, ancient or modern," she said, "are any number of words found more touching and eloquent than his speech on November 19, 1863."

Still, Lincoln's more legalistic Emancipation Proclamation received most of the attention in the subsequent decades, and when painters of the late nineteenth century portrayed the president, it was as the Great Emancipator. Gabor Boritt, author of *The Gettysburg Gospel*, has noted that the address gained popularity in the early twentieth century for a number of reasons, not all of them laudable. As Reconstruction was abandoned, and Jim Crow laws reestablished second-class citizenship for blacks in Southern states, many American people wanted to remove the Emancipation Proclamation from its pedestal. The Gettysburg Address was not as overt a racial document. Lincoln's abstract phrase— "new birth of freedom"—was originally interpreted as a poetic reference to the freeing of slaves. Yet later, the phrase was increasingly interpreted as referring to white men restoring a democratic nation almost torn in two. Progressives of the early twentieth century, seeking a fairer distribution of wealth and the end to political corruption, embraced the phrases "all men are created equal" and a "government of the people, by the people, for the people."

Americans also came to appreciate the elegance of the address's words. The speech was taut and simple, written with modern brevity. "I should be glad," Everett wrote in a note to Lincoln after their day on the podium, "if I could flatter myself that I came as near to the central idea of the occasion, in two hours, as you did in two minutes." Later, Lincoln would tell James Speed, his attorney general, that he "had never received a compliment he prized more highly."

A PHOTOGRAPH OF LINCOLN AT GETTYSBURG

The chief of the Still Pictures Branch of the National Archives stumbled across the only known image of Abraham Lincoln at Gettysburg while she was clearing out her files before retiring in 1952. Lincoln can be seen in the center of the photo, without a hat, seated near a bearded man wearing a stovepipe hat, who is standing. It's estimated that the photo was taken a few hours before Lincoln delivered his Gettysburg Address.

CHICKAMAUGA— THE CONFEDERATES' LAST HURRAH IN THE WEST

WEEK 36

WILLIAM ROSECRANS SENDS BRAXTON BRAGG FLEEING THROUGH TENNESSEE

The war strategy of Abraham Lincoln and General Ulysses Grant was simple—fight everywhere and at all times to prevent one Confederate army from reinforcing another. To this end, the Lincoln administration had pushed William Rosecrans and his Army of the Cumberland to mount a third front in Tennessee in the spring of 1863 to complement Grant's moves around Vicksburg and Joseph Hooker's in Virginia.

But Rosecrans had resisted pressure to make an attack against Confederate General Braxton Bragg in early 1863. The bloodbath at Stones River on New Year's Eve had convinced him not to attack until he had all the supplies and troops he wanted—and perhaps more. Rosecrans's hesitation frustrated Lincoln, especially when he discovered that some of Bragg's troops had been moved to Mississippi.

Yet when Rosecrans's army finally did move on June 24, it moved with precision. In just over a week, the Army of the Cumberland had pressed Bragg's forces eighty miles while suffering only 570 casualties. And Rosecrans had done it despite a stew-like mud caused by June rains. "No Presbyterian rain, either," recalled one soldier who was there, "but a genuine Baptist downpour."

Bragg, who confessed that his retreat had been "a great disaster," was perhaps the least liked commander in either army. He was considered impatient, nervous, and explosive; a tyrant who didn't treat his men well. The Tennessee soldier Sam Watkins put it plainly:

> None of General Bragg's soldiers ever loved him. They had no faith in his ability as a general. He was looked upon as a merciless tyrant. The soldiers were very scantily fed. Bragg was never a good feeder. . . . He loved to crush the spirit of his men. The more of a hang-dog look they had about them, the better was General Bragg pleased.

Rosecrans thought he could take Chattanooga, the only rail hub that connected the eastern and western portions of the Confederacy and a door to an invasion of Georgia. In mid-August, he finally feinted an approach north of Chattanooga, but crossed below it, surprising Bragg. Bragg, fearing he'd be trapped in Chattanooga, abandoned it without a fight and retreated to northern Georgia on September 8.

Jefferson Davis declared: "We are now in the darkest hour of our political existence."

DESERTERS, NORTH AND SOUTH

Abraham Lincoln once said that holding men in the army was like shoveling fleas. An estimated three hundred thousand soldiers, two-thirds of them Union men, deserted during the war. Those who left the ranks are often portrayed as soldiers afraid of dying. "I remember a man by the name of Smith stepping deliberately out of the ranks and shooting his finger off to keep out of the fight . . ." wrote the Tennessee soldier Sam Watkins, "and . . . others suddenly taken sick with colic." But soldiers had many good reasons to leave the front: resentment toward officers; disgust with politicians; worries about their families at home.

Desertion was sometimes overlooked by officers, but usually not. Many of the punishments were passing: deserters sometimes had their heads shaved or were forced to wear a barrel for a shirt. But sometimes it included tougher measures. Watkins remembered one deserter who had left the ranks without permission for ten days, "stripped to the naked skin. Then a strapping fellow with a big rawhide would make the blood flow and spurt at every lick, the wretch begging and howling like a hound, and then he was branded with a red hot iron with the letter D on both hips, when he was marched through the army to the music of the 'Rogue's March.'"

In the first cold month of 1863, after the Union Army had suffered the brutal defeat at Fredericksburg, with its killing field on Marye's Heights, desertion increased to two hundred men a day. By late January, one in four men were gone without permission. After the draft in 1863, desertion increased, since many Northern soldiers were conscripts or hired substitutes.

Yet many soldiers deserted the army because of the privations of family members at home. One Virginian asked, "What man is there that would stay in the armey and no that his family is sufring at home?"

Even Watkins, a soldier throughout the war, deserted for a short while. "I loved a maid . . ." he explained. "When I went to see my sweetheart that night I asked her to pray for me, because I thought the prayers of a pretty woman would go a great deal further 'up yonder' than mine would. I also met Cousin Alice, another beautiful woman . . . and told her that she must pray for me, because I knew I would be court-martialed as soon as I got back. . . ."

Upon return, Watkins was sentenced to thirty days of fatigue duty and docked four months' pay. "The Confederate States of America were richer by forty-four dollars," Watkins said.

A UNION DISASTER AT CHICKAMAUGA CREEK, THE RIVER OF BLOOD

In June 1863, U.S. General William Rosecrans chased Confederate Braxton Bragg and his army southeast toward Chattanooga and, as an officer in his army put it, Old Rosy "expected to drive Bragg to the sea." The usually cautious Rosecrans split his army into three parts and hastily sent them marching through mountain passes below Chattanooga to finish off the fleeing Confederates.

But Braxton Bragg was not running. He had decided to counterattack along a creek about fifteen miles south of Chattanooga, named Chickamauga, a Cherokee name meaning River of Blood. He would have help. President Jefferson Davis had decided to send twelve thousand of James Longstreet's troops to throw back the Union advance in Tennessee he feared might destroy the Confederacy.

The battle began on the morning of September 19, 1863, in a wooded area thick with underbrush along the river. With visibility poor and maneuverability poorer, it quickly disintegrated into, as one federal soldier put it, "a mad, irregular battle, very much resembling guerrilla warfare on a vast scale, in which one army was bushwhacking the other, and wherein all the science and the art of war went for nothing."

Bragg hit the Union hard for two days. In the morning of the second day, Rosecrans ordered troops to the embattled Union left to fill a gap that wasn't there, mistakenly opening another gap, a quarter-mile wide, in the Union center. The newly arrived Longstreet, seeing the opportunity, sent fifteen thousand men pouring through the hole in the line. "On they came like an angry flood," remembered one Union officer. A third of Rosecrans's army fled to the crossroads of Rossville, five miles north of the battlefield. With them went Rosecrans himself, who kept running all the way to Chattanooga.

Late in the afternoon, Rosecrans sent his commander Henry Halleck a telegram: WE HAVE MET WITH A SERIOUS DISASTER; EXTENT NOT YET ASCERTAINED. ENEMY OVERWHELMED US, DROVE OUR RIGHT, PIERCED OUR CENTER, AND SCATTERED TROOPS THERE.

Would Rosecrans's entire Army of the Cumberland be destroyed? The answer would lay in the hands of Major General George Thomas, who decided not to flee but to stand.

THE ROCK OF CHICKAMAUGA—
MAJOR GENERAL GEORGE THOMAS

While the Union right collapsed, Major General George Thomas pulled back. Although he was from Virginia, he had decided to fight for the Union. Confederates hated him for the decision; his sisters never spoke to him again.

At Chickamauga, Thomas took command of a defensive line of scattered and exhausted regiments on Snodgrass Hill and Horseshoe Ridge, high ground to the west. In effect, they were shielding Rosecrans and the other fleeing troops. Starting at one p.m., Confederates threw division after division, including James Longstreet's men, at Thomas's forces, who repelled charge after charge. By early afternoon, Thomas's men were almost out of ammunition. The Confederates smelled victory.

Six miles away, Union Reserve Corps Commander Gordon Granger had heard the sounds of battle and wondered: should he stay put as he had been ordered to do, or should he join the battle? "I am going to Thomas," he declared, "orders or no orders!" He marched toward the sounds of battle, and as a soldier later said, "The whole country was on fire, fences, woods, haystacks, houses."

Thomas saw a column advancing toward his rear, but was uncertain whether they were allies or attackers. It was Granger and 3,900 fresh troops, and, rumbling behind them on wagons, 95,000 rounds of ammunition. The reinforcements helped Thomas hold off the Confederates until nightfall, when he made an orderly retreat. Thomas had avoided total disaster and was nicknamed "The Rock of Chickamauga" for holding back the Confederate onslaught.

Meanwhile, in Chattanooga, one officer searching out General William Rosecrans for orders found him weeping and seeking spiritual succor from his staff priest. Lincoln would call him "confused and stunned, like a duck hit on the head."

Chickamauga was a victory for the Confederates, but one that fell far short of what it might have been. It was the last time Confederates would threaten to destroy a major Union army, but Jefferson Davis would send no more troops to Bragg's Army of Tennessee—there were none. He also kept Bragg in command, despite James Longstreets's comment that "nothing but the hand of God can help as long as we have our present commander." In contrast, Lincoln sent 37,000 men to shore up the Army of the Cumberland as well as a new commander—Ulysses S. Grant.

AFTER THE BATTLE—"TO SEE ALL THOSE DEAD, WOUNDED AND DYING HORSES . . ."

Tennessee's Sam Watkins was on the winning side at Chickamauga. "We raise one long, loud, cheering shout. . . ." he wrote. "We do not stop to look around to see who is killed and wounded, but press right up their breastworks, and plant our battle-flag upon it. They waver and break and run in every direction. . . ."

Watkins remained on the battlefield through the night, surrounded by the spoils of the day's battle: Union artillery, wagons, provisions, and prisoners of war. But it also left them with the most brutal remains of the fiercest bloodbath in the western theater. "A battlefield, after the battle, is a sad and sorrowful sight to look at," he wrote.

Men were lying where they fell, shot in every conceivable part of the body. Some with their entrails torn out and still hanging to them and piled up on the ground beside them, and they still alive. Some with their under jaw torn off, and hanging by a fragment of skin to their cheeks, with their tongues lolling from their mouth, and they trying to talk. Some with both eyes shot out, with one eye hanging down on their cheek. In fact, you might walk over the battlefield and find men shot from the crown of the head to the tip end of the toe. And then to see all those dead, wounded and dying horses, their heads and tails drooping, and they seeming to be so intelligent as if they comprehended everything. I felt like shedding a tear for those innocent dumb brutes.

LOOKOUT MOUNTAIN AND MISSIONARY RIDGE— THE UNION COMES BACK

By the time Rosecrans's Army of the Cumberland retreated from Chickamauga to Chattanooga, it had lost sixteen thousand men. On September 24, 1863, Rosecrans evacuated Lookout Mountain, the commanding heights south of Chattanooga. Confederate General Braxton Bragg quickly brought artillery up the mountain, and added more infantry to Missionary Ridge to the east. By placing artillery on high, the Confederates blocked federal supplies from the city.

U.S. Secretary of War Stanton convinced Lincoln to send twenty thousand men on a circuitous twelve-hundred-mile railroad route, and they got there in eleven days, one of the longest and fastest movements of troops before the twentieth century. The Union made another momentous change, putting Ulysses S. Grant in control of the army between the Mississippi and the Appalachian Mountains.

On November 24, Joseph Hooker, wanting to prove himself after leading the Union debacle at Chancellorsville, sent his men through a dense fog to take Lookout Mountain, winning what was poetically called the "Battle Above the Clouds."

The next day, Grant sent Thomas to attack the midsection of the Confederate line. With the Union was General Phil Sheridan, a 115-pound son of an Irishman, and a fighter. When Sheridan and his men reached the base of the ridge, he toasted the Confederate gunners above him, shouting, "Here's at you." The Confederates responded by firing on him and his men, spraying them with dirt. "That was ungenerous!" shouted Sheridan. "I'll take your guns for that!" His men stormed up the slope. Grant, a mile in the rear, watched regimental flags flutter up the ridge. He asked Thomas: "Who ordered those men up the hill?" Thomas answered, "I did not." The men had gone up spontaneously with a new battle cry, "Chickamauga! Chickamauga!"

"A column of Yankees swept right over where I was standing," Sam Watkins remembered later. "I saw Day's brigade throw down their guns and break like quarter horses. I heard [Bragg] say, 'Here is your commander,' and the soldiers hallooed back, 'Here is your *mule.*'" The Army of Tennessee fled southeastward into Georgia.

Chickamauga had energized the South; Lookout Mountain and Missionary Ridge had chastened it. In the spring, the Army of the Cumberland would use Chattanooga as a base for its sweep through Georgia. Davis replaced Bragg with General Joseph Johnston. "Calamity . . . defeat . . . utter ruin," wrote a Southern official. "Unless something is done . . . we are irretrievably gone."

GENERAL GRANT AND FIVE OTHER SOLDIERS
AT LOOKOUT MOUNTAIN, TENNESSEE

General Ulysses S. Grant, shown on the left with a cigar in his mouth, and five other Union soldiers stand on Lookout Mountain, Tennessee, where they defeated General Braxton Bragg and the Army of Tennessee.

The PEOPLE,
WEARY *of* WAR
(1864)

INTRODUCTION

L ike confident heavyweight boxers at the end of an evenly contested match, the Union and the Confederacy moved into 1864 each believing they could win the war. The Union was coming off significant victories at Gettysburg, Vicksburg, and Chattanooga in 1863, and the new Yankee commander, Ulysses S. Grant, believed he could finish the job by fighting everywhere simultaneously, overwhelming the Confederates with his larger armies. His aim was to crush the Rebel army before the fall elections.

Confederate General Robert E. Lee, the Confederacy's hero, believed he could win the war by fighting defensively to inflict overwhelming losses on the Union Army. That would convince Northerners to abandon Abraham Lincoln in November, instead electing politicians who would sue for peace without victory and grant the Confederates independence.

The grimmest casualties of the entire war came during the spring. In one four-week stretch, the Union Army suffered 44,000 casualties and the Confederates 25,000. Lee's defensive tactics inflicted almost two casualties for every one of his own, and by July, Union casualties totaled 100,000. Soldiers and civilians on either side doubted whether the staggering casualties would lead to a victory. In August, Lincoln, abandoned by many of his allies, expected to lose the fall presidential election.

Then, five hundred miles from the capitals of Richmond and Washington, a Confederate city would fall. As happened so many times before, a battle would redraw the war's political landscape, and this time the landscape favored the Union.

ANOTHER
YEAR OF WAR

WEEK 37

DAY
1

FREDERICK DOUGLASS INTERPRETS
THE MEANING OF THE WAR

On January 13, 1864, Frederick Douglass spoke before the Women's Loyal League at the Cooper Institute in New York City. In his address, called "The Mission of the War," he eloquently expressed his views about the meaning of the war.

I know that many are appalled and disappointed by the apparently interminable character of this war. . . . I . . . often said it: once let the North and South confront each other on the battlefield, and slavery and freedom be the inspiring motives of the respective sections, the contest will be fierce, long and sanguinary. . . . the world has not seen a nobler and grander war than that which the loyal people of this country are now waging against the slaveholding rebels. The blow we strike is not merely to free a country or continent, but the whole world, from slavery; for when slavery falls here, it will fall everywhere. . . .

The hour is one of hope as well as danger. But whatever may come to pass, one thing is clear: . . . the obvious requirements of the age, and every suggestion of enlightened policy demand the utter extirpation of slavery from every foot of American soil, and the enfranchisement of the entire colored population of the country. Elsewhere we may find peace, but it will be a hollow and deceitful peace. . . . Elsewhere we may find greatness and renown, but if these are based upon anything less substantial than justice they will vanish, for righteousness alone can permanently exalt a nation.

I end where I began—no war but an Abolition war; no peace but an Abolition peace; liberty for all, chains for none; the black man a soldier in war, a laborer in peace; a voter at the South as well as at the North; America his permanent home, and all Americans his fellow countrymen. . . . If accomplished, our glory as a nation will be complete . . .

GRANT COMES TO WASHINGTON AND MEETS LINCOLN

After Ulysses S. Grant's victories at Vicksburg and Chattanooga, Secretary of War Edwin Stanton invited him to come to Washington for a reception. The desk clerk at the Willard Hotel, seeing nothing special in Grant, told the general and his thirteen-year-old son, Fred, that nothing was available but a small room on the third floor. Then the clerk saw the entry in the register—U. S. Grant and son, Galena, Illinois—and immediately upgraded their room.

Lincoln pumped Grant's hand when they met, and said, "Why, here is General Grant. Well, this is a great pleasure, I assure you!" Secretary of State Seward took Grant to the East Room of the White House. The general was wearing a badly fitted and wrinkled uniform and some more mannered guests characterized him as a "stumbling seedy hick" and an "awkward hayseed." Seward persuaded Grant to step up on a couch so the crowd could see the squat general while he gave his speech. It was three sentences long—the general was admired for his clear, concise commands—but it was a disappointment to many. "The General had hurriedly and almost illegibly written his speech on a half sheet of note paper, in lead pencil," wrote Lincoln's secretary John G. Nicolay afterward, "and being quite embarrassed by the occasion, and finding his own writing so very difficult to read, made rather sorry and disjointed work of enunciating his reply." It didn't matter—the capital had many talkers but few successful generals.

The next day, Grant was promoted to general-in-chief of the U. S. Army, a position last held by George Washington. Afterward, in private, Lincoln asked Grant whether it was possible to take Richmond. Yes, Grant replied, if I have the troops. He would have them, the president told him. Grant soon departed Washington with his son, glad to leave what he called the "show business" atmosphere of the nation's capital.

THE DAVISES BRING HOME A FOSTER CHILD—
A BLACK ONE

On February 16, 1864, Mary Chesnut, a friend to the Davises, wrote in her diary that while visiting the Confederate executive mansion, she saw a "little negro Mrs. [Varina] Davis rescued yesterday from his brutal negro guardian. The child is an orphan. He was dressed up in Little Joe's clothes and happy as a lord. He was very anxious to show me his wounds and bruises, but I fled."

On the back of a surviving photo of the boy is a note Varina wrote: "James Henry Brooks adopted by Mrs. Jefferson Davis during the War. . . . A great pet in the family and known as Jim Limber." In her 1890 memoirs, Mrs. Davis said her husband "went to the Mayor's office and had [Jim's] free papers registered to insure Jim against getting into the power of the oppressor again."

When Varina fled Richmond, she took the boy with her family and wrote about him in an April 19 letter to her husband: "The children are well and very happy—play all day—Billy [a Davis son] & Jim fast friends as ever . . ." When federal forces caught Varina and her family, the Davises put the boy in the trust of an old family friend, Union General Rufus Saxton. "He quietly went," Varina Davis wrote in her memoirs, "but as soon as he found he was going to leave us he fought like a little tiger and was thus engaged the last we saw of him."

A Boston woman named Elizabeth Hyde Botume, who went South to teach freed slaves, said teachers took Brooks to the North, where he was "well-trained in all ways, having . . . a good practical education, until he was old enough to support himself." Some modern accounts say the Davises tried to find Brooks after the war, but there's little evidence of this. "I hope he has been successful in the world for he was a fine boy. . . ." Varina wrote. "Some years ago we saw in a Massachusetts paper that he would bear to his grave the marks of the stripes inflicted upon him by us. We felt sure he had not said this, for the affection was mutual between us, and we had never punished him."

SOLDIERS TRY TO DIE WITH A NAME

What was done to make sure soldiers didn't die nameless, identified "by the significant word UNKNOWN," as the poet Walt Whitman put it? Both the North and the South made attempts to keep records of the number of dead and their names, but neither army ever sent a notification of a death to a soldier's family. More often, newspapers printed the lists of the dead. It was expected that close friends of the dead would send the news home in a letter, and later in the war, relief agencies such as the Union's Sanitary Commission, committed to giving "immediate and accurate information of the wounded and dead to those who waited," sent thousands of letters home. The letters often included the last words of a son, husband, or father.

Soldiers often wrote their name and address in the pocket Bible many carried into battle, as well as the names and addresses of their next of kin. Oliver Wendell Holmes Jr., the future Supreme Court Justice, was shot at Antietam. Semiconscious, and fearing he'd die without identification, he scribbled on a piece of paper, "I am Capt. O. W. Holmes 20th Mass. V Son of Oliver Wendell Holmes, M.D. Boston." Holmes's father rushed to Maryland, and said afterward, "Our son and brother was dead and is alive again, and was lost and is found." Holmes kept the scrap of paper for the rest of his life. But despite all these attempts to die with a name, roughly half of all the soldiers who died in the Civil War died nameless, a fate more common for the Rebel soldier.

Mistakes were often made. After the Battle of Antietam, the Yankee private Henry Struble not only appeared on a list of the dead but his grave was given a marker. The confusion came when a dead soldier was found with Struble's canteen, which Struble had given him before he died. After the war, Struble sent flowers to the unknown soldier's grave each Memorial Day to acknowledge the anonymous soldier—and perhaps acknowledge that it might have been him.

WILLIAM QUANTRILL, "BLOODY" BILL ANDERSON, AND JESSE JAMES—GUERRILLA WARFARE PLAGUES THE WEST

The Civil War was not fought between just blue- and gray-uniformed soldiers who marched in columns and fought in formation. Both sides also waged a "shadow war," especially in the western states and territories, fought by guerrillas who conducted raids, robberies, and often the murder of civilians. Some of the groups, such as John Mosby's Rangers, were disciplined, but many were not. Union generals often treated these "partisan rangers" as outlaws, and ordered their men to "Pursue, strike, and destroy the reptiles."

Confederates also were concerned about their lawlessness. On June 30, 1862, Confederate Major General M. J. Thomson wrote President Davis about rangers who had been "induced to believe that they are to be a band of licensed robbers, and are not the men to care whether it be friend or foe they rob." The Confederate Congress repealed the Partisan Ranger Act in February 1864, but by then men such as William C. Quantrill didn't need official approval to terrorize the Missouri-Kansas corridor.

Here, an area plagued by violence since the "Bloody Kansas" conflicts of the 1850s, was where guerrillas waged the bloodiest fighting of the war. Kansas senator James H. Lane organized Union bushwhackers, who sacked and burned towns that had Confederate-leaning populations. But the most savage killer was Quantrill, who counted among his deputies "Bloody" Bill Anderson, a man who tied the scalps of his victims to his horse's bridle. Quantrill would school other cold-blooded killers—the legendary Cole Younger and the brothers Frank and Jesse James were in his band—who would continue their outlaw activities after the war.

The violence escalated in the summer of 1863 when a building collapsed on some jailed women, Confederate sympathizers who included sisters of Quantrill's gang, killing five.

Seeking revenge, Quantrill gathered 450 men and marched to Lawrence, Kansas, a free-soil town. Quantrill's gang killed 182 men and boys. Missouri Union Commander Thomas Ewing responded by issuing Order No. 11, which forcibly evicted civilians from the four Missouri counties bordering Kansas, displacing some ten thousand people, leaving the area barren for years.

Quantrill left Missouri in the spring of 1865 to go east to murder Abraham Lincoln. But a Union patrol caught him first in Kentucky, and killed him.

SAM WATKINS STEALS FOOD FROM AN OLD WOMAN— AND REGRETS IT

Union and Confederate troops often relied on civilians to feed them, often taking what was not freely given. In his memoirs, the Tennessee soldier Sam Watkins recounted how he and a few other soldiers had spotted a "neat looking farm house" and "had found a fine fat sow in a pen near the house. Now, the plan . . .

> we formed was for two of us . . . to go into the house and keep the inmates interested and the other was to . . . drive off the hog. I was in the party which went into the house. There was no one there but an old lady and her sick and widowed daughter. They invited us in . . . and soon prepared us a very nice and good dinner. The old lady told us of all her troubles and trials. Her husband had died before the war, and she had three sons in the army, two of whom had been killed, and the youngest, who had been conscripted, was taken with the camp fever and died in the hospital at Atlanta, and she had nothing to subsist upon, after eating up what they then had. . . . I soon went out, having made up my mind to have nothing to do with the hog affair. . . . I had heard the gun fire and knew its portent. I . . . soon overtook my two comrades with the hog, which had been skinned and cut up, and was being carried on a pole between them. . . . On looking back I saw the old lady coming and screaming at the top of her voice. It was too late to back out now. . . .
>
> I had a guilty conscience, I assure you. The hog was cooked, but I did not eat a piece of it. I felt that I had rather starve, and I believe that it would have choked me to death if I had attempted it."

A short time afterward, Watkins returned to the woman's house and offered to give her $100 he'd received from his father.

> "Well, sir," says she, "money is of no value to me; I cannot get any article that I wish; I would much rather have the hog." Says I, "Madam, that is an impossibility; your hog is dead and eat up, and I have come to pay you for it." The old lady's eyes filled with tears.

Watkins helped the woman harvest vegetables from her garden, brought in wood for the fire, and shared a dinner with her. "I laid the money on the table and left," he said. "I have never in my life made a raid upon anybody else."

UNION SOLDIERS, WHITE & AFRICAN AMERICAN, AT A LOG CABIN CANTEEN

In April 1864, these soldiers from the Sixth New York Artillery were photographed standing at Brandy Station, Virginia, in front of a log cabin company kitchen.

THE OVERLAND CAMPAIGN—
THE BLOODIEST
OF THE WAR—
BEGINS

WEEK 38

GRANT AND LEE PLAN HOW TO WIN THE WAR IN 1864

Early in the war, General Robert E. Lee was dismissed as "Granny Lee" for not holding western Virginia, but his leadership since 1862 earned him near God-like status. In two years, despite having a far smaller army than his Union opponents, he stopped General McClellan's attack on Richmond and drove him out of Virginia, defeated John Pope at the Second Battle of Manassas, destroyed Ambrose Burnside at Fredericksburg, and crushed Joseph Hooker at Chancellorsville. By the beginning of 1864, his officers respected him, his troops revered him, and the enemy feared him.

Lee's plan was to fight defensively, not his usual way, forcing the larger Union forces to attack fortified positions, thereby inflicting tens of thousands of war-wearying casualties. Lee hoped these losses, and depriving the Union of victory for a fourth year, would convince Northerners to abandon the fight and its chief proponent, Abraham Lincoln, who was up for reelection in the fall. Peace—and the Confederacy—would prevail.

Lee would employ the strategy against a general he had not yet tested: Ulysses S. Grant, who now oversaw all the Union armies. Grant, too, had a new strategy. "Before this time," Grant wrote, "these various [Union] armies had acted separately and independently of each other . . . I determined to stop this. . . . My general plan was now to concentrate all the force possible against the Confederate armies in the field." Grant's overall intention was to destroy the Confederate armies before the November elections, guaranteeing Lincoln's victory. George Meade, with Grant, would take 110,000 troops and fight Lee, not with the aim of taking Richmond, the Union's original goal, but of crushing Lee's army. "Wherever Lee goes," Grant told Meade, "you will go also."

In early May, Grant moved his Army of the Potomac across the Rapidan River into northeastern Virginia, and Sherman began his march from Chattanooga into Georgia, with Atlanta as his ultimate destination. Marching armies would now test Grant's war strategy.

UNION GENERALS SIGEL, BANKS, AND BUTLER ATTACK IN EARLY MAY—AND LOSE

As Grant and Meade began to pound away at Robert E. Lee's army in Virginia, Grant ordered Union generals to hit other Confederate armies to keep them too busy to join Lee. Sherman was ordered to break up Joseph Johnston's army and to destroy crops, cities, and homes. Grant also gave marching orders to three political generals—Benjamin Butler's Army of the James on the Virginia Peninsula; Nathaniel Banks's Army of the Gulf in Louisiana; and Franz Sigel's forces in the Shenandoah Valley and West Virginia.

But Banks faced fifteen thousand men under Confederate General Richard Taylor, who hit Banks's men at Sabine Crossroads, driving the Union forces back, and attacked again a second day. Banks retreated, and as a result, Taylor brought Johnston his fifteen thousand men, troops Grant was trying to keep from him.

Butler had a real chance at glory, steaming thirty thousand soldiers up the James River and landing them between Richmond and Petersburg on May 5. Just five thousand Rebel troops defended the city, and their commander, Pierre Beauregard, hadn't yet arrived. If Butler had immediately attacked, he might have marched into the capital. But by the time Butler moved, Beauregard and reinforcements were in place.

The Confederates took the initiative, attacking at Drewry's Bluff. Butler's men retreated to Virginia's Bermuda Hundred Peninsula, between the James and Appomattox Rivers. Beauregard's men dug trenches across the peninsula's exit, sealing off Butler's army.

At the same time, Sigel got thumped in what had become the Confederate lion's den—the Shenandoah Valley. On May 15, Sigel's 6,500 men were moving south through the valley to Staunton, when John Breckinridge hit him at New Market with 4,000 troops. Some 247 Virginia Military Institute cadets between fifteen and seventeen years old had marched eighty miles in four days to get to Breckinridge's army, and entered Civil War history when a gap of a hundred yards opened in the Confederate lines. One of his staff urged him to send in the VMI boys. "I will not do it," Breckinridge said. "General, you have no choice," the aide replied. Breckinridge relented. "Send the cadets in, and may God forgive me."

The VMI boys led the charge. Ten were killed, forty-five wounded, but the Union line broke. Sigel retreated. The three commanders had failed, unable to even divert, much less defeat, their opponents. That made Grant's job of crushing Lee's army all the more difficult.

THE BATTLE OF THE WILDERNESS—LEE CATCHES UNION TROOPS IN THE WOODS AGAIN

"Whatever happens," Ulysses S. Grant told Abraham Lincoln before setting out in the spring of 1864, "there will be no turning back."

The Virginia wilderness that Grant's army entered in May 1864 was the same wilderness where Robert E. Lee had beaten Joseph Hooker a year before, crushing his right flank at Chancellorsville. Spring rains had revealed shallow graves from the 1863 battle, and one of the green Union soldiers saw a veteran poke his bayonet into the ground and "suddenly rolled a skull on the ground before us and said in a deep, low voice: 'That is what you are all coming to, and some of you will start toward it tomorrow.'"

Grant wanted to move the men quickly through the dense woods to fight Lee's army on open ground; Lee planned to destroy Grant's army while it was still tangled there, knowing that landscape would undermine the advantage Grant had in troops—120,000 soldiers to Lee's 64,000—and make it difficult to maneuver and target his army's superior artillery.

At about noon on May 5, Confederate General Richard S. Ewell's corps hit while the Army of the Potomac was still in the woods.

"The woods and brush were so thick and dark that the enemy could not be seen," Rhode Island's Elisha Hunt Rhodes wrote later, "but we knew they were in our front from the terrible fire we received." The forest ignited in patches. Entire units became lost, with soldiers on both sides struggling to distinguish enemy from friend. "Up through the trees rolled dense clouds of battle smoke circling about the pines and mingling with the flowering dogwoods," remembered one Northern soldier. "Each man fought on his own grimly and desperately."

On the first day, the Union Army had the edge. On the second day, both Grant and Lee planned to attack in the morning, but Grant struck first, and the Union Army drove the Confederates a mile through the woods. Lee, on his horse, Traveller, watched veteran men in gray retreat past him. At that moment, Lee stood nearly alone on his horse, considering a charge to lead his men in a counterattack against the rolling Union Army.

WHY GENERALS—INCLUDING ROBERT E. LEE—
WERE MORE LIKELY TO DIE DURING THE CIVIL WAR

Robert E. Lee's impulse to lead a counterattack during the Battle of the Wilderness would not have surprised his troops if he were a bit lower in the officer corps. That's because many top officers on both sides, including generals, literally led their troops into battle in the Civil War.

On the second day of the Battle of the Wilderness, Union Generals Alexander Hays and James S. Wadsworth were killed. Confederate General Micah Jenkins of South Carolina was also shot down. Because they often led from the front, the number of officers killed in combat during the Civil War was 15 percent higher than the percentage of enlisted men killed. Generals fared even worse, 50 percent more likely to die in combat than a private.

On the morning of the second day of the Battle of the Wilderness, General Lee watched from his horse, Traveller, as a charging Union Army came within two hundred yards. Confederates were passing him, fleeing, when a score of fresh Confederate soldiers came up from the rear. "Who are you, my boys?" Lee shouted to the men.

"Texas boys!" they yelled. "Hurrah for Texas!" said Lee, standing in his stirrups and waving his hat. Lee knew that these were the first reinforcements from General James Longstreet's First Corps, and the Texans soon saw that their commander was planning on leading a countercharge with the fresh troops.

"Go back!" they shouted at Lee. "We won't go on unless you go back!" Brigadier General John Gregg brought his horse in front of Traveller to prevent him from galloping off, and a sergeant grabbed Traveller's reins to lead him back to safety. Then the yelping Texans and Longstreet's corps launched a counterattack, almost driving the bluecoats back to where they had started that day.

But before the Union troops were routed, tragedy struck five miles from where "Stonewall" Jackson was killed by friendly fire a year earlier. This time, Longstreet took a bullet to his shoulder and throat, shot by Confederate soldiers confused by the smoky woods. The event arrested the Confederate counterattack. But Longstreet would be lucky: he recovered in five months, returned to the battlefield, and would outlive many generals and privates, dying in 1904 just short of his eighty-third birthday.

THE BATTLE OF THE WILDERNESS—DESPITE LOSSES, GRANT PUSHES FORWARD

Late on the second day of the Battle of the Wilderness, Confederate General John B. Gordon launched a surprise attack on the Union's unprotected right flank. Veteran soldiers panicked, fearing that Lee would again destroy the Union Army as he'd done at the first Battle of the Wilderness. "I am heartily tired of hearing what Lee is going to do," General Grant said. "Some of you always seem to think he is suddenly going to turn a double somersault, and land on our rear and on both our flanks at the same time. Go back to your command, and try to think what we are going to do ourselves, instead of what Lee is going to do."

Elisha Hunt Rhodes wrote of the second day: "Our Brigade charged into the swamp six times, and each time were driven out. . . . During the night the brush caught fire, and many of the wounded burned to death."

The battle, gruesome as it was, was a tactical victory for the Confederates. In two days, the Union Army suffered eighteen thousand casualties—nearly one in six men—compared to seven thousand for the Confederates. Union veterans expected a retreat back across the Rapidan River to recover, as they'd done after their losses at Fredericksburg and Chancellorsville.

But Grant was different from Generals Burnside and Hooker. The general ordered his men to get their backpacks together and marched them to a crossroads. A right turn would send them north, back over the Rapidan. But the officers made a left, toward Lee's army and Richmond. William Tecumseh Sherman would call Grant's decision to move south that day the most important of his friend's life. One veteran saw Grant's fateful decision to move forward after defeat as the turning point of the war. "Our spirits rose, we marched free," the veteran recalled. "The men began to sing."

"A HISSING CAULDRON OF DEATH"—SPOTSYLVANIA

The Union Army marched into the night on May 7 to get to the cross-roads village of Spotsylvania, located twelve miles to the south, and leapfrog past General Lee's army to Richmond. As General Grant passed his troops on his big horse, Cincinnati, the men responded. "Wild cheers echoed through the forest," recalled Horace Porter, one of Grant's staff. "Men swung their hats, tossed up their muskets, and pressed forward to within touch of their chief, clapping their hands, and speaking to him with the familiarity of comrades. Pine-knots and leaves were set on fire. . . . The night march had become a triumphal procession."

But the cheering was premature. Lee predicted Grant's move, and had dug his men into Spotsylvania. Grant attacked the flanks of Lee's army, and tried to bust through the lines in a frontal assault, but had little success. But at dawn on May 12, Winfield Scott Hancock's Second Corps caught the enemy by surprise and broke through Lee's line at a point called the Mule Shoe, for its shape, splitting the Confederate Army and capturing most of the legendary Stonewall Division. A Confederate counterattack produced some of the most frenzied fighting of the war at what became known as the Bloody Angle. Soaked by the rain, the men would fight from morning until midnight. "The horseshoe was a boiling, bubbling and hissing cauldron of death," wrote one Union officer. "Clubbed muskets, and bayonets were the modes of fighting for those who had used up their cartridges, and frenzy seemed to possess the yelling, demonic hordes on either side."

The battle continued at a lower pitch for another week, and by its end, Grant had lost eighteen thousand men, the Confederates ten thousand. "We have met a man this time who either does not know when he is whipped," a Southerner said of Grant, "or who cares not if he loses his whole army." During the battle, Grant sent a message to Lincoln: "[I] propose to fight it out on this line if it takes all Summer."

ULYSSES S. GRANT
HOLDS A WAR COUNCIL

General Ulysses S. Grant holds a "Council of War" with his commanders in the yard of Massaponax Church as his troops marched from Spotsylvania Court House in May 1864.

THE COLD HARBOR
FIASCO

WEEK 39

GRANT DECIDES TO ATTACK AT COLD HARBOR

The first month of what was called General Grant's Overland Campaign had been brutal. In only four weeks, the Union Army had suffered 44,000 casualties and the Confederates about 25,000. The war had changed. Previously, after battles like the Wilderness and Spotsylvania, one of the armies—usually the Union's—had retreated, recuperated, and then reengaged. But here, the two armies moved southward, locked like two wrestlers, marching, fighting, or digging defensive trenches almost every day. The men began to suffer from what, in later years, would be called shell shock. "Many a man has gone crazy since this campaign began from the terrible pressure on mind & body," wrote the young captain Oliver Wendell Holmes Jr.

After Grant realized he could not defeat Lee at Spotsylvania, he tried to lure Lee's army into the open by moving his army southward. His destination was Cold Harbor, a tiny crossroads eight miles northeast of Richmond. But Lee's army had beaten Grant's to Cold Harbor, and his men dug in again, waiting for the blow from the 109,000-man Union Army.

Grant could try another flanking maneuver, but he knew that could easily send Lee to Richmond, which had been fortified with near-impenetrable defenses. Expiring enlistments would also mean the Union Army would lose about a dozen regiments in July, another reason to strike quickly.

"Lee's army is really whipped," Grant had written Chief of Staff Henry Halleck a few days before the battle. "The prisoners we now take show it, and the action of his army shows it unmistakably. A battle with them outside of entrenchments cannot be had. Our men feel that they have gained the morale over the enemy and attack with confidence."

On June 3, Grant ordered an attack, knowing a victory could mean the fall of Richmond and the end of the war. It was a straight-on sledgehammer assault by three corps, fifty thousand men in all. Grant would say soon after it was made: "I regret this assault more than any one I have ever ordered."

THE DISASTROUS UNION CHARGE AT COLD HARBOR

It was easy for both the federal troops and Rebels in Cold Harbor to see that the place was misnamed. It wasn't near a harbor—and even in June, it was hot, not cold, and dry and dusty. In just a few days, the Confederates had carved one of the most formidable bulwarks of the war. A newspaperman described the trenches built along a six-mile line this way: "They are intricate, zig-zagged lines within lines, lines protecting flanks of lines. Lines built to enfilade an opposing line, lines within which lies a battery . . . a maze and labyrinth of works within works and works without works, each laid out with some definite design either of defense or offense."

"The whole army," said New York Private Frank Wilkeson, "seemed depressed the night before Cold Harbor." At about four thirty a.m., an artilleryman fired a cannon, the signal for fifty thousand Union soldiers to step out against the invisible enemy. Rebel guns appeared over the edge of the earthen parapets, and soon the attackers were hit with a hail of bullets, canister, and shell along their front and both their flanks. "It had the fury of the Wilderness musketry," wrote one of the veteran Union gunners afterward, "with the thunders of the Gettysburg artillery super-added." At one point, a Union commander, seeing a stand of charging men drop to the ground, prodded them with his sword to get up until he realized they'd all been shot dead in one fell swoop. Those not killed or wounded bellied down to the ground and furiously dug improvised foxholes to protect themselves.

In just half an hour, seven thousand Union men were killed or wounded, five times the casualties in Lee's army. Grant didn't deny the enormity of the failure. The night after the battle he told his shaken staff that he'd expected the "stern necessity" of the battle "would bring compensating results; but no advantages have been gained sufficient to justify the heavy losses suffered." A few days after the assault, as soldiers from both sides buried the dead, one Confederate officer said to a Yankee: "It seemed almost like murder to fire upon you."

WAS GRANT A BUTCHER?

From May 4 to June 18, the Union Army lost 65,000 men, half as many as it lost in the three previous *years* of the war. The rolling battles that took place over a hundred miles were the bloodiest six weeks of the war. The casualty percentages were about equal in both armies, but the overwhelming numbers of Northern soldiers killed and wounded left many families mourning across the North that spring. Many, already weary of war, thought Grant had crossed the limits of tolerable human losses, a conclusion amplified in Northern newspapers.

Elizabeth Keckley, Mary Todd Lincoln's seamstress, noticed the first lady began referring to Grant as a "butcher." When Abraham argued that Grant had been successful, Mary didn't back down. "Yes, he generally manages to claim a victory, but such a victory! He loses two men to the enemy's one. . . . He has . . . no regard for life. If the war should continue four years long . . . he would depopulate the North. I could fight an army as well myself."

But was he a butcher? Grant told a friend, "They call me a butcher, but do you know I sometimes could hardly bring myself to give an order of battle. When I contemplated the death and misery that were sure to follow, I stood appalled." He also stayed away from the gore of the battlefield so that the suffering did not undermine his will and judgment. And Grant was not the only general who suffered ghastly battlefield casualties. Union General George McClellan lost 11,657 soldiers in one day of fighting at Antietam; General Ambrose Burnside lost 10,900 men at Fredericksburg; Confederate General Robert E. Lee lost 16,914 men at Gettysburg; and General Braxton Bragg lost 16,986 men at Chickamauga.

The truth was that attacking armies suffered the highest casualties. In the six battles in 1862 and 1863 in which the Confederates were on the offensive, they lost 89,000 men to the Union's 69,000. During Grant's driving Overland Campaign in the spring of 1864, he suffered almost twice the casualties of Lee's army.

Historians have sometimes said that Grant was engaged in a strategy of attrition. But during the Overland Campaign, Grant wasn't trying to grind Lee's army down; he was trying to maneuver Lee's army into the open, where he hoped to defeat it once and for all. The problem was that Lee repeatedly hunkered his army into trenches, hoping the enormous casualties he could inflict would turn the North against the war—and turn the populace against Lincoln in his reelection.

WHY DID SO MANY MEN DIE, SO QUICKLY, IN SO MANY BATTLES?

The overwhelming casualties at Cold Harbor and in other battles—during Pickett's Charge at Gettysburg and the Union assault on Marye's Heights at Fredericksburg, for example—were caused by generals who used outmoded strategies against more deadly weapons. In the Napoleonic Wars, which West Pointers studied, or the Mexican War, which many Civil War commanders fought in, attacks were made in open terrain against lines of men wielding smooth-bore muskets. These attacks were often successful because the musket had a short range and a relatively long reloading time. Defenders could get off only one, maybe two shots, before attackers swarmed them.

But in the Civil War, the introduction of rifled guns—those with spiraled grooves in the barrel that spun a bullet, enabling it to bore straight through the air—changed the mathematics of casualties during an assault. Rifles had a range of up to 400 yards—three to five times that of a musket. Defenders with rifles could inflict five times more casualties on charging troops than their musket-wielding predecessors. These long-distance sharpshooters also made cavalry charges obsolete, because they could pick off horses long before their riders reached enemy lines. The Enfield or the Springfield model rifles used by both Union and Confederate soldiers accounted for 85 percent of the war's casualties.

Killing was now done at a distance. Of the 245,000 wounds that Union surgeons treated during the war, only about a thousand were caused by bayonets. The minié ball—named after Claude Étienne Minié, the Frenchman who invented it in 1848, but called "minnies" by the soldiers—also caused messy wounds. The ball was relatively large and mushroomed when it hit, tearing apart intestines and shattering and splintering bone, a major reason for the huge number of amputations during the war.

Despite these deadlier weapons, generals persisted with suicidal charges. Soldiers on the front lines, though, knew that they were safer hunkered down in trenches, waiting for the enemy to make such a foolhardy charge.

HOW DO MEN SUMMON THE COURAGE
TO CHARGE INTO BATTLE?

Before the disastrous Union charge at Cold Harbor, Union soldiers knew what they were in for, and one officer watched soldiers "calmly writing their names and home addresses on slips of paper, and pinning them on to their coats, so that their bodies might be recognized and their fate made known to their families." Another soldier wrote this diary entry: "June 3. Cold Harbor. I was killed." The diary was found on his body.

What drove men to willingly march into a hail of fire, knowing that death was likely? After the war, Joshua Chamberlain, the Maine soldier who charged into ferocious fire at Fredericksburg and Petersburg and rose to the rank of general, ruminated about what convinced men to make what often seemed like suicidal charges.

Curious people often ask the question whether in battle we are not affected by fear, so that our actions are influenced by it; and some are prompt to answer, "Yes, surely we are, and anybody who denies it is a braggart or a liar." I say to such, "Speak for yourselves. . . ." Most men . . . are aware of the present peril, and sometimes flinch a little by an instinct of nature . . . as when I have seen men pin their names to their breasts that they may not be buried unknown. . . .

But, as a rule, men stand up from one motive or another—simple manhood, force of discipline, pride, love, or bond of comradeship— "Here is Bill; I will go or stay where he does." And an officer is so absorbed by the sense of responsibility for his men, for his cause, or for the fight that the thought of personal peril has no place whatever in governing his actions. The instinct to seek safety is overcome by the instinct of honor.

One soldier put peer pressure at the top of the list. "You ask me if the thought of death does not alarm me," wrote a soldier to his sister. "I will say that I do not wish to die. . . . I myself am as big a coward as eny could be, but give me the bullet before the coward when all my friends and companions are going forward."

LEE MISJUDGES GRANT'S INTENTIONS AT PETERSBURG

After the Union debacle at Cold Harbor, Lee expected that Grant would keep hammering at his army and push south toward Richmond. But on June 13, the Confederate Army awoke at Cold Harbor to find the 115,000-man Union Army gone. Grant had moved his army toward Petersburg, a hub of four separate rail lines twenty-two miles south of Richmond, which was considered the capital's "back door," providing the city with food, soldiers, and supplies. To get there, Union engineers built a 2,100-foot bridge, 13 feet wide, perhaps the longest pontoon military bridge ever constructed, across the James River in just eight hours. The massive Union Army started a four-day crossing, putting it on the south side of the James River.

Grant ordered the sixteen thousand federal troops under General W. F. ("Baldy") Smith to attack Petersburg on June 15. But Smith dawdled, and when he did attack, it was tentative. Little did he know that General Pierre Beauregard had only 2,200 men entrenched in the Petersburg lines. "Petersburg at that hour," wrote Beauregard later, "was clearly at the mercy of the Federal commander, who had all but captured it." Grant scrambled to bring more men in, but disorganized Union assaults faltered as Confederate reinforcements arrived.

After Cold Harbor, the Union soldiers were also reluctant to attack dug-in troops. General George Meade, known for his temper, pushed his troops to attack, and on June 18 he snapped at one immobile commander in a telegram: "What additional orders to attack you require I cannot imagine." At one point, a converted heavy artillery regiment, inexperienced in such assaults, got ready to charge the breastworks, and was told by some veterans to "Lie down, you damn fools!" But the regiment went ahead anyway, losing 632 of 850 men in the assault. Even Joshua Chamberlain, one of the heroes of Gettysburg, resisted orders to attack the well-manned breastworks at Petersburg.

SOLDIERS' REMAINS
AT COLD HARBOR'S BATTLEFIELD

An African-American soldier sits next to a stretcher with the remains of soldiers who died in the battles of Gaines' Mill and Cold Harbor.

PETERSBURG,
AND THE BATTLE
OF THE CRATER

WEEK 40

THE RELUCTANT ATTACK OF COLONEL JOSHUA LAWRENCE CHAMBERLAIN AND THE TWENTIETH MAINE

On June 18, Union General George Meade ordered Joshua Chamberlain and his men from Maine to make a frontal assault on Rives' Salient outside the city of Petersburg. Chamberlain, who had proved his mettle at Gettysburg the previous summer, didn't like the orders. His men would have to cross a long, open, marshy field, a stream, and then they'd have to climb up a hill without cover. He feared all his men would be wiped out before they got to the enemy lines. He asked Meade to call off the attack, but his commander insisted.

Chamberlain then drew his sword and ordered his men to attack the 7,500 Confederate men behind the formidable Rebel fortifications. When his color-bearer was shot dead, Chamberlain grabbed the flag and was holding it high when a minié ball cut through both his hips, severing arteries and grazing his bladder. He propped his sword into the ground to support himself and then waved his men forward until he collapsed, bleeding profusely.

The attack was repulsed and surgeons at the field hospital said there was little they could do to save Chamberlain. But his brother found two physicians who stitched him back together, although they still believed his wounds were lethal. For weeks, Chamberlain was in severe pain, sliding from fevers to chills. He dictated a farewell letter to his wife.

On the day of Chamberlain's assault, the veterans from Lee's army began pouring into the Petersburg lines. Hesitation during the original attacks and poor execution had undermined Grant's surprise attack. He ended the assault on Petersburg. The siege of Petersburg began.

While still ill, two generals asked Chamberlain what they could do for him, and he requested a promotion to brigadier general. General Grant awarded him the promotion, the only such battlefield promotion of the war. Although obituaries in several Northern newspapers mourned his passing, Chamberlain slowly recovered. While he healed, Grant had his men extended the trenches around Petersburg, forcing Lee, with his smaller army, to extend his line close to its breaking point.

EARLY TRENCH WARFARE

After the initial attacks by the Union Army failed at Petersburg, General Grant said, "We will rest the men and use the spade for their protection until a new vein has been struck."

Much of the time was spent waiting, and Elisha Hunt Rhodes, promoted to captain on June 26, wrote about life in the trenches. "Fighting is going on every hour on some part of the line, and our turn will come again soon enough," he wrote. "Yesterday some of my men discovered an ice house full of ice, and we have been having a luxury in the way of iced water." The next day the men found a way to enhance the ice. "We have found a supply of lemons and have iced lemon aid in abundance."

But lemonade did not save the men from the heat. On the second day of July, Rhodes wrote, "We are back in the lines again, and I have an arbor of green boughs to shield me from the sun. The thermometer stands today at 124, and the men are suffering severely."

The trench life foreshadowed the four-hundred-mile stalemate on the Western Front during World War I. While the men weren't engaged in anything close to a full-fledged battle, neither were they safe. Rhodes wrote, "Yesterday, Sergeant Major George F. Polley, Tenth Massachusetts Volunteers, showed me a board on which he had carved his name, date of birth and had left a place of the date of his death. . . . I asked him if he expected to be killed and he said no, and that he had made his head board only for *fun*. Today he was killed by a shell fired by a rebel battery."

A PENNSYLVANIA MINER'S PLAN TO
"BLOW THAT DAMNED FORT OUT OF EXISTENCE"

As Brigadier General E. Porter Alexander, responsible for Confederate artillery defenses during the siege of Petersburg, patrolled the Confederate lines, he saw something at Elliott's Salient that made him uneasy. The gunfire had dropped off at either end of the Union lines, but not at the salient, located in front of the road that ran north into Petersburg, where "the popping of the muskets seemed to increase." He also wondered why federal troops hadn't pushed the lines forward, as attacking armies usually did during a siege. One day, "suddenly a light broke in on me. They were coming, but it was not above ground . . . they were coming underground. They were mining us!"

He was right. Union Lieutenant Colonel Henry Pleasants, a civil engineer engaged in railroad tunneling before the war, was in charge of the Forty-eighth Pennsylvania, mostly coal miners. One day Pleasants heard one of his men say, "We could blow that damned fort out of existence if we could run a mine shaft under it." Pleasants forwarded the plan and General Ambrose Burnside approved it. Digging began at noon on June 25, 1864.

General Grant later admitted he regarded the project "as a means of keeping the men occupied," and General George Meade said he didn't think "there was any reasonable chance of success." Still, the 210 men of the Forty-eighth Pennsylvania worked around the clock, two at a time, filling boxes of dirt and then dragging them out of the tunnel. By July 23, the Pennsylvanian miners had completed the longest tunnel ever used in warfare until that time—511 feet long—which ended 20 feet underneath the salient.

General Lee ordered countermining measures, but Confederate soldiers took them up in a desultory manner. They joked that federal troops, frustrated by Confederate entrenchments, were digging a train tunnel underneath to Petersburg, which would become apparent when engine steam filtered up through the city's cobblestone. In just days, something far more deadly than steam would rise beneath their feet.

BAD UNION DECISIONS
BEFORE THE BATTLE OF THE CRATER

By the end of July, Grant thought it was time to "do something in the way of offensive movement" regarding Richmond, and he moved troops to destroy railroad tracks north of the Confederate capital. Lee, aware of the troop movements, transported four Confederate divisions north to defend Richmond, leaving only three divisions, or about eighteen thousand men, at Petersburg. This sudden subtraction of Confederate forces at Petersburg piqued Grant's interest in the mining expedition. He ordered General George Meade, overseeing the Petersburg operations, to explode the mine.

On July 27, Meade ordered the Pennsylvanian miners to load the tunnel with gunpowder. For six hours, they lugged 320 kegs of black powder, weighing twenty-five pounds each, underneath Elliott's Salient. Meade told General Ambrose Burnside to "spring his mine" at three thirty a.m. on Saturday, July 30.

But just twenty-four hours before the detonation was planned, Meade and Grant countermanded Burnside's battle plan for the mine attack. For two weeks, Burnside had trained Petersburg's freshest division to rush forward across the no-man's-land after the massive explosion and then widen the gap in the enemy lines so that three following divisions could get to higher ground and make their way into Petersburg.

Meade, however, considered these fresh troops to be woefully inexperienced. He and Grant also had another issue: the division was the only one of U.S. Colored Troops in the Army of the Potomac at the time. Grant worried that if the assault was a disaster, people might say "that we were shoving these people ahead to get killed because we did not care anything about them." It was a remarkable decision. For the first time in the war, Union leaders were putting the well-being of black troops before those of whites.

Devastated, Burnside had to decide which of the remaining three commanders of white divisions would lead the assault. Instead of selecting one himself, he let them draw straws, and the winner was Brigadier General James Ledlie, a political appointee whom many considered the least competent general in the entire Army of the Potomac. He was also a drunkard and a coward, traits that soon would reveal themselves in the Battle of the Crater.

"A DETONATION OF THUNDER"—THE EXPLOSION
AT PETERSBURG

Shortly after three a.m. on July 30, Lieutenant Colonel Henry Pleasants entered the mine his men had spent over a month digging and lit the fuse to the gunpowder. The expected time of the explosion came and went, and after an hour General Grant considered telling Burnside to forget the explosion and make the assault. Instead, two more miners crawled into the mine, relit the fuse, and scurried out just before four forty-four a.m., when eight thousand pounds of gunpowder blew.

"A slight tremor of the earth for a second, then the rocking as of an earthquake," is how one Union captain remembered it, "and, with a tremendous blast which rent the sleeping hills beyond, a vast column of earth and smoke shoots upward to a great height, its dark sides flashing out sparks of fire, hangs poised for a moment in mid-air, and then, hurtling down with a roaring sound, showers of stones, broken timbers and blackened human limbs, subsides—the gloomy pall of darkening smoke flushing to an angry crimson as it floats away to meet the morning sun." Intimating an even greater explosion that would be unleashed eighty years later, another soldier said the earth rose "full of red flames and carried on a bed of lightning flashes . . . [and] spread out like an immense mushroom whose stem seemed to be of fire and its head of smoke." What they witnessed was the largest man-made explosion in the Western hemisphere up until that time.

With dust and smoke still covering the carnage, the first of Brigadier General James Ledlie's division sprinted across the no-man's-land toward the steaming, desolate crater, sixty feet wide, two hundred feet long, and ten to thirty feet deep.

At the crater's rim, many Union soldiers stood paralyzed by the horrors below. One Union soldier from New York later recalled "the heads or limbs of half-buried men wriggled in the loose earth." Of 300 South Carolinians sleeping when the tunnel exploded, 278 were killed or wounded. The pause above the smoldering crater might have been the pinnacle of the Union assault during the Battle of the Crater.

THE BATTLE OF THE CRATER—"THE SADDEST AFFAIR I HAVE WITNESSED IN THIS WAR"

When they reached the crater, the troops under Brigadier General James Ledlie did not fan out to make room for the two following divisions as planned, or even march forward to the critical high ground. Instead, they descended into the crater and helped Confederate survivors—a humanitarian response but one that would doom the attack. If a commander were with them, he might have ordered the men to keep moving to take advantage of the explosive surprise. But Ledlie, as was his way, had retreated four hundred yards behind the battle, sequestering himself in a bombproof shelter to gulp down rum he had borrowed from a staff surgeon.

A second and third Union division entered the crater. Forward progress was stopped by a thirty-foot-high wall of dirt to the crater's rear, which couldn't be climbed without ladders. From point-blank range, Rebels lobbed shells at the fifteen thousand Union soldiers in the quarter-acre fishbowl and fired guns from the lip of the crater at soldiers so tightly packed they couldn't aim their guns. Some in the bloody pit stacked dead men as parapets to defend themselves. The heaviest casualties were among the Colored Troops, who lost 1,327 of 4,000 men. Over the next few hours, the battle turned into a slaughter. Confederates, infuriated by the surprise explosion and the first use of black soldiers in a major battle, killed many black soldiers who tried to surrender. Those who could, retreated.

Afterward, Grant dismissed General Ledlie and sent Burnside home on leave, never to return to active duty. Back in Rhode Island, Burnside would go on to have a successful business and political career that would include three terms as governor and two as a U.S. senator. This, his last battle, resulted in four thousand Union casualties. Confederates lost about a third that number. By nightfall, the men had returned to their siege lines, nothing changed except for a long, jagged scar of brown earth, visible and lifeless in the Confederate line.

THE BATTLE OF THE CRATER,
JULY 30, 1864

Union soldiers advance on mounds of dirt and the crater created by the
explosion of a mine dug underneath the Confederate lines at Petersburg.

AUGUST'S DARK DAYS— LINCOLN EXPECTS TO LOSE HIS REELECTION

WEEK 41

ALL—INCLUDING LINCOLN—EXPECT HE WILL LOSE HIS REELECTION

By August 1864, Union optimism for a quick victory after the Gettysburg and Vicksburg successes the previous summer had evaporated. In the spring, General Lee's defensive tactics had inflicted almost two casualties for every Confederate one, and by July, Union casualties totaled a hundred thousand. Now Grant appeared stalled at Petersburg. Confederate General Joseph Johnston had so far prevented General Sherman from taking Atlanta. Tens of thousands of captured Union soldiers also languished in Confederate prisoner-of-war camps with mortality rates that exceeded those on the battlefield. And in mid-July, Jubal Early added insult to injury when he swept toward the capital and took his Rebel army just a few miles from the White House.

"Our troops have suffered much," wrote Secretary of the Navy Gideon Welles in his diary in early summer, "and accomplished but little." The frustration felt with the war's progress translated into a frustration with Lincoln. Lincoln expected the hammering he received from Peace Democrats—especially with their party convention scheduled for August 28. But Lincoln's friends and political allies were also beginning to slide away. Former Illinois Senator Orville Browning, one of Lincoln's closest friends, invited to stay at the White House when Willie was dying, wrote a friend that he had never "been able to persuade myself that [Lincoln] was big enough for the position. . . . And I fear he is a failure." By early August, Thurlow Weed, the veteran Republican leader, believed that "Lincoln's reelection [is] an impossibility. . . . The people are wild for peace."

Lincoln's secretary John Nicolay, one of his most loyal aides, sensed the sudden flight from Lincoln, calling it "a disastrous panic—a sort of political Bull Run." When a Radical Republican told Lincoln privately and without feathers that the president would be beaten unless the fortunes of war changed, Lincoln agreed. "You think I don't know I am going to be beaten," Lincoln, always the astute politician, replied, "*but I do* and unless some great change takes place *badly beaten.*"

CONFEDERATE SABOTEURS MAKE TROUBLE
ACROSS THE NORTH

Come 1864, Confederate leaders knew their best chance for victory was to unseat the resolute Abraham Lincoln and his Republicans in the fall 1864 election. Confederate leaders knew their allies in the North were the Copperheads, the antiwar and anti-Lincoln Democrats, and to help them win election, Confederates looked for ways to harass the Union war effort, disrupt the economy, and undermine resolve to continue the war.

On February 15, 1864, the Confederate legislature secretly appropriated $5 million to support a fifth column of the Confederacy, which called on Captain Thomas C. Hines and other saboteurs to go to Canada and launch what Jefferson Davis called "appropriate enterprises of war against our enemies." In the spring and summer of 1864, Maine coastal residents reported seeing a group of fifty or so artists sketching the coastline; but they were Confederate topographers making maps of secluded coves and inlets. The idea was to locate harbors to hide two armed steamers, the *Tallahassee* and the *Florida*, which could raid and terrorize the undefended Maine coast. In late July, these "artists" tried to rob a bank in Calais, Maine, but they were caught.

Another plot involved freeing ten thousand Confederate prisoners from Camp Douglas, outside Chicago, and then having them wreak havoc in the Union's unprotected west. The Confederates placed their hopes in the Sons of Liberty, a loosely knit organization of devoted anti-Lincoln Northerners. But when the Confederate operatives met with Chicago's Sons of Liberty leaders, they found the group more yelp than bite. Protest was relatively risk-free; aiding the enemy risked getting themselves shot or hanged. The Sons of Liberty chose inaction, especially when dethroning Lincoln at the polls looked possible. Disgusted, the saboteurs slipped back into Canada.

In October, the men descended on the northern Vermont community of Saint Albans and walked into three banks with pistols, identified themselves as Confederates, and rode off with $208,000. They rode horses back into Canada, and it looked like a success until Canadian authorities caught them and returned $88,000 they found on the men to the banks. On November 25, Confederate agents again came down from Canada, this time to New York City, and attempted to set fires to nineteen prominent city hotels. While some of the hotels were damaged, the hoped-for conflagration never got started. The conspirators again fled back to Canada.

THE PRESIDENT IS SHOT—THROUGH HIS HAT

In 1864, the number of death threats arriving at the White House multiplied. Lincoln kept these letters in a desk drawer at the White House, and once showed them to a journalist, saying, "I know I am in danger; but I am not going to worry over threats like these." One Wisconsin newspaper, edited by a rabid Lincoln-hater, said that if Lincoln were reelected, "We hope that a bold hand will be found to plunge the dagger into the Tyrant's heart for the public welfare."

A "Lizzie W.S." wanted to protect him, warning in July of "hordes of Secesh-sympathizers" who might shoot the president on his commute to the Soldiers' Home, the Lincolns' cool and private summer cottage three miles north of the city.

"If, you value your life!" wrote Lizzie, "*do* I entreat of you *discontinue* your visits, out of the City!" Lincoln commuted to the Soldiers' Home by horse or carriage, often alone. On an August evening, at about eleven o'clock, after an exhausting day at the White House, Lincoln rode to the cottage by horse. A private at the gate of the Soldiers' Home heard a gunshot, and moments later, the horse galloped into the compound, Lincoln holding on, bareheaded. Lincoln explained that a gunshot had gone off "at the foot of the hill," which sent the horse galloping so fast it jerked his hat off. Two soldiers went out and found Lincoln's hat— with bullet holes on either side. Lincoln asked them to keep the incident quiet—he didn't want to worry Mary.

Afterward, Lincoln spoke to Ward Lamon, his self-appointed bodyguard, saying, "I can't bring myself to believe that anyone has shot at me or will deliberately shoot at me with the deliberate purpose of killing me." The president said the shot might have come from "someone on his return from a day's hunt." Lamon, incredulous at Lincoln's naiveté, considered resigning. He had threatened to do so before, when Lincoln had gone out in public with Senator Charles Sumner and Baron Gerolt, an elderly Prussian minister, "neither of whom," Lamon said, "could defend himself against an assault from any able-bodied woman in this city." That incident occurred at a place where Lincoln often went to escape the war's worries: the theater.

LINCOLN FINDS RELIEF IN ATTENDING THE THEATER

As a boy, Abraham Lincoln owned William Scott's *Lessons in Elocution* and had memorized Shakespeare's soliloquies, which were included in the book. In Springfield, Lincoln had owned a collection of Shakespeare's plays and said he had read *King Lear*, *Richard III*, *Henry VIII*, *Hamlet*, and *Macbeth* "perhaps as frequently as any unprofessional reader," he wrote an actor he had seen play Falstaff in *Henry IV*. "I think nothing equals *Macbeth*," he wrote. "It is wonderful."

But Lincoln had never seen a performance of Shakespeare's plays until he became president. In February and March of 1864, Lincoln saw *Hamlet*, *Richard III*, *Julius Caesar*, and *The Merchant of Venice*. Each of them starred the great tragic actor Edwin Booth, brother to Lincoln's future assassin, John Wilkes Booth, whom Lincoln had seen in *Richard III* the previous year. The president attended Grover's Theatre on E Street, over a hundred times during his presidency. Other times he would go to Ford's Theatre on Tenth Street, where the Lincolns had box seats.

Mary encouraged her husband to go to the theater, and would often join him. Secretary of State William Seward also joined the president, as did his secretaries, friends, and his son Tad. Other nights he was happy to go alone. "It gave him an hour or two of freedom from care and worry," noted friend and journalist Noah Brooks, "and what was better, freedom from the interruption of office-seekers and politicians. He was on such terms with the managers of two of the theaters that he could . . . slip into the stage boxes without being seen by the audience."

His theatrical tastes were often lowbrow: he enjoyed Barney Williams, the Irish comedian who acted the blackface minstrel, for example. But his favorite playwright was Shakespeare. During one performance of *Henry IV*, an assistant observed of Lincoln, "He has forgotten the war. . . . He is out of politics. He is living in Prince Hal's time."

LINCOLN SUGGESTS FREDERICK DOUGLASS
LEAD AN UNDERGROUND RAILROAD

If Abraham Lincoln lost the fall 1864 election, he knew there was a great possibility that not only would the Confederacy succeed, but that slavery would survive as well. With this in mind, a meeting was arranged with the abolitionist Frederick Douglass—their second—and on August 19, 1864, Douglass found Lincoln in an "alarmed condition." "The dimmed light in his eye, and the deep lines in his strong American face, told plainly the story of the heavy burden of care that weighed upon his spirit." Lincoln said he had hoped that the Emancipation Proclamation, signed eighteen months earlier, would lead to an exodus of slaves, but that "the slaves are not coming so rapidly and so numerously to us as I had hoped." The reason, Douglass responded, was that slaveholders kept the news of the proclamation from their slaves.

Then Lincoln proposed that a "band of scouts, composed of colored men, whose business should be somewhat after the original plan of John Brown, to go into the rebel states, beyond the lines of our Armies, and carry the news of emancipation, and urge the slaves to come within our boundaries." It was a momentous request. A year before the war began, Lincoln had condemned John Brown's actions at Harpers Ferry. Now Lincoln was proposing a mission to establish an official Underground Railroad that bore Brown's stamp.

"He treated me as a man," Douglass said later that day. "He did not let me feel for a moment that there was any difference in the color of our skins! The president is a most remarkable man. I am satisfied now that he is doing all that circumstances will permit him to do." Lincoln called Douglass "one of the most meritorious men in America." Ten days later, Douglass sent Lincoln an outline of a plan to place a small band of African Americans along the Union front to help slaves escape. It was dated August 29—the same day that George McClellan, the man whom Lincoln expected to defeat him in the fall election, was nominated by the Democrats in Chicago.

LINCOLN'S CHALLENGERS—TWO FORMER GENERALS
AND A CABINET MEMBER

Two failed Civil War generals and a member of his own cabinet wanted Lincoln's job in 1864. The first challenger was Salmon Chase, Lincoln's secretary of the treasury, who believed he should be president ever since he lost the Republican Party's nomination in 1860.

In February, a group of anti-Lincoln politicians sent around a circular that said the president needed to be replaced by Chase on the ticket. The promotion blew up in Chase's face, and most Republican organizations quickly endorsed Lincoln.

Major General John C. Frémont challenged Lincoln from the left in the spring, under the Radical Democratic Party. Frémont, a legendary Western explorer and one of California's first two senators, had been badly defeated by Democrat James Buchanan when Republicans nominated him as their first candidate in 1856. Lincoln had appointed him as a commander in the West, but poor management and the issuance of his own emancipation proclamation—without telling Lincoln—led to his dismissal. He was sent to West Virginia, where Thomas "Stonewall" Jackson chased him around. He eventually resigned, but was still a darling to radical German Americans and the abolitionists. But few came to the Radical Democratic Party's convention in Cleveland on May 31, and Frémont withdrew from the race.

Next, Republicans wondered whether Grant might be interested. Lincoln heard the rumors and sent John Eaton, a Union chaplain, to feel him out. Grant told Eaton that he thought it "as important for the cause that [Lincoln] should be elected as that the army should be successful in the field."

The Northern discontents on the right came together behind George McClellan, the Union commander Lincoln had dismissed in 1862. The Democrats opposed an emancipation war, and seemed willing to exchange peace for recognition of the Confederacy, but many were confused on just where they stood.

"The truth is," wrote one Republican editorialist, "neither you, nor I, nor the Democrats themselves, can tell whether they have a peace platform or a war platform. . . . Upon the whole, it is both peace and war, that is peace with the rebels but war against their own government." Despite their platform, which smelled defeatist, Lincoln still expected to lose the election. But then something happened in Atlanta.

This Currier & Ives Democratic Party campaign poster from 1864 depicts Democratic presidential nominee and former Union commander George McClellan (on the left) and his running mate, vice-presidential candidate George H. Pendleton.

UNION TRIUMPHS
IN GEORGIA AND
IN THE SHENANDOAH VALLEY

JUBAL EARLY KNOCKS AT THE GATES OF WASHINGTON— AND LINCOLN SEES BATTLE

During the siege at Petersburg, General Robert E. Lee ordered cavalry-man Jubal Early to push northward to drive Union troops out of the Shenandoah Valley. Lee's aim was to regain access to the valley's bounty, pull Grant's men away from besieged Petersburg, and perhaps even harass Washington, DC. Early's fifteen thousand men moved, crossing the Potomac on July 6, and on July 11 his forces appeared at Washington defenses five miles north of the White House. Because Grant had sent Washington army units to Virginia, all that was left to defend the lines was a ragtag band of convalescents and local militia. Weeks earlier, Northern leaders imagined taking Richmond; now Rebel troops were at the gates of Washington.

The War Department sent frantic cables to Grant, who dispatched the battle-tested Sixth Corps to man the fortifications just in time. Elisha Hunt Rhodes of Rhode Island came with them and was stationed at Fort Stevens, in Washington's suburbs, which he had helped build in 1861.

On July 12, at Fort Stevens, Rhodes noticed, along the fort's parapet, a man in a stovepipe hat, who kept poking his head over the wall as Rebel bullets whistled by. One of the Sixth Corps' captains—the future Supreme Court Justice Oliver Wendell Holmes—also noticed the tall civilian, and before he recognized who he was, yelled, "Get down, you damn fool, before you get shot!" Lincoln, amused, kept his head down.

Early, facing an army ahead of him and more gathering behind, retreated back to Virginia virtually unharmed. Grant created a new Army of the Shenandoah and put it under the command of the energetic cavalryman Phil Sheridan, with orders to "pursue Early to the death."

But such intent was lost on a discouraged Northern press and public. After Early's jaunt, a writer for the London *Times* commented that "the Confederacy is more formidable than ever." On July 18, Lincoln called upon the states to deliver another 500,000 soldiers, with a draft before the fall elections to make up for any shortfall. The New York diarist George Templeton Strong wrote, "The blood and treasure spent on this summer's campaign have done little for the country." One Democratic editor, looking ahead to the fall elections, observed, quite grimly, that "Lincoln is deader than dead."

THE ATLANTA CAMPAIGN—SHERMAN IS STYMIED AT KENNESAW MOUNTAIN

During the summer of 1864, the Confederates were holding out for time, trying to prevent any major Union victories before the fall election. Grant had ordered Sherman to move against Johnston's army, to break it up and to destroy Southern resources. Sherman, leading 100,000 men, had his eyes on Atlanta. To get there, he had to go through the rugged terrain south of Chattanooga and get past Johnston and his 63,000 troops.

By nature, Joseph Johnston was a defensive fighter. He had retreated from Manassas and Yorktown in 1862, and avoided a fight with Grant over Vicksburg in 1863. Johnston was adored by his men—some said because he so deftly kept them from the battlefield. As he moved southward, Sherman kept swinging around Johnston's left flank, but Johnston refused to fight Sherman's superior forces in the open. And Sherman, despite his fierce reputation, refused to charge against entrenched troops.

The Confederate government and the press criticized Johnston for his constant retreats. "The truth is we have run until I am getting out of heart," wrote one of Johnston's soldiers to his wife, "& we must make a Stand soon or the army will be demoralized. . . ." At the end of May, rains turned the clay into slip. Just north of Marietta, the Confederates dug in along Kennesaw Mountain—Cherokee for "burial ground."

Sherman was losing his patience, and worried over his three-hundred-mile supply line. He decided to "feign on both flanks and assault the center. It may cost us dear but in results would surpass an attempt to pass around." About thirteen thousand Union soldiers charged the Confederate center, but the Confederates were well-established behind breastworks that approached those at Petersburg. "I've heard men say that if they ever killed a Yankee during the war they were not aware of it," Sam Watkins would write later. "I am satisfied that on this memorable day, every man in our regiment killed from . . . twenty to one hundred each. All that was necessary was to load and shoot. . . ."

In the middle of the afternoon, General George Thomas sent Sherman the message that "one or two more such assaults would use up this army." Sherman called it off. The Confederates had killed or wounded three thousand Union men; Union forces inflicted six hundred Confederate casualties. The victory buoyed Southerners. Atlantan Mary Mallard wrote that "everyone feels unbounded confidence in General Johnston" and an Atlanta journalist wrote that Sherman's army would be "cut to pieces."

THE FALL OF ATLANTA CHANGES EVERYTHING

General Sherman shook off the defeat at Kennesaw Mountain and immediately started flanking General Johnston's army again, backing it toward Atlanta, and Richmond leaders became jittery. President Jefferson Davis, seeking a way of "averting calamity," sent the unpopular Braxton Bragg on a fact-finding mission, and he recommended John Bell Hood replace Johnston. But General Robert E. Lee advised against the move, because he thought Hood was too reckless—"All lion, none of the fox." On July 16, Davis asked Johnston for "your plan of operations," and Johnston hinted he might abandon Atlanta. That was unacceptable: Atlanta was the major rail hub of the South, which sent food to Lee's army in Virginia, and had also become a manufacturing center. Besides, the city was one of the symbols of the Confederacy.

Davis, who preferred generals who fought, replaced Johnston with Hood. Two days after taking command, Hood attacked Sherman. In three battles over the last eight days of July, Hood lost fifteen thousand men to Sherman's six thousand. As Atlantans began to flee their city, the Southern press touted the battles as Confederate victories. "Sherman will suffer the greatest defeat that any Yankee General has suffered during the war. . . ." wrote one Georgia newspaper. Confederate troops retreated to Atlanta's heavily fortified ramparts, beginning a siege. Sherman showed no mercy, lobbing shells onto Atlanta's streets, noting, "War is war, and not popularity-seeking."

The two sides sparred until August 26, when the Union Army disappeared from its trenches on the edge of Atlanta. Hood thought they'd retreated, but they were sweeping twenty miles south of the city to cut off roads and railroads, just as Northern Democrats at their Chicago convention were declaring the war a failure. When he realized what was happening, Hood struck at the Union forces but he was beaten badly, and on September 1, he abandoned the city to prevent being surrounded. The next day, the Union Army marched into Atlanta, and Sherman sent Lincoln a telegram: "Atlanta is ours, and fairly won." Sherman was hailed as the greatest general since Napoleon, and Lincoln's reelection, apparently impossible just days earlier, became possible again.

"Since Atlanta I have felt as if all were dead within me, forever," Mary Chesnut wrote. "We are going to be wiped off the earth."

THE PEOPLE OF ATLANTA PROTEST THE EVACUATION OF THEIR CITY

After taking Atlanta on September 2, 1864, Sherman gave an order that all civilians must evacuate the city. Here is the response from the remaining government in Atlanta, dated September 11.

Maj. Gen. W. T. SHERMAN:
  SIR: We, the undersigned . . . petition you to reconsider the order requiring [the people] to leave Atlanta . . . [W]e are satisfied . . . it will involve . . . consequences appalling and heart-rending.
  Many poor women are in advanced state of pregnancy; others now having young children, and whose husbands, for the greater part, are either in the army, prisoners, or dead. Some say, "I have such a one sick at my house; who will wait on them when I am gone?" Others say, "What are we to do? We have no house to go to, and no means to buy, build, or rent any; no parents, relatives, or friends to go to. . . ."
  . . . [B]efore your arrival here a large portion of the people had retired south, so that the country south of this is already crowded and without houses enough to accommodate the people . . . This being so, how is it possible for the people still here (mostly women and children) to find any shelter? And how can they live through the winter in the woods? . . . [W]hat has this helpless people done, that they should be driven from their homes to wander strangers and outcasts and exiles, and to subsist on charity?
  . . . [W]e most earnestly and solemnly petition you to reconsider this order, or modify it, and suffer this unfortunate people to remain at home and enjoy what little means they have.

  Respectfully submitted.
  JAMES M. CALHOUN, Mayor.
  E. E. RAWSON, S. C. WELLS, Councilmen.

SHERMAN'S RESPONSE—"WAR IS CRUELTY . . ."

Nine days after receiving the letter from Atlanta's officials pleading for mercy, Sherman responded to Atlanta's officials. In the letter, Sherman reveals his theory of war, in which war's sufferings are not just visited upon soldiers but on civilians.

September 12, 1864

GENTLEMEN: I have your letter of the 11th, in the nature of a petition to revoke my orders removing all the inhabitants from Atlanta. I . . . give full credit to your statements of the distress that will be occasioned, and yet shall not revoke my orders, because they were not designed to meet the humanities of the case, but to prepare for the future struggles in which millions of good people outside of Atlanta have a deep interest. We must have peace, not only at Atlanta, but in all America.

The use of Atlanta for warlike purposes is inconsistent with its character as a home for families. . . . Why not go now . . . instead of waiting till the plunging shot of contending armies will renew the scenes of the past month? . . . War is cruelty, and you cannot refine it; and those who brought war into our country deserve all the curses and maledictions a people can pour out. . . . I had no hand in making this war, and . . . I will make more sacrifices to-day than any of you to secure peace. But you cannot have peace and a division of our country. . . . the only way the people of Atlanta can hope once more to live in peace and quiet at home, is to stop the war. . . . But, my dear sirs, when peace does come, you may call on me for any thing. Then will I share with you the last cracker, and watch with you to shield your homes and families against danger from every quarter.

Now you must go, and take with you the old and feeble, feed and nurse them, and build for them, in more quiet places, proper habitations to shield them against the weather until the mad passions of men cool down, and allow the Union and peace once more to settle over your old homes at Atlanta.

Yours in haste,
W. T. SHERMAN, Major-General commanding.

UNION COMMANDER PHILIP SHERIDAN LAYS WASTE
TO THE SHENANDOAH VALLEY

After Early threatened Washington in July 1864, General Grant put cavalryman Philip Sheridan in charge of the newly formed Army of the Shenandoah and charged him with two tasks: destroy Confederate General Jubal Early's army, which was running loose in the Shenandoah Valley, and decimate the fertile valley, the breadbasket of the Confederacy. The orders were an extension of Sherman's total-war philosophy being practiced in Georgia.

"Take all provisions, forage and stock wanted for the use of your command," Grant told Sheridan. "Such as cannot be consumed, destroy." Grant wanted the valley left so barren that "crows flying over it . . . will have to carry their provender with them."

Sheridan obeyed, sending Early "whirling through Winchester" at the battle in that Virginia town on September 19. He used his superior forces three days later to overwhelm Early at the Battle of Fisher's Hill, a high bluff dominating the valley at its narrowest point. But on the morning of October 19, Early launched a surprise attack at Cedar Creek that sent Sheridan's Army of the Shenandoah reeling. Sheridan was in Winchester, on his way to a war conference in Washington, and when he heard the news, he raced to the battle on his large black horse, Rienzi. When the men started to chant his name, Sheridan yelled, "God damn you! Don't cheer me. Fight! We will lick them out of their boots!"

Early fled, and the Confederates would never again return to the Shenandoah Valley. To celebrate, General Grant fired a second hundred-gun volley into the enemy trenches at Petersburg. At one point during the campaign, Sheridan proudly reported the devastation he had wreaked in the valley. "I have destroyed over 2,000 barns filled with wheat, hay, and farming implements; [and] over 70 mills; . . . have driven in front of the army 4,000 head of stock and have killed 3,000 sheep. . . . When this is completed, the Valley . . . will have but little in it for man or beast."

Northerners considered the devastation in the valley essential; Southerners called the destruction wrought there "the Burning."

Before launching General Sherman's march to the sea, Union troops set fire to Atlanta, leaving much of it in ruins.

PROSPECTS DARKEN
FOR THE CONFEDERACY

WEEK 43

SOLDIERS—AND THE REST OF THE NORTH—
VOTE FOR LINCOLN

On the morning of November 8, Election Day, Tad Lincoln, the president's eleven-year-old son, told his father to look out his office window at the South Lawn. There, Lincoln's White House guards, soldiers from the 150th Pennsylvania, were lined up to cast their votes. At noon, Lincoln spoke with Noah Brooks, a journalist and friend, noting that "about this thing I am very far from being certain."

Despite his worries, the president earned a decisive victory, receiving 2.2 million votes to McClellan's 1.8 million, and winning the Electoral College by a vote of 212 to 21. Lincoln had carried all of the participating states besides New Jersey, Kentucky, and Delaware. Soldiers overwhelmingly supported him. Lincoln's sixty-three guards had all voted for him, not much of a surprise. Of the 150,635 soldiers' votes identified, Lincoln received 116,887. Although one in two soldiers was a Democrat when he joined the army, more than three out of four soldiers voted for Lincoln.

Why had the soldiers, who had suffered more than other Americans, voted for Lincoln and a continuation of the war? To vote for the Democrats was to agree that the war was a failure. After nearly four years of war, that was a tough pill to swallow. "We want peace too," said an Ohio officer who had switched from the Democratic to the Republican Party, "*honorable* peace, won in the full light of day at the bayonet's point, with our grand old flag flying over us as we negotiate it, instead of a cowardly peace purchased at the price of national dishonor." The people had endorsed Lincoln's steadfast determination to continue to an unconditional victory. "I am astonished," observed one British war correspondent, "the more I see and hear of the extent and depth of [this] determination . . . to fight to the last."

The politically astute Lincoln had his own analysis, which he shared with his secretary John Nicolay: "I am here by the blunders of the Democrats. If, instead of resolving that the war was a failure, they had resolved that I was a failure, and denounced me for not prosecuting it more vigorously, I would not have been reelected."

"TO MAKE GEORGIA HOWL!"—
SHERMAN'S MARCH TO THE SEA

A week after Lincoln's reelection, William Tecumseh Sherman led his 62,000 men southeast out of Atlanta, leaving it, as Sherman said, "smouldering and in ruins." Sherman planned cutting a 225-mile wasteland through Georgia on his way to Savannah. Lincoln, as well as Generals Grant and Halleck, had resisted the idea at first—Lincoln said the plan made him "*anxious*, if not fearful"—but they had relented to Sherman's vision. "If we can march a well-appointed army right through [Jefferson Davis's] territory, it is a demonstration to the world, foreign and domestic, that we have a power which Davis cannot resist. . . . " Sherman said. "I can make the march, and make Georgia howl!"

Even without a battle, Sherman planned the "utter destruction of [Georgia's] roads, houses and people," acts intended to convince "sensible men" that further resistance was pointless. He left behind rail links and telegraph links—he didn't want to have to guard them in his rear— which meant no one in the North would know how he fared until—or if—he got to Savannah. When Senator John Sherman asked the president about his brother, Lincoln replied, "I know the hole he went in at, but I can't tell you what hole he will come out of."

The army marched off with twenty days worth of food, herding along three thousand beef cattle, taking the rest of their food from Georgians along the way. Sherman's troops were originally ordered to only take supplies they needed, and to avoid entering Southern homes. But the destruction soon knew few limitations. In the words of one soldier, the army "destroyed all we could not eat, stole their niggers, burned their cotton & gins, spilled their sorghum, burned & twisted their R. Roads and raised Hell generally." Slave mansions became a favorite target of arsonist soldiers. Sherman broke his army into different columns, and at night they could locate each other by the flames from the homes they'd torched. Confederates dubbed Sherman "the Attila of the West."

Sherman's army was adopting their commander's vision; to increase the pain inflicted on Georgians, they believed, would shorten the war. "Anything, Everything," wrote one soldier to his family in Wisconsin, "if it will help weaken them, is my motto." After four weeks, Sherman's army arrived in Savannah and discovered that the city's ten thousand militia had abandoned the city's fortifications. "I beg to present to you as a Christmas-gift," Sherman cabled Lincoln, "the city of Savannah."

CONFEDERATES REFUSE TO GIVE UP BLACK PRISONERS— AND ALL EXCHANGES ARE HALTED

In 1862, with the capture of Union and Confederate soldiers at battles at Fort Donelson, Shiloh, and on the Virginia Peninsula, the number of prisoners held by both sides skyrocketed. Public pressure in the North and South demanded that prisoners come home, and despite problems, both sides exchanged prisoners through 1862.

But Lincoln's Emancipation Proclamation, and its call for the enlistment of African-American soldiers, complicated matters. President Jefferson Davis and the Confederate Congress responded by declaring that black soldiers would be considered escaped slaves rather than prisoners of war, and were turned over to the states to handle, which meant they could be executed. The U.S. government said they would retaliate by executing Confederate officers, but both sides backed down from those harsh measures. Exchanges broke down.

Then, in mid-April of 1864, the Confederate cavalry commanded by Nathan Bedford Forrest captured the Union-occupied Fort Pillow, Tennessee, on the Mississippi River. Many of the Union's African-American troops surrendered, and surviving prisoners said Forrest's men executed black prisoners. President Lincoln considered retaliation but then decided that "blood can not restore blood, and government should not act for revenge." Still, captured soldiers weren't exchanged. Prisoners captured during General Grant's Overland Campaign in the spring of 1864 overwhelmed Rebel and Yankee prisoner-of-war camps, with mortality rates often exceeding those in battle.

Despite increasing pressure from the Northern public to bring home prisoners of war languishing in Southern prisons, Northern leaders resisted. "It is hard on our men held in southern prisons not to exchange them," General Grant wrote to General Butler, "but it is humanity to those left in the ranks to fight our battles. Every man we hold, when released on parole or otherwise, becomes an active soldier against us at once either directly or indirectly. If we commence a system of exchange which liberates all prisoners taken, we will have to fight on until the whole south is exterminated. If we hold those caught they amount to no more than dead men."

Still, public pressure led to an exchange of some prisoners at the beginning of 1865, including several hundred black soldiers. But by then, the war was nearly over.

"THIS HELL ON EARTH"—ANDERSONVILLE AND OTHER
DISMAL PRISONER-OF-WAR CAMPS

On Thanksgiving Day 1864, a company of Indiana soldiers in Sherman's army at Milledgeville, Georgia's capital, were feasting on dinner when a small group of emaciated Union soldiers shuffled into the camplight. The men had escaped from a Georgia prison camp established in early 1864 in an impenetrable swampy pine forest.

The prison, Andersonville, became a symbol of dismal prisoner treatment during the war. It was meant to hold 10,000 prisoners. But by August 1864, it held 33,000, making it the fifth largest city in the Confederacy, although it was built on a dozen acres. Illness and disease—diarrhea, dysentery, gangrene, and scurvy among them—killed soldiers faster than any artillery battery could. Gross mismanagement meant latrines often overflowed into a stagnant stream used for washing and drinking water.

Because of the filth, the most innocuous wounds—a blister, a mosquito bite, a splinter—often turned gangrenous. Gangrenous limbs were amputated, and amputations almost always led to death.

The Confederacy could barely feed their soldiers, much less their prisoners, so many starved to death. On some days, the men got a half pint of raw meal, or a repulsive mixture of swamp water and cornmeal, or a brackish stew of dirty pea pods, if anything at all. About thirteen thousand men perished at Andersonville, a third of the deaths in all Southern prisons. This outnumbered Union soldiers killed at the battles of Antietam and Gettysburg *combined*. Secretary of War Edwin Stanton concluded that "there seems to have been a deliberate system of savage and barbarous treatment." But historians generally agree that the abysmal conditions were most likely caused by inept administration, limited Confederate resources, and a tottering infrastructure incapable of transporting food.

The outrage over Andersonville seemed to blind Yankees to how poorly they treated Rebel soldiers in their own prison camps. The mortality rate at the prisoner-of-war camp in Elmira (called "Helmira" by many imprisoned there), New York, was 24 percent.

Of the 400,000 Union and Confederate soldiers imprisoned in the war, 55,000 died in captivity, nearly 10 percent of all fatalities.

ANOTHER SUICIDAL ASSAULT—THE BATTLE OF FRANKLIN

When General Grant approved General Sherman's march from Atlanta to the sea, he knew that Sherman would be leaving behind Confederate General John Bell Hood to roam freely. Sherman believed General George Thomas could handle Hood, and in late November, Thomas and Hood were in a race to reach Nashville. The stakes were high. If Hood leaped ahead of Thomas, he could use Nashville as his base to threaten undefended cities such as Louisville and Cincinnati, potentially drawing troops from Sherman and Grant. Strategically, having Thomas hold Nashville was more important than having Sherman take Savannah.

Hood was battle-scarred. His right arm had been badly wounded at Gettysburg. He'd lost his right leg at Chickamauga. He was still a fighter, and his men strapped him into his saddle before battles. He faced Thomas, a cautious general who had fought well at the Battle of Bull Run, Shiloh, and had earned fame as the "Rock of Chickamauga" for his stand at the northern Georgia battlefield in 1863.

On the morning of November 30, Union troops under Brigadier General John Schofield arrived at the town of Franklin, twenty miles south of Nashville, just before Hood. Wanting to keep Hood from striking Thomas's supply lines headed toward Nashville, Schofield dug into fortifications on the southern edge of town, which had been left the previous year by Union General William Rosecrans. Hood arrived at Franklin the same day, and at about four p.m. he ordered a frontal assault.

"I do not like the looks of this fight," said Confederate Corps Commander Benjamin F. Cheatham. The Confederates would have to cover two miles of open ground to breach the Union breastworks, about twice the distance that Pickett and his men covered at Gettysburg in that doomed charge.

Close to three p.m., about twenty thousand Confederate soldiers stepped out. Confederate bands played tunes such as "Dixie," "Bonnie Blue Flag," and "The Girl I Left Behind Me," one of the few times music was played during an assault in the war. Then the songs were drowned out by the sound of Union artillery, and a battle began that would rage for five hours.

THE CONFEDERATES ARE ROUTED AT FRANKLIN— AND NASHVILLE AS WELL

At Franklin, Confederate General John Bell Hood's men made a dozen thrusts at the Union breastworks, sweeping forward "as steady . . . as a tidal wave." It was the last disastrous frontal assault of the war; in four years, generals such as Hood still hadn't learned that modern warfare made such charges suicidal. "At every discharge of my gun there were two distinct sounds," wrote Captain Aaron Baldwin of the Sixth Ohio light artillery, "first the explosion, then the [shattering of] bones."

Even Hood saw the futility of the charges, and called off the slaughter at nine p.m. In the night, the Union Army retreated, usually a sign of defeat, but the Confederates had lost far more men. The Union had suffered 2,326 casualties; the Confederates 6,252, nearly as many as Grant lost in his catastrophic frontal assault at Cold Harbor in the spring. Six Confederate generals were killed in the battle, their worst single-day loss of the war, decimating the Confederate command.

Union Brigadier General John Schofield had retreated to the safety of Nashville, and Hood, undeterred, followed, but even he knew that to attack the city, which had been occupied by Union forces for thirty-three months, would be ruinous. Thomas readied his troops for two weeks—Grant almost dismissed him because of his slow preparation— and then he hit Hood's men outside of Nashville on December 15. The Confederate lines began to crumble that afternoon.

"I beheld for the first and only time," Hood stated afterward, "a Confederate Army abandon the field in confusion." That night, Thomas was out with the cavalry going after stragglers, repeating almost glee-fully, "Didn't I tell you we could lick'em? Didn't I tell you . . ." In the Confederate camp, a Rebel private mistakenly entered Hood's tent and found the general weeping. Less than a month later, disgraced and abandoned, he would resign.

UNION GENERAL WILLIAM TECUMSEH SHERMAN
SURVEYING THE PROSPECTS

General William Tecumesh Sherman is shown here sitting on his horse in the Atlanta area sometime in the fall of 1864. After he forced Confederate General John B. Hood to evacuate Atlanta, Sherman remained there for nearly two and a half months longer, resting his men and accumulating supplies for his devastating march through Georgia.

The "MIGHTY SCOURGE" ENDS, *the* NATION *is* TRANSFORMED (1865)

INTRODUCTION (1865)

"The winter of 1864–1865 was the coldest that had been known for many years," remembered the Tennessee soldier Sam Watkins, who had fought in many of the major battles of the war, including Shiloh, Chattanooga, Chickamauga, Missionary Ridge, and Atlanta. "The ground was frozen and rough, and our soldiers were poorly clad, while many, yes, very many, were entirely barefooted. . . . Everything and nature, too, seemed to be working against us. Even the keen, cutting air that whistled through our tattered clothes . . . seemed to lash us."

The Confederacy was also lashed by its inability to feed and supply its dwindling army, but more so by the increasingly muscular Union Army, now commanded by two men—Ulysses S. Grant and William Tecumseh Sherman. Sherman's army, which his foe Joseph Johnston concluded was as impressive as any since the times of Julius Caesar, pressed northward into South Carolina, an invasion that moved like a giant scythe through the heartland of the Confederacy. Ulysses S. Grant squeezed Robert E. Lee's defenses around Petersburg, which protected Richmond, stretching the Confederate lines thinner and thinner, until Lee would flee westward, only to be trapped at a little town named Appomattox Station. The Confederacy would not only see its landscape destroyed, it would watch as the North laid the groundwork for the destruction of Southern society. In the new year, the U.S. Congress debated the Thirteenth Amendment to free the slaves, and the Confederacy, grasping at any way to survive, even considered freeing their slaves and arming them—treasonable ideas four years earlier.

"It was perhaps better for the country and for mankind that the good man could not know the end from the beginning," Frederick Douglass said of Abraham Lincoln years after the Civil War ended. "Had he foreseen the thousands who must sink into bloody graves, the mountains of debt to be laid on the breast of the nation, the terrible hardships and sufferings involved in the contest, and his own death by an assassin's hand, he too might have adopted the weak sentiment of those who said, 'Erring sisters, depart in peace.'"

THE BEGINNING
OF THE END

WEEK 44

TAKING FORT FISHER, THE LAST ATLANTIC HARBOR
FOR BLOCKADE RUNNERS

By the end of 1864, the last port open to Confederate blockade runners on the Atlantic seaboard was Wilmington, North Carolina, protected by Fort Fisher, at the mouth of the Cape Fear River. The blustery Ben Butler, a politically appointed general, led the Union attack on the fort at the end of December 1864. His plan consisted of floating a boat loaded with 215 tons of gunpowder to the fort to blow up its ramparts in the night. The boat exploded, but did so little damage that the Confederates mistook it for an exploding boiler. Butler then landed men on the fort's banks, but when they were met with blistering artillery fire and land mines, he put the men back on their boats and declared the fort invincible.

Since Lincoln's position had been solidified by his reelection, he and Grant no longer had to smile at Butler's incompetence. They relieved Butler of his generalship, sent him back to Massachusetts, and put A. H. Terry and Rear Admiral David Porter in charge. Porter assembled the largest fleet of the war—nearly sixty warships—and on January 13, he ordered a two-day bombardment, raining eight hundred tons of shot and shell on the fort's defenders, disabling most of the fort's guns. On January 15, forty-five hundred men attacked the fort's north side, with two thousand more making an assault from sea. Although they took one thousand casualties, the fort was breached and its two thousand men surrendered.

Wilmington soon fell, and the coast of North Carolina was now in Yankee hands. The Anaconda Plan, devised by old General Winfield Scott nearly four years earlier to surround and then squeeze the Confederacy to death, had finally been completed. No open port on the Atlantic was left in the Confederacy that could accept foreign supplies. Confederacy Vice President Alexander Stephens called the loss of the fort "one of the greatest disasters that had befallen our Cause from the beginning of the war."

CONFEDERATE SOLDIERS DESERT IN DROVES

In early months of 1865, the Confederacy was falling apart. The governor of Georgia was threatening to secede, and the governor of North Carolina only allowed his own state's troops to wear the state's 92,000 uniforms. "If the Confederacy falls," Jefferson Davis said privately, "there should be written on its tombstone: 'Died of a Theory.'"

Robert E. Lee's army, which included some of the most devoted troops of the Civil War, began to desert in droves. They deserted because they were under-clothed, underfed, and barefoot—symptoms of a country that was unable to feed and supply its civilians or its soldiers. Some were so hungry and hopeless they surrendered themselves to the enemy they'd been trying to murder for years, knowing that they'd at least be provided with food and clothes.

One soldier in the Petersburg trenches, counting forty Confederate soldiers who had surrendered in two days, noted that "if we stay here, the Johnnies will all come over before the 4th of July." In one month alone, eight percent of the Army of Northern Virginia deserted.

Soldiers also left the battlefield because their families at home were desperate. Tens of thousands of Southern women, their land destroyed, their prospects bleak, begged their men to come home. "We haven't got nothing in the house to eat but a little bit of meal," one woman wrote to her husband, a soldier. "Try to get off and come home and fix us all up some and then you can go back. If you put off coming, t'wont be no use to come, for we'll all hands of us be out there in the garden in the old graveyard with your ma and mine."

One Confederate officer noted that "the chief and prevailing reason [for desertion] was a conviction among them that our cause was hopeless and that further sacrifices were useless." Lee recognized the desertions had reached "epidemic" proportions. "Unless it can be changed," he said, "[it] will bring us calamity."

LINCOLN ATTENDS PEACE TALKS ON THE *RIVER QUEEN*

At the start of 1865, Lincoln felt public pressure to at least look as though he was open to a peaceful reconciliation, and agreed to discuss peace with a three-man Confederate delegation led by Vice President Alexander Stephens at Fort Monroe in Virginia. Lincoln didn't need to be there, but he couldn't stay away, and attended the meeting on the *River Queen*, a steamer that served as a floating White House. Lincoln had not seen Stephens since they were both Whigs in the House of Representatives sixteen years ago, and when they met, the president shook his hand and smiled.

The four hours of discussion on February 3 began with Stephens suggesting that the Union and Confederates join forces to kick the French out of Mexico "until the passions of both sides might cool." But another Confederate delegate admitted that the Southern people "would be found unwilling to kindle a new war . . . on any such pretence," and that subject was closed. Lincoln was not interested.

The Southerners wanted an armistice and a convention to discuss peace terms, but Lincoln would only agree to an armistice after the Confederates committed to giving up their arms and coming back into the Union, a *"sine qua non* with me." In one of his few concessions, Lincoln told the Confederates that if they surrendered, their leaders would not lose their property or be jailed.

The two sides also discussed slavery. William Seward, U. S. secretary of state, told the Southern representatives that the Union would not "retract or modify" the Emancipation Proclamation, and informed them that Congress had just passed a constitutional amendment banning slavery. Lincoln told the commissioners he would be willing to "remunerate the Southern people for their slaves," saying he believed the "people of the North" would approve "an appropriation as high as Four Hundred Millions of Dollars for this purpose."

The talks ended with no movement by either side, much less agreement. Davis used Lincoln's stiff peace conditions to denounce the president as "His Majesty Abraham the First," predicting that Lincoln and Seward would learn that "they had been speaking to their masters" and that Confederate armies would yet "compel the Yankees, in less than twelve months, to petition us for peace on our own terms."

"LOTS OF WISDOM IN THAT DOCUMENT. . . ." —LINCOLN'S REMARKABLE, REFLECTIVE SECOND INAUGURAL ADDRESS

Inauguration Day March 4, 1865, began cold, windy, and rainy, as had Lincoln's first inauguration four years earlier. But as Lincoln began to speak, the clouds opened and the sun bathed the fifty thousand or so who were gathered at the Capitol. "It made my heart jump," Lincoln said afterward.

As interesting as what Lincoln included in the speech is what he left out. He neither recited his administration's accomplishments nor laid out his postwar policy, not even in broad strokes. The speech did not affirm the moral superiority of the North, or call upon his supporters and God to help the North to finish the war. "The prayers of both [sides] could not be answered; that of neither has been answered fully," Lincoln said. "The Almighty has His own purposes." To Frederick Douglass and to others, the address felt "more like a sermon than a state paper," as Lincoln quoted the Bible four times in only seven hundred words. He ended the speech calling for reconciliation:

> *With malice toward none; with charity for all; with firmness in the right, as God gives us to see the right, let us strive on to finish the work we are in; to bind up the nation's wounds; to care for him who shall have borne the battle, and for his widow, and his orphan—to do all which may achieve and cherish a just, and a lasting peace, among ourselves, and with all nations.*

But the most remarkable part of the speech was not its ending, but the preceding section. Here he adopted the abolitionist belief that the war was necessary to wash the country of its original sin—"American slavery"—and restore the promise of the country's founding principles. "Fondly do we hope—" Lincoln said, "fervently do we pray—

> *that this mighty scourge of war may speedily pass away. Yet, if God wills that it continue, until all the wealth piled by the bond-man's two hundred and fifty years of unrequited toil shall be sunk, and until every drop of blood drawn with the lash, shall be paid by another drawn with the sword, as was said three thousand years ago, so still it must be said "the judgments of the Lord, are true and righteous altogether."*

THE TEXT OF LINCOLN'S SECOND INAUGURAL ADDRESS

"I know not how many times and before how many people I have quoted these solemn words of our martyred President," Frederick Douglass said years after Lincoln delivered his Second Inaugural Address. "They struck me at the time, and have seemed to me ever since to contain more vital substance than I have ever seen compressed in a space so narrow. . . ."

. . . On the occasion corresponding to this four years ago all thoughts were anxiously directed to an impending civil war. All dreaded it, all sought to avert it. While the inaugural address was being delivered from this place, devoted altogether to saving the Union without war, urgent agents were in the city seeking to destroy it without war—seeking to dissolve the Union and divide effects by negotiation. Both parties deprecated war, but one of them would make war rather than let the nation survive, and the other would accept war rather than let it perish, and the war came.

One-eighth of the whole population were colored slaves, not distributed generally over the Union, but localized in the southern part of it. These slaves constituted a peculiar and powerful interest. All knew that this interest was somehow the cause of the war. To strengthen, perpetuate, and extend this interest was the object for which the insurgents would rend the Union even by war, while the Government claimed no right to do more than to restrict the territorial enlargement of it. Neither party expected for the war the magnitude or the duration which it has already attained. Both read the same Bible and pray to the same God, and each invokes His aid against the other. It may seem strange that any men should dare to ask a just God's assistance in wringing their bread from the sweat of other men's faces, but let us judge not, that we be not judged. The prayers of both could not be answered. That of neither has been answered fully. The Almighty has His own purposes. . . . Fondly do we hope, fervently do we pray, that this mighty scourge of war may speedily pass away. Yet, if God wills that it continue . . . so still it must be said "the judgments of the Lord are true and righteous altogether."

With malice toward none, with charity for all, with firmness in the right as God gives us to see the right, let us strive on to finish the work we are in, to bind up the nation's wounds, to care for him who shall have borne the battle and for his widow and his orphan, to do all which may achieve and cherish a just and lasting peace among ourselves and with all nations.

FREDERICK DOUGLASS FIGHTS TO GET IN THE WHITE HOUSE TO PAY HIS RESPECTS TO THE PRESIDENT

Though no African American had ever attended an inaugural reception, Frederick Douglass decided that he would come to this one to personally congratulate the president, whom he'd met twice before. Douglass recounted that event in his autobiography:

We ... moved slowly towards the executive mansion. ... I regret to be obliged to say, however, that ... on reaching the door, two policemen stationed there took me rudely by the arm and ordered me to stand back, for their directions were to admit no persons of my color. ... I told the officers I was quite sure there must be some mistake, for no such order could have emanated from President Lincoln. They then ... assumed an air of politeness, and offered to conduct me in. We followed their lead, and soon found ourselves walking some planks out of a window, which had been arranged as a temporary passage for the exit of visitors.

We halted so soon as we saw the trick, and I said to the officers, "You have deceived me. I shall not go out of this building till I see President Lincoln." At this moment a gentleman who was passing in recognized me, and I said to him, "Be so kind as to say to Mr. Lincoln that Frederick Douglass is detained by officers at the door." It was not long before ... I walked into the spacious East Room, amid a scene of elegance such as in this country I had never witnessed before. Like a mountain pine high above all others, Mr. Lincoln stood, in his grand simplicity, and home-like beauty.

Recognizing me, even before I reached him, he exclaimed, so that all around could hear him, "Here comes my friend Douglass." Taking me by the hand, he said, "I am glad to see you. I saw you in the crowd today, listening to my inaugural address; how did you like it?"

I said, "Mr. Lincoln, I must not detain you with my poor opinion, when there are thousands waiting to shake hands with you."

"No, no," he said, "you must stop a little, Douglass; there is no man in the country whose opinion I value more than yours. I want to know what you think of it?"

I replied, "Mr. Lincoln, that was a sacred effort."

"I am glad you liked it!" he said, and I passed on ...

PRESIDENT LINCOLN DELIVERS
HIS SECOND INAUGURAL ADDRESS

President Abraham Lincoln delivered his inaugural address on the East Portico of the U.S. Capitol on March 4, 1865. Above, on the balcony, stood John Wilkes Booth.

THE DEATH THROES
OF SLAVERY

WEEK 45

LINCOLN BEGS AND BORROWS FOR VOTES TO PASS THE THIRTEENTH AMENDMENT

During his reelection campaign, Lincoln promised to pursue a Thirteenth Amendment banning slavery, and he took his overwhelming victory as a mandate for its passage. The amendment would change the Constitution, which had sanctioned slavery since it was written. But passing an amendment was a formidable challenge. The Twelfth Amendment had been passed in 1803, some sixty years earlier, and the first twelve amendments had dealt with strictly governmental powers. The Thirteenth Amendment was a sweeping social reform that would affect the daily lives and fortunes of millions of Americans, touching on property rights as well as civil rights.

If Lincoln had been willing to wait for the seating of the new Congress, passage would have been easier. To get the two-thirds majority necessary, Lincoln and the Republicans would have to win votes from lame-duck Democrats, whose official policy was that the Thirteenth Amendment was unwise and impolitic. But other Democrats saw change as necessary to the survival of their party. Lincoln may have relied on more than moral persuasion to get the necessary votes. One Democrat "yes" vote received an appointment to the navy, and an Indiana Republican said afterward that the success of the amendment "depended upon certain negotiations . . . the particulars of which never reached the public."

On January 31, 1865, the amendment passed by 119 to 56. The gallery erupted in cheers, "the like of which," said one partisan witness, "probably no Congress of the United States ever heard before." The amendment read: "Neither slavery nor involuntary servitude, except as a punishment for crime . . . shall exist within the United States. . . ." To many, it must have seemed a lifetime ago that Congress and Lincoln approved of another Thirteenth Amendment, which *forbade* Congress from ever banning slavery in a state. But it had been four long years.

"I have felt, ever since the vote," a Republican congressman wrote later, "as if I were in a new country."

AN AFRICAN-AMERICAN MINISTER ADDRESSES CONGRESS FOR THE FIRST TIME AND CALLS FOR CIVIL RIGHTS AS WELL AS FREEDOM

Less than two weeks after Congress's passage of the Thirteenth Amendment to the Constitution, Henry Highland Garnet, a New York City minister and an abolitionist, came to the hall of the U.S. House of Representatives to commemorate the passage of the Thirteenth Amendment. Garnet had been born into slavery, and in 1824 he had escaped as a nine-year-old boy with his parents through the Underground Railroad.

During the Civil War, he recruited black soldiers for the Union cause. In the summer of 1863, he and his family eluded the antiblack mobs rampaging through New York City when his daughter chopped off the family name from the door of their home. Garnet spoke on February 12, 1865, Lincoln's fifty-sixth birthday, and was the first African-American to speak before Congress. In his sermon, titled "Let the Monster Perish," he called for more than emancipation.

It is often asked when and where will the demands of the reformers of this and coming ages end? It is a fair question, and I will answer. . . . When emancipation shall be followed by enfranchisement, and all men holding allegiance to the government shall enjoy every right of American citizenship. . . . When the men who endure the sufferings and perils of the battlefield in the defense of their country, and in order to keep our rulers in their places, shall enjoy the well-earned privilege of voting for them. . . . When there shall be no more class legislation and no more trouble concerning the black man and his rights than there is in regard to other American citizens. When, in every respect, he shall be equal before the law, and shall be left to make his own way in the social walks of life.

We ask, and only ask, that when our poor, frail barks are launched on life's ocean, Bound on a voyage of awful length And dangers little known, that, in common with others, we may be furnished with rudder, helm and sails and charts and compass. . . .

THE EMANCIPATION OF AMERICAN SLAVES—
A LONG, POPULAR STRUGGLE

The day following the passage of the Thirteenth Amendment, Salmon P. Chase, once Lincoln's secretary of the treasury and now a Supreme Court Justice, admitted a Massachusetts lawyer named John Rock to practice before the Supreme Court. As well as an attorney, John Rock was a physician, a dentist, and an orator who spoke both French and German. He was also an African-American. Six years earlier, Chase's predecessor, Justice Roger B. Taney, had handed down the Dred Scott decision, writing that black people were "beings . . . so far inferior, that they had no rights which the white man was bound to respect."

The Thirteenth Amendment and John Rock's promotion were made possible because for decades, black and white abolitionists had agitated in the streets and in the voting booth. When existing political parties didn't respond to their call, they created the Republican Party, elected an antislavery Northern Congress, and nominated Lincoln himself, whom they pushed to act politically on his personal antislavery beliefs. Activists also fought to allow black men to take up arms in the struggle. In the summer of 1864, antislavery activists—a majority of them women such as Susan B. Anthony and Elizabeth Cady Stanton—sent 400,000 signatures to Congress, calling for the end to slavery. Before the war, abolitionist and freed slave Frederick Douglass spoke to the struggle for change he was engaged in:

> The whole history of the progress of human liberty shows that all concessions yet made to her august claims have been born of struggle. . . . If there is no struggle there is no progress. Those who profess to favor freedom and yet deprecate agitation, are men who want crops without plowing up the ground. They want rain without thunder and lightning. They want the ocean without the awful roar of its many waters. The struggle may be a moral one; or it may be a physical one; or it may be both moral and physical, but it must be a struggle. Power concedes nothing without a demand. It never did and it never will.

SHERMAN GIVES "FORTY ACRES AND A MULE" TO FREED SLAVES

Union General William Tecumseh Sherman resisted the recruitment of blacks into his army until the very end of the Civil War. That's why it came as a surprise to many that he would be the author of one of the most revolutionary acts regarding race during the entire war: his "Special Field Orders No. 15."

As Sherman moved his army from Atlanta to Savannah, Georgia, thousands of escaped African-American slaves flocked under the protective wing of his army. Rumors streamed North that Sherman and his officers were not treating these freed men, women, and children well, so Secretary of War Edwin Stanton traveled South to assess the situation. To get a sense of what was happening, Stanton met with twenty leaders from the refugee camp and one question he asked was how they could become independent now that they were free. "The way we can best take care of ourselves," came the answer, "is to have land, and turn and till it by our labor. . . . We want to be placed on land until we are able to buy it, and make it our own."

Both Stanton and Sherman agreed with that sentiment, and on January 16, 1865, Sherman issued "Special Field Orders No. 15." It gave freed slaves land abandoned by plantation owners on South Carolina's Sea Islands and the South Carolina and Georgia coast. The head of a freed-slave family would be given forty acres of land. By June, the Union Army had given forty thousand slaves about four hundred thousand acres. Word spread, and freed slaves throughout the South soon expected they, too, would receive what became known as "forty acres and a mule."

But the program was halted when President Andrew Johnson assumed the presidency after Lincoln's assassination in April 1865. Johnson was far more sympathetic to the interests of Southern whites, and in August he ordered the transferred land returned to its former Confederate slave-owners, and it was.

"When you turned us loose," Frederick Douglass, the ardent abolitionist, said in 1876, "you gave us no acres; you turned us loose to the sky, to the storm, to the whirlwind, and, worst of all, you turned us loose to the wrath of our infuriated masters."

RECRUITING MORE CONFEDERATE SOLDIERS— *BLACK* ONES

As the Confederacy hobbled into 1865, Southerners were now considering what was once unthinkable: arming slaves to provide soldiers for the outmanned Confederacy. In January 1864, Major General Patrick Cleburne argued that the South was losing the war because "slavery, from being one of our chief sources of strength at the commencement of the war, has now become, in a military point of view, one of our chief sources of weakness." Escaped slaves were fighting for the Union. The South's embrace of slavery also had turned European nations against the Confederacy. Thus, the Confederacy was threatened with "the loss of all we now hold most sacred—slaves and all other personal property, lands, homesteads, liberty, justice, safety, pride, manhood." To preserve all but slavery, Cleburne concluded that the South would need to arm the slave and "guarantee freedom within a reasonable time to every slave in the South who shall remain true to the Confederacy."

Jefferson Davis at first ordered his generals not to discuss the notion, but in February 1865, Davis said, "We are reduced to choosing whether the negroes shall fight for or against us." Yet the irony of freeing slaves to fight for a nation that cemented slavery in its Constitution was lost on no one. "The day you make soldiers of [African Americans] is the beginning of the end of the revolution," wrote Georgian Howell Cobb, a leading secessionist. "If slaves will make good soldiers our whole theory of slavery is wrong."

The country waited to hear General Robert E. Lee's views. Arming African Americans was "not only expedient but necessary," wrote the general. On March 13, 1865, the Confederate Congress voted by a narrow margin to pass the Negro Soldier Bill, which armed slaves and granted them freedom after the war.

The next week, people in Richmond saw something few could have predicted: two companies of *black* hospital orderlies marching with three companies of *white* convalescents from Chimborazo Hospital up Main Street to strains of "Dixie." But less than three weeks later, white Richmonders fled the city before Union troops, many of them black soldiers.

PRESIDENT DAVIS PROPOSES TO EMANCIPATE
THE SLAVES FOR FOREIGN RECOGNITION

Through the winter of 1864–1865, the Confederate Army began to stagger. In December, Major General George Thomas had chased John Hood's Army of Tennessee south into Alabama and Mississippi. Just before Christmas, General Sherman had finished his march through Georgia and taken Savannah. At the siege of Petersburg, General Grant kept extending his lines westward, forcing General Lee to extend the lines of his smaller army precariously thin.

In mid-January, Davis sent wealthy Louisiana planter and congressman Duncan F. Kenner to France and England on a secret mission. Kenner, who had long been telling Davis that slavery was the major obstacle to European recognition, traveled with an offer: the Confederacy would consider emancipating the slaves, he would tell French and English leaders, in exchange for recognition of the Confederacy.

In Paris, Napoleon III responded through intermediaries that France would follow England on the matter. In London, Prime Minister Lord Palmerston also gave his response through intermediaries. Lord Palmerston and Great Britain had equivocated on recognition for years, but that was over. There would be no recognition, especially "when the events of a few weeks might prove [the South's attempt at independence] a failure," Palmerston said quite bluntly.

It was a strange affair: the president of a country that had assumed slavery and states rights in its constitution had acted secretly to free the slaves. It was a desperate act of a desperate nation.

FREED SLAVES JOIN RHODE ISLAND SOLDIERS IN WASHINGTON, DC

These African Americans, freed by Union forces when they moved into Confederate states, are pictured here with Rhode Island troops in Washington, DC.

FINALLY
ON TO RICHMOND

WEEK 46

CORNELIA McDONALD AND HER FAMILY
CAN BARELY FEED THEMSELVES

In January 1865, Winchester's Cornelia Peake McDonald, a widow since December, was approached by a neighbor who told her that some young women in Lexington wanted drawing lessons. McDonald wrote in her memoirs,

> *The thought of being daily obliged to meet strangers, of not having the privilege of retirement in my present state of distress was dreadful to me; but the alternative was starvation. So the classes came, and I taught them in the morning for three or four hours, and in the afternoon two other young ladies came to read poetry and history. With this there was no time for grief, besides there was plenty of work to keep the children's knees and elbows covered. With all I could do we had barely enough food to keep from actual want; and that of a kind that was often sickening to me. I generally went all day with a cup of coffee and a roll. The children could eat the beans and the sorghum molasses, but I could not. We seldom saw butter, but some idea may be formed of the difficulty of getting food when I say that I sent one hundred dollars (the proceeds of two weeks teaching) up town, and got for it a pound of fat bacon, three candles, eighteen dollars for the three, and a pound of bad butter.*
>
> *The quartermaster proposed to me to let my boys cut wood in the woods for the Government, and that they should have one cord out of every three they cut, and the Government wagons would haul it for me. I joyfully agreed. . . . So we were supplied with wood, indeed never wanted for it, and a bright cheerful fire was a great comfort and delight to us.*

PETERSBURG FINALLY FALLS—
THE BATTLE OF FIVE FORKS

For months, Generals Grant and Lee had stared each other down at Petersburg along a front that extended 37 miles. The stalemate suited neither general. Lee had plans to break out and join the only other Confederate army left, that of General Joseph Johnston. Grant wanted to destroy Lee's army. Lee tried to break out at Fort Stedman on March 24, but a counterattack caused Lee's army four thousand casualties, to two thousand Union ones. Now Grant decided to attack Lee's right flank and force the Confederates to retreat or come into the open.

To help, Union cavalryman Phil Sheridan destroyed what was left of Jubal Early's cavalry near Waynesborough and took twelve thousand men to Lee's right flank, near a crossroads known as Five Forks. Lee sent a mix of cavalry and infantry to hold Five Forks, because he knew that without his supply line, he and Richmond were doomed. George Pickett, the man made famous by his charge at Gettysburg, had initial success, but Sheridan organized a counterattack. At the end of the day, Grant and other officers at headquarters got the news: it was a Union rout. Grant then went over to the telegrapher's tent and came back, saying, "I have ordered an immediate assault all along the lines."

Grant ordered an attack on April 2 at Petersburg because he believed that Lee's forces had been crippled by the defeats at Fort Stedman and Five Forks. But all the Union soldiers could see were the most formidable breastworks of the war. The men darkly pinned their names and addresses to their uniforms. Before dawn, what was the most intense artillery fire of the war began, and fourteen thousand Union men moved into the no-man's-land at the center of Lee's line.

By dawn, Petersburg's trenches were filled with Union soldiers, and the Confederates had fled Petersburg and Richmond. Lee now played his last card, planning to move his men south, to join forces with Johnston's. But Union forces, led by the vigilant Sheridan, cut off that retreat, and Lee's men scrambled west, bedraggled and desperate.

RICHMOND IS ABANDONED

General Ulysses S. Grant attacked the Petersburg line on the morning of April 2. At eleven a.m., at a Palm Sunday service at Saint Paul's Church in Richmond, a messenger slipped down the aisle and handed President Davis a telegram from Lee. "My lines are broken in three places," Lee wrote. "Richmond must be evacuated this evening." A woman seated near him remembered a "gray pallor" overcoming Davis's face, and he hurriedly left the church.

Soon the news had darted through the city, and Richmond residents scrambled to find transportation to flee. Many took a ramshackle train to Danville, Virginia, 140 miles to the south. A slave-dealer tried to get fifty chained slaves aboard one overcrowded train, but a soldier with a bayonet stopped him. Finally, the slave-dealer unlocked the $50,000 worth of property, suddenly free. Mobs scoured the stores for essentials, and Confederacy Rear Admiral Raphael Semmes blew up what was left of their navy on the James, blasts that shattered glass throughout the city.

Davis sent his wife and children to Charlotte, North Carolina. Before he left, he gave a marble bust of himself to a slave, asking that he hide it from the Yankees so they would not ridicule him. The president and his cabinet took the last train out, consisting of freight trains filled with key governmental records. On the sides of different freight cars were written: TREASURY DEPARTMENT, QUARTER MASTERS DEPARTMENT, and WAR DEPARTMENT. Traveling on the train was also the Confederacy's gold reserve. The same night that residents fled Richmond, Lee's army retreated across the Appomattox River, knowing the last hope for the Confederates was the preservation of his Army of Northern Virginia.

Retreating Confederates set fire to the tobacco houses, a general fire erupted, and one retreating captain described what he saw behind him as he left: "Every now and then, as a magazine exploded, a column of white smoke rose . . . instantaneously followed by a deafening sound. The ground seemed to rock and tremble. . . ."

LINCOLN VISITS RICHMOND AND SITS IN DAVIS'S CHAIR

President Lincoln visited General Grant at Petersburg the day after Lee's army fled. To meet the general, Lincoln had to ride by the battlefield at Petersburg, which still included dead bodies, and a bodyguard noted that his "face settled into its old lines of sadness." He met with Grant, and afterward the president received the word of Richmond's fall. "Thank God I have lived to see this," the president told Admiral David D. Porter. "It seems to me that I have been dreaming a horrid dream for four years, and now the nightmare is gone. I want to see Richmond."

When the Union soldiers arrived in Richmond on April 3, they worked to restore order and put out the lingering flames. Richmond slaves, suddenly free, welcomed the Union soldiers, including the all-black Twenty-fifth Corps. "Our . . . servants were completely crazed," a Richmond matron noted. "They danced and shouted, men hugged each other, and women kissed . . . Imagine the streets crowded with these people!"

After Lincoln arrived at the fallen Confederate capital on April 4, he walked about a mile through the streets, holding his son Tad's hand, surrounded by a dozen Union soldiers and sailors. Soon he was mobbed by freed slaves, many of whom tried to reach out and touch him. Porter looked up at the windows overlooking the street, afraid of stray snipers. "Bless the Lord!" shouted one freed slave. "The great Messiah! I knowed him as soon as I seed him. He's been in my heart four long years. Come to free his children from bondage. Glory, Hallelujah!"

"Don't kneel to me," the president told one old freedman. "That is not right. You must kneel to God only, and thank Him for the liberty you will enjoy hereafter." The day was warm, and Lincoln took off his overcoat. Soldiers took him to the Confederate White House and he sat in a chair in Jefferson Davis's study.

"Richmond has never before presented such a spectacle of jubilee," T. Morris Chester, a journalist for the *Philadelphia Press*, wrote that day. "What a wonderful change has come of the spirit of Southern dreams." Chester was a black man.

JEFFERSON DAVIS WANTS A GUERRILLA WAR

Confederacy President Jefferson Davis gave his last presidential address on April 4, 1865. Petersburg was lost, and Richmond, which Lee had defended so well for so long, had been reduced to ashes. Many in the North and South thought the war was over, but Davis, defiant, claimed instead that the conflict had entered a "new phase." He pledged the Confederate armies to continue the battle and to wage what is now known as a guerrilla war against the Union Army. "To the People of the Confederate States of America:" he wrote,

> *. . . It would be unwise, even were it possible, to conceal the great moral as well as material injury to our cause that must result from the occupation of Richmond by the enemy. It is equally unwise and unworthy of us, as patriots engaged in a most sacred cause, to allow our energies to falter, our spirits to grow faint, or our efforts to become relaxed under reverses, however calamitous. . . .*
>
> *The hopes and confidence of the enemy have been constantly excited by the belief that their possession of Richmond would be the signal for our submission to their rule and relieve them from the burden of war which, as their failing resources admonish them, must be abandoned if not speedily brought to a successful close.*
>
> *It is for us, my countrymen, to show by our bearing under reverses how wretched has been the self-deception of those who have believed us less able to endure misfortune and fortitude than to encounter danger with courage.*
>
> *We have entered a new phase of a struggle, the memory of which is to endure for all ages and to shed ever increasing luster upon our country. Relieved from the necessity of guarding cities and particular points . . . with our army free to move from point to point and strike in detail the detachments and garrisons of the enemy; . . . nothing is now needed to surrender our triumph certain but the exhibition of our own unquenchable resolve. Let us but will it, and we are free; and who, in the light of the past, dare doubt your purpose in the future? . . .*
>
> *Let us not then [d]espond, my countrymen, but, relying on the never failing mercies and protecting care of our God, let us meet the foe with fresh defiance, with unconquered and unconquerable hearts.*

LEE'S ARMY SEARCHES FOR FOOD

After abandoning Petersburg, General Lee hoped to move quickly southward to join forces with General Joseph E. Johnston's army, then retreating through the Carolinas from General Sherman. Lee was undoubtedly disappointed in the course the war had taken, but he was not hopeless. "I have got my army safe out of its breastworks, and in order to follow me, my enemy must abandon his lines and can derive no further benefit from his railroads and the James River," he reported.

He pushed his men forty miles west in less than two days. They were hungry and malnourished. The general looked forward to the meat and bread and 350,000 meals, amassed in Richmond, that he'd arranged to have sent to Amelia Court House, a community on a railroad line. But when the shipment was opened, what was seen was not food but 96 loaded caissons, 200 crates of ammunition, and 164 boxes of artillery harnesses.

At the news, a cavalry staffer said that Lee's face gained "an anxious and haggard expression." It was little wonder. He'd lost 4,000 men in each of the battles of Fort Stedman and Five Forks, and now his force was 55,000, less than half of Grant's 120,000-man army. Lee had no choice but to delay his flight from the Union Army—a dangerous thing to do—and send men into the countryside to find food. They went out with a letter addressed to "the Citizens of Amelia County," asking them to "supply as far as each one is able the wants of the brave soldiers who have battled for your liberty for four years." The appeal was signed by "R. E. Lee."

The next morning, April 5, the commissary wagons returned almost as empty as they'd left. The farmers had nothing left to give, their land already scoured by both armies. Lee gave orders to continue the westward march, which a later observer called "the most cruel marching order the commanders had ever given the men in four years of fighting." As the men marched, some planted their weapons, bayonet down, monuments to weariness.

"It is now," wrote one soldier, "a race for life or death."

THE RUINS OF
RICHMOND, APRIL 1865

A man sits amid the burned-out ruins of the Richmond & Petersburg
Railroad depot in Richmond, the Confederate capital.

THE ROAD TO
APPOMATTOX

WEEK 47

"HAS THE ARMY BEEN DISSOLVED?"—CONFEDERATE DEFEAT AT SAILOR'S CREEK

As General Grant's armies chased Robert E. Lee's men westward, they picked up the detritus of a faltering Confederate army—bedrolls, muskets, wagons, men, and more. "Dropped in the very middle of the road from utter exhaustion," one pursuer recalled, "old horses, literally skin and bones, [were] so weak as scarcely to be able to lift their heads when some soldier would touch them with his foot to see if they really had life."

Grant's armies harassed the fleeing army from behind, and Lee's army began to disassemble. On April 6, Lee began to worry about the whereabouts of two of his generals and their missing corps. He rode to a ridge overlooking a valley carved by Sailor's Creek, and saw what had happened. Union guns were firing from another ridge, destroying the remnants of the gray corps consisting of "hurrying teamsters with their teams and dangling traces, infantry without guns, many without hats—a harmless mob."

"My God," Lee said, overlooking the slaughter. "Has the army been dissolved?" About eight thousand Confederates were lost or taken prisoner. General Philip Sheridan, the Union cavalry leader who had pushed for the attack, wired Grant: "If the thing is pressed, I think that Lee will surrender." Grant forwarded it to Lincoln. "Let the *thing* be pressed," replied Lincoln.

The next day Grant sent Lee a letter: "The result of the last week must convince you of the hopelessness of further resistance. . . . I . . . regard it as my duty to shift from myself the responsibility of any further effusion of blood, by asking of you the surrender of that portion of the Confederate States Army known as the Army of Northern Virginia."

One of Lee's officers advised him to surrender, but Lee angrily asked what the country would think of him if he did not persevere in battle. Lee and his men were soon trapped in the town of Appomattox Court House. They tried to break out on April 9 but they failed. "Then there is nothing left for me to do but go and see General Grant," Lee told his commanders, "and I would rather die a thousand deaths."

LEE'S SECOND MOST IMPORTANT DECISION:
HIS REJECTION OF A GUERRILLA WAR

After Confederate troops failed to break free from Appomattox Court House on April 9, General Robert E. Lee asked General James Longstreet whether surrender was the right decision. Longstreet said, "Your situation speaks for itself." But Brigadier General E. Porter Alexander, Lee's twenty-nine-year-old chief of artillery, urged Lee to dissolve the army into the woods and resist as scattered bands of soldiers, a development that was feared by President Lincoln and his generals. "We would be like rabbits or partridges in the bushes," Alexander explained, "and they could not scatter to follow us." Alexander was recommending a guerrilla war, as Jefferson Davis had recommended five days earlier.

This was Lee's most important decision of the war, next to his decision to fight for Virginia. To bless a guerrilla war would mean that the Union would have to keep its army in the field to battle as many as 175,000 scattered Rebel troops and that for the war to end, the "Confederacy would have been reduced to smoldering wilderness," as Ambassador Charles Adams put it. The war would continue for months and perhaps years. An exhausted Union might eventually concede the Confederacy, slavery and all.

But Lee rejected that path. "We must consider its effect on the country as a whole," he replied. "Already it is demoralized by the four years of war. If I took your advice, the men would be without rations and under no control of officers. They would be compelled to rob and steal in order to live. They would become mere bands of marauders, and the enemy's cavalry would pursue them and overrun many sections they may never have occasion to visit. We would bring on a state of affairs it would take the country years to recover from."

"I had not a single word to say in reply," Alexander said years later. "He had answered my suggestion from a plane so far above it that I was ashamed of having made it."

"THE WAR BEGAN IN MY FRONT YARD AND ENDED IN MY FRONT PARLOR"—GRANT AND LEE MEET IN WILMER McLEAN'S HOME

General Joshua Chamberlain, one of the heroes of Gettysburg, remembered Generals Lee and Grant passing through his lines at Appomattox Court House on April 9, 1865.

A commanding form, superbly mounted, richly accoutered, of imposing bearing, noble countenance, with expression of deep sadness overmastered by deeper strength . . . [Then] not long after, by another in leading road, appeared another form . . . plain, simple and familiar . . . but as much inspiring awe as Lee in his splendor and his sadness. It is Grant. Slouched hat without cord . . . high boots mud-splashed to the top . . . no sword . . . sitting his saddle with the ease of a born master . . . all his faculties gathered into intense thought. . . .

Lee arrived first, on Traveller, his dappled gray horse, and he directed his secretary Colonel Charles Marshall to find a meeting place. A friendly man, out for a stroll, led Marshall to a building, but the colonel found it too small and poorly furnished. Then the man reluctantly took Marshall to his own home, a two-story brick house with a large front porch. The man's name was Wilmer McLean, an ardent Confederate supporter who had previously crossed paths with the war.

In 1861, at the First Battle of Bull Run, Confederate General Pierre Beauregard used McLean's house, near Manassas Junction in northern Virginia, as his headquarters. Southern regiments camped on his farm, and wounded soldiers were brought to his barn. His home was fired upon, and one shell is said to have come down his chimney and exploded in a stew cooking in the fireplace.

McLean had gathered his family and fled to the tiny crossroad village of Appomattox Court House, ninety miles west of Richmond, of little importance to either side, thinking that the location would allow his family to sidestep the scourge of war.

"Here," he assured his family, "the sound of battle will never reach you." He was wrong, of course, and would later boast, "The war began in my front yard and ended in my front parlor."

LEE'S ARMY SURRENDERS

At one thirty in the afternoon on April 9, 1865, Generals Grant and Lee began their historic meeting in the parlor of Wilmer McLean's house by engaging in small talk. "I met you once before, General Lee," Grant told the Virginian, recalling a visit Lee had made to Grant's brigade when both men were soldiers in Mexico. "I have always remembered your appearance and I think I should have recognized you anywhere." Lee nodded. "Yes, I know I met you on that occasion," he replied, "and I have often thought of it and tried to recollect how you looked. But I have never been able to recall a single feature." If it was a slight, Grant never acknowledged it. "What General Lee's feelings were I do not know," Grant wrote in his *Memoirs*.

> *As he was a man of much dignity, with an impassible face, it was impossible to say whether he felt inwardly glad that the end had finally come, or felt sad over the result, and was too manly to show it. . . . [B]ut my own feelings . . . were sad and depressed. I felt like anything rather than rejoicing at the downfall of a foe who had fought so long and valiantly, and had suffered so much for a cause, though that cause was, I believe, one of the worst for which a people ever fought, and one for which there was the least excuse. . . .*

Grant offered generous conditions for peace. Officers could keep their possessions, their side arms, and their horses. More important, Grant promised that "each officer and man will be allowed to return to his home, not to be disturbed by United States authority. . . ." This was amnesty; there would be no retaliation against the enemy, much less witch hunts, war trials, and hangings, as there so often were after civil wars. Lee must have been relieved, because some of his staff feared the Confederate Army would be sent to a prison camp. When Lee read the terms, he said to Grant, "This will have a very happy effect upon my army. It will be very gratifying and will do much toward conciliating our people."

Lee, though, had two more requests. He asked if the enlisted men as well as the officers could keep their horses. Grant hesitated, but then agreed. Lee also said his men were hungry. Grant offered 25,000 rations.

The men shook hands. Lee left. It was just before four p.m. on Palm Sunday. The next day, nearly thirty thousand Confederate soldiers were paroled and sent home, scattered like seeds in the wind.

GENERAL LEE'S FAREWELL TO HIS TROOPS

At about three p.m., on April 9, 1865, Lee mounted Traveller in front of Wilmer McLean's porch. Grant and his officers stepped off the porch and removed their hats. Lee saluted and rode slowly away. Confederate soldiers lined the road to Lee's camp.

"As he approached," one of the men remembered, "we could see the reins hanging loose . . . and his head was sunk low on his breast. As the men began to cheer, he raised his head and hat in hand as he passed by, his face flushed, his eye ablaze." The men began "reaching up a thousand hands to wring his own, to touch his horse or Lee himself." One officer recalled that the men seemed to go through an emotional passage. "[Each] group began in the same way with cheers and ended in the same way with sobs, all the way to his quarters. Grim, bearded men threw themselves on the ground, covered their faces with their hands, and wept like children." A crowd of soldiers, weeping openly, waited in front of Lee's tent. "Men," the general said to them, "I have done for you all that it was in my power to do. You have done your duty. Leave the rest to God. Go to your homes and resume your occupations. Obey the laws and become good citizens as you were soldiers. My heart is too full to say more." Then he retreated into his tent.

Cornelia Peake McDonald, the Winchester widow and mother, wrote that "I can never forget the effect [Lee's surrender] had on me and on my family. I felt as if the end of all things had come, at least for the Southern people. Grief and despair took possession of my heart, with a sense of humiliation that till then I did not know I could feel. . . . Yet some seemed relieved to be rid of the awful strain, and to be content with defeat if it brought rest and peace."

SOUVENIR COLLECTORS ROB WILMER McLEAN'S HOUSE

When Generals Lee and Grant left Wilmer McLean's home, officers began pilfering it. "Relic hunters charged down upon the manor house," a staff colonel would remember, "and began to bargain for the numerous pieces of furniture."

Union cavalry commander Philip Sheridan gave $20 in gold for the table Grant had used to write down the surrender terms, but McLean refused to take any money, tossing some on the floor in disgust. Sheridan took the table anyway, presenting it to General Custer's pretty wife. The chairs Lee and Grant had sat in were also forcibly purchased. Sheridan's brother Michael, a captain on his brother's staff, took the stone inkstand, and another brigadier made off with two brass candlesticks.

"Cane-bottomed chairs were ruthlessly cut to pieces," a reporter wrote afterward, "the cane splits broken into pieces a few inches long and parceled out among those who swarmed around." Flowers were cut from the McLeans' garden, pressed in wallets and carried homeward.

Afterward, men who had tried to kill each other in battles large and small crossed their lines peaceably. "We were glad to see them," Union Private Theodore Gerrish remembered of Confederate soldiers who came to visit. "We received them kindly, and exchanged pocket knives and sundry trinkets, that each could have something to carry home as a reminiscence of the great event."

The Rhode Island soldier Elisha Hunt Rhodes tried to sum up what was gained by peace. "No more suffering, no more scenes of carnage and death," he wrote. "Thank God it is over and that the Union is restored. And so at last I am a simple citizen. . . . The Governor has given me a commission as Colonel for gallant conduct during the war. But what are honors now, compared to the delights of peace and home."

THE McLEAN FAMILY HOME, WHERE ROBERT E. LEE SURRENDERED

This is the home of Wilmer McLean and his family at Appomattox Court House, Virginia, where General Robert E. Lee surrendered to General Ulysses S. Grant on April 9, 1865.

PRELUDE
TO AN ASSASSINATION

WEEK 48

LINCOLN AND WASHINGTON, DC, REJOICE OVER
LEE'S SURRENDER

"We are scattered," South Carolina's Mary Chesnut wrote in her diary, "stunned; the remnant of heart left alive is filled with brotherly hate. . . . Whose fault? Everybody blamed somebody else. Only the dead heroes left stiff and stark on the battlefield escape." Instead of again joining the nation with members of the "perfidious, malignant and vile Yankee race," Edmund Ruffin, the old Virginia secessionist who had fired one of the first shots at Fort Sumter four years ago, wrapped himself in the Confederate flag and put a bullet through his head.

In the North, the day after Lee's surrender became an impromptu holiday. In Washington, a celebratory band of Treasury workers skipped to the White House and serenaded the president with "Praise God from Whom All Blessings Flow" and "The Star-spangled Banner" while the president ate breakfast. By noon, three thousand people gathered outside the White House, with cheers hitting a crescendo when young Tad waved a Confederate flag in the window.

Lincoln gave an impromptu speech and asked three bands that had gathered to play his favorite tune. "I have always thought 'Dixie' one of the best tunes I ever heard," Lincoln told the crowd. "Our adversaries over the way attempted to appropriate it, but I insisted . . . that we fairly captured it [yesterday]. I presented the question to the Attorney General and he gave it as his legal opinion that it is our lawful prize. I now request the band to favor me with its performance."

A few blocks away, a man stopped by a darkened room at the National Hotel just to see if his friend, an actor, was in, and asked him if he'd like to go out for a drink. "Yes," said John Wilkes Booth, who was now drinking brandy by the quart. "Anything to drive away the blues."

JOHN WILKES BOOTH, WHITE SUPREMACIST, OPPOSES "NIGGER CITIZENSHIP"

On Tuesday, April 11, all of Washington, DC, took to the streets and taverns to celebrate the end of the war. People illuminated their homes, and the Capitol dome was lit as well. Across the Potomac River in Arlington, Lee's hometown, freed slaves gathered to sing "The Year of Jubilee." Thousands of people swarmed the driveway to the White House and called for the president to speak. Finally, Lincoln appeared in a second-story window as "cheers upon cheers, wave after wave of applause, rolled up."

At first, the president tried to hold a candle himself as he read his prepared remarks, but he found this difficult, and handed the candle to his friend Noah Brooks to hold. Lincoln dropped each page to the floor after he finished it, and his son Tad picked them up.

"We meet this evening, not in sorrow, but in gladness of heart," began the president, expressing hope that the recent Northern victories "give hope of a righteous and speedy peace." He thanked the soldiers, and then his speech took a turn into policy. He talked about how best to reconstruct the country, especially the Southern states, whose political structures had collapsed in defeat. Some of the crowd wandered off before the speech was finished.

The president weighed black suffrage in Louisiana, a state that had just drawn up a constitution that forbade blacks to vote. "I would myself prefer that it [voting privileges for blacks] were now conferred on the very intelligent," Lincoln said, "and on those who serve our cause as soldiers." These were views that Lincoln had expressed before privately, but this was the first time an American president had publicly announced he favored black suffrage.

"That means nigger citizenship," a man in the crowd sputtered to a friend standing next to him, and then declared, "That is the last speech he will ever make." He urged another friend, Lewis Paine, to shoot the president right there. When Paine refused, John Wilkes Booth announced, "By God, I'll put him through."

ABRAHAM LINCOLN'S FINAL MORNING

On Good Friday, April 14, 1865, the final day of his life, Abraham Lincoln arose at seven a.m., as was his habit. He put on his robe over his long white nightshirt, stepped into his large slippers, and walked down the hallway to the sitting room. As usual, he started his day by opening the family Bible and reading from it.

He then went to his corner office, where he could see the Potomac River, which had separated the Union and the Confederacy for four wearying years. He sat down at the long wooden table, the same table where he'd signed the Emancipation Proclamation two years prior, and began looking at the letters his secretaries had winnowed from the five hundred or so he received daily.

He read a letter from James H. Van Alen, who urged the president to be more careful about his safety. Lincoln replied, "I intend to adopt the advice of my friends and use due precaution," although he added that he hoped the time would come when Americans wouldn't have to worry about such things. He told Van Alen that he wanted to build more than functioning states in the South; he wanted to build a "Union of hearts and hands."

He went back to his bedroom, dressed for breakfast, and went to the dining room around eight a.m., where Mary; his youngest son, Tad; and his oldest son, Robert were gathered. Robert had just returned from Virginia, where he had served under General Grant. Lincoln listened as Robert spoke of his service. The son then showed his father a souvenir he'd picked up in the South: a small photograph of General Robert E. Lee. Lincoln examined the photograph for some time. "It is a good face," he said finally. "It is the face of a noble, noble, brave man. I am glad the war is over at last." He then told his son that he was happy he had arrived home safely, saying, "We soon shall live in peace."

ASSASSINATION PLANS ARE READIED

On Friday morning, Abraham Lincoln sent word to Ford's Theatre, one of Washington's most popular theaters, that he and Mary would attend *Our American Cousin*, an old comedy playing that evening. At ten a.m., an actor who often performed at the theater ate breakfast at his hotel and then had the hotel's barber shave his face. The mirror showed a handsome young man with curly hair and a full mustache: John Wilkes Booth. At about noon, Booth stopped by Ford's Theatre to pick up his mail and heard theater hands buzzing that the president and General Grant were expected that evening. It was the opportunity John Wilkes Booth had been waiting for.

Booth still saw hope in the Confederate cause despite the defeat of General Lee. President Davis was still at large, and Joseph Johnston's army was still intact in North Carolina. Booth abandoned plans to kidnap the president and exchange him for thousands of Confederate prisoners. Instead, he stepped into the role of Brutus, the tyrant-killer.

He would work with coconspirators to also kill Vice President Andrew Johnson and Secretary of State William Seward, thereby destabilizing the North and giving the South another chance to scrap for independence. "Our cause being almost lost," he said, "something decisive and great must be done."

Shortly before the play began, Booth went to Taltavul's, a saloon next door to Ford's Theatre, and a drunken customer who recognized the well-known actor, called out, "You will never be the actor your father was!"

"When I leave the stage," Booth replied calmly, "I will be the most talked about man in America."

A UNION CELEBRATION AT FORT SUMTER

Robert Anderson, the Union commander who surrendered Fort Sumter on April 14, 1861, was enfeebled by the end of the war. In early 1865, Secretary of War Edwin Stanton asked him to attend a special ceremony at the fort on April 14, 1865, where Anderson would raise the same flag he had pulled down from the fort exactly four years earlier.

Abner Doubleday, who had fired the first shot in defense of the fort, was there, as was abolitionist William Lloyd Garrison, who stopped at Charleston's former slave market and led a large crowd in the singing of "Roll, Jordan, Roll," and "John Brown's Body." Thousands of visitors who came to the fortress, now largely rubble, walked through a line of white soldiers and a line of black soldiers. Those in the crowd talked about the surrender of General Lee to General Grant, which happened just five days earlier.

From a battered old mailbag, the ripped U.S. flag that had flown over Fort Sumter was held up, and the crowd roared. Then Anderson stood. He put his hat under his arm, and his thin white hair blew in the bay's breeze. He reached out for the halyards and said, "I thank God that I have lived to see this day, and to be here, to perform this, perhaps the last act of my life, of duty to my country." He needed help pulling the rope to raise the flag, described by one woman as "weather-beaten, frayed, and shell-torn."

That evening, at a dinner at the Charleston Hotel, dignitaries toasted the enlisted men at Fort Sumter. Anderson gave a toast to "a man who now could travel *all* over our country with millions of hands and hearts to sustain him. I give you the good, the great, the honest man, Abraham Lincoln." He made the toast a few minutes after ten o'clock, almost the precise moment when, at Ford's Theatre in Washington, DC, John Wilkes Booth quietly slipped into the presidential box with an assassin's gun in one hand and a knife in the other.

LINCOLN IS SHOT!

When the Lincolns arrived at Ford's Theatre late, the pit orchestra interrupted the performance by striking up "Hail to the Chief." The audience gave the president a standing ovation and he responded with a "smile and a bow" before he sat back in an armchair in the box seat, Mary at his side. Later, Mary leaned close to Abe and whispered, "What will Miss Harris think of my hanging on to you so?" referring to the young woman who had joined them in the box. Mary later said her husband replied with a smile, saying, "She won't think any thing about it." Those were the last words Abraham Lincoln would ever speak.

John F. Parker, the Metropolitan policeman assigned to protect Lincoln, left at intermission to go next door to have a drink at Taltavul's, perhaps crossing paths with John Wilkes Booth, who spent the early evening there. Parker left the president's box guarded by Charles Forbes, a White House assistant. As the third act began, Booth made his way to the box, showed Forbes his calling card, and Forbes, recognizing the famous actor, gladly gave Booth entrance into the Lincolns' box. When the audience responded with a burst of laughter, Booth stepped through the inner door, raised his gun just inches behind Lincoln's head, and pulled the trigger. It was ten thirteen p.m.

The shot silenced the theater. Major Henry Rathbone, who had joined the Lincolns in the box with his fiancée, Clara Harris, tried to seize Booth, but the actor cut Rathbone's arm badly with a hunting knife. Booth then leaped over the balustrade, an easy leap for the athletic actor, but the spur on his heel snagged on the flags hanging in front of the box, and he landed awkwardly on one foot, breaking a bone above his ankle. He shouted, "*Sic semper tyrannis*"—"Thus always to tyrants"—Virginia's state motto, and some in the audience thought they heard him add, "The South is avenged!" The crowd was at first confused, some thinking Booth might be part of the play. Then Mary Lincoln let out a curdling shriek and screamed, "They have shot the President! They have shot the President!"

A WEARY ABRAHAM LINCOLN, FEBRUARY 1865

This photograph was taken by Alexander Gardner on a Sunday in February 1865, just two months before Lincoln was assassinated. The president had aged considerably in his four years in office, and he looks weary, his expression here revealing what Walt Whitman called "a deep latent sadness."

THE BITTER END

WEEK 49

Charles A. Leale, the first doctor who reached Lincoln, found him being held up by Mary, his eyes closed and his head bowed on his chest. Leale first thought the president was dead. He searched for the wound and found "the perfectly smooth opening made by the ball," and removed the blood clot there. Then he performed artificial respiration, which produced feeble breathing and a heartbeat. Men then carried Lincoln out of the crowded theater, and someone suggested they bring him to the White House, but Leale thought the jostling would kill him. When they carried the president into the street, a man called out, "Bring him in here, bring him in here!" The president was laid down in a room in the back of a boardinghouse, on a bed too short for his body.

The doctors removed his clothes to search for other bullet holes and noticed Lincoln's strong chest and muscular arms, evidence that the legend of the man's strength was true. His body was cold, so they brought in hot-water bottles and heated blankets, and they spread a warm mustard paste over his body. Mary became hysterical, repeatedly kissing her husband's face and begging him to speak to her. She was led away to the front parlor.

Those gathered knew it was a deathwatch. At one point, the doctors tried to remove the bullet with long needles, but it was too deep for them to reach. Robert Lincoln, the president's oldest son, broke down when he saw his father in the bed, but then regained control. When his mother began to keen, Robert said, "Mother, please put your trust in God and all will be well." Before a three a.m. visit by Mary, the men covered the bloody pillow with a clean white napkin. Politicians and friends came and went until seven twenty-two a.m., when Lincoln exhaled one last time.

Reverend Phineas Gurley gave a brief prayer. "God," he asked, "please accept this good man, Abraham Lincoln, into the kingdom of heaven." The men in the room whispered, "Amen." "Now," Secretary of War Edwin Stanton said, "he belongs to the ages."

DAVIS, STILL DEFIANT, IS CAUGHT

On the afternoon of May 2, 1865, Confederate President Jefferson Davis convened what he called a "council of war" in Abeville, South Carolina, attended by his secretary of war John C. Breckinridge, his friend Major General Braxton Bragg, and a handful of brigade commanders. General Joseph E. Johnston had surrendered his Army of Tennessee a week before, and General Lee had surrendered two weeks before that. Union troops were now hunting Davis, who was being escorted by an elite group of tattered Rebels.

"It is time," Davis told the men, "that we adopt some definite plan upon which the further prosecution of our struggle shall be conducted." Davis hoped to join Lieutenant General Richard Taylor in Alabama, not knowing that Taylor had surrendered that same day. The gathered men were dumbstruck, and told Davis that the Southern people were broken and hungry and unable to continue. They said that after Davis was ushered to safety, the soldiers expected to go home. Davis then acknowledged what he'd refused to accept for months. "All indeed is lost," he said, and stumbled away.

Secretary of the Navy Gideon Welles recalled what Lincoln said he wanted to do with captured Confederate leaders. " 'Frighten them out of the country, open the gates, let down the bars, scare them off,' said [Lincoln], throwing up his hands as if scaring sheep. 'Enough lives have been sacrificed. We must extinguish our resentments if we expect harmony and union.' " President Andrew Johnson had set a much harsher tone. "Treason is a crime," he said, "and the crime must be punished." Davis was falsely accused as a conspirator in Lincoln's assassination and a $100,000 reward was offered for his capture.

The Fourth Michigan and First Wisconsin surrounded Davis before dawn on May 10, 1865, near Irwinsville, Georgia, where Davis had come to meet his wife, Varina, and their children, also in flight. Davis considered trying to escape, but Varina pleaded for him to surrender. "God's will be done," he muttered.

Davis was imprisoned in Fort Monroe, Virginia, and put in shackles. After a public outcry, the shackles were removed a week later.

In 1866, Davis was indicted for treason, but he was never brought to trial, the government perhaps wishing to avoid questions over the legality of secession. Charges against Davis were dropped on December 25, 1868. Years later, Davis said, "Tell the world I only loved America."

THE *SHENANDOAH* FIRES THE WAR'S LAST SHOT— TWO MONTHS AFTER LEE SURRENDERS

The last shot in the Civil War was not fired by soldiers in Virginia or Texas, but by sailors on a Confederate ship named the *Shenandoah*. To do damage to the Union cause, Lieutenant James Waddell, the ship's captain, was ordered in the fall of 1864 to go after "the great American whaling fleet, a source of abundant wealth of our enemies" and a supplier of oil that lubricated the daunting Union war machine.

During its tenure as a raider, the ship traveled south around Africa and then across the Indian Ocean, around Australia, and then north into the Pacific. The *Shenandoah* did most of its damage after it reached the Bering Sea on June 16, 1865. In six days, the ship's crew burned twenty-four New England whaling vessels. That same month, a captured sailor told Waddell that Richmond had fallen, that General Robert E. Lee had surrendered, and that President Abraham Lincoln had been assassinated. Disbelieving, the men continued to August 2, when other sailors confirmed the news.

"We now have no country, no flag, no home," wrote one of the ship's officers. To dock at a U.S. port meant they'd be tried as pirates, as they attacked U.S. ships after the war's end, and that would subject them to imprisonment and hangings. So they decided to sail 9,000 miles to Liverpool, England, without stopping at port. In a little over a year, the *Shenandoah* had captured thirty-eight ships and taken more than a thousand prisoners.

British leaders, who had sympathies for the Confederacy and perhaps pitied the men's fate, let them go. After the war, the U.S. government demanded monetary compensation from Britain for their covert role in supporting the *Shenandoah* and the Confederate Navy, thereby damaging the U.S. commercial shipping and whaling industry. In 1872, after an international commission decided the case in favor of the U.S., Britain paid $16 million in damages for losses caused by the *Alabama*, the *Shenandoah*, and the *Florida*. The settlement was considered a milestone in peaceful settlements of international disputes and a step forward for the international rule of law.

DAY
4

WAR—"THE SHIELD OF THE OPPRESSED"
OR SIMPLY "HELL"?

At the Battle of Antietam, one of the wounded that Clara Barton treated was a young woman who was dressed in a Union uniform. The girl, named Mary, had cut her hair short and come to the front disguised as a man to find a Lieutenant Harry Barnard of the Third Wisconsin, with whom she had fallen in love during the war. At Antietam, she had been shot in the neck and was terrified she would die. Barton comforted her and fetched a surgeon, who removed the bullet.

Soon after that battle, Barton was serving in a hospital caring for the wounded at Antietam, and she came across a distraught wounded soldier with a card at the head of his bed that read "H.B., 3rd Wisconsin." It was Harry Barnard, Mary's love.

When he was told his arm would have to be amputated, he resisted, delirious from fever and the pain, and called out, "No, no, I want Mary." Barton knew where Mary was and brought her to Barnard. Mary convinced him to have his arm removed. As Barton told the story, he was sedated, his arm was amputated, and when he awoke, Mary was by his side, his "wildness" abated.

After the war, Barnard would tell his children: "War is the scourge of tyrants, the shield of the oppressed, the nurseling of brave men and lofty deeds; the theatre where heroes enact melo-dramas on the worlds' stage to the thunderous music of bursting artillery."

Barton emerged from the war with a far less romantic view. "Men have worshiped war," she asserted, "till it has cost a million times more than the whole world is worth, poured out the best blood and crushed the fairest forms the good God has ever created.—Deck it as you will, war is—'Hell.' . . . All through and through, thought, and act, body and soul—I hate it. . . . Only the desire to soften some of its hardships and allay some of its miseries ever induced me, and I presume all the other women who have taken similar steps, to dare its pestilence and unholy breath."

ROBERT E. LEE'S HOME IS TURNED INTO A GRAVEYARD

When Virginia seceded from the Union, Robert E. Lee and his wife, Mary, were living in a mansion on an 1,100-acre Virginia estate called Arlington, which overlooked the Potomac and Washington, DC. It had been built for Mary's father, George Washington Parke Custis, who was George Washington's adopted grandson. Lee left the property to serve in the Confederate Army, and Mary fled before federal troops crossed the river and occupied the estate.

In 1863, the Union government confiscated the estate for nonpayment of $92.07 in taxes. Mary had been unwilling to cross Union lines and pay in person, and the government refused to accept payment from her agent. At a public sale on January 11, 1864, the property was purchased by a tax commissioner for "government use, for war, military, charitable and educational purposes."

Meanwhile, the U.S. government gave 1,100 freed slaves land on the estate to farm, and they became part of a model community for freed slaves, called Freedman's Village. On June 15, 1864, with Washington-area cemeteries rapidly filling, Montgomery Meigs, the Union's quartermaster general and a former aide to Lee, used parts of the estate as a cemetery, intending to make the house uninhabitable if the Lee family ever wanted to return. A burial vault for the remains of eighteen hundred Bull Run soldiers was built under the estate's former rose garden.

Robert and Mary Lee quietly investigated reclaiming Arlington, but no action was taken before Mary died in 1873. But in 1877, their oldest son, George Washington Custis Lee, sued the federal government, claiming the property had been confiscated illegally. In 1882, by a five-to-four margin, the Supreme Court gave it back to him. What to do with an estate whose ground was filled with corpses? George Lee sold it back to the government for $150,000. Eventually, 250,000 soldiers would be buried in what became Arlington National Cemetery.

CORNELIA McDONALD AGAIN FINDS A WAY TO SURVIVE

"Getting food was the great difficulty," wrote Cornelia McDonald, a Virginia war widow, during the last year of the war. "What I earned by teaching [drawing] supplied little more than bread, beans and a little fat bacon, which last was nearly all consumed by the servant. The breakfast was bread and water, except the cup of coffee for me, which I believe I would have died without. The dinner was bean soup and bread, of which I never ate a particle. . . . The children ate it, and if they did not enjoy it, did not complain. Supper we had none, for there was not bread to spare for a third meal."

The war ended, but the family's privations did not. The pantry was barren. No money remained for the rent. "I felt that God had forsaken us, and I wished, oh! I wished that He would at one blow sweep me and mine from the earth. There seemed no place on it for us, no room for us to live."

McDonald had scalded her foot badly with a pot of boiling water during the summer and had to give up teaching her drawing classes. In October, she went for a walk to the cemetery, fearful of another winter about to blow in. There, she bumped into a friend, who said, "What can be the matter, you look so dreadfully?" She held McDonald's hands and begged her to explain.

"We are starving, I and my children," McDonald said. The woman replied, "Comfort yourself. I meant to have come and told you that help is coming for you." A relief fund had been created for widows and orphans of Confederate soldiers, and McDonald was to receive $100. "I went to bed that night," wrote McDonald, "with a happy heart and a thankful one."

In the same month, McDonald was offered a $300 loan from a woman who had received an inheritance from her brother, killed at Chickamauga. "I accepted it," McDonald remembered, "and with a light and happy heart set about making provision for the winter."

SOLDIERS STAND
IN FRONT OF ROBERT E. LEE'S
FORMER HOME

This photo, taken in 1864, shows Union soldiers, including African Americans, in front of the Custis-Lee Mansion, or Arlington House, Robert E. Lee's former home.

WHY DID THE NORTH WIN— OR THE SOUTH LOSE?

WEEK 50

THE LOST CAUSE—THE SOUTHERN VIEW

Napoleon once said that God was on the side of the heaviest battalions, and the common wisdom is that Lady Victory, if not God, went with the superior forces—men, munitions, and money—of the North. This theory is part of a larger framing of the war held by many Southerners, called the Lost Cause, which holds that Confederates lost because of the overwhelming odds against them.

In an 1872 address on Robert E. Lee, Confederate General Jubal A. Early said, "General Lee had not been conquered in battle . . . [H]e surrendered . . . the mere ghost of the Army of Northern Virginia, which had been gradually worn down by the combined agencies of numbers, steam-power, railroads, mechanism, and all the resources of physical science." Early was echoing Lee himself, who told his soldiers at Appomattox that he had been compelled to surrender by the enemy's "overwhelming numbers and resources."

In population, the twenty-three states in the Union had a five-to-two advantage over the eleven states in the Confederacy, a larger advantage if the slave population, accounting for a third of the Confederacy's population, is subtracted. Northerners also had a three-to-one advantage in wealth. "The important fact remains demonstrated," President Lincoln said in his annual message to Congress in December 1864, "that we have *more* men *now* than we had when the war *began*; that we are not exhausted, nor in the process of exhaustion; that we are *gaining* strength, and may, if need be, maintain the contest indefinitely." President Davis couldn't make such claims.

But historians have noted that outmanned and outgunned armies— the Davids in history—sometimes fell Goliaths. Might other factors have contributed to the Southern defeat?

DID THE SOUTH LOSE THE WAR BECAUSE OF
INTERNAL DIVISIONS?

Did the South sow the seeds of its own demise? The argument that internal conflicts sapped the strength of the Confederacy was first put forward by Frank Owsley in his book *State Rights in the Confederacy*, published in 1925.

He argued that war's demand for a powerful centralized government was undermined by the centrifugal forces of states rights, civil liberties (at least for white men), and individualism. The resistance to a powerful government came from local officials, such as Governor Joseph Brown of Georgia, but also from those inside Davis's administration, such as Vice President Alexander H. Stephens, who denounced conscription (which "outraged justice and the constitution"), federal taxes, martial law, and the suspension of the writ of habeas corpus ("a blow at the very 'vitals of liberty'"). Owsley wrote that the epitaph carved on the tombstone of the Confederacy should read: "Died of States Rights." The Civil War scholar David Donald expanded the epitaph to read, "Died of Democracy."

But more recently, historians have argued that the theory stands on a shaky foundation. Despite dissent, they point out, the South conscripted soldiers a year before the North, and had a larger percentage of soldiers who were drafted. And while Abraham Lincoln jailed more dissenters, the Confederate government came down ruthlessly on Union sympathizers in Tennessee and North Carolina. The Confederacy may have talked states rights, but its power was centralized.

Besides, as Civil War historian James McPherson notes, the North experienced similar internal fractures and Lincoln took a fiercer and more public flogging than Davis. When Lincoln jailed war dissenters and suspended the writ of habeas corpus, many labeled him a despot. New York's Irish were so incensed at being conscripted for an emancipation war that they rioted, causing the worst civil insurrection in American history. Through much of the war, vocal Peace Democrats called Lincoln and the war a failure and wanted to negotiate a peace and let the Confederates go. If Lincoln had lost his reelection of 1864, McPherson points out, we might be making the argument that internal dissent was the reason the *Union* lost the war.

DID THE SOUTH LOSE THE WILL TO FIGHT?

Some historians have raised a larger question: Did the South at some point lose the *will* to fight? Were the Confederates missing a fire behind their cause?

Authors of *Why the South Lost the Civil War* argue that despite the initial outburst of war fever in the South, the Confederates started the war with a weak premise. President Jefferson Davis, responding to the North's mobilization of troops, spoke to his Congress on April 29, 1861, saying, "All we ask is to be let alone"—hardly the inspirational cry that comes off the lips of most successful revolutionaries. While states' rights were paid lip service, many Southerners were ashamed or at least uncomfortable with the real cause of the war—protecting slavery.

Many poor Southerners resented slave-owners, especially larger ones, who were exempted from the draft, an exemption sanctioned by the Confederate Congress. And even those willing to fight for slavery lost their cause by the last year of the war, when Southern leaders, including Robert E. Lee, offered to arm slaves and free them if they fought for the Confederacy. Perhaps the strongest argument that the South lost the will to fight is that in the early fall and winter of 1864–1865, 40 percent of Confederate soldiers east of the Mississippi deserted.

James McPherson, though, argues in *Battle Cry of Freedom* that this "loss of will" thesis suffers because it doesn't recognize that the will to fight often pivots on military success and failure. "Defeat causes demoralization and loss of will," McPherson writes, "victory pumps up morale." During the summer of 1864, for example, devastating casualties and a stalled offensive nearly undermined Northern morale to such a degree that Lincoln expected to lose his reelection. But the taking of Atlanta and Philip Sheridan's rout of Jubal Early's army in the Shenandoah Valley created a "depth of determination . . . to fight to the last" that "astonished" one British journalist.

What about the quality of leadership? If Abraham Lincoln and his commanders were switched with Jefferson Davis and his, would the Confederacy have won?

WHAT IF THE LEADERS WERE REVERSED?
WOULD THE SOUTH HAVE WON?

Did the superior quality of Northern leadership win the war for the Union? The Union hardly had the edge in leadership at the war's launch. "I fought, bled, and came away" after "charges upon the wild onions," Abraham Lincoln said about his military experience in the Mexican War, and "a good many bloody struggles with the mosquitoes." His only national political experience was an ineffectual term as a congressman, after which he said, "I neither expect, seek, or deserve" to return to Washington—and he didn't. By contrast, Jefferson Davis was a West Pointer who had served admirably in the Mexican War and was elected a congressman, a senator, and then appointed U.S. secretary of war by President Franklin Pierce.

But as the war progressed, Lincoln revealed himself the more capable leader. Davis bickered with those who disagreed with him; Lincoln chose his rivals during the presidential campaign for his cabinet members and always valued winning the war over winning an argument. And while Davis often got lost in the war's details, Lincoln concentrated on the larger strategic picture, one that would win the war once he found a general to execute it.

What about each side's military leaders? Southern generals in the early war, such as Albert Johnson, Pierre Beauregard, and "Stonewall" Jackson, were superior to Northern bumblers such as George McClellan, John Pope, Joseph Hooker, and Ambrose Burnside. And Robert E. Lee is generally praised as the best tactician of the war.

But the best military strategist of the Civil War was probably General Ulysses S. Grant. "The first quality of a general-in-chief," Napoleon once said, "is to have a cool head which receives exact impressions of things, which never gets heated, which never allows itself to be dazzled, or intoxicated, by good or bad news." Of all the generals in the war, that description best sums up Grant. He, Lincoln, and William Tecumseh Sherman understood that the way to win the war was to fight it all-out, everywhere at once, against armies and civilians, and that's what they did in 1864.

EMANCIPATION AND ARMING OF THE EX-SLAVES— THE DECIDING FACTOR?

Americans have always understood that the Civil War emancipated the slaves. But did the freeing of slaves during the war and the arming of the African-Americans after 1863 actually provide the Union victory?

From the very start of the war, slaves slipped away from Southern homes and plantations to find safety behind Union lines. By the time the war ended, between 500,000 and 700,000 slaves would escape to freedom. That was 15 to 20 percent of the Confederacy's slave population, but the impact they had, writes Joseph T. Glatthaar in his essay "Black Glory: The African-American Role in Union Victory" was "so much greater than their numbers."

As slaves disappeared across enemy lines, fewer hands were available to make weapons or grow the crops that fed both Southern civilians and soldiers. "So long as the rebels retain and employ their slaves in producing grains, [etc.]," wrote Union General-in-Chief Henry Halleck to Ulysses S. Grant on March 31, 1863, "they can employ all the whites in the field [of arms]. Every slave withdrawn from the enemy is equivalent to a white man put *hors de combat* [out of action]." This mass flight also undermined one of the core Southern ideologies behind the war—that slaves were contented with their position.

This mass exodus, and the recruitment of freed blacks into the U.S. military, also made it clear that the war was not about keeping the Union—"a goal too shallow to be worth the sacrifice of a single life," according to Civil War scholar Barbara Fields—but a historic struggle to free the slaves. Fighting a "freedom war," as African Americans called it, released a new energy for the war in the North and also discouraged European leaders from joining pro-slavery Confederates.

The double-barreled policy of black emancipation and enlistment may have turned the war. "I believe it is a resource which, if vigorously applied now, will soon close the contest," Lincoln told Grant in 1863. "It works doubly, weakening the enemy and strengthening us."

Roughly 300,000 black men served in the Union army; 180,000 black men would see combat, 10,000 more served in the navy. They would engage in over 40 major battles and 450 smaller ones. Eighty-five percent of the eligible black population in the North signed on; in the war's final year, 120,000 black soldiers enlisted. By the time of Appomattox, about one in every eight Union soldiers was a black recruit.

DID CHANCE PLAY A ROLE IN THE UNION VICTORY?

Historians have long acknowledged that small events can have momentous historical consequences. Was this true of the Civil War? Would minor alterations in a battle or a political decision have turned a grinding Union victory into a Confederate one? Such musings lead to many "what-if"s of the Civil War that many history buffs have played since the day General Lee surrendered.

What if the eight border states had all sided with the South instead of splitting between the two sides? Might the added men and resources have swung the balance of power to the Confederacy? And if the British government had listened to its textile lobby and recognized the Confederacy, wouldn't British domination of the seas have destroyed the Union blockade, brought more supplies to the South, and put the Confederacy over the top to victory?

What if two Union soldiers drinking coffee had not picked up the plans for Lee's invasion of Maryland, wrapped around three cigars? Would Lee have whipped Union General George McClellan at Antietam, perhaps destroying his army, and then marched on to Washington and sent the U.S. government fleeing?

And what if Brigadier General Gouverneur Warren had not put out the frantic call to Union soldiers to mount Little Round Top at Gettysburg just minutes before the Confederate attack on the Union's left flank? Would the Confederates have taken Round Top, crumbled the Union line, and won Gettysburg and the war?

One more: What if General William Sherman's march into Atlanta on September 2, 1864, had been delayed by ten weeks? Might former Union general and Democratic presidential candidate George McClellan beaten Lincoln, forcing Lincoln to make peace with the Confederacy? Might you now be reading about Lincoln as a failed president, who oversaw the end of the American democratic experiment and who failed to slow the expansion of slavery on the continent?

"TO COLORED MEN!
FREEDOM, PROTECTION, PAY,
AND A CALL TO MILITARY DUTY!"

TO COLORED MEN!

FREEDOM,

Protection, Pay, and a Call to Military Duty!

On the 1st day of January, 1863, the President of the United States proclaimed FREE-DOM to over THREE MILLIONS OF SLAVES. This decree is to be enforced by all the power of the Nation. On the 21st of July last he issued the following order:

PROTECTION OF COLORED TROOPS.

"WAR DEPARTMENT, ADJUTANT GENERAL'S OFFICE,
WASHINGTON, July 31.

"*General Order, No. 233.*

"The following order of the President is published for the information and government of all concerned:—

EXECUTIVE MANSION, WASHINGTON, July 30.

"It is the duty of every Government to give protection to its citizens, of whatever class, color, or condition, and especially to those who are duly organized as soldiers in the public service. The law of nations, and the usages and customs of war, as carried on by civilized powers, permit no distinction as to color in the treatment of prisoners of war as public enemies. To sell or enslave any captured person on account of his color, is a relapse into barbarism, and a crime against the civilization of the age.

"The Government of the United States will give the same protection to all its soldiers, and if the enemy shall sell or enslave any one because of his color, the offense shall be punished by retaliation upon the enemy's prisoners in our possession. It is, therefore, ordered, for every soldier of the United States, killed in violation of the laws of war, a rebel soldier shall be executed; and for every one enslaved by the enemy, or sold into slavery, a rebel soldier shall be placed at hard labor on the public works, and continued at such labor until the other shall be released and receive the treatment due to prisoners of war.

"ABRAHAM LINCOLN."

"By order of the Secretary of War.
"E. D. TOWNSEND, Assistant Adjutant General."

That the President is in earnest the rebels soon began to find out, as witness the following order from his Secretary of War:

"WAR DEPARTMENT, WASHINGTON CITY, August 3, 1863.

"SIR: Your letter of the 3d inst., calling the attention of this Department to the cases of Orin H. Brown, William H. Johnston, and Wm. Wilson, three colored men captured on the gunboat Isaac Smith, has received consideration. This Department has directed that three rebel prisoners of South Carolina, if there be any such in our possession, and if not, three others, be confined in close custody and held as hostages for Brown, Johnston and Wilson, and that the fact be communicated to the rebel authorities at Richmond.
"Very respectfully your obedient servant,

"EDWIN M. STANTON, Secretary of War.

"The Hon. GIDEON WELLES, Secretary of the Navy."

And retaliation will be our practice now—man for man—to the bitter end.

LETTER OF CHARLES SUMNER,

Written with reference to the Convention held at Poughkeepsie, July 15th and 16th, 1863, to promote Colored Enlistments.

BOSTON, July 13th, 1863.

"I doubt if, in times past, our country could have expected from colored men any patriotic service. Such service is the return for protection. But now that protection has begun, the service should begin also. Nor should relative rights and duties be weighed with nicety. It is enough that our country, aroused at last to a sense of justice, seeks to enrol colored men among its defenders.

"If my counsels should reach such persons, I would say: enlist at once. Now is the day and now is the hour. Help to overcome your cruel enemies now battling against your country, and in this way you will surely overcome those other enemies hardly less cruel, here at home, who will still seek to degrade you. This is not the time to hesitate or to higgle. Do your duty to our country, and you will set an example of generous self-sacrifice which will conquer prejudice and open all hearts.

"Very faithfully yours,
"CHARLES SUMNER."

This recruitment poster was aimed at recruiting African-American men into the Union Army to defeat the Confederacy.

WHAT DID
THE WAR DECIDE?

WEEK 51

WHAT TO CALL THE WAR?

The American Civil War did not always go by that name. Generals, writers, and partisans have given the war many names, often infused with politics and passions, subtle and not so subtle, by those on either side of the conflict. Southern resentment of the Union Army's invasion into the South was expressed in their name, the War Against Northern Aggression. Another popular Southern name, the Second American Revolution, connected their cause with that of the patriots of the Revolutionary War. (Scholar Charles Beard also called the conflict the Second American Revolution, but his name referred to the ascendancy of capitalism and the North after the war.) Confederate General Joseph Johnston called the conflict the War Against the States, framing the war as one waged by the federal government against Southern states and states' rights.

Many of the official records for the war referred to the conflict as the War of the Rebellion, and Walt Whitman, emphasizing the failure of the Confederacy, called it the War of *Attempted* Secession. Others, willing to recognize the separation had been more than attempted, called it simply the War of Secession. Southerners also gave it names that alluded to noble causes, calling it the War of Southern Independence, the War for Southern Rights, or the War for Southern Freedom. Slaves and former slaves also evoked freedom in the name they gave to the war, but not freedom *of* the Confederacy, but freedom *from* it. They called the war the Freedom War.

Some names, such as the War Between the States or the Brothers' War, are more neutral. Perhaps that's the appeal of the generic Civil War, the overwhelming choice for the war's name since the early twentieth century. In a country that has emphasized binding the wounds of the bitter conflict over the last century and a half, it lays no blame, makes no interpretation, takes no sides.

THAT SLAVES WERE FREE—BUT NOT COMPLETELY

At the beginning of the war, Abraham Lincoln would have willingly accepted a peace that brought Southern states back into the Union with slavery intact. His condition for peace was simple: he wanted the country restored as it was.

But by 1862, the constant abolitionist push for emancipation and the flight of escaped slaves into Union lines changed the lives of slaves and the purpose of the war. When Lincoln said at Gettysburg in the fall of 1863 that the war was fought and men died so "that this nation under God shall have a new birth of freedom," he was referring to a societal birth that broke the nation free from the bonds of slavery. The North's victory meant the largest slave republic in the world was toppled, a change codified by the Thirteenth Amendment to the Constitution.

"If I stay here," said one freed slave from South Carolina, "I'll never know I am free." Others chose surnames for themselves associated with American freedom, such as Washington. Free to leave their former masters, they tracked down their separated children and spouses and they married under the law.

But emancipation was incomplete at best. The right to vote, the right to testify in court, the right to attend quality schools, the right to sell their labor freely, the right to protection from mob violence—these would be won in fits and lost in starts. Unlike the aftermath of civil wars in France, Spain, and Russia, the losing side, the Southern aristocracy, was not executed, robbed of their land, or even prevented from holding positions of influence. Within a decade, politicians of the Old South found their way back into power—the Virginia general William Mahone, for example, became a senator after the war.

In the 1890s, these Southern leaders passed Jim Crow laws that segregated Southern society, giving African-Americans the lesser half of schools and other institutions, and intimidated blacks with organizations such as the Ku Klux Klan, which used tactics such as lynchings to ensure blacks remained second-class citizens, both politically and socially. It would take a hundred years and another major social upheaval—the Civil Rights movement of the 1950s and 1960s—to make substantial gains in these rights and freedoms.

THAT WE ARE ONE COUNTRY—NOT A UNION OF STATES

Before the Civil War, many people traveled no more than fifty or a hundred miles from their home in a lifetime and they identified with the states they lived in. Even during the war, these attachments persisted. Soldiers enlisted with others from their hometowns; they served in the Fifty-fourth Massachusetts or the Twentieth Maine or the Army of Northern Virginia. Lee didn't decline command of the Union Army because he wanted to fight for the Confederacy; he wanted to defend his beloved Virginia.

After the war, local allegiances were diminished; the war had forged all into one nation. Secession was never considered again. Historian Shelby Foote put it this way: "Before the war, it was said, 'The United States are . . .' Grammatically, it was spoken that way and thought of as a collection of independent states. After the war, it was always 'The United States *is* . . .'—as we say today without being self-conscious at all. And that sums up what the war accomplished. It made us an '*is*.'"

Lincoln maintained throughout the war that it was about preserving the unity of a democracy. "Our popular government has often been called an experiment," Lincoln told Congress on July 4, 1861. ". . . [This] presents to the whole family of man, the question, whether a constitutional republic, or a democracy . . . can or cannot, maintain its territorial integrity, against its own domestic foes."

With unity came a much more powerful centralized government. Before the war, the only contact the average American had with the federal government was through the postal service. Afterward, the federal government imposed taxes on all citizens, and a revenue bureau was in place to collect those taxes. Federal courts became more powerful and men were drafted. Eleven of the first twelve amendments to the U.S. Constitution limited the federal government's powers. Six of the next seven, including the Thirteenth Amendment, expanded the powers of the national government.

THAT FEW EVER CAN PREDICT THE CARNAGE OF WAR

On May 23, 1865, two weeks after Jefferson Davis was caught, the surviving soldiers from the Army of the Potomac marched down Pennsylvania Avenue, Philip Sheridan's cavalry in front, many of the corps bearing their war-torn flags. Instead of singing the bright patriotic songs that dominated at the beginning of the war, the enormous crowd sang more mournful ones, such as "When This Cruel War Is Over" and "When Johnny Comes Marching Home." Patriotism had survived, but it was tempered by four years of unrelenting death.

When Southerners first voted for secession, some predicted less than a thimbleful of blood would be spilled by the political conflict. But the war had been far more brutal than nearly all had expected, including Abraham Lincoln. Some 360,000 federal troops had died in the war, and 260,000 more Rebels. For the Union, which kept more careful records, about 110,000 men had died in combat from wounds, with another 224,000 killed by disease. Union surgeons had performed thirty thousand amputations, most of them delaying, at best, the deaths of soldiers whose bodies had been ripped and shattered by gunshots and cannon fire. Some battles had 30 percent casualties; today, 10 percent is considered a bloodbath.

The four-year ordeal ended up leaving more men dead than in all America's other wars combined. Twice as many Americans died in the Civil War than in World War II. To have matched the number of deaths proportionally, 2.5 million Americans would have had to have died in World War II, seven times the actual number. To the dead were added the walking wounded: some 275,000 federal soldiers and almost 200,000 Confederates were physically diminished for the rest of their lives. The losses seem almost biblical in proportion, and as Lincoln said in his Second Inaugural Address, it was as if "every drop of blood drawn with the lash shall be paid by another drawn with the sword. . . . Neither party expected for the war the magnitude or the duration which it has already attained. Neither anticipated that the cause of the conflict might cease with, or even before, the conflict itself should cease. . . . The prayers of both could not be answered; that of neither has been answered fully. The Almighty has His own purposes."

THAT NINETEENTH-CENTURY WOMEN HAD A PLACE OUTSIDE THE HOME

Clara Barton's devotion to nursing Union soldiers made her the best-known woman of the war. "I appear to be known by reputation by every person in every train I enter and everywhere," she confessed to her diary. She decided to use her fame to make a living, going on the lecture circuit in 1866, reliving her war experiences in variations of an address called "Work and Incidents of Army Life." Although she had long feared speaking publicly, she soon found she had a knack for it, and her talents earned her as much as 100 dollars an appearance, a fee on par with the top male lecturers of the day.

She would take her listeners back to the field hospitals of Second Bull Run, Antietam, and Fredericksburg and would ask rhetorically why she talked about her "own little personal doings in the war. . . . [T]o show you that from first to last I have been the soldiers' friend and have an honest right to speak for him."

But she also spoke for women who had stepped out, often out of necessity, from their domestic roles prior to the war. She spoke openly about the inhibitions that prevented her from serving in 1861 and 1862. "I struggled long and hard with my sense of propriety," she told the large crowds, "with the appalling fact that I was a woman . . . Only an opportunity was wanting for woman to prove to man that she could be in earnest, that she had character, and firmness of purpose—that she *was* good for something in an emergency." During the war, more than eighteen thousand women worked in Northern military hospitals as *paid* matrons, nurses, laundresses, and cooks, with thousands more volunteering their services. Some two thousand of these women were black, many of them escaped slaves. Women also campaigned for Lincoln and other Republicans and established the National Women's Loyal League, which collected 400,000 signatures in support of the Thirteenth Amendment, abolishing slavery.

Women in the North and South worked as hospital workers, government employees, retail workers, farmers, and war factory workers, filling vacancies left by men who went to war. By the end of the war, Barton told a group in Boston that American women were more than "fifty years in advance of the normal position which continued peace and existing conditions would have assigned her."

THAT THE NORTH BECAME DOMINANT

In 1869, a retired Harvard professor mused that the Civil War had created a "great gulf between what happened before in our century and what has happened since, or what is likely to happen hereafter. It does not seem to me as if I were living in the country in which I was born."

The country was not only transformed; its center of power and wealth shifted radically. The North's power, built on growing industry, new immigrants, and accruing wealth, was ascending before the Civil War—Abraham Lincoln could not have been elected otherwise—but it picked up speed in the postwar era. With emancipation, two-thirds of the assessed wealth of the South, much of it contained in slaves, was taken from Southerners, a loss with little parallel in world history. The Union war machine had also destroyed what Southern industry existed at the war's beginning.

"I chant the new empire, grander than before," said Walt Whitman. "I chant commerce coming!" The commerce that came usually arrived in the ex-Union states. "The truth is," said Ohio politician John Sherman, the brother of General William Sherman, "the close of the war with our resources unimpaired gives an elevation, a scope to the ideas of leading capitalists, far higher than anything ever undertaken before. They talk of millions as confidently as formerly of thousands." The Fisks, Rockefellers, Carnegies, and Morgans would soon build entire industries and make many millions, and they would do it in the North.

Northerners also dominated the centers of governmental power in post–Civil War America. Before the conflict, the U.S. Supreme Court always included a majority of Southerners. Afterward, only about one in five Supreme Court justices came from Southern states. Before the war, twenty-three of thirty-six speakers of the House—two-thirds— had come from Confederate states. A Southern speaker would not oversee the House for another fifty years. Until 1861, the U.S. presidency was held by a Southerner for two out of every three terms. A Southerner from an ex-Confederate state wouldn't be elected president again for a century.

VETS SHAKING HANDS

This photograph, taken in 1913, nearly half a century after the Civil War ended, shows a Confederate and a Union soldier shaking hands.

WHAT BECAME OF THEM?

WEEK 52

THE DAVISES

After Jefferson Davis was released from prison in 1868, the Davises and their children went abroad and considered living in London or Paris. But the former president soon grew homesick and he took a job with the Carolina Life Insurance Company in Memphis. After that company failed in 1873, he went abroad again looking for work, although he told Varina, his wife, he could not "run round begging for employment" and returned to Memphis. In 1876, he said he felt like a "waif" and feared he might end up old and homeless. He then spent four years on his memoirs, *The Rise and Fall of the Confederate Government*, and when its sales were slight, he said he hadn't written it for profit but to "set the righteous motives of the South before the world." Davis died on December 6, 1889, Varina by his side.

Afterward, Varina took up writing, and settled in New York City after newspaper magnate Joseph Pulitzer, who was a relative of hers by marriage, gave her an entrée into the publishing world. But she might also have stayed because in New York she was but one of many famous players from the Civil War, not the first lady of the Confederacy.

Although Varina Davis once confessed to a friend that her time in the Confederate White House seemed like a "troubled dream," she tried not to focus on the past, saying that most people's lives became "swallowed up by time and the world knows them no more." She advocated reconciliation with Northerners, and for that view, and her New York City residency, many Southerners considered her a traitor. On October 16, 1906, Varina Davis, eighty years old, died of pneumonia, and as her coffin was lowered into the ground next to her husband's at Richmond's Hollywood Cemetery, a U.S. military band played "Dixie."

"She was one of the last living mementoes of the Confederate government," wrote the *Richmond New Leader*, "one of the last of all to die."

NORTHERN GENERALS

David G. Farragut was appointed vice admiral of the Navy in 1864, the country's first admiral in 1866, and died in 1870, having served the U.S. Navy since he was a twelve-year-old in the War of 1812. Ambrose Burnside, convinced he was not qualified to serve as a general, which he proved at Fredericksburg, died a senator. George Armstrong Custer, a dashing young cavalry hero, would be remembered for leading a few hundred men into a massacre by Plains Indians at the Battle of Little Bighorn in 1876, where he was killed.

In 1868, four years after the Civil War ended, Ulysses S. Grant was elected president of the United States and then reelected in 1872, the first of seven Civil War soldiers who would become presidents (the last was William McKinley, elected in 1897 and killed by an assassin). Despite persistent scandals that dogged his administration, Grant pushed for civil rights for blacks and deployed the army to ensure freedmen's rights. He avoided war with Spain over Cuba and rebuilt relations with Great Britain. He also prevented the complete annihilation of the Plains Indians, and instead forwarded a policy that called for their assimilation. He pushed for civil service reform and also kept the economy on an even keel.

He lost all his money in a Wall Street swindle in 1884. He contracted throat cancer soon after and spent the last weeks of his life writing his memoir so his family would have money to avoid destitution. He died on July 23, 1885, four days after he finished his manuscript, which Mark Twain published. Over 1.5 million people watched the funeral procession in New York City. Grant had requested his pallbearers include an equal number of Southern and Northern generals, and the slogan from his first election campaign was put on his tomb, paid for by donations of the American people: "Let Us Have Peace." His memoirs became a bestseller.

There was talk of drafting William Sherman as a Liberal Party candidate in the 1872 presidential election, but he responded, "What do you think I am, a damned fool? Look at Grant! . . . What wouldn't he give now if he had never meddled in politics!" At Sherman's funeral in February 1891, Joseph Johnston, one of the Confederate generals Sherman defeated in the war, was a pallbearer. Johnston insisted on taking off his hat in the bitter cold, and when someone expressed concern, he replied, "If I were in his place and he were standing here in mine he would not put on his hat." Johnston caught pneumonia and died five weeks later.

SOUTHERN GENERALS

At war's end, Robert E. Lee was fifty-eight years old, his thirty-nine-year-long military career over. The Union had confiscated his family estate and he had no home for his invalid wife, Mary, and their three daughters. He had probably suffered a mild heart attack in 1863, and his ongoing heart problems often caused him chest pains and left him weary. "I could have taken no other course without dishonor," Lee would say after the war, "and if it all were to be done over again, I should act in precisely the same manner."

Other Southern generals clung to bitterness. Nathan Bedford Forrest, the flamboyant cavalryman, was part of a group of unemployed Confederate veterans who established the Ku Klux Klan in Pulaski, Tennessee, in December 1865. He became the KKK's first Imperial Wizard, although escalating violence, including lynchings, led him to resign.

Lee moved his family into a borrowed house west of Richmond and expected to live quietly and write a history of the Army of Northern Virginia. Then, in 1865, he was made an unexpected offer by a trustee of Washington College in Lexington, Virginia. Would the general serve as president of the tired and underfunded school?

Lee took the job, noting that "I think it the duty of every citizen in the present condition of the Country to do all in his power to aid in the restoration of peace and harmony." He raised money from all over the country, planting trees, building the school's library, hiring faculty, erecting buildings, and adding practical departments, such as chemistry, law, and engineering. In the late 1860s, his rides on his horse Traveller became less frequent. While he was still collecting materials for his memoirs, he suffered a stroke on September 28, 1870, and died on October 11. In the days after his death, the school was renamed Washington *and Lee* University.

The soldiers lasted longer than their generals. The last meeting of the Grand Army of the Republic was held in 1949; six came to the meeting. Three former soldiers from the United Confederate Veterans held their last reunion two years later, in 1951. After that, the war became one step removed, part of family folklore, saved in daguerreotypes and soldier diaries, history.

JAMES LONGSTREET—SOUTHERN TRAITOR OR REALIST?

At Appomattox, when General Lee worried that General Grant would set harsh terms for surrender, Longstreet advised: If that happens, come back and we'll fight. But after the war, Longstreet decided the path to restoring Southern greatness and prosperity lay in accepting defeat and complying with Northern political wishes. In June 1867, Longstreet was living in New Orleans when a local newspaper asked him how Louisiana should respond to a federal law that required former Confederate states to give black males the vote. Longstreet responded that the South should obey. His argument: Might makes right.

"The ideas that divided political parties before the war—upon the rights of the States—were thoroughly discussed by our wisest statesmen, and eventually appealed to the arbitrament of the sword," he said. "The decision was in favor of the North . . . and should be so accepted." For supporting black suffrage, Longstreet was immediately denounced by many Southerners as a traitor. The next day, "old comrades passed me on the streets without speaking," he later wrote in his memoirs. Hatred for him was fanned in 1874, when he led black troops to put down a white supremacist mob in New Orleans. For supporting the Republicans' Reconstruction policies, Longstreet was given plum government positions, such as a customs official post in New Orleans and an ambassadorship to Turkey.

After Robert E. Lee died in 1870, a group led by ex–Confederate General Jubal Early, who had fought with Longstreet at Gettysburg, assailed him for delaying an attack on the battle's second day. But Early and others took it further, arguing that Longstreet, not Lee, was responsible for the Gettysburg disaster. Longstreet denied the accusations, and in his memoirs, published in 1896, he said the blistering post-war attacks were payback for his support of black suffrage. He added that Lee had been wrong to put him in command of the Gettysburg attack: "He knew that I did not believe that success was possible; . . . he should have put an officer in charge who had more confidence in his plan." Who should have led the attack instead of him? With more than a hint of bitterness, Longstreet suggested Early.

FREDERICK DOUGLASS BATTLES FOR REAL FREEDOM

When the abolitionist William Lloyd Garrison suggested disbanding the Anti-Slavery Society a month after the Civil War ended, Frederick Douglass protested, arguing that slavery is not abolished "until the black man has the ballot," and that the group's work would not be done until the word "white" was deleted from every law in the country. Without the vote, he told the Massachusetts Anti-Slavery Society, "liberty is a mockery."

"We want it because it is our *right*, first of all," he said. "We want it again as a means for educating our race." And he believed it would be a bulwark to preventing Southerners from undermining the freedom of African-Americans.

"Let the civil powers of the [Confederate] States be restored," he wrote, and

> the old prejudices and hostility to the Negro will revive. Aye, the very fact that the Negro has been used to defeat this rebellion and strike down the standards of the Confederacy will be a stimulus to all their hatreds, to all their malice, and lead them to legislate with greater stringency towards this class than ever before. The American people are bound—bound by their sense of honor . . . to extend the franchise to the Negro.

"What I ask for the Negro," he said, "is not benevolence, not pity, not sympathy, but simply *justice*." He lived long enough to see the rise of the Ku Klux Klan, the resurgence of racist Democrats in the South, and the vote and other civil rights given and then taken away from blacks.

In 1881, the former slave wrote *Life and Times of Frederick Douglass*, which relayed stories of the Civil War, including his contact with Abraham Lincoln. He urged Americans not to forget their history of slavery and reminded white America that black America was not yet free, but the book sold poorly. On February 20, 1895, Douglass attended a women's rights rally. Afterward, he came home and mimicked some of the ponderous speakers for his second wife, Helen, sinking to his knees for dramatic effect. Then he fell to the floor, dead.

CLARA BARTON MEETS A SOLDIER

After the war, following one of her lectures at a local YMCA, a man approached Clara Barton. He was wearing a light blue soldier's coat and walking with a limp. She recognized his face, excused herself from well-wishers, and approached him.

"Have we met before?" she asked. "Yes," he said. "Three times." As she clasped his hand, she said, "Tell me."

"At the battle of Second Bull Run when I was shot through the body and had lain on the field for days with nothing to eat," he said, "you came out of the woods and met the wagon that was taking me off and climbed up onto the wheel and fed me."

"I remember," Clara said softly.

"Before my wound had entirely healed," he said, "I rejoined my regiment at Falmouth—and next day went to the battle of Old Fredericksburg, had this leg shattered in the charge of Saturday and lay out on the field in the cold till Monday night—my hands and feet were frozen. . . . You had the men scrape the snow off the ground and gave us warm drink and kept hot bricks about us all night—you had them heated in the camp fires."

"I remember," Clara said. Her lips trembled.

"I lost you then for nearly two years—when one terribly hot day in front of Petersburg, when from our marching nearly our whole brigade fell with exhaustion and sunstroke, I among the first—for I hadn't the strength I had at Bull Run—and while I lay there on the ground you came with whiskey and water for us all and had me taken to the hospital tents and you bound my head in ice and I was too crazy to tell you that I knew you but I did—and your care saved my life."

When he ended his recollections, Clara took her hand from his and touched the cheek of the small child who was with the man. "And is this your little girl?"

"Yes," he said, stroking the girl's hair. "She is almost three years old and we call her Clara Barton."

GENERAL ULYSSES S. GRANT'S
FUNERAL PROCESSION

Over 1.5 million people watched General U. S. Grant's funeral
procession, shown coming down Fourteenth Street in New York
City on August 8, 1885.

ENDNOTES

PRELUDE TO A WAR:
SPARKS BEFORE THE FLAME

Introduction

Different historians weigh in on the causes of the Civil War in the collection *Why the War Came*, edited by Gabor S. Boritt.

Slavery and Its Discontents

HARRIET TUBMAN ESCAPES SLAVERY AND RIDES THE UNDERGROUND RAILROAD

For more on the Underground Railroad, see Fergus M. Bordewich's *Bound for Canaan: The Underground Railroad and the War for the Soul of America.*

Going West, Pulling Apart

COMPROMISES AND MORE COMPROMISES TO PUT OFF THE CONFLICT

David Potter's *The Impending Crisis, 1848–1861* is a narrative of the sectional differences that led up to the Civil War.

UNCLE TOM'S CABIN—THE STORY BEHIND THE BOOK

This account largely comes from *Bound for Canaan: The Underground Railroad and the War for the Soul of America*, by Fergus M. Bordewich. For the role Stowe and other women played in the crusade for freedom, see Glenna Matthews's "'Little Women' Who Helped Make this Great War" in *Why the Civil War Came,* edited by Gabor S. Boritt.

PASSIONS ARE INFLAMED BY THE LAST AMERICAN SLAVE SHIP—THE *WANDERER*

For more on Charles A. L. Lamar, the fire-eaters, and the *Wanderer*, see Erik Calonius's book, *The Wanderer.*

John Brown—Meteor of the Civil War

JOHN BROWN INVITES FREDERICK DOUGLASS TO JOIN HIS RAID

This account is largely taken from the former slave's autobiography, *The Life and Times of Frederick Douglass.*

FAILURE AT HARPERS FERRY

For an overview, with accompanying documents, of the raid and its aftermath, see *John Brown's Raid on Harpers Ferry*, by Jonathan Earle.

JOHN BROWN'S TRIAL TURNS HIM INTO A NORTHERN MARTYR

A classic biography of John Brown is Stephen B. Oates's *To Purge This Land with Blood.*

PRAISE AND VILIFICATION—JOHN BROWN DIVIDES THE COUNTRY

Was John Brown mad, a terrorist, or a martyr in the fight against slavery? To read an overview of different historical answers to this question, see "Chapter 3. John Brown and his Judges" of *Our Fiery Trial*, by Stephen B. Oates.

JOHN BROWN'S HANGING AND THE PROPHET'S PREDICTION

A classic volume on Brown that portrays him as a hero is W. E. B. Dubois's *John Brown*. For a sympathetic modern portrayal, see *Patriotic Treason*, by Evan Carton.

Lincoln Is Elected—and the Deep South Secedes

LINCOLN IS ELECTED—"GOD HELP ME, GOD HELP ME"

For more on Lincoln's election and the secession that followed, see Harold Holzer's book, *Lincoln President-Elect: Abraham Lincoln and the Great Secession Winter 1860–1861*.

THE OTHER SOUTH—SAM HOUSTON AND THE ANTI-SECESSIONISTS

To read about Southerners who opposed secession and slavery, read Carl N. Degler's book, *The Other South—Southern Dissenters in the Nineteenth Century*.

THE DEEP SOUTH GOES OUT—AND THE FATHERS OF THE CONFEDERACY MEET IN MONTGOMERY

For more on the Montgomery convention, read William C. Davis's *"A Government of Our Own": The Making of the Confederacy*. For more on the political affairs of the Confederate nation, especially prewar nationalism, see Emory M. Thomas's *The Confederate Nation, 1861–1865*.

WERE THE SECESSIONISTS REBELS OR CONSERVATIVES?

For more on whether the Confederates were rebels or conservatives, see Chapter 8, "The Counterrevolution of 1861" in James McPherson's *Battle Cry of Freedom*.

THE COUNTRY EXPLODES, THE CANNON IS FIRED (1860–1861)

The Creation of the Confederate States of America

"DIXIE"—A SONG STOLEN FROM BLACK MUSICIANS BY AN OHIO WHITE SONGWRITER FOR A MINSTREL SHOW?

To read about the evolution of the song "John Brown's Body," read Sarah Vowell's essay by that name in the book *The Rose and the Briar: Death, Love and Liberty in the American Ballad*, edited by Sean Wilentz and Greil Marcus. To read about the theory that "Dixie" was written by African-Americans, read *Way Up North in Dixie: A Black Family's Claim to the Confederate Anthem*, by Judith and Howard Sacks.

WAS SLAVERY THE PRIMARY REASON FOR SECESSION?

For more on the causes of the Civil War, see Edward L. Ayers's *What Caused the Civil War?: Reflections on the South and Southern History*. For the theory that the war was caused by a conflict between two economic systems, see *The Rise of American Civilization*, by Charles and Mary Beard. A compelling case that the participants in the political conflict saw slavery as the cause for the war is made in the book *Apostles of Disunion: Southern Secession Commissioners and the Causes of the Civil War*, by Charles B. Dew.

HARRIET TUBMAN HAS A VISION THAT THE SLAVES WILL BE FREED

For this and other accounts of Tubman's life, read *Harriet Tubman: Imagining a Life*, by Beverly Lowry.

MONEY, MEN, AND MUNITIONS—THE RISE OF THE CONFEDERATE NATION

For a political, social, and economic history of the Confederacy, see William C. Davis's *Look Away! A History of the Confederate States of America.*

Failed Compromises to Save the Union

LINCOLN DISGUISES HIMSELF TO ESCAPE FROM FEARED ASSASSINS—AND REGRETS IT

For more on this train ride to Washington, D.C., see Victor Searcher's *Lincoln's Journey to Greatness: A Factual Account of the Twelve-Day Inaugural Trip.*
For more on this alleged plot to kill Lincoln, see Norma B. Cuthbert's *Lincoln and the Baltimore Plot.*

The Gun Is Fired—Fort Sumter

WILLIAM SEWARD CHALLENGES LINCOLN'S AUTHORITY

To learn more about Lincoln's secretary of state, read *William Henry Seward: Lincoln's Right Hand Man,* by John M. Taylor.

DID LINCOLN PROVOKE THE SOUTH?

A summary of the different historical perspectives on Lincoln's motivation in resupplying Fort Sumter is presented by Richard Current in *Lincoln and the First Shot.*

Innocence Before the Slaughter

CLARA BARTON AIDS THE UNION'S FIRST RECRUITS, ATTACKED IN BALTIMORE

For a detailed account of this story and the life of Clara Barton during the conflict, see Stephen B. Oates's *A Woman of Valor: Clara Barton and the Civil War.*

RHODE ISLAND'S ELISHA HUNT RHODES ENLISTS "WITH MINGLED FEELINGS OF JOY AND SORROW"

For more on Elisha Hunt Rhodes, read his wartime journal and his collection of letters published as *All For the Union*, by a great-grandson.

SAM WATKINS—" 'HIGH PRIVATE' IN THE REAR RANKS OF THE REBEL ARMY"—AND OTHERS ENLIST

For more on Sam Watkins, see his memoir, *"Co. Aytch."*

Bull Run (Manassas)—the Great Skedaddle

THOMAS "STONEWALL" JACKSON AND THE REBEL YELL

To learn more about this shy, religious, and driven general, read *Thomas Stonewall Jackson: A Biography of General Thomas J. Jackson*, by James Robertson.

ROSE O'NEALE GREENHOW IS ARRESTED FOR SPYING

To learn more about Rose O'Neale Greenhow, read *Wild Rose*, by Ann Blackman.

The Making and Unmaking of Soldiers, Spies, and Munitions Manufacturers

DID SHERMAN GO INSANE?

For more on the relationship between the two great Union generals, read Charles Bracelen Flood's *Grant and Sherman: The Friendship that Won the Civil War.*

Lincoln Resists a War of Freedom

NO BLACKS NEED APPLY—WHY BLACKS WERE KEPT OUT OF THE UNION ARMY

A classic book about the history of African Americans in the conflict is *The Negro in the Civil War*, by Benjamin Quarles.

THREE SLAVES ESCAPE IN A CANOE—AND BEGIN TO CHANGE WHAT THE WAR IS ABOUT

For more on this topic read, "Black Glory: The African-American Role in Union Victory," by Joseph T. Glatthaar in *Why the Confederacy Lost*, edited by Gabor S. Boritt.

FREDERICK DOUGLASS LOBBIES TO MAKE BLACK MEN SOLDIERS

Free at Last: A Documentary History of Slavery, Freedom, and the Civil War, edited by Ira Berlin, et al., consists of testimonies from African-Americans in the Civil War.

A BLOODY WAR—FOR FREEDOM
(1862)

The War Is Pressed

THE "BATTLE HYMN OF THE REPUBLIC"—AN ABOLITIONIST SONG?

To learn more about Julia Ward Howe, read *Diva Julia: The Public Romance and Private Agony of Julia Ward Howe*, by Valarie H. Ziegler. For a family account of Howe's writing of the hymn, see *The Story of the Battle Hymn of the Republic*, by Florence Howe Hall, Julia's daughter.

THE DRAMATIC ESCAPE BY NATHAN BEDFORD FORREST FROM FORT DONELSON

For more on Forrest and other Southern generals, read *Leaders of the Lost Cause*, edited by Gary W. Gallagher and Joesph T. Glatthaar.

A Battle Named After a Church—Shiloh

THE DEAD AND WOUNDED GATHER AROUND BLOODY POND

To learn more about the evolution of the most pivotal friendship of the Civil War—between Ulysses Grant and William Sherman—read Charles Flood's *Grant and Sherman: The Friendship That Won the Civil War.*

NATHAN BEDFORD FORREST—THE LAST SOLDIER WOUNDED AT THE BATTLE OF SHILOH

For a complete account of the battle, see *Shiloh: Bloody April,* by Wiley Sword or *Shiloh and the Western Campaign of 1862*, by O. Edward Cunningham.

Ironclads

MIGHT THE *VIRGINIA* ATTACK NEW YORK CITY?

An account of the *Virginia*'s shortcomings, as well as the entire first battle of ironclads, can be found in James L. Nelson's *Reign of Iron.*

THE CONFEDERACY RULES THE SEAS—FOR A DAY

For essays on various aspects of the battle and what it meant, read *The Battle of Hampton Roads,* edited by Harold Holzer and Tim Mulligan.

THE *MONITOR* NEARLY SINKS BEFORE THE FIRST BATTLE OF IRONCLADS

For a compact biography of the *Monitor,* including its dangerous trip south, see *Monitor,* written by naval historian James Tertius deKay. To see the *Monitor,* visit the Mariner's Museum, The U.S.S. Monitor Center in Newport News, Virginia.

The Naval War

WHY DIDN'T KING COTTON BRING EUROPE TO ITS KNEES?

For more on the Southern attempts to use the cotton trade to get Europe to intervene on their behalf, see Howard Jones's *Blue and Gray Diplomacy: A History of Union and Confederate Foreign Relations.*

THE *HUNLEY*—A DARK AND DANGEROUS CONFEDERATE SUB

The story of the *Hunley* and its dramatic recovery in 2000 is recounted on the Web site www.hunley.org. For more about subs in the war, see Mark K. Ragan's *Submarine Warfare in the Civil War.*

The First Cracks in the Institution of Slavery

MARY TODD LINCOLN'S SEAMSTRESS HELPS BLACK REFUGEES IN WASHINGTON

To read more about the Capital during the war, read *Freedom Rising—Washington in the Civil War,* by Ernest B. Furgurson.

ONE SLAVE FAMILY SEEKS REFUGE WITH THE UNION ARMY

The Federal Writers' Project collected more than 2,300 first-person accounts of slavery and 500 black-and-white photographs from 1936–1938. They are available at http://memory.loc.gov/ammem/snhtml/snhome.html

WHICH SIDE ARE YOU ON? NOT ALL SLAVES FLED THE PLANTATIONS

This account comes from Andrew Ward's *The Slaves War,* which uses diaries, letters, memoirs, and interviews to provide a slave's perspective on the Civil War.

HARRIET TUBMAN LEADS A FREEDOM RAID

To learn more about Harriet Tubman, read *Bound for the Promised Land: Harriet Tubman, Portrait of an American Hero,* by Kate Clifford Larson.

Of Privates and Generals—the Men Who Fought

WHO WERE THE SOLDIERS WHO FOUGHT THE WAR?

For a soldier's-eye view of the Civil War, read *Civil War Soldiers,* by Reid Mitchell.

"POLITICAL GENERALS" APPOINTED NEXT TO MILITARY ONES

For more about Union generals, see Philip Katcher's *American Civil War Commanders: Union Leaders in the East.*

NEVER ENOUGH SHOES—SCAVENGING FOR CLOTHES IN THE CONFEDERATE ARMY

For more on the life and clothing of the soldier, see David Williams's *The People's History of the Civil War.*

"On to Richmond!"—the Peninsula Campaign Begins

MAGRUDER'S BATTLEFIELD THEATRICS DECEIVE McCLELLAN

To learn more about Yorktown and the entire Peninsula Campaign, read the Stephen W. Sears book, *To the Gates of Richmond.*

GEORGE McCLELLAN'S HABIT OF MISCALCULATING EVERYBODY'S TROOP STRENGTH

To read more about the enigmatic general who led the Union army for the first phase of the Civil War, read *George B. McClellan: The Young Napoleon*, by Stephen W. Sears.

AERIAL RECONNAISSANCE AND THE YORKTOWN BALLOONS

For more on how balloons were used as reconnaissance, see *The War of the Aeronauts: A History of Ballooning In the Civil War*, by Charles M. Evans.

The Peninsula Campaign and the Rise of Robert E. Lee

THE ECCENTRIC "STONEWALL" JACKSON ATTACKS IN THE SHENANDOAH VALLEY

For more on "Stonewall" Jackson's famous Shenandoah Valley military campaign, read *Stonewall in the Valley*, by Robert G. Tanner.

JEB STUART CIRCLES McCLELLAN'S ARMY—AND IS PROUD TO DO SO

To read more of the first-person accounts regarding McClellan's Peninsula Campaign, read Richard Wheeler's *Sword Over Richmond.*

LEE BEATS BACK McCLELLAN IN THE SEVEN DAYS' BATTLES

For more on the Peninsula Campaign, see Bruce Catton's *Mr. Lincoln's Army.*

Women to the Rescue—Medical Care and Clara Barton

WITH HER FATHER'S BLESSING, CLARA BARTON BECOMES A NURSE

For more about Clara Barton and the state of American medicine during the Civil War, read Stephen B. Oates's *Woman of Valor: Clara Barton and the Civil War.*

FILTHY HOSPITALS, "GUILLOTINE" AMPUTATIONS, AND DEADLY INFECTIONS

For a history of medical care in the Civil War, read *Bleeding Blue and Gray: Civil War Surgery and the Evolution of American Medicine*, by Ira Rutkow.

HOSPITAL CLEANLINESS IMPROVES AS WOMEN BECOME NURSES

Much of this account comes from David Williams's *The People's History of the Civil War.* For more on medical care during the Civil War, see George Worthington Adams's *Doctors in Blue* or H.H. Cunningham's *Doctors in Gray.*

TO TREAT THEIR WOUNDED, CONFEDERATES BUILD CHIMBORAZO HOSPITAL IN
RICHMOND
For an account of life at Chimborazo, read Phoebe Pember's memoir, *A Southern Woman's Story.*

The Bloodiest Day In American Military History—Antietam (Sharpsburg)

SECOND BATTLE OF BULL RUN—JOHN POPE BOTCHES THE BATTLE

To learn more about the Second Battle of Bull Run and the Confederate decision to invade the North, read *Return to Bull Run*, by John J. Hennessy.

THE DEAD IN FRONT OF DUNKER CHURCH IN ANTIETAM, MARYLAND (IMAGE)

For high-quality images of Antietam, see *America's Bloodiest Day: The Battle of Antietam*, by William A. Frassinito. For more of Brady's Civil War photos, see *In the Wake of Battle: The Civil War Images of Mathew Brady.*

Approaching the Emancipation Proclamation

LINCOLN ADVOCATES SENDING FREED SLAVES ABROAD

For more on this issue, see Eric Foner's "Lincoln and Colonization" in the collection of essays *Our Lincoln: New Perspectives on Lincoln and His World.*

ABOLITIONISTS BLAST LINCOLN'S COLONIZATION PROPOSAL

For an account of the complicated political relationship between Lincoln and Douglass, see James Oakes's book, *The Radical and the Republican.*

ANTIETAM CHANGES THE WAR—AND MAKES THE EMANCIPATION PROCLAMATION POSSIBLE

For more discussion of how Antietam changed the war, see Gary W. Gallagher's essay, "The Maryland Campaign in Perspective," and other essays in his book, *Essays on the 1862 Maryland Campaign.*

Signing the Emancipation Proclamation

LINCOLN'S HAND SHAKES AS HE SIGNS THE PROCLAMATION

For a classic account of how Lincoln's thinking evolved regarding emancipation, read *The Emancipation Proclamation*, by John Hope Franklin.

AFTER THEY ARE READ THE PROCLAMATION, BLACK SOLDIERS SING "MY COUNTRY 'TIS OF THEE"

Accounts of the response to the Emancipation Proclamation can be found in volume 5 of Page Smith's *Trial by Fire: A People's History of the Civil War and Reconstruction.*

Fredericksburg—Northern Exasperation as Lee Triumphs Again

NEW RECRUITS—MAINE'S JOSHUA CHAMBERLAIN AND OTHERS SIGN UP

To learn more about Joshua Chamberlain and his Twentieth Maine, read *In the Hands of Providence: Joshua L. Chamberlain and the American Civil War*, by Alice Rains Trulock.

To read about this letter and some of Lincoln's other memorable writings, see the illustrated young adult book, *Abraham Lincoln, the Writer: A Treasury of His Greatest Speeches and Letters*, by Harold Holzer.

AN ALL-CONSUMING BATTLE
(1863)

A Brother's War, a Bitter War

CHANCELLORSVILLE I

For a thorough account of the Chancellorsville campaign, see *Chancellorsville* by Stephen Sears.

CHANCELLORSVILLE II—LEE'S GREATEST VICTORY

For more on the Battle of Chancellorsville, see the National Parks Service Web site, Fredericksburg and Spotsylvania County Battlefields Memorial, at www.nps .gov/frsp/index.htm.

Food and Drink—the Edible, Inedible, and Coffee, Always

HARD *TACK* COME AGAIN NO MORE

For more on other foods foraged and cooked by Civil War soldiers, see *Beyond the Battlefield—The Ordinary Life and Extraordinary Times of the Civil War Soldier*, edited by David Madden.

BEGGING, BUYING, AND STEALING FOOD FROM CIVILIANS

For more accounts of what soldiers ate and how they lived, see the classic Civil War books *The Life of Billy Yank* and *The Life of Johnny Reb*, by Bell Irvin Wiley, filled with many colorful first-person accounts.

Fire in the Rear—Lincoln and Antiwar Politicians Duke It Out

LINCOLN SUSPENDS THE WRIT OF HABEAS CORPUS

To learn more about Abraham Lincoln's controversial restriction of civil liberties, read *The Fate of Liberty*, by Mark E. Neely, Jr.

OHIO POLITICIAN CLEMENT VALLANDIGHAM IS JAILED FOR SPEAKING AGAINST THE WAR

To learn more about Clement Vallandigham, read *The Limits of Dissent: Clement L. Vallandigham and the Civil War*, by Frank Klement.

More Dissent at Home—the Richmond Food Riot
and the New York City Draft Riot

JEFFERSON DAVIS CONFRONTS HUNGRY WOMEN ON THE STREETS OF RICHMOND

For more on the Bread Riots in Richmond and a history of how Richmond was transformed by the war, see Ernest Furgurson's *Ashes of Glory: Richmond at War*.

LINCOLN PERSISTS WITH A NEW YORK CITY DRAFT

To learn more about the struggles of New York City's African-Americans, see Iver

Bernstein's essay "Securing Freedom: The Challenges of Black Life in Civil War New York," in *Slavery in New York*, edited by Ira Berlin and Leslie Harris.

More than Glory—the Fifty-fourth Massachusetts Volunteer Regiment Is Born

SHOULD WE JOIN? BLACKS QUESTION WHETHER THEY SHOULD FIGHT FOR THE NORTH

For more on the life of George E. Stephens and to read his letters to the *Anglo-African*, see *A Voice of Thunder*, by Donald Yacovone.

BRAVERY, SACRIFICE, AND RESPECT—THE EFFECTS OF FORT WAGNER

To learn more about the relations between African-American soldiers and their white officers, read *Forged in Battle: The Civil War Alliance of Black Soldiers and White Officers*, by Joseph T. Glatthaar.

The Vicksburg Campaign

"MISSISSIPPIANS DON'T KNOW . . . HOW TO SURRENDER"—FAILED ATTEMPTS TO TAKE VICKSBURG

For more about Ulysses S. Grant's attacks on the "Fortress on the Hill," read Terrence J. Winschel's *Vicksburg: Fall of the Confederate Gibraltar*.

WAS GRANT A DRUNKARD? AND DID LINCOLN CARE?

For a discussion about the debate about Grant's drinking, see Brooks Simpson's first volume on Grant, *Ulysses S. Grant: Triumph Over Adversity, 1822–1865*. To read about the debate of Sylvanus Cadwallader's account, read the "Introduction" by Brooks D. Simpson in Cadwallader's memoirs, *Three Years with Grant*.

"I WAS NOW IN THE ENEMY'S COUNTRY"—GRANT CROSSES THE MISSISSIPPI TO GET AT VICKSBURG

For more on the Vicksburg campaign, read *Vicksburg Is the Key—Struggle for the Mississippi River*, by William L. Shea and Terrence J. Winschel.

The Siege of Vicksburg

WAS VICKSBURG THE MOST IMPORTANT VICTORY OF THE WAR?

A good one-volume overview of Vicksburg is *Vicksburg: The Campaign That Opened the Mississippi*, by Michael B. Ballard.

Stumbling into Battle—Gettysburg Unfolds as Another Confederate Victory

JEB STUART WANDERS OFF—AND LEE IS LEFT BLIND

For more on Jeb Stuart's controversial ride before Gettysburg, see Mark Nesbitt's *Saber and Scapegoat: J. E. B. Stuart and the Gettysburg Controversy*.

DID CONFEDERATES COME TO GETTYSBURG ON A SEARCH FOR SHOES?

A short book that introduces Gettysburg—and the debate of the shoes—to those who have never visited the battlefield is James McPherson's *Hallowed Ground*. For a firsthand account of the initial attack, read *The Memoirs of Henry Heth*, edited by James Morrison, Jr.

To read more about Humiston and his ambrotype, see Mark H. Dunkelman's *Gettysburg's Unknown Soldier: The Life, Death, and Celebrity of Amos Humiston*.

The Battle Turns—Day Two and Day Three of Gettysburg

DANIEL E. SICKLES STEPS FROM LITTLE ROUND TOP—AND INTO HISTORY

To learn more about the life of Daniel E. Sickles, read *American Scoundrel*, by Thomas Keneally. For more detail about his decisions at Gettysburg, read *Sickles at Gettysburg*, by James Hessler.

DID DANIEL E. SICKLES WIN THE BATTLE OF GETTYSBURG—OR ALMOST LOSE IT?

Did Sickles's forward movement win or almost lose the Battle of Gettysburg? To read more about this debate, read Harry W. Pfanz's *Gettysburg—The Second Day*.

THE BOYS OF MAINE—AND NEW YORK AND MICHIGAN—DEFEND LITTLE ROUND TOP

For a balanced account of Chamberlain's life, read Thomas A. Desjardin's *Stand Firm Ye Boys from Maine: The 20th Maine and the Gettysburg Campaign*.

Gettysburg—the Aftermath

WHO WAS TO BLAME FOR THE DEFEAT AT GETTYSBURG?

For a discussion of Robert E. Lee's strengths and weaknesses as a general, see Gary W. Gallagher's "'Upon Their Success Hang Momentous Issues': Generalship," in Gabor S. Boritt, ed., *Why the Confederacy Lost*.

GENERAL MEADE FAILS TO FOLLOW UP ON GETTYSBURG

For a concise, modern perspective on Gettysburg, see Steven E. Woodworth's *Beneath a Northern Sky: A Short History of the Gettysburg Campaign*.

AFTER THE BATTLE—A LANDSCAPE OF FILTH AND DEATH

How does an entire nation cope with such overwhelming casualties? This is the subject of the book *This Republic of Suffering: Death and the American Civil War*, by Drew Gilpin Faust.

The Gettysburg Address

DID LINCOLN WRITE THE GETTYSBURG ADDRESS ON THE BACK OF AN ENVELOPE?

How Lincoln wrote the Gettysburg Address is explored in the book *Did Lincoln Own Slaves? And Other Frequently Asked Questions About Abraham Lincoln*, by Gerald J. Prokopowicz.

DID LINCOLN'S GETTYSBURG ADDRESS DISAPPOINT HIS AUDIENCE?

For an analysis of Lincoln's speech, read Gabor Boritt's *The Gettysburg Gospel: The Lincoln Speech That Nobody Knows*.

TIME'S ASSESSMENT: WHY THE GETTYSBURG ADDRESS HAS LASTED

In his book, *Lincoln at Gettysburg: The Words that Remade America*, Gary Wills maintains that Lincoln's address was a revolutionary document in American history.

Chickamauga—the Confederates' Last Hurrah in the West

A UNION DISASTER AT CHICKAMAUGA CREEK, THE RIVER OF BLOOD

For a military history of this or any other battle of the Civil War, read the one volume, *How the North Won: A Military History of the Civil War*, by Herman Hattaway and Archer Jones.

THE PEOPLE, WEARY OF WAR
(1864)

Another Year of War

THE DAVISES BRING HOME A FOSTER CHILD—A BLACK ONE

For more information on Jim Limber, see the article "What Do We Really Know About 'Jim Limber'?" by John M. Coski in the winter 2008 issue of *Museum of the Confederacy Magazine*.

SOLDIERS TRY TO DIE WITH A NAME

This passage was derived from "Chapter 4. Naming: The Significant Word Unknown" in Drew Gilpin Faust's book, *This Republic of Suffering—Death and the American Civil War*.

WILLIAM QUANTRILL, "BLOODY" BILL ANDERSON, AND JESSE JAMES—GUERRILLA WARFARE PLAGUES THE WEST

To learn more about the Confederate outlaw Jesse James, read *Jesse James: Last Rebel of the Civil War*, by T. J. Stiles.

The Overland Campaign—the Bloodiest of the War—Begins

THE BATTLE OF THE WILDERNESS—LEE CATCHES UNION TROOPS IN THE WOODS AGAIN

For more on the Southerners' view of the war, see Gary Gallagher's *The Confederate War*.

WHY GENERALS—INCLUDING ROBERT E. LEE—WERE MORE LIKELY TO DIE DURING THE CIVIL WAR

This account comes largely from the book *1864: Lincoln at the Gates of History*, by Charles Bracelen Flood.

The Cold Harbor Fiasco

HOW DO MEN SUMMON THE COURAGE TO CHARGE INTO BATTLE?

For more on why men enlisted to fight in the Civil War, the reasons they fought, and what convinced them to risk their lives, see James McPherson's *For Cause and Comrades*.

Petersburg, and the Battle of the Crater

A PENNSYLVANIA MINER'S PLAN TO "BLOW THAT DAMNED FORT OUT OF EXISTENCE"

A comprehensive work on this battle is *The Horrid Pit: The Battle of the Crater, the Civil War's Cruelest Mission*, by Alan Axelrod.

"A DETONATION OF THUNDER"—THE EXPLOSION AT PETERSBURG

For a thorough account of the Petersburg campaign, read *The Last Citadel: Petersburg, Virginia, June 1864–April 1865*, by Noah Andre Trudeau.

August's Dark Days—Lincoln Expects to Lose His Reelection

CONFEDERATE SABOTEURS MAKE TROUBLE ACROSS THE NORTH

For more on the Democrats attempt to defeat Lincoln in 1864, sometimes conspiring with Confederate spies, see *Copperheads: The Rise and Fall of Lincoln's Opponents in the North*, by Jennifer Weber.

THE PRESIDENT IS SHOT—THROUGH HIS HAT

This account is based largely on an account of the incident in the book *1864, Lincoln at the Gates of History*, by Charles Bracelen Flood.

LINCOLN FINDS RELIEF IN ATTENDING THE THEATER

For more on Lincoln and his love of the theater, see David C. Mearns, "Act Well Your Part," in his *Largely Lincoln*.

Union Triumphs in Georgia and in the Shenandoah Valley

THE PEOPLE OF ATLANTA PROTEST THE EVACUATION OF THEIR CITY

For more on the taking of Atlanta by Sherman's army, read *War Like the Thunderbolt: The Battle and Burning of Atlanta,* by Russell S. Bonds.

Prospects Darken for the Confederacy

"TO MAKE GEORGIA HOWL!"—SHERMAN'S MARCH TO THE SEA

For a soldier's eye view of Sherman's march through Georgia, read *The March to the Sea and Beyond: Sherman's Troops in the Savannah and Carolinas Campaigns,* by Joseph T. Glatthaar and *Southern Storm: Sherman's March to the Sea,* by Noah Andre Trudeau.

CONFEDERATES REFUSE TO GIVE UP BLACK PRISONERS—AND ALL EXCHANGES ARE HALTED

A book that explores the complicity of Union and Confederate leaders in the poor treatment of prisoners-of-war is *While In the Hands of the Enemy: Military Prisons of the Civil War*, by Charles S. Sanders.

"THIS HELL ON EARTH"—ANDERSONVILLE AND OTHER DISMAL PRISONER-OF-WAR CAMPS

To read a first-person account and see images drawn by an Andersonville prisoner, read *Eye of the Storm*, by Robert Knox Sneden, edited by Charles F. Bryan, Jr., and Nelson D. Lankford.

<h1>THE "MIGHTY SCOURGE" ENDS,
THE NATION IS TRANSFORMED</h1>
(1865)

The Beginning of the End

"LOTS OF WISDOM IN THAT DOCUMENT. . . ."—LINCOLN'S REMARKABLE, REFLECTIVE
SECOND INAUGURAL ADDRESS

For more on Lincoln's Second Inaugural Address, read *Lincoln's Greatest Speech*, by Ronald White.

The Death Throes of Slavery

RECRUITING MORE CONFEDERATE SOLDIERS—*BLACK* ONES

For more on this Southern view regarding the arming of slaves, see *The Gray and the Black: The Confederate Debate on Emancipation*, edited by Robert F. Durden.

Finally on to Richmond

CORNELIA McDONALD AND HER FAMILY CAN BARELY FEED THEMSELVES

For more from Cornelia Peake McDonald, see her *A Woman's Civil War: A Diary, with Reminiscences of the War, from March 1862*, edited by Minrose C. Gwin.

The Road to Appomattox

"HAS THE ARMY BEEN DISSOLVED?"—CONFEDERATE DEFEAT AT SAILOR'S CREEK

For an account of the final phase of the war, see Bruce Catton's *Stillness at Appomattox*.

Prelude to an Assassination

LINCOLN IS SHOT!

Three books about the plotters who killed Lincoln are: *Blood on the Moon*, by Edward Steers Jr.; *American Brutus: John Wilkes Booth and the Lincoln Conspiracies*, by Michael W. Kauffman; and *Manhunt: The 12-Day Chase for Lincoln's Killer*, by James L. Swanson.

The Bitter End

THE *SHENANDOAH* FIRES THE WAR'S LAST SHOT—TWO MONTHS AFTER LEE
SURRENDERS

Much of this account comes from the book *Last Flag Down: The Epic Journey of the Last Confederate Warship*, by John Baldwin.

Why Did the North Win—or the South Lose?

THE LOST CAUSE—THE SOUTHERN VIEW

To explore the Lost Cause perspective, see chapter 4 of Gaines M. Foster's *Ghosts of the Confederacy: Defeat, the Lost Cause, and the Emergence of the New South*.

DID THE SOUTH LOSE THE WAR BECAUSE OF INTERNAL DIVISIONS?

For more on the theory that internal fractures cost the Confederacy the war, read

Why the South Lost the Civil War, by Richard E. Beringer, Herman Hattaway, Archer Jones, and William N. Still Jr.

WHAT IF THE LEADERS WERE REVERSED? WOULD THE SOUTH HAVE WON?
For a fuller discussion of this view, read T. Harry Williams's essay "The Military Leadership of North and South" in *Why the North Won the Civil War,* edited by David Donald.

EMANCIPATION AND ARMING OF THE EX-SLAVES—THE DECIDING FACTOR?
For the argument that freed slaves led the way to their own emancipation, read "Who Freed the Slaves?" by Barbara Fields, in Geoffrey Ward's *The Civil War.*

DID CHANCE PLAY A ROLE IN THE UNION VICTORY?
For a look at how different battlefield decisions might have changed the war's outcome, read *How the South Could Have Won the Civil War,* by Bevin Alexander.

What Did the War Decide?

THAT FEW EVER CAN PREDICT THE CARNAGE OF WAR
To learn more about the death wrought by the Civil War, and how the country dealt with it, read Drew Faust's *Republic of Suffering.*

THAT NINETEENTH-CENTURY WOMEN HAD A PLACE OUTSIDE THE HOME
For more on the contributions of Northern women to the war effort, read Jeanie Attie's *Patriotic Toil: Northern Women and the American Civil War.*

What Became of Them?

THE DAVISES
For more on Varina Davis, see *Civil War Wives: The Lives and Times of Angelina Grimke Weld, Varina Howell Davis, and Julia Dent Grant,* by Carol Berkin.

SOUTHERN GENERALS
To learn more about Robert E. Lee, see *Reading the Man: A Portrait of Robert E. Lee Through His Private Letters,* by Elizabeth Brown Pryor.

JAMES LONGSTREET—SOUTHERN TRAITOR OR REALIST?
For more on Longstreet, read *General James Longstreet: The Confederacy's Most Controversial Soldier,* by Jeffry D. Wert.

CLARA BARTON MEETS A SOLDIER
This account was largely taken from *A Woman of Valor: Clara Barton and the Civil War,* by Stephen B. Oates.

INDEX

Page numbers in *italics* refer to illustration captions.

Currier & Ives, *353*
Curtin, Andrew, 235
Curtis, George William, 233
Custer, George Armstrong, 404, 440
Custis, George Washington Parke, 419

Daily Journal, 232
Dana, Charles A., 256
Davis, Garret, 89
Davis, Jefferson, 13, 33, 34, 35, 41, 44,
    46, *47,* 51, 59, 61, 66, 70, 154, 158,
    177, 209, 218, 303, 306, 308, 357,
    410
  black soldiers and, 387
  capture of, 416, 434
  Chickamauga and, 305
  child adopted by, 317
  conscription and, 143
  council of war convened by, 416
  Cuba and, 14
  death of, 439
  Emancipation Proclamation and, 193
  and European recognition of the
    Confederacy, 388
  and end of Confederacy, 376
  and factors in Confederate defeat,
    423, 425
  and fall of Richmond, 393, 394
  food riots and, 239, 240
  generals appointed by, 144, 145
  Greenhow and, 78
  guerrilla war called for by, 395, 400
  inauguration of, 41
  Johnston and, 109
  leadership of, 426
  Lee and, 160, 289
  Lincoln's assassination and, 416
  in peace talks, 377
  photograph of, *47*
  political experience of, 426
  postwar life of, 439
  prisoners and, 365
  rangers and, 319
  saboteurs and, 348
  Sherman's march and, 364
  Vicksburg and, 254, 259, 262
Davis, Varina, 33, 35, 135, 158, 416
  child adopted by, 317
  death of, 439
  postwar life of, 439
Declaration of Independence, 5, 34, 49
  Gettysburg Address and, 295, 297

Delaware, 89
Democrats, 10, 144, 187, 241, 243, 443
  in elections of 1864, 351, 352, *353,*
    357, 363
  Peace (Copperheads), 177, 188, 229,
    230, 235, *236,* 288, 347, 348,
    424
  Thirteenth Amendment and, 383
Derby, Richard, 154
deserters, 304, 376
Devil's Den, 279, *292*
Dickey, Cyrus, 110, 114
disease, 238
  soldiers and, 166, 213, 223, 241, 255,
    265, 366, 434
Dix, Dorothea, 170
"Dixie," 41, 211, 367, 387, 407, 439
Dixon, George E., 131
Dodson, Jacob, 89
Donald, David, 424
Doubleday, Abner, 270, 411
Douglas, Stephen, 90, 91, 191
Douglass, Charles, 246
Douglass, Frederick, 50, 91, 92, 93, 94,
    95, 134, 135, 249
  black soldiers and, 246, 248
  Brown and, 22, 23
  death of, 443
  on emancipation, 386
  Emancipation Proclamation and,
    192, 193, 194
  on Lincoln, 373
  Lincoln's colonization proposal and,
    185
  Lincoln's meeting with, 351, 443
  Lincoln's second inauguration and,
    378, 379, 380
  "Mission of the War" speech of, 315
  photograph of, *95*
  postwar life of, 443
  on struggle for change, 385
Douglass, Lewis, 246, 249
Douglass' Monthly, 94
Downsville, Maryland, 222
draft, 143, 202, 241, 242, 243, 304,
    355, 424
draft riots, 241, 242, 243, *244,* 424
Dred Scott, 90, 229, 385
Drewry's Bluff, 324
Dubois, W.E.B., 44
Dubuque Herald, 229
Duck River, 222

South Carolina, *11,* 18, 31, 33, 39, 43, 44, 51, 59, 60, 139, 343, 373
Spain, 58, 440
Speed, James, 300
Spotsylvania, 328, *329,* 331
Stanton, Edwin, 102, 121, 151, 256, 308, 316, 366, 386, 411
   in depiction of Emancipation Proclamation reading, *189*
   Lincoln's assassination and, 415
   press and, 234
   Sickles and, 279
Stanton, Elizabeth Cady, 385
State Rights in the Confederacy (Owsley), 424
states' rights, 33, 42, 44, 82, 143, 231, 424
Staunton River, 160
Stephens, Alexander H., 33, 43, 44, 128, 375, 377, 424
Stephens, George E., 246, 248, 251
Stephens, Susan, 251
Stevens, Simon, 86
Stones River, 211–12, 303
Stonewall Brigade, 75
Storey, Wilbur, 234
Stowe, Harriet Beecher, 15, 16, *19,* 194, 300
Strong, George Templeton, 29, 134, 229, 242, 355
Struble, Henry, 318
Stuart, J. E. B. "Jeb," 23, 62, 75, 161, 162, 274
   at Chancellorsville, 215–16, 217
   character of, 161
   at Gettysburg, 272, 278, 286
submarines, 131, *132*
Sullivan, Timothy O., *227*
Sumner, Charles, 18, 134, 230, 349
Supreme Court, 31, 50, 385, 419, 436
   Dred Scott decision of, 90, 229, 385
Susquehanna River, 177

Tallahassee, 348
Taney, Roger B., 229, 385
tariffs, 7
Taylor, Richard, 324, 416
Tennessee, 59, 62, 187, 303
Tennessee River, 103, 158
Terry, A. H., 375
Texas, 13, 32, 33, 254
Thanksgiving, 299

Third South Carolina Volunteers, 251
Thirteenth Amendment, 53, 373, 377, 383, 384, 385, 432, 433, 435
Thomas, Benjamin, 256
Thomas, Emory M., 42
Thomas, George, 305, 306, 356, 367, 368, 388
Thomson, M. J., 319
Thoreau, Henry David, 25
Toledo, Ohio, 242
Tompkins, Sally Louisa, 163, 170
Toombs, Robert, 59, 270
Tremont Temple, 194
trench warfare, 340
Tubman, Harriet, 9, 194
   freedom raid of, 139
   vision of, 45
Turner, Nat, 8
Twain, Mark, 298, 440
Tweed, William, 243
Twelfth Amendment, 383
Twentieth Maine, 202, 203, 339, 433
Twenty-first Massachusetts, 225

Uncle Tom's Cabin (Stowe), 16, *19,* 300
Underground Railroad, 8, 9, 16, 45, 139, 384
   Lincoln's suggestion for, 351
United States Sanitary Commission, 170, 213, 318

Vallandigham, Clement L., 134, 231, 232–33, 234, 235
Valley of Death, 279
Van Alen, James H., 409
Vermont, 90
veterans, *437,* 441
Vicksburg, 188, 209, 254, 255, 256, 257, 258, *260,* 262, 263, 264, 265, 289, 303, 313, 316, 347, 356
   defenses of, 259, *268*
   importance of Union victory at, 267
   Lincoln and, 254, 257, 288, 289, 299
   reaction to Union victory at, 288
   siege of, 263, 264, 265, *268*
   surrender of, 266, 267
Vincent, Strong, 281
Virginia, 10, 30, 39, 50, 52, 59, 60, 62, 68, 81, 93, 144, 303, 323, 324, 355, 419
Virginia, CSS (USS *Merrimack*), 117, 118, 119, 120, 121, 122–23, *124*

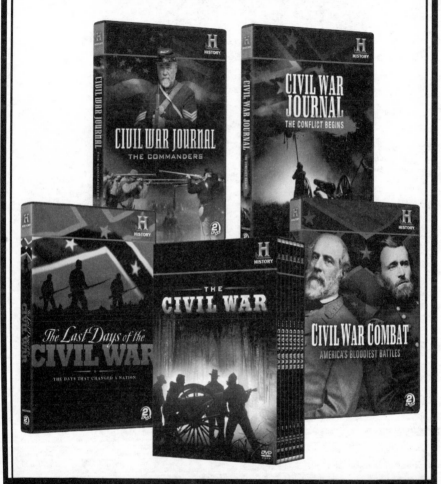